THE DEVELOPMENT OF A CULTURE-BASED TOOL TO PREDICT TEAM PERFORMANCE

A doctoral thesis submitted in partial fulfilment of the requirements
for the award of
Doctor of Philosophy of Loughborough University

October 2014

© 2014 by Allan Hodgson

Acknowledgements

I would like to thank my supervisors, Professor Carys Siemieniuch and Dr Ella Hubbard, for their guidance, advice and encouragement over the period of the PhD. I would also like to acknowledge the patience and forbearance of friends, former industrial colleagues and academic colleagues who provided information on the various teams that they had worked with; this information formed an important part of my research.

I would also like to thank my wife, Christine, for her patience and support, and son and daughter, Alec and Leonie, for their unwavering confidence in my ability to succeed – confidence that I did not always possess myself.

Finally, I would like to thank my friend and colleague, Pavel, for his insights, support, advice and encouragement.

Abstract

The effect of national culture on the performance of teams is becoming an increasingly important issue in advanced western countries. There are many interlinked reasons for this, including the increasing globalisation of companies and the use of joint ventures for the development of expensive platforms. A further issue relates to the export of complex sociotechnical systems, where a culture clash between designer/-manufacturer and user can lead to significant problems.

This report describes research work that was carried out to analyse the cultural factors that influenced the performance of teams (including researchers, designers, operators and crews), and to determine whether these factors could be captured in a tool to provide assistance to team managers and team builders. The original point of interest related to the development of increasingly complex sociotechnical systems, for example nuclear power stations, oil refineries, offshore oil platforms, hospital systems and large transport aircraft. Answers that might be sought, in particular by the senior managers of global companies, included (1) the best teams (or best national locations) for fundamental research, industrial research & development, product/system improvement and other key activities, and (2) the implications for system performance and, as a result, for system design, of targeting an eastern Asian market, a South-American market, etc.

A literature review was carried out of the effects of culture on team performance, of culture measures and tools and of task classifications; in addition, empirical evidence of the validity of measures and tools was sought. Significant evidence was found of the effects of culture on teams and crews, but no national-culture-based team performance prediction tools were found. Based on the findings of the literature review, Hofstede's original four-dimension cultural framework was selected as the basis for the collection and analysis of data, including the results of studies from the literature and the researcher's own empirical studies. No team or task classification system was found that was suitable for the purposes of linking culture to team performance, so a five-factor task classification was developed, based on the literature review, to form the basis of the initial modelling work.

A detailed analysis of results from the literature and from the author's pilot studies revealed additional culture-performance relationships, including those relating to cultural diversity. Three models were incorporated into software tools that offered performance prediction capabilities. The first model was primarily a test bed for ideas; the second model incorporated a detailed task/behavioural approach that achieved limited success; the third and final model was evaluated

Abstract

against a range of team and crew performance data before being tested successfully for acceptability by users.

The research results indicated that the effects of cultural diversity must be sought at the individual cultural dimension level not at the composite level, that the effects of national culture on team performance were consistent and strong enough to be usefully captured in a predictive culture tool and that the relationships between culture and behaviour were moderated by contextual factors.

CONTENTS

CONTENTS

CONTENTS

CONTENTS

LIST OF FIGURES

LIST OF TABLES

LIST OF TABLES

GLOSSARY OF TERMS

Acronym or term	Meaning
Anglo	A person of British descent, typically taken to include British, Australians, Canadians, Irish, New Zealanders, Anglo-Americans and Anglo-South Africans.
ASAP	Aviation Safety Action Program (originated in USA)
ASRS	Aviation Safety Reporting System (originated in USA)
ATP	Air transport pilot (licencing).
BASIS	British Airways Safety Information System
BEA	Bureau d'Enquetes et d'Analyses pour le Securite de l'Aviation Civile (France).
BFU	Bundesstelle für Flugunfalluntersuchung – the German Federal Bureau of Aircraft Accidents Investigation.
CAA	Civil Aviation Authority (originated in UK).
CHIRP	Confidential Human Factors Incident Reporting Programme (originated in UK)
COL (or COLL)	Collectivism – a cultural dimension, a term sometimes used to represent the opposite 'end of the scale' to 'individualism'.
CRM	Crew resource management.
CVF	Competing Values Framework – a model and framework for interpreting many organisational phenomena.
DCI	Design and Creativity Index.
EPO	European Patent Office.
ESS	Europe Social Survey – an academic-based social survey and database to track and explain interactions and attitudes within Europe.
FAA	Federal Aviation Authority (USA).
FLE	Full (hull) loss equivalent, refers to aircraft accidents and incidents.
FMC	Flight management computer.
GCI	Global Creativity Index.
GII	Global Innovation Index.
GPA	Grade point average (typically referring to student examination and coursework marks).
GS	Google Scholar.
HFACS	Human Factors Analysis and Classification System.
IDV	Individualism (versus collectivism) - a cultural dimension.
IJV	International joint venture.
IND	Indulgence (versus restraint) – a cultural dimension.
IVS	Indulgence vs. restraint – a cultural dimension.
LOSA	Line Operations Safety Audit – An approach to pilot technical skill rating, which records all threats and errors, how they were managed and their outcomes.
LTO	Long term orientation – a cultural dimension.
LTO-WVS	The 'new' version of long term orientation.

MAS	Masculinity (versus femininity) – a cultural dimension.
MODAF	The UK's Ministry of Defence Architecture Framework.
NATO	North Atlantic Treaty Organization
NEO-FFI	A five-factor personality scale.
OCAI	Organizational Culture Assessment Instrument – based on the theoretical model that underlies the Competing Values Framework (CVM).
OGC	Office of Government Commerce (UK).
PRA	Pragmatic (versus normative) – a cultural dimension
PDI	Power distance – a cultural dimension.
PMBOK	Project Management Body of Knowledge.
R&D	Research and development.
RAE	The UK's Research Assessment Exercise, applied periodically to universities.
RAE2008	The UK's 2008 Research Assessment Exercise.
SOP	Standard operating procedure.
TACARE	TAiwan Civil Aviation safety REporting system
TCT	Team Culture Tool (the three tools – TCT1, TCT2 and TCT3 that were develop during the research described in this thesis).
TEM	Threat and Error Management – a flexible approach to practical risk management aimed at improving aviation safety.
UAI	Uncertainty avoidance – a cultural dimension.
USPTO	United Stated Patent and Trademark Office.
WVS	World Values Survey.

Obtaining the culture tools

The culture tools that were developed during (and following) the research described in this thesis can be downloaded from the following web page:

http://www.allanhodgson.com/culture

These software tools were produced using Microsoft Excel 2010.

The author can be contacted via the following email address:

allanhodgson@outlook.com

Any constructive comments or information on typos and errors will be gratefully received.

1 Introduction

1.1 Overview

Multinational companies design and produce complex sociotechnical systems (large transport aircraft, ships, nuclear power plants, oil refineries, etc.) that are utilised and/or installed round the World. As such companies grow, they acquire subsidiaries in increasingly diverse regions, and these subsidiaries become increasingly viable options for research, development, product design and manufacture.

The area of particular interest for the work of this thesis relates to the interplay of cultures. Engineers and designers are products of their cultures; their approaches to research, development, design and manufacture are culture-bound, and they build their cultural assumptions into their products, systems and procedures. Users of sociotechnical systems are similarly culture-bound and, therefore, culture-related problems can occur when designer and operator cultures differ.

Teams, in particular project teams, are increasingly being utilised to develop sociotechnical systems and their sub-systems. In Europe and in Anglo[1] countries, such teams are often multicultural due, in particular, to the influx of foreign graduate engineers and scientists. Elsewhere, project teams are often created at subsidiaries by multinational companies and may be of a single culture (or dominant culture) that is different to that of the companies' base countries. Sociotechnical systems are, in turn, operated by organised action teams such as aircrews or refinery crews who are typically (but not always) nationals of the countries where or from which they operate.

Although there now exists a large amount of practical experience and theoretical understanding of teams, much of this body of knowledge relates to North European and Anglo teams, and has been amassed by researchers and practitioners from within those cultures; as a result, many of the tacit assumptions behind this body of knowledge are culture-

---

[1] Anglo refers to people of British descent, e.g. British, Irish, Canadian, Anglo-American, New Zealander, Australian and Anglo-South African.

bound. Although North European and Anglo companies began to use multicultural teams (and different culture teams via their subsidiaries) increasingly widely in the 1980s, the effects of differing cultures on team performance were not well understood, and early experiences of different-culture teams and multicultural teams were not very positive. For managers, the development of multicultural teams, in particular, has been fraught with problems (Wolf, 2002) and the performance outcomes have been discouraging (Hambrick, Davison, Snell, & Snow, 1998).

Note that the terms 'multicultural' and 'multinational' are not synonymous. There are single nationality teams (e.g. comprising USA Hispanics and USA Anglos) whose members have significantly different ethnic cultures; there are multinational teams (e.g. comprising Belgians and French) whose members have very similar ethnic cultures. In addition, cultural misunderstandings and conflicts in many team-based projects have arisen from differing *organisational* and *professional* cultures, rather than differing *ethnic* cultures.

The work described in this report was centred on teams (single- or multicultural) and the effects of cultural differences – whether internal or external to the team, i.e. whether these differences were associated with other individuals in the team or were built into the systems that the team members utilised. The primary aims of the research were to gain an understanding of the culture-related factors that influenced the effectiveness of single- and multicultural teams, and to develop a methodology and tool that could assist managers to predict the effects of culture on existing and proposed teams; it was also intended that such a tool could function as part of an educational suite on teams and team working.

1.2 Background

1.2.1 'Other culture' teams and multicultural teams

Technically advanced companies have faced higher competition and an accelerating pace of change over the last few decades, and have increasingly adopted team-based approaches to task execution and problem solving. Originally, these work teams were typically homogeneous, single-cultural and, as experience and analysis brought a better understanding of the dynamics of such teams, they proved increasingly useful for bringing a sharp focus to bear on important or urgent tasks and problems. However, these single-culture work teams were increasingly replaced by multicultural and 'other culture' work teams and this trend has shown no sign of abating, particularly in the UK. Some of the key factors contributing to the increasing incidence of multicultural work teams in the UK are described in the following points:

- The annual UK output of graduate engineers and scientists who chose to enter engineering/science-related occupations has been in decline for more than a decade; this has necessitated the recruitment of foreign engineers and scientists to fill the gap between the supply of graduates and industrial requirements.

- The huge costs associated with bringing new high technology products to market has resulted in an increasing trend towards major international joint ventures aimed at the global market, for example between international vehicle manufacturers; this has necessitated the utilisation of multinational, multicultural teams.

- Global companies have increasingly chosen to place research and development operations at foreign subsidiaries due to differential skills, costs and/or subsidies.

Similar factors have applied in most Western European countries and in other Anglo countries. Therefore the utilisation of 'other culture' teams and multicultural teams has become the norm, rather than the exception for multinational companies.

1.2.2 Teams - problem areas

Individuals and groups are heavily 'programmed' by their cultures (based on a combination of ethnic, organisational and professional cultural backgrounds). Culture affects values, attitudes, expectations, interaction styles, signals, behaviours and emotions. Therefore, when individuals of two or more cultures meet, or even when they interact remotely, their differing actions, signals, etc., tend to be misinterpreted to negative effect, unless there are joint understandings of their cultural differences and effective means in place to address these differences.

It has become increasingly clear that the nature of interactions between individuals of different cultures is more complex than those between individuals that share the same or a similar culture; assumptions that are taken for granted by members of single-culture teams are no longer valid, and team members cannot rely on informal processes to come into play to enable a team ethos to form. Snow et al. (1996) carried out a two-year study of multicultural teams at thirteen companies; they came to the conclusion that a precondition for multicultural team effectiveness was the development of clear processes for communicating, for decision-making and for handling conflicts and disagreements. In the absence of adequate measures to remedy or ameliorate such problems, multicultural teams typically underperformed when compared to single-culture teams, despite the wider range of experience that they could often bring to tasks and projects. However, where effective integration was achieved within multicultural teams, they could perform as well as, and in some cases better than, single-culture teams; in particular, their wider range of thinking styles could result in higher creativity and innovation, improved decisions and higher performance (DiStefano & Maznevski, 2000; Earley & Gibson, 2002).

Our limited understandings have related not only to multicultural teams, but also to 'other culture' teams (teams with members of a culture different to ours). Complex sociotechnical systems exported from the West have typically been crewed or operated by 'other culture' teams, i.e. teams of different national cultures to those who designed the systems. In addition, research & development work has been increasingly delegated to foreign subsidiaries, to be carried out by 'other culture' teams.

Theories of motivation and teaming that were developed in the West (in particular in Anglo countries) contained cultural assumptions that were not universal. For example, Maslow's hierarchy of needs (Maslow 1943; Maslow 1997, Ch. 5) placed *self*-actualisation at the top of the hierarchy, whereas *group* actualisation would be more important for the collectivistic majority in the World. The second element of Tuckman's *forming, storming, norming, performing* model of team development (Tuckman & Jensen, 1977) would not be acceptable in collectivistic cultures due to the risks of loss of face. Some of Belbin's team roles (R M Belbin, 1993) would have been difficult to fill (or even unacceptable) in collectivistic societies, for example the *shaper* role, which included arguing, disagreeing and displaying aggression in the pursuit of goals.

1.2.3 Sociotechnical systems – problem areas

As stated earlier, cultural mismatches between complex sociotechnical systems and their operators have occurred due to the cultural assumptions that designers have built into their complex systems and standard operating procedures. Designers' default assumptions have typically been that the system operators would behave similarly (i.e. have the same cultural values) as them. These assumptions have resulted in degraded operational effectiveness and reduced safety.

1.3 Initial assumptions of the proposed research programme

The initial assumptions included the following:

- The cultural properties (i.e. 'cultural profiles') of teams could be usefully modelled[2] by quantifying team member cultural values along a limited number of 'cultural dimensions'.

---

[2] In this context, 'usefully modelled' implied that the cultural profiles captured the key differences between teams that influenced relative team performance.

4

- The tasks that teams performed[3] (i.e. the teams' task profiles) could be modelled in terms of factors that were directly affected by team culture.

- Relationships between culture trait/attribute/dimension scores and the performance of task factors could be established.

- Models that incorporated team cultural profiles and task profiles could be used to predict the effects of team culture on team performance.

One or more of the above initial assumptions could have been shown to be false in the literature review or subsequent data collection exercises; in that case, the programme of research would have been adapted to account for this.

1.4 Aims and objectives of the research

The primary aims of the research were to develop an improved under-standing of the cultural factors that influenced the effectiveness of teams, and to create a methodology and toolset for the evaluation of project teams and sociotechnical system operators and crews.

The associated objectives were as follows:

- to identify the culturally-related factors that contributed most to variances in team performances,

- to identify a task classification relevant to culturally-moderated team performance,

- to build a model that incorporated the above factors for the prediction of the effects of culture on team performance when tackling specified types of task, and

- to develop tools that encompassed the above model in order to:
  - o facilitate the creation of successful work teams in given situations, and
  - o enable the prediction of the effects of culture on team performance, and likely success or failure, of existing or proposed teams.

---

[3] Many complex sociotechnical systems are highly automated and, for most of the time, crews are acting as system monitors rather than operators. To be useful, a task (or mission model must capture the functionalities and capabilities required at *critical times*, e.g. when performing complex tasks or dealing with emergencies.

1.5 Main contributions to knowledge

The main contributions to knowledge were intended be a cultural theory of work team performance and a validated, quantitative methodology and tool that would enable the culturally-based assessment and improvement of teams.

1.6 Stakeholders and potential users

The main stakeholders and potential users of the outputs of the research were considered to be:

- organizations that designed or built complex sociotechnical systems
- organisations that utilised complex sociotechnical systems
- organizations that utilised multicultural (or different culture) teams for project and problem-solving work
- education and training organisations

1.7 Scope and boundaries of the work

1.7.1 Culture

The primary area of focus for the research described in this thesis was that of culture and its effects on teams, products and systems. Person-ality, leadership, qualifications, training, experience, age, health and many other factors impinge on the performance of teams; where bene-ficial to the research, the effects of these additional factors was to be explored to a limited degree, inasmuch as they affected an individual's and team's culture.

The research was **not** primarily concerned with the technical skill sets required to complete specific tasks.

1.7.2 Team types

A further limitation to the scope of the research related to the types of team under consideration. The primary focus of the research was on formal work teams, not informal or ad-hoc groups; such work teams:

- were formally created for one or more purposes,
- existed within a work environment, and
- either:

o included individuals who were involved in activities that could be associated with the creation of sociotechnical systems or products (e.g. research, development, design, planning, manufacture), or

o included individuals that were operating sociotechnical systems (e.g. crewing aircraft or power plants)

1.7.3 Tasks

The research was not concerned with analysing and categorising tasks other than from the point of view of the constraints and demands that those tasks placed on culture-moderated aspects of team organisation, communication and performance.

1.8 Background to the research methodology

Most of the articles and books covering multicultural and 'other culture' teams were anecdotal and qualitative. In contrast, the development of predictive cultural models required a quantitative, statistical approach. Coverage of the topics proposed in this thesis therefore required a *mixed methods research approach*, i.e. combining the (largely) inductive reasoning of qualitative methods and the (largely) deductive reasoning of quantitative methods; this resulted in the *inductive-deductive research cycle*.

It was important that the outputs of the research had potential applicability and, to that end, a compromise between explanatory power and usability was required. The researcher therefore adopted the approach known as *dialectical pragmatism*, where the value of a theory was judged on the basis of its 'workability', i.e. its applicability and predictive power (Teddlie & Tashakkori, 2009, Table 4.1):

"Theories are viewed instrumentally (they are "true" to differing degrees based on how well they currently work; workability is judged especially on the criteria of predictability and applicability)."

The research methodology is described in more detail in Chapter 2.

1.9 Structure of this report

This chapter (Chapter1) provides an introduction to the problem areas, initial assumptions, aims and objectives, scope and research methodology. Chapter 2 discusses the problem areas and research methodology in more detail, introduces the proposed problem solution in terms of theories, methodologies and software-based tools and lists the main areas to be studied in the literature review of Chapter 3.

Chapter 3 explores the current state of knowledge and opinion about the effects of national culture on teams, the tools that are available to evaluate and predict the performance of such teams, and the empirical evidence that is available to support such tools.

Chapter 4 describes research decisions that were based on the literature review of Chapter 3. A specific cultural framework was selected as the basis for data collection, analysis and tool-building, and a measure of cultural diversity was defined. A detailed set of culture-affected team/-task/mission factors was developed, and a set of task/mission dimensions was also proposed as an alternative basis for the quantitative description of team tasks. Three research questions relating to specific cultural factors are also asked in Chapter 4, because qualitative and quantitative studies in the literature relating to the effects of these cultural factors had been found to be limited and contradictory.

Chapter 5 describes the collection of statistical data from the literature, the collection of anecdotal information via questionnaire and interview, and the generation of statistical data by the author from pilot studies; this data was combined and utilised for the evaluation of the research questions of Chapter 4 and for the development of models of culture/-task-performance relationships that would be utilised by the team culture tools described in later chapters.

Chapter 6 describes a first team culture model and tool that utilised the team cultural profile to predict, directly, the team culture-related performance for a limited range of team and task types. Chapter 7 describes a second version of the model and tool that took account of the issues and limitations that were revealed during the evaluation of the first model. This second model and tool used an extended team cultural profile and a task profile based on the set of detailed team/task/mission factors developed in Chapter 4. The second model and tool used a different approach to prediction to that of the first model and tool; prediction was based on the discrepancies between the actual team cultural profile and a 'desirable cultural profile' generated from the task profile. Chapter 8 describes the third and final version of the model and tool. The third model and tool utilised the team cultural profile of the second model, but utilised a different, dimension-based approach for mission representation; this was, in part, because users had found this aspect of the second model to be problematic.

Chapter 9 presents an overview of the work and a discussion and analysis of the research results, models and tools. Chapter 10 offers conclusions and recommendations for further work.

Figure 1-1 presents an overview of the thesis structure and contents.

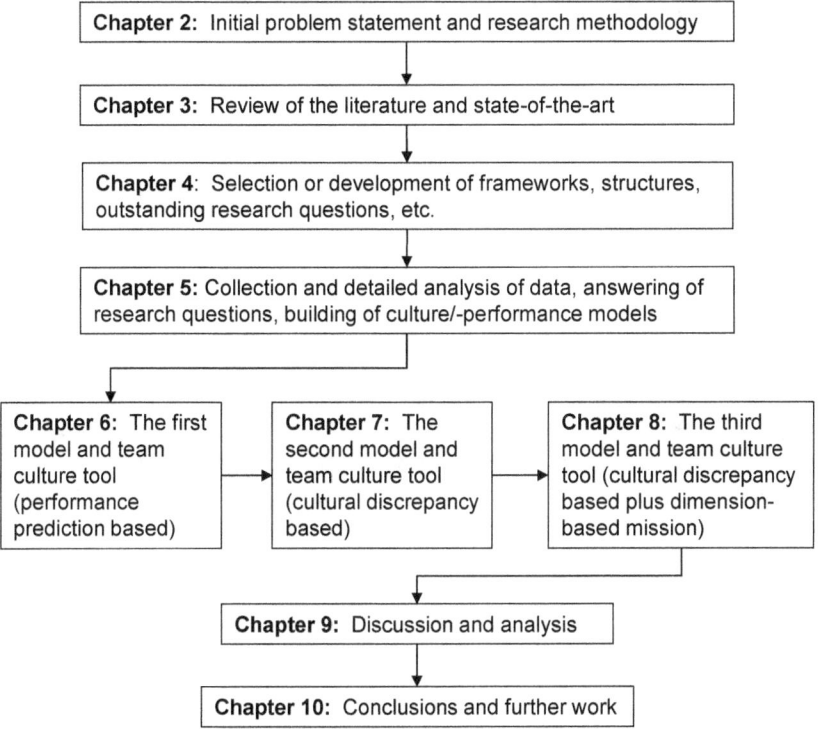

Figure 1-1: Thesis organisation

2 Problem statement and research methodology

2.1 Introduction

The purpose of this chapter is to define the problem area, problem statement (in detail), purpose and research question, and to describe the research methodology and solution approach. The purpose statement provides a focus for the research project and enables the definition of a key research question. The research question leads to the definition of sub-questions that impose structure and boundaries on the literature review.

2.2 The problem area

2.2.1 Background

All humans are products of the cultures in which they are immersed; culture heavily colours what people perceive (particularly in social situations), how they interpret what they perceive, how they react to it and how they behave towards each other. The products and systems of various cultures are increasingly exported to customers of different cultures, and people of differing cultures now intermix and collaborate more than ever before. Therefore, issues arising from differing culturally-based world views are impinging on a wide range of organisations, for example:

- **Companies exporting complex sociotechnical systems to other parts of the World:** Such systems include oil refineries, power generation systems and commercial transport aircraft. As systems have become more complex, formal systems modelling methods have improved; however, these methods primarily capture the specification and design of the *technical* sub-systems; the *human* components of such systems are captured in much less detail, and *cultural* aspects are not formally captured at all. To compound the problem, cultural assumptions are unconsciously built into sociotechnical systems; these assumptions lead to reduced performance and safety when such systems are exported to culturally-distant countries (see next paragraph).

- **Operators (or crews) of complex sociotechnical systems:** Cultural differences between designers and operators of complex sociotechnical systems with regard to communication, handling uncertainty, prioritising and decision-making result in differing safety performances in the operation of complex socio-technical systems; these differences can be seen, for example, in the safety records of national airlines.

An improved understanding of the effects of cultural traits on the factors that contribute to performance and safety would enable system designers, planners and implementers to take account of culture in system design, standard operating instructions, training, etc.

2.2.2 An initial problem statement

For several decades, multinational companies have been outsourcing a growing proportion of their research and development (R&D) activities to foreign subsidiaries; international joint ventures have also become more common over this period, for example to develop new multi-company vehicle platforms. Such companies have faced increasing choices when placing a new R&D project. It has become clear that different countries (with differing national cultures) tend to offer differing strengths that fit better with particular types of R&D than others. In addition, many teams have become internally more diverse, thus introducing further complex-ities. The R&D location decision has become more complicated.

A further issue relates to the safe and effective operation of complex systems. Although accidents involving safety-critical sociotechnical systems have occurred infrequently, they have typically been associated with high costs in terms of loss of life and destruction of resources. Worldwide, approximately seventy percent of sociotechnical system failures have been assigned to human error (Hollywell 1996; Amalberti 2001); however there have been clear differences in the error rates (and the corresponding accident rates) of operators of different nationalities. In particular, the accident rates amongst operators of similar cultures to those of the (typically European or North American) original system designers have tended to be low, whereas the accident rates amongst those of significantly different cultures have been much higher.

Although there are methodologies and tools to aid in the specification and design of the technical aspects of complex systems and systems-of-systems, there are no equivalent methodologies or tools to aid in the specification or definition of the cultural and social aspects of these systems; as a result, designers have unwittingly built their own cultural assumptions into such systems. Evidence is presented in the literature review of significant variations in accident rates amongst users of different cultural backgrounds.

The problems of particular interest to the author are detailed in the following subsections. The research has therefore covered these areas, but has not been limited to them because, in order to develop models of the relationships between team member cultural traits and team performances, it has been necessary to utilise data from a wide variety of team types.

a) The project team, including the sociotechnical system design team

The primary focus of interest was the effect of team member culture on the ability of the team to achieve a satisfactory level of performance.

Performance-limiting problems that could arise in **single-culture teams** (depending on the ethnic, professional and organizational cultures of the team) included:

- reluctance to suggest or support new ideas
- excessive consensus-seeking ("groupthink")
- low creativity

Additional problems that could arise in **multicultural teams** included:

- poor communication, misunderstandings and conflict
- fragmentation and social loafing
- poor decision-making

A multinational company might have many national branches that have the resources (human, physical, organisational) required for product design. However, differing cultural backgrounds could result in different branches performing better at specific stages of the research and development cycle, such as 'blue-skies' research, focused research, new system/product development, product mid-term upgrade or detailed process improvement.

b) The sociotechnical system operator team or crew

The primary focus of interest was the potential mismatch between system designers' default cultural assumptions about system operators and the cultural reality.

Problems that could arise from this mismatch included the following:

- **Inadequate representations (or specifications) of the operators of sociotechnical systems:** As a result, unanticipated problems could arise during operation, including those that increased the risk of catastrophic failure.

- **Unrecognised cultural assumptions built into products and systems:** These assumptions related not only to the physical equipment and software of the product or system, but also to the associated standard operating procedures, operator training and support systems. As a result, users who were culturally distant from system builders operated such systems and products less effectively and typically suffered higher accident and failure rates.

2.2.3 The primary stakeholders

It was important, in defining the problem area and scope, to consider the primary stakeholders (listed below); this encouraged a more focused approach.

- **Organisations that design or build complex sociotechnical systems:** The designers and engineers (in particular systems engineers) of such organisations should be aware of their own cultural traits, and should be enabled to specify the cultural traits of the system users, and to take these traits into account in their systems.

- **Organisations that utilise complex sociotechnical systems:** These organisations should be interested in the effects of culture on the training requirements, safety and performance capabilities of their operators or crew.

- **Organisations that utilise different culture or multicultural teams for project or problem-solving work:** These organisations (which could also be the sociotechnical system designers of the first point, above), should have an interest in the effects that team culture could have on creativity, decision-making, etc.

- **Education and training organisations:** Many of these organisations have a responsibility to impart team-working experience and training to their students. Most Anglo and European university engineering undergraduate courses include at least one team-based project during their students' second and third years. These teams are often culturally mixed, therefore an introduction to culture and a hands-on investigation of its effects, via the tools that form an output of this research, would help students to understand, respect and take advantage of cultural differences.

In particular, it was intended that outputs from the proposed research should provide assistance or guidance in two ways:

- Enabling engineers to take into account the effects of user (operator, crew) culture on the performance of their systems, when specifying and designing those systems.

- Enabling managers to compose or select single-culture or multi-cultural systems/product design teams that could potentially deliver the best results; this might be at the level of assembling a new team at a particular location, assembling a virtual team distributed across the globe, or assigning work to an existing team based at one of many locations across the globe.

2.3 Purpose statement, research questions and delimitations

2.3.1 Purpose statement

Based on the problem descriptions of the previous subsections, the purpose statement was as follows:

> The purpose of this research is to investigate relationships between team cultural traits and team performances for teams associated with the design and operation of sociotechnical systems, and to capture those relationships in methodologies or tools to assist in the design and operation of sociotechnical systems.

2.3.2 Research question

The associated research question was stated as:

> Is it feasible to predict, to a practicable degree, the performances of teams involved in the design or operation of sociotechnical systems, on the basis of those teams' members' national cultures?

2.3.3 Research sub-questions

The above research question provided three sub-questions, to form the basis of the literature review and subsequent research activities:

1. What do we know about 'different culture' and multicultural teams?

2. What tools are available to evaluate them?

3. What empirical evidence is available about the validity of such tools?

2.3.4 Delimitations of scope

The proposed research and culture tool would have to take account of situations where no information was available about the individuals who would make up a team, other than their likely national cultures and, perhaps, their educational attainments. Therefore, factors associated with individual team members' personalities, their experiences and skills would not be investigated. As a result the following topics were not, in themselves, of primary interest[4]:

- cultural/intercultural competence and the associated measurement tools and methods
- individual team member personalities and their effects on team performance
- the effects of informed leadership on team performance (e.g. inter-culturally competent team leaders)

In addition, when designing complex sociotechnical systems, it was unlikely that detailed information on the organisational and safety cultures of user organisations would be available; therefore, the following topics were not of primary interest[5]:

- safety culture and the associated measurement/assessment tools and methods
- organisational culture and the associated measurement/assessment tools and methods

2.4   Research methodology

Many of the most relevant articles retrieved during the literature review described in this thesis, including those on team or crew attitudes to automation in complex sociotechnical systems and those on the efficacy and effectiveness of multicultural teams, were found to be highly anecdotal and qualitative in nature. Other articles, for example many of those that examined cultural traits, were quantitative in their approach. In addition to this reliance on both qualitative and quantitative research

---

[4] Except where the associated methods or tools could be adapted to the prediction or assessment of the effects of national culture on relevant aspects of team performance.
[5] As above.

sources, the work described in this thesis also relied on qualitative and quantitative methods in order to collect evidence, to develop and evaluate hypotheses and to create demonstration tools.

The main implication of the findings described in the above paragraph was the necessity to apply a mixed method research approach, as described in Teddlie & Tashakkori (2009).

As described earlier in this thesis, the issues and problems associated with multicultural and 'different culture' teams had important consequences for many organizations. It was therefore important that the theories and tools that arose out of this work could offer *practical* predictions or guidance with regard to the conduct and performance of multicultural teams. The culture-moderated interactions between operators and their sociotechnical systems were highly complex, as were the internal interactions of multicultural teams and groups; a very wide range of qualitative and quantitative factors could be considered (and had been considered elsewhere) as candidates for new theories of culture-moderated team performance. Although it would have been very valuable to develop a theory that was highly explanatory, there was little benefit in developing a toolset that incorporated so many factors that it was unusable in typical situations due to the unavailability of data or due to the restrictions of data protection laws. It was therefore necessary to adopt the *pragmatist* approach in order to develop a theory that could form the basis of a practical toolset, see Teddlie & Tashakkori (2009), Table 4.1, p.74. Point (5) of this table stated the pragmatist principle:

> *"Theories are viewed instrumentally (they are "true" to differing degrees based on how well they currently work; workability is judged especially on the criteria of predictability and applicability)."*

The above statement concurred with the view of the philosophy of science scholar Laudan; he advocated that the criteria for assessing the development of a theory should relate to that theory's problem-solving effectiveness, rather than to its falsifiability (Laudan, 1978).

The toolset had to balance the effort of application against the value of the answers that it produced. To that end, it might have been possible to reduce the number of factors required in the toolset, or at least to enable trade-offs between accuracy and cost/effort.

2.5   Study design

The central subject area of the research related to sociotechnical systems, and the driving rationale behind the research activities was to develop and test a culture tool. The study design was intended to reflect the associated requirements. An outline of the study design is presented in Figure 2-1.

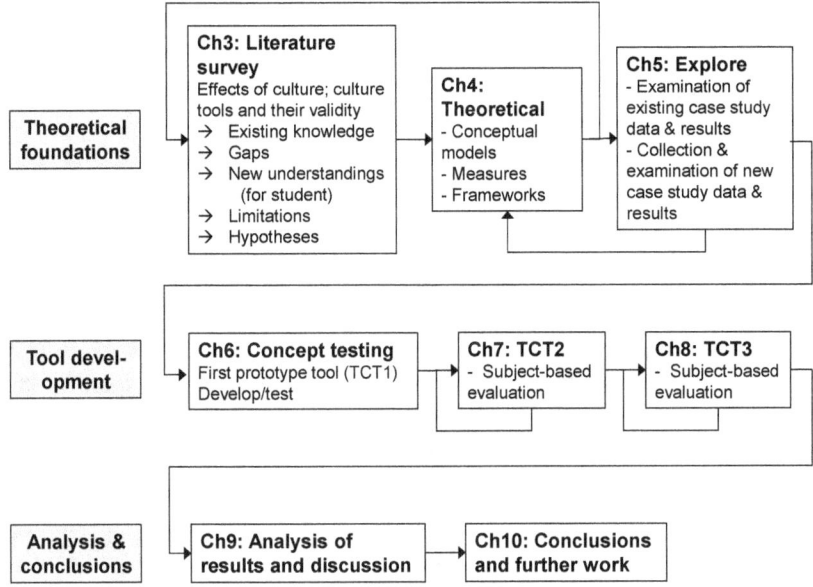

Figure 2-1: Study design

Based on the three research sub-questions, the literature review provided insights as to the effects of national culture on team activities, the availability of culture-based tools to predict various aspects of team performance, and the validity of such tools. Based on the outputs of the literature review, gaps and limitations were identified and several hypotheses were generated. Appropriate methodologies were adapted from the literature, where available, and initial conceptual models were proposed. Selected case study material from the literature was supplemented via the collection of qualitative anecdotal data and by studies carried out by the author; the studies were statistically analysed, in part to answer earlier-generated hypotheses. Based on the results, sets of relationships between team national cultures and team performance factors were generated to form the basis of the team performance prediction methodologies.

A first prototype tool was produced as a proof-of-concept. Following an analysis of this, a second tool was developed; this was validated and tested with real data prior to a subject-based evaluation. Following user feedback, a final version of the tool was developed, and similarly validated, tested and subject-evaluated.

Finally, the results were analysed and the limitations of such tools (and the underlying theories and assumptions) were discussed within a wider context. Conclusions were drawn and recommendations were made for further work.

2.6 Approach adopted and activities undertaken

The high-level requirement for any culture tool developed by the author was that it should enable the prediction of the effects of team cultural traits on team performance (as measured or evaluated externally). In order to achieve this capability, it would be necessary, firstly, to obtain or develop a capability to capture team cultural traits, based on no more than team member nationalities and educational levels[6]. Secondly, it would be necessary to obtain or develop a capability to capture the culture-affected task, skill or mission factors that were associated with key aspects of teams' performance. Thirdly, it would be necessary to associate specific cultural trait levels or scores with optimum achievement of these factors. Finally, it would be necessary to be able to assess any team based on its closeness to the ideal represented by the above optimum cultural trait levels or scores.

It was difficult to establish a set of detailed requirements at the outset because an examination of academic sources revealed little literature on cultural tools other than that relating to a range of cultural frameworks; these frameworks were typically based on cultural dimensions or attributes that enabled the placing of groups or populations in cultural space. There were, in addition, several academically-developed questionnaire-based tools that assessed individual team members' cultural intelligence (or similar) from their personalities and cultural attitudes as captured in the questionnaire responses. The author also examined non-academic sources of various commercial and community-produced 'culture tools'. Such tools were typically intended for the provision of advice or training to individuals who were travelling to other cultural zones, for the assessment of individuals' cultural preferences, for the assessment of individuals' cultural competences or for the assessment of companies' organisational or safety cultures.

The author discussed aspects of the requirements with, amongst others, Geert Hofstede (developer of the most widely-used cultural framework)

---

[6] A key potential application of any culture tool produced by the author was as an adjunct to a suite of system design tools; as such, the only information available about potential operators or crew would be their nationalities and likely educational levels.

18

and Peter Richerson (joint author of the book 'Not by Genes Alone – How Culture Transformed Human Evolution').

No tools were found that enabled the effective assessment of the performance of various types of team on the basis of (default) team national culture. Although this finding demonstrated that there was a dearth of such tools, it was still necessary to obtain evidence of the effects of culture on performance (and of a corresponding need for culture tools) and to define the detailed requirements for such tools.

The first part of the literature review ('what we know about different-culture and multicultural teams') revealed empirical evidence of the effects of culture on the performance of various types of teams, e.g. research/design team creativity and innovation performance, sports team performance and operator/crew safety and accident rates. In addition, evidence was found about the effects of culture on skill or task factors associated with team performance, for example, communication, management and leadership, training and situation awareness. However, no evidence was found to suggest that the effects of team culture were specifically taken into account to-date by designers of complex systems and standard operating procedures.

The second part of the literature review ('the tools that are available to evaluate or predict the performance of such teams') revealed very little information about tools that could utilise team member national culture to estimate or predict team performance. There were many cultural frameworks that enabled the positioning of individuals (or teams consisting of 'same culture' members) in culture space, but only one national culture-based model and one national culture-based tool attempted to provide further analysis of likely performance, or optimum team cultural traits; neither of these provided an effective capability to predict team performance in a range of sociotechnical situations.

As the second part of the literature review had revealed that there were no relevant theoretical models or practical team culture tools, the third part of the literature review ('empirical evidence about the validity of the tools') examined the validity of various tools, models, frameworks and taxonomies that could provide the building blocks of such a tool.

Based on the literature review, a widely-used cultural framework was selected as the basis for scoring team members' default cultural traits, algorithms were developed to produce team cultural trait and cultural diversity values from these scores, and a five factor skill/task set was developed.

Detailed results from the literature review were combined with further data collection and analysis by the author in order to assign optimal cultural dimension scores to sub-factors of the above five skill/task factors. In addition, questionnaires were employed to gather anecdotal information about individuals' cross-cultural experiences in order to ascertain the degree to which they observed and reacted according to their country-level scores. Long, unstructured interviews were held with several experts who had significant experience in various team types, in order to ascertain their personal observations about cultural effects on team member performances.

The process of detailing and testing the requirements included the building of an initial 'Aunt Sally' tool in order to 'test the water'; this captured a cultural representation of a team, a simplified representation of the required tasks/skills and produced a measure of team performance based on culture. This initial tool attempted to generate an absolute measure of a team's effectiveness, expressed as a percentage. However, the potential complexity of the equations and the difficulty associated with justifying the weightings chosen in the equations convinced the author that this approach could not be extended satisfactorily; it would also be extremely difficult to update in the light of improved knowledge. Although the tool's measure of effectiveness was unsatisfactory, it did demonstrate the capability of the method that had been developed to produce a team cultural profile. As a result of building and testing this initial culture tool, a revised requirement for establishing cultural 'fitness for purpose' was devised, which was based directly on the level of discrepancy between actual and optimum or desirable culture trait scores.

The second tool utilised a similar team cultural profiling method to the first, but utilised the earlier-developed full set of five task/skill factors as the basis for establishing a 'desirable cultural profile'. The tool produced a 'cultural discrepancy score' that indicated the degree of mismatch between a team's actual and desirable cultural profile. The use of a discrepancy score avoided the complexity problems of the first tool and allowed the use of a more detailed set of task skill sub-factors. Individual factor and sub-factor discrepancies could be analysed to highlight the types of problems that the discrepancies signified. This tool was verified and validated before being user-tested. Feedback from the users indicated that some had difficulties when scoring the task/skill factors; this was unsurprising in hindsight, as this scoring task required a high level of understanding of skill requirements that would only develop with training and experience in team selection.

The third tool was developed in order to overcome user difficulties with the second tool's task/skill scoring requirement. Based on the task/skill factors used in the second tool, the author produced optimal scores for a range of teams for each of two cases: sociotechnical system design/-project teams, and organised action teams (e.g. airline crew, ship crews, power station operators). Users were presented with a two-dimensional matrix containing a range of 'exemplar' teams and were required to select the location on the matrix that represented their team via a process of comparison with the exemplar teams.

2.7   Summary of problem statement and methodology

Section 2.2 defined the main problem area of research interest to include sociotechnical system design teams and sociotechnical system operator teams; the main stakeholders were identified as the designers and users of complex sociotechnical systems, their managers, and education and training organisations.

A mixed method research methodology was chosen, and a *pragmatist* approach was selected for theory development to ensure that it could form the basis of a reliable, practical toolset.

The proposed solution approach included the selection of relevant areas of the literature to review and, from these, the identification of methodologies that could be utilised and gaps that required to be filled or circumvented, the collection of and analysis of data and, on the basis of the analysis results, the development of a culture-based theory of team performance; this theory was incorporated in culture-based performance prediction methodologies and tools.

3   Review of the literature and state-of-the-art

3.1   Introduction

The state-of-the-art literature review was based on the three-stage review process as described by Levy & Ellis (2006), see Figure 3-1.

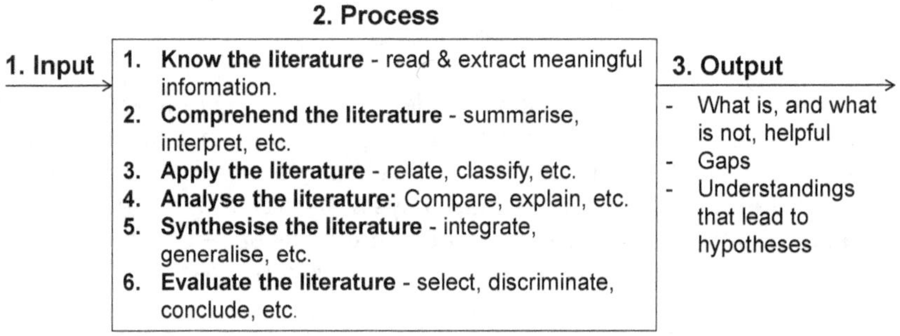

2. Process

1. Input	1. **Know the literature** - read & extract meaningful information. 2. **Comprehend the literature** - summarise, interpret, etc. 3. **Apply the literature** - relate, classify, etc. 4. **Analyse the literature:** Compare, explain, etc. 5. **Synthesise the literature** - integrate, generalise, etc. 6. **Evaluate the literature** - select, discriminate, conclude, etc.	3. Output - What is, and what is not, helpful - Gaps - Understandings that lead to hypotheses

Figure 3-1: The literature review process of Levy & Ellis

The review question was:

Is it feasible to predict, to a practicable degree, the performance of teams involved in the design or operation of sociotechnical systems, on the basis of those teams' members' national cultures?

The state-of-the-art review was split into three areas (see subsections 3.3 to 3.5) that sought to answer the following questions:

1. What do we know about (the effects of culture on the performance of) 'different culture' and multicultural teams?

2. What tools are available to evaluate these teams?

3. What empirical evidence is available about the validity of such tools?

The number of relevant publications varied greatly within and between the three areas. For example, many publications were retrieved on studies into the effects of culture on team performance and on cultural frameworks, but few publications were retrieved on the topic of culture-based performance prediction tools, and those that were found were concerned with safety culture or organisational culture, not national culture.

Key findings that directly affected subsequent research towards the aims and objectives of this thesis are detailed in this chapter's summary.

3.2 Overview of the literature review

3.2.1 Literature review design

As stated above, the literature review was split into three major parts. For the first research sub-question, a dozen or so key researchers and their publications (journal papers and academic books) were initially identified, read and commented upon. Following this activity, potentially relevant forward and backward citations[7] were followed. Sets of key words and phrases (and their synonyms) were then selected, based in part on the most relevant publications on each topic and sub-topic; in addition, after initial evaluative literature searches, key 'exclusion words' were identified. This enabled complex search logic statements to be built up, e.g. *culture AND (framework OR tool OR methodology) AND team AND performance NOT "safety culture" NOT "organizational culture"*[8]. These keywords (and their synonyms) and phrases were utilised in several citation databases and search engines. In sub-topic areas where many publications were amassed, then, following reading and commentary, the sets of subjects and authors were pruned to enable more focused citation and keyword searches to be carried out. See Appendix 1A for more details of keyword searches.

For the second part of the literature review, only one relevant article was initially found in the search for national culture-based team performance prediction models, methods and tools, despite widening the search and evaluating a wide range of articles and websites. As a result, the search was broken into 'sub-searches' for potential components of such models, methods and tools. At this stage, the literature review process followed that of the first part of the review, except that the range of published materials was extended to include professional magazines, commercial tools, websites, blogs, etc.

---

[7] Potential relevance was identified via comments in the text of the citing paper, by cited paper title and/or by author.
[8] Note that the various citation databases and search engines differed in the form and complexity of logic that they could interpret; in some cases, only the simplest of logic statements could be used.

For the third part of the literature review, the search for material was driven by the tools found in the second part of the literature review.

3.2.2 Literature review sources

Several citation/database sources were initially accessed via the university library portal, and new sources were added to these as they became available. These sources were evaluated by searching for a range of previously identified papers in relevant areas and via keyword searches. The evaluated sources are listed below; more details of the results of the evaluation of sources are presented in Appendix 1B.

- **CiteSeerX:** Initial test searches on the CiteSeerX demonstrated that it performed poorly across the range of topic areas.

- **EBSCO:** Initial test searches on the *EBSCO* database confirmed that it would only retrieve literature from a limited range of subject areas.

- **ERIC (Education Resources Information Center):** Many *ERIC* thesaurus descriptors were related to culture, but few relevant papers were returned by the *ERIC* database due, probably, to its extreme focus on education-related research.

- **Google/Google Scholar:** The ability to express the search logic very precisely in *Google/Google Scholar* enabled the author to 'tune' the search to cope with the very wide range of sources and forms of data that were available (compared to all other search engines). The author was able to discover relevant blogs, wikis, bulletin boards, discussion forums, newsletters, etc., as well as the more usual academic sources of information. Overall, *Google/Google Scholar* was the most useful single source of information for the literature review. In addition, Google Scholar's 'live' author citation-tracking facility enabled the author of this thesis to track new citations of key authors, e.g. Salas, Helmreich and Hollenbeck.

- **Mendeley:** *Mendeley* was the reference manager system used by the author for the latter half of his PhD project due to recurring problems with the original reference manager, which had been recommended by the university. Although the *Mendeley* database was by no means comprehensive, it was convenient to use it to search for previously-identified papers because successful search results could be entered into the author's list of references at the touch of a button.

- **PubMed:** Although limited to the *MEDLINE* references and abstracts database, *PubMed* produced a surprisingly high return rate of relevant articles.

- **PsycINFO:** The author was only able to access a limited subset of the *PsycINFO* database, as the university did not have a full subscription to the database.

- **Scopus:** The *Scopus* bibliographic database provided abstracts and citations for a very wide range of disciplines, but it appeared to have less coverage of pre-1985 articles than the *Web of Science.*

- **SSCI** (Social Science Citation Index): Accessed as part of the *Web of Science.*

- **Web of Science:** The *Web of Science* provided advanced search facilities for its 'core' collection, but only basic search facilities for the full collection. Its forward and backward citation following facilities proved very effective and fast. In addition, the search facility was efficient, producing a higher proportion of relevant articles than most search engines (including Google/-Google Scholar).

- **Individual journal searches:** In the late stages of the literature review, two journals of high relevance to the research described in this thesis were subjected to a 100% article-by-article exam-ination of abstracts (when in doubt, the whole paper was perused). Out of 108 articles deemed as relevant to the PhD research, 98 had already been retrieved; of the previously omitted 10 articles, only one was deemed to be of sufficient importance to be cited in the thesis.

To summarise the literature search sources: The most useful sources were found to be *Google/Google Scholar,* which retrieved a significantly wider range of publications than all other sources, and *Web of Science,* which not only accessed a wide (though lesser) range of publications, but also included useful forward and backward citation-chasing capabilities.

3.2.3 Key authors

Based on prior reading and knowledge, a small number of key authors, and their most relevant publications, were initially identified for each research sub-question; the literature review was then extended via forward and backward citations.

The first literature review topic aimed to answer the question "What do we know about (the effects of culture on the performance of) different-culture teams and multicultural teams?" For this topic, the initially-identified researchers were Helmreich & Merritt, Sherman and Harris (for sociotechnical system operators and crew), Shane, Barjak, Herbig &

Jones (for design innovation teams) and Stahl et al. (for studies concentrating on multicultural teams).

The second part of the literature review aimed to answer the question "What tools are available to evaluate or predict the performance of such ('different culture' and multicultural) teams?" An initial search revealed no relevant national culture tools; however, a range of *cultural frameworks* had been developed and, for these, the initially-identified authors were Hofstede, House et al., Triandis, Schwartz and Earley & Gibson; academic books detailing many of these frameworks were available, and represented a useful starting point. The initially-perused academic books associated with these authors included "Culture's Consequences" (G H Hofstede, 1980), "Cultures and Organizations" (Geert Hofstede, 1991), "Culture, Leadership and Organizations" (House, Hanges, Javidan, Dorfman, & Gupta, 2004), "Culture and Social Behavior" (Triandis, 1993), "Beyond Individualism/Collectivism" (S H Schwartz, 1994) and "Multinational Work Teams: A New Perspective" (Earley & Gibson, 2002). Academic papers by these authors, and reviews by other authors of their work were then retrieved and examined before expanding the literature review via forward and backward citations.

As stated above, detailed forward and backward citation searches for the second literature review topic revealed no publications on methodologies and tools for the assessment or prediction of *national* culture's effects on the performance of teams, and a subsequent extensive search of the academic literature, utilising a wide range of search terms, only revealed one publication on this topic (other than the author's own publications). As a result a further search was carried out in order to retrieve academic publications on safety culture/organisational culture tools, and non-academic sources of culture tools. The intention of this activity was to examine any culture- and task-related factors utilised in these tools, and to determine whether any of them could be re-used in a national culture tool.

The third part of the literature review aimed to answer the question "What empirical evidence is available about the validity of such (culture-based team evaluation and prediction) tools?" As no relevant tools had been found, this section was devoted to an examination of the validity of the previously-identified cultural frameworks, diversity indices and team/-task/behaviour classifications. As any evaluations of such frameworks and classifications would cite the relevant developers, the initial starting point for this third topic was similar to the second, i.e. tracing citations of the same key papers; indeed many relevant papers had been retrieved during the literature search activity for the (above) second topic. The keyword searches employed for this third review topic included additional search terms, e.g. 'evaluation', 'validity', 'criticism' and 'limitations'.

For this third literature review topic, the research was spread across a very wide range of fields, with limited cross-connection. As a result, the author of this thesis had to rely heavily on keyword searches. Appendix 1C provides an incomplete list of journal papers, learned society and professional society publications that were cited in this thesis.

3.3 The effects of culture on team performance

This section is divided into two parts. The first part reviews the literature that addresses 'external' aspects of team performance, i.e. how effectively teams of various cultures performed in terms of their missions. The second part reviews the literature that addresses 'internal' aspects of team performance that are affected by culture, e.g. communication and decision-making. These divisions are somewhat artificial, but assist in identifying intermediate variables that could be used later in the research.

Note that many of the references in this section refer to 'cultural dimensions' such as individualism, power distance, uncertainty avoidance and masculinity. Descriptions of these cultural terms are provided in Chapter 4, tables 4-1 to 4-4.

3.3.1 Effects of culture on external measures of performance

Particular attention has been paid to the two key areas of interest for the research described in this thesis, i.e. complex sociotechnical system design and sociotechnical system operation.

a) Teams involved in creativity and innovation

Complex, automated sociotechnical systems are the products, directly and indirectly, of various levels of research, invention and technical development. As producers of sociotechnical systems have become increasingly multinational (e.g. via expansion, takeover or merger), they have gained access to a wider range of choices when placing research, development and manufacturing activities. The purpose of this sub-section is to examine evidence about relationships between national cultural traits (or scores) and various levels of research and innovation performance.

The term 'creativity' has had differing meanings in different cultures (Berthrong, 1998; Lubart, 1999; Niu & Sternberg, 2002). In many western cultures, creativity was considered to be associated with the creation of new knowledge, paradigms, novel systems, products or processes; in many eastern cultures, creativity was considered to be associated with the search for, or a revealing of, a truth that is temporarily hidden from view. Even where a degree of common understanding was reached, there were likely to be cultural differences in emphasis, for example Morris & Leung (2010) claimed that there was evidence that westerners prioritised novelty over usefulness whereas easterners prioritised usefulness over novelty. Simonton & Ting (2010) suggested a definition of creativity as the product of novelty x usefulness, i.e. that creativity only occurred where the result was both novel (or original) and useful. However, the concept of innovation was already associated with usefulness, as it was the process of developing an idea or invention into a product or service that customers wanted; therefore Simonton & Ting's definition merely added confusion. The lack of a universal classification or agreement about the various forms of knowledge creation and application has made it difficult to accurately categorise differing forms and levels of creative output. For example, the following capabilities or activities have produced new knowledge and/or led to new products or services: Academic/fundamental/blue-skies research[9], industrial research & development (R&D), creativity/creation, inventiveness, innovation, improvement, implementation. Would it be feasible to identify differing human capabilities associated with each of these forms of creative output? Simple subdivisions, e.g. of R&D activities into basic research, applied research, and development activities (as suggested by Pearce (1990) and others) were inadequate because they did not cover the full gamut of activities that led to new products and services.

The author of this thesis did not have the resources to explore further the issues of research, creativity, inventiveness and innovation. Therefore, the Western view of 'creativity-as-novelty' (rather than creativity-as-usefulness') was chosen, as this emphasis on 'novelty' helped to differentiate between creativity and innovation, each of which required different skill sets as suggested earlier.

Education has played a major part in enabling the creativity and innovation potential of a population. However, the primary purpose of education in high-individualism nations has been to *'learn how to learn'*, whereas the primary purpose in low-individualism (high-collectivism) nations has been to *'learn how to do'* (Geert Hofstede, 1986); most nations could be placed somewhere on the continuum between the

---

[9] In many ways, blue-skies research <u>could</u> be associated with the *eastern* view of creativity, i.e. the search for, or a revealing of, a truth that is temporarily hidden from view. The (western) creative aspects of fundamental research are perhaps associated with the development of novel tools to carry out the research, rather than with the research itself.

above two 'educational extremes'. 'Learning how to learn' encouraged the search for new ideas, i.e. western-type creativity and innovation, whereas 'learning how to do' encouraged the implementation of prior innovations and improvements in tangible products and services. In support of this view, Herbig & Palumbo (1996) suggested that western cultures favoured breakthrough innovations, and eastern cultures fostered incremental innovations. Kirton's adaptation–innovation inventory of cognitive styles (Kirton, 1976) was informative, as its extremes appeared to describe some of the strengths of eastern and western approaches to innovation. Kirton described an adapter as one who reduced problems via incremental improvements, utilised tried and tested means, was cautious, sensitive to people and maintained cooperation; he described an innovator as one who tried to do things differently, was undisciplined, created dissonance and shock, challenged rules and did not require consensus.

In the remainder of this subsection, published studies on the effects of national culture on the generation and development of new ideas (by both academic and industrial teams) are examined. Such studies covered basic (or blue skies) research, applied research, product and process development and improvement. Some studies, for example that of Mihaela, Ogrean, & Belascu (2011) grouped countries into regions prior to the examination of cultural effects; such studies have been omitted from the following examination because of the wide intraregional ranges in culture traits (in some cases much wider than those of the corresponding interregional ranges. Other studies, for example that of Vecchi & Brennan (2009) concentrated on the relationships between national culture and innovation-related *inputs*; such studies have also been omitted.

i) Research

The effects of cultural and disciplinary diversity on the performance of academic research teams in the life sciences were examined by Barjak (2006). The outperforming teams had 20-25% of foreign-educated members[10]; low cultural diversity teams and high cultural diversity teams (those containing 40-45%) performed less well, resulting in an inverted 'U'-shaped performance curve.

Following the above study, a larger study was carried out on a representative sample of life science teams, based on 468 usable questionnaire returns (Barjak & Robinson, 2008). Research performance was based on numbers of papers per researcher and average number of citations.

---

[10] Foreign-educated in the sense that the team member's last degree was obtained outside the host country.

Research team diversity was measured separately for PhD students and post-docs, based on the Shannon diversity index applied to countries of origin; international collaboration was based on papers co-authored with researchers based in the USA, EU and other foreign countries. Twelve regression models were produced that variously included inputs relating to knowledge pooling (from internal cultural diversity and/or external collaboration), characteristics of team leaders, team size, etc., and included measures of performance based on output quantity, output quality. The results of Barjak & Robinson's (2008) analysis indicated that the most successful academic life science research teams had a strong domestic base (with a minority of foreign team members), a moderate amount of collaboration with foreign research teams and a small proportion of research students. They also found that small teams (optimum size seven members) produced the maximum number of publications per capita, and also the highest number of citations per publication. The average cultural diversity of post-docs (based on Shannon's diversity index) was 0.38; based therefore on the qualitative recommendations (limited cultural diversity within team), it would appear that academic research teams in the life sciences should have a Shannon's diversity index of somewhere below 0.38, in line with Barjak's earlier findings.

The results of a study of eight hundred industrial and academic research units in Austria, Belgium, Finland and Sweden were reported by Kedia et al. (1992). This study revealed that higher research productivity occurred in high masculinity/low power distance countries than in low masculinity/low power distance countries, i.e. that high masculinity appeared to contribute to researchers' ideas initiation.

ii) Industrial research & development

Cozzi & Giordani (2011) carried out an analysis of the effects of ambiguity aversion on countries' R&D performances; they utilised OECD and United Nations data sources to highlight a strong negative relationship between national uncertainty avoidance scores and research performance as exhibited by the level of R&D intensity and the proportion of researchers in each country. They found that the negative correlation between uncertainty avoidance scores and research performance was stronger across European countries than across OECD or a wider range of countries. Niebuhr (2010) carried out a regression analysis of innovation performance in the various German regions, the results of which suggested that diverse cultural backgrounds in the team or workforce could enhance R&D performance. The maximum proportion of high-skilled workers (those that we would associate with R&D) in any region was 12.92 percent, the lowest was near-zero; even the highest figure (12.92%) would be considered low in terms of diversity within an R&D team. Because Niebuhr's work was carried out at the regional, rather than team level, there were issues with its validity. Also, when time lags were applied (to represent delayed outputs), the correlations between cultural diversity and R&D performance were significantly lower. In addition, the measure of cultural diversity appeared to be based on the proportion of non-German workers in each region; this was a poor measure of diversity.

Jones & Davis (2000) produced a taxonomy of company (or subsidiary) R&D focus, with associated optimum cultural scores (all other things being equal) based on their analysis of studies:

- locally-supported support/adaption – low individualism, high power distance, high masculinity, high uncertainty avoidance and long term orientation

- locally-orientated R&D - medium/high individualism, low/medium power distance, low/medium masculinity, low/medium uncertainty avoidance and long term orientation

- globally-orientated R&D – high individualism, low power distance, low masculinity, low uncertainty avoidance and long term orientation

Rinne et al. (2013) analysed the relationships between cultural dimension scores and two creativity indices, the Global Creativity Index (GCI) and the Design and Creativity Index (DCI). They found a strong positive relationship between individualism and the two creativity indices, but no significant relationship between power distance or uncertainty avoidance and the creativity indices. Willems (2007) investigated the relationships between national culture, social capital and innovation (as measured in terms of patents registered in Europe (EPO) and the USA (USPTO)); he found that individualism had the highest correlation (positive) with innovation, followed by power distance (negative), masculinity (positive) and uncertainty avoidance (negative).

iii) Innovation

Herbig and Miller (1992) considered several levels of innovation, concluding that higher order innovation was best served by high individualism, low uncertainty-avoidance societies. Shane's (1992) investigation of early stage per-capita inventiveness and innovation rates across 33 countries indicated that power distance (negative) and individualism (positive) had strong correlations with per-capita inventiveness and innovation. Willems (2007) found that individualism had the highest correlation (positive) with innovation, as measured in terms of European and US patents, followed by power distance (negative), masculinity (positive) and uncertainty avoidance (negative).

Bouncken & Winkler (2008) found that differences in power distance among team members were particularly damaging to the performance of bicultural global innovation teams. Rothwell & Wissema (1986) presented two models of the process of technical innovation and discussed the role that culture played in these models with particular reference to the innovation diffusion process. They identified characteristics associated with low power distance, long term orientation and low uncertainty avoidance as promoting technical innovation. Herbig & Dunphy (1998) found that national culture played a significant role in the adoption of innovative technologies, in particular if the adoption implied changes in behaviour; they cited several studies that identified high individualism, low power distance and low uncertainty avoidance scores as promoting technical innovation.

Halkos & Tzeremes (2011), who studied the effects of national culture on innovation efficiency, found that masculinity was positively correlated with innovation up to a score of 70-80[11]. The emphasis on relationships and agreement-seeking within a low-masculinity culture, rather than on externally-measured goals, was similar to that of low-individualism communities; such an emphasis could lead to reduced performance when faced with high creativity or blue-skies research goals. The same authors later carried out analyses of the innovation efficiency and performance of 25 European countries (G. E. Halkos & Tzeremes, 2013); these analyses revealed that high uncertainty avoidance had the greatest effect on innovation, followed by high power distance – in both cases, the effects were negative. As part of a three-decade multi-level review of the application of Hofstede's cultural framework, Taras, Kirkman & Steel (2010) found that uncertainty avoidance was strongly negatively related to innovation.

Efrat (2014) examined the impacts of national culture on innovation in 35 countries for the years 1998, 2004 and 2008; innovation output measures were based on patents, journal articles and high-technology exports (obtained from the World Bank database). He found that power distance had little effect, high individualism contributed positively to publications but negatively to patents, uncertainty avoidance had a general negative effect, and that high masculinity contributed negatively to publications and positively to patents. There were several issues with the results of Efrat's study. Firstly, the results were based on national, not team values; research teams often contain many foreign members, therefore the default national values may not have been accurate. Secondly, journal articles tend to be produced by academic research teams, patents by industrial innovation teams, and high technology

---

[11] Perhaps adjusted to 55-65 following Bosland's education corrections for 16 years FTE.

exports (the end of a long chain) often depend significantly on lower level process and product improvements; these three outputs represent significantly different levels of creativity or innovation, and should be distinguished from each other.

iv) Product development (initiation)

Nakata & Sivakumar (1996) carried out a literature review in order to understand the relationships between national culture and new product development. They split the product development process into two stages, as suggested by Johne (1984), i.e. initiation (idea generation, screening, concept testing) and implementation (product development, test marketing, product launch). Nakata & Sivakumar found that the best-performing national cultures at the *initiation* stage had high individualism, low power distance, low uncertainty avoidance and low masculinity scores (i.e. as in Nordic cultures); the low masculinity scores contrast with the findings of Kedia et al. and Halkos & Tzemeres. They found that the best-performing national cultures at the *implementation* stage had low individualism, but high power distance, uncertainty avoidance and masculinity scores (e.g. Japan, Taiwan and Mexico).

D'Iribarne et al. (1998, Ch.IV) reported on a joint venture between Renault of France (high power distance, high masculinity and high uncertainty avoidance) and Volvo of Sweden (low power distance, low masculinity and low uncertainty avoidance) for the development of a new car. According to d'Iribarne, the hierarchically-organised French team members produced the most innovative designs and defended them aggressively; the democratically-organised Swedish team members sought consensus to such a degree that they were limited in the range of ideas that they could even conceive. The joint venture failed and was subsequently dissolved. D'Iribarne highlighted the fact that the French, with their supposedly creativity-limiting high uncertainty avoidance, were able to out-innovate the Swedes. Geert Hofstede referred to this case during a conversation with the author of this thesis at a Loughborough University workshop (Fellows, 2011), highlighting the Swedish high femininity (low masculinity) score; he suggested that this had caused the need for consensus to overrule the purpose of the joint venture. This low masculinity/inadequate product development result contradicts that of Nakata & Sivakumar (above).

Rinne et al. (2012) utilised Hofstede's cultural framework to investigate the effects of national culture on innovation in 66 countries, as measured by the 2008-2009 Global Innovation Index (INSEAD, 2009). A multiple linear regression analysis highlighted that power distance was strongly negatively related to innovation performance, whereas individualism was strongly positively related; no statistically significant relationship with uncertainty avoidance was found. The 2008-2009 Global Innovation

Index measure of performance was based on five input measures (institutions, human capacity, uptake of infrastructure, market sophistication, and business sophistication) and two output measures (scientific outputs, and creative outputs & wellbeing).

Kaasa and Vadi (2010) analysed the effects of culture on innovation in European countries, using patenting activity as a measure. They found a strong negative relationship between national uncertainty avoidance scores and indicators of patenting intensity; however, the relationship did not appear to be linear. In addition, high power distance and masculinity scores reduced innovation, but their effects could be counteracted to some extent by high individualism scores.

Shane (1993) utilised Hofstede's cultural framework to investigate the effects of national culture on the innovation rates of 33 countries over the period 1975 to 1980, using (this time) trademarks filed in the USA as a measure of the countries' innovation rates. He included two economic independent variables that are known to influence innovation rates – per capita income, and percentage of total value added accounted for by industries that typically generated large numbers of innovations. A least squares multiple regression analysis highlighted uncertainty avoidance as the most important cultural variable (it was also more significant than either of the two economic control variables; a *low* uncertainty avoidance score promoted innovation. High individualism and low power distance scores each also promoted innovation to a lesser extent. Shane later examined the effects of culture on attitudes towards the role of innovation champions, finding, again, that a low uncertainty avoidance score was an indicator of high support (Shane, 1995). Shane's measures of innovation performance were very different from those used by Rinne et al. (see earlier), which might at least partially explain why the results of the two investigations, in terms of cultural influences, differed significantly.

v) Product and process implementation

Herbig & Miller (1992) proposed that low-IDV, high PDI (collectivist) societies were pre-eminent in lower order innovations, in particular those societies with high MAS. Ambos & Schlegelmilch (2008) carried out a study of 139 R&D laboratories (located in 21 countries) and found that the optimum 'cultural environment' for capability-exploitation laboratories (those whose aim was to bring that technology to market) was high power distance, low individualism, high masculinity and high uncertainty avoidance.

Nakata & Sivakumar's (1996) literature review found that the best-performing national cultures at the *implementation* stage had low individualism, high power distance, high uncertainty avoidance and high masculinity scores (e.g. Japan, Taiwan and Mexico).

Lin's (2009) study examined major car manufacturers in fourteen countries in order to assess the impacts of national culture on their process management and technical innovation. However, from his description of technical innovation and its measurement, the study appears to relate primarily to automobile and process detailed development and implementation, rather than any form of novel innovation. Lin found that high uncertainty avoidance and long term orientation positively influenced performance.

Herbig and Jacobs (1998) described Japanese culture in detail and explained the strengths and weaknesses of Japanese research and development. Japan excelled in improving process and product technology but, with the exception of a small number of scientists, did not produce radical innovations or extend basic knowledge. This was reflected in technology transfers to Japan from the USA and Europe, which were almost four times greater than transfers from Japan. High masculinity (with the resultant aggressive competitiveness) had the potential to be a hindrance to the performance of low/medium-creativity improvement processes; however, in the case of Japan, the country's history and its cultural combination of high power distance, mid-low individualism, high uncertainty avoidance and high masculinity resulted in a fierce competitiveness at the company level, rather than at the individual level.

vi) Acceptance and promotion of new technologies

Although this subsection does not specifically refer to project teams, such teams are typically involved in the adoption and implementation of new technologies.

Hasan and Ditsa (1999) analysed attitudes to the take-up of new technologies across Australia, West Africa and the Middle East. They found that West Africans were more favourable to the adoption of information technology than were Middle Easterners, and considered that this was due to the West Africans' much lower uncertainty avoidance scores. Van Everdingen and Waarts (2003) carried out a large study of the effects of national culture on the adoption of enterprise resource planning software in ten European countries. They concluded that high national scores for power distance, uncertainty avoidance and masculinity negatively influenced the adoption of enterprise resource planning; individualism appeared to play a positive role in only the early adoption of enterprise resource planning software.

Menzel et al. (2006) analysed the literature on the wider topic of entre-preneurship as the basis of support and technical knowledge required for radical innovation. Based on their analysis, they proposed an ideal supportive culture, which included very low power distance and uncertainty avoidance scores, medium individualism and masculinity scores, and medium-to-high long-term orientation scores (the latter cultural dimension was not used in the later research of this PhD).

vii) Complex projects involving significant political or social issues

Almost every large, complex sociotechnical project was unique and, in addition to technology issues, many such projects had significant additional complexities imposed on them due to political or social issues (D. Hodgson & Cicmil, 2008). These complexities could have been due to the involvement of multiple partners, for example in the negotiation of large international defence contracts involving commercial rivals and civil service organisations, or they could have been due to multiple customer stakeholders, or both. Examples of such projects included new generation strike aircraft, aircraft carriers, nuclear power stations, high-speed rail links, airports, bypasses and motorways. However, many smaller projects also had significant cultural, personal and vested interests (often undisclosed), which could add to complexity, time delays and costs. It was almost impossible to analyse such projects on a comparative, quantitative basis, as there was no equivalent of a 'level playing field' on which one could gauge their performances. We could, however, examine qualitatively the key reasons why complex projects have often failed.

A large proportion of complex technical and social projects failed to a greater or lesser degree – cost and time overruns were 'the norm'; the 2012 UK Olympics project was (of course) delivered on time, but the costs had escalated by 200% over the original estimates. The Bull Survey (Spikes Cavell Research Company, 1998) revealed that the largest single cause of project failure was poor communications between the relevant parties on the project. The UK government's OGC best practice report entitled 'Common Causes of Project Failure' (Office of Government Commerce, 2005) identified two of the eight major causes of failure in government-funded projects as lack of understanding/lack of contacts at senior levels, and lack of project team integration between clients and supplier team. Anderson (2011) identified bad communications as the largest single root cause of project failure. It appeared from the above (and from many other references) that failures in communication and understanding, particularly across departmental and organisational boundaries, were the leading causes of failure in complex projects.

Buckle & Thomas' (2003) study of the Project Management Body of Knowledge, PMBOK, (PMI, 2000) revealed an embedded masculine set of values. Masculine cultures tended be highly competitive, assertive and aggressive (G H Hofstede 2001, Ch.6), and tended to apply impersonal problem-solving approaches (Daley & Naff, 1998) and decision-making styles (Baxter Magolda, 1992). Contrastingly, feminine cultures tended to value relationships and seek consensus (G. H. Hofstede 2001, Ch.6). However, project management typically attracted masculine-orientated individuals (Cartwright & Gale, 1995), even from within more feminine cultures. Given the earlier-described primary causes for the high rates of project failure, it is probable that personnel with lower masculinity scores, perhaps applying alternative project management methods, e.g. the Scandinavian approach (Lichtenberg, 1983), would perform more effectively in socially or politically complex projects.

viii)   Conclusions with regard to teams involved in creativity and innovation

The results are summarised in Tables 3-1 to 3-5; empty cells imply that the particular cultural dimension was not evaluated. Note that these tables attempt to cover a range of types of creativity, from blue-skies research (Table 3-1) to product implementation (Table 3-4).

Researchers	Creativity/innovation type	Optimum cultural dimension scores (low, high, or [optimum value])				
		PDI	IDV	MAS	UAI	Cultural diversity
Kedia et al. (1992)	Academic R&D	Low		High	Little effect	
Barjak (2006)	Academic R&D					20-25%*
Barjak & Robinson (2008)	Academic R&D					Low/Med
Jones & Davis (2000)	Globally orientated R&D	Low	High	*Low*	Low	
Rinne et al. (2013)	National creativity	Little effect	High		Little effect	
Shane (1992)	Inventiveness	Low	High			
Rothwell & Wissema (1986) [B]	Technological developments	Low			Low	
Cozzi & Giordani	R&D (including patenting)				Low	
PDI = power distance; IDV = individualism; MAS = masculinity; UAI = uncertainty avoidance. * * Optimum percentage of team members who obtained their most recent degree in a different country; diversity vs. performance produced an inverted 'U' shape.						

Table 3-1: High creativity – academic R&D and inventiveness

As there are no 'hard and fast' definitions of what is meant by innovation, nor are all forms of product initiation likely to require the same levels of innovation, it is unsurprising that there are some contradictory results. However, despite these contradictory results, there are some clear trends in terms of culture trait values vs. levels of creativity.

From a synthesis and evaluation of the literature on creativity and innovation, taking into account the 'majority vote' from tables 3-1 to 3-4, it appeared that different combinations of cultural scores suited differing levels of creativity, as expanded in the following paragraphs:

High creativity – academic R&D and inventiveness (original thinking) (Table 3-1): This appeared to benefit from low power distance, high individualism, low uncertainty avoidance (but this may not have had a large effect) and low-to-medium diversity (optimum of under 30% non-nationals). The results with regard to masculinity were inconsistent, with optimal values varying from low to high; however, evaluations such as that of D'Iribane (and Hofstede's supporting comments) suggested that low masculinity resulted in group-think that prevented beneficial conflict and exploration of options. Overall, a medium-high masculinity (optimum score of approximately 70) appeared to be the optimum, avoiding both group-think and excessive conflict.

Researchers	Creativity/-innovation type	Optimum cultural dimension scores (low, high, or [optimum value])				
		PDI	IDV	MAS	UAI	Cultural diversity
Niebuhr (2010)	Industrial R&D					Low
Kaasa & Vadi (2010)	Industrial R&D	Low	High	*Low*	Low	
Kedia et al. (1992)	Industrial R&D	Low		High	Little effect	
Herbig & Dunphy (1998)	Lifestyle-changing innovation	Low	High		Low	
Halkos & Tzeremes (2011)	Innovation efficiency			High		
Halkos & Tzeremes (2011)	Innovation	Low			Low	
D'Iribarne/Hofstede	Industrial R&D/innovation			NOT low		
Herbig & Miller (1992)	High order innovations	Low	High		Low	
Nakata & Sivakumar (1996)	New product (initiation)	Low	High	*Low*	Low	

Table 3-2: Industrial R&D/high level innovation

Industrial R&D/high level innovation (Table 3-2): This appeared to benefit from low power distance, high individualism, low uncertainty avoidance (again, this probably had only a limited effect); one result (low) was reported for cultural diversity. Contradictory results were reported for masculinity.

38

Researchers	Creativity/-innovation type	Optimum cultural dimension scores (low, high, or [optimum value])				
		PDI	IDV	MAS	UAI	Cult div.
Taras, Kirkman & Steel	Innovation				Low	
Rinne et al. (2012)	Innovation	Low	High	Little effect	Little effect	
Willems (2007)	Innovation	Low	High	High	(Low)	
Shane et al. (1993)	Industrial innovation	(Low)	(High)	Little effect	Low	
Jones & Davis (2000)	Locally-supported R&D	Low/med	Med/-high	Low/-med	Low/-med	
Lin (2009)	Industrial innovation	(Low)	Little effect	Little effect	High	

Table 3-3: Medium innovation

Medium innovation (Table 3-3): This appeared to benefit from low power distance, medium/high individualism and low uncertainty avoidance; little effect was reported for masculinity. No results were available for cultural diversity.

Researchers	Creativity/innovation type	Optimum cultural dimension scores (low, high, or [optimum value])				
		PDI	IDV	MAS	UAI	Cult div.
Herbig & Miller (1992)	Lower order innovation		Low	High	Any	
Ambos & Schlegelmilch (2008)	Exploitation laboratories	High	Low	High	High	
Nakata & Sivakumar (1996)	New product (implementat'n)	High	Low	High	High	
Jones & Davis (2000)	Locally-supported adaptation	High	Low	High	High	
Lin (2009)	Process & product improvement	No effect	No effect	No effect	High	
Herbig & Jacobs (1998)	Process & product improve't	High	Low	High	High	

Table 3-4: Low innovation/product & process improvement

Low innovation, product & process improvement, implementation (Table 3-4): This appeared to benefit from high power distance, low individualism, high masculinity and high uncertainty avoidance. No results were available for cultural diversity, although it appeared unlikely that the wider breadth of knowledge and experience that diversity could bring would counteract for the loss in output due to reduced communication. Note that high masculinity could be detrimental if not counterbalanced by low individualism (see later comments on interaction between cultural traits).

Projects management of complex social issues (Table 3-5): There was very little culture-related literature associated with this area but, based on the many qualitative analyses of the high failure rates of large, complex projects, the primary causes of failure appeared to be communication and understanding. It appeared probable that low masculinity project teams would perform significantly better in terms of communication, compromise-seeking and working together than high masculinity teams.

Researchers	Creativity/innovation type	Optimum cultural dimension scores				
		PDI	IDV	MAS	UAI	Cult. div.
[SEVERAL]	Any that have significant social issues			Low?		

Table 3-5: Project management of complex developments

Note that there appeared to be interactions between cultural traits, for example:

- Low masculinity might counteract the positive effects of high-individualism/low-uncertainty avoidance (willingness to disagree, to think differently) when in a situation that demanded creative thinking.
- Low individualism might counteract the negative effects of high masculinity (aggressive competitiveness) when in the low-innovation stage of product implementation.

These interactions could either confound or overcome (to some extent) the benefits or limitations of cultural traits, and add to the complexity of forecasting performance on the basis of culture.

To summarise the above: It appeared that, as the requirements placed on a team shifted from original thinking, high creativity activities to low innovation, routine activities (e.g. minor product or process improvements), the optimum team cultural traits shifted from high individualism, low power distance, low uncertainty avoidance to low individualism (high collectivism), high power distance, high uncertainty avoidance. Of the above three cultural dimensions, individualism appeared to have the strongest effects, followed by power distance, then uncertainty avoidance.

With regard to masculinity, the picture was less clear than with the other cultural dimensions. Low masculinity appeared to impede the expression of original, novel ideas, and high masculinity appeared to benefit the performance of relatively routine team requirements. The picture was complicated further when considering projects that faced complex social issues, where qualitative evidence suggested that reduced masculinity enhanced the likelihood of success.

Figure 3-2 presents an initial estimate of the optimum culture scores based on the literature review of innovation teams. The reviewed studies of higher creativity situations, presented some contradictory results, in particular with regard to masculinity (MAS). A range of MAS values was therefore suggested, as shown in Figure 3-2.

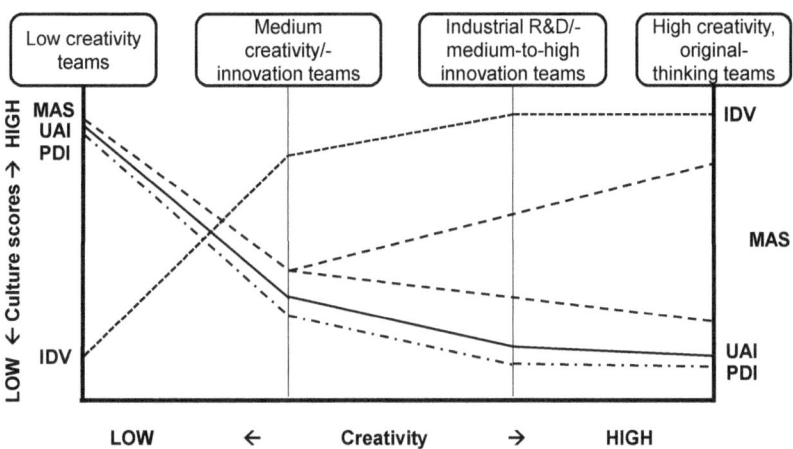

Figure 3-2: Optimum culture values for innovation teams

Finally, the lack of a widely-accepted framework for categorising creativity-related activities (see next subsection) has made the task of this part of the literature review more difficult.

ix) Issues linked to the validity of published study results

Lack of a practicable research/creativity/innovation framework

As stated earlier, the author found it difficult to place the various studies (and their results) in the spectrum of creative/innovative activities, as there was wide variation in the studies' usage of creativity/innovation-linked terms; this difficulty affected the accuracy of the results of this review. Many innovation frameworks have been proposed, for example Balachandra & Friar's (1997) contingency cube, Jones & Davis' (2000) three levels of R&D, Cooper's (1998) three-dimensional model or Baragheh, Rowley & Sambrook's (2009) six-component model; however, these frameworks were typically too limited in scope (e.g. concentrating on innovation to market), or covered organisational, administrative and societal factors, resulting in excessive complexity. A framework was needed that enabled the *positioning* of innovation-related activities, rather than the *planning and execution* of such activities. Taking into account the eastern and western viewpoints introduced in the discussion at the beginning of this subsection on creativity and innovation (Subsection 3.3.1(a)), three potentially independent activities or processes could be identified – searching for truth, creativity/lateral thinking/-invention, and adaptation to needs/markets. These or similar groupings could form the basis of a three (or more) dimension framework, such as the example illustrated in Figure 3-3.

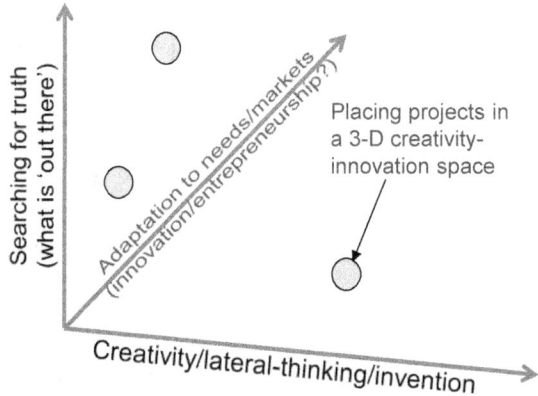

Figure 3-3: A potential 3-D framework

Each of the above three activities could require significantly different skillsets and, as such, would probably be optimised in different cultures; however none, in isolation, would benefit society. As an example, one could suggest that nuclear fusion research has relied extensively, to-date, on searching for truth (understanding the fundamentals of fusion in all its aspects) and creativity/lateral-thinking/invention (conceiving, prod-ucing and testing a wide range of novel ideas for the achievement of controlled fusion). Now, with the achievement of the technical milestone of energy-breakeven, fusion has arrived at the stage where the long process of adaptation to meet the World's energy needs could begin (S. Lee & Saw, 2011; Tokimatsu, Fujino, Konishi, Ogawa, & Yamaji, 2003).

The placing of projects and project studies in a multidimensional framework such as that of Figure 3-3 would enable improvements in the generalisation of study results, and a consequent better understanding of the effects of culture on various types and levels of creativity. However, note that each of these dimensions could be subject to more detailed structuring.

Use of patents as a measure of innovation output

Patenting rates were utilised in many published innovation-related studies as a measure of innovation output. Where patent quality was taken into account, e.g. in terms of citations and income generated, patents may have represented a reasonable measure of innovation. However, the *raw* number of patents per head of population has become increasingly susceptible to changing governmental and industrial policies. For example, in recent years the Chinese government has strongly encouraged and supported its universities to increase the level of patenting of their outputs; this has resulted in a large increase in the quantity of patents without a commensurate increase in their quality or potential value (Fisch, Block, & Sandner, 2013). Patenting rates have increased far more rapidly in the Far East than in the West - in 2012, Asia filed 56% of all patents and 70% of all industrial designs (WIPO, 2013); in 2013, three of the World's top five patenting countries were Far Eastern. As patenting rates increased, so did the proportion of patents relating to minor design features; in many cases, such features (both in the East and West) had little intellectual content, but served the purpose of preventing rivals from competing on a 'level playing field'. Examples of minor patents included mobile phone responses to finger-tapping on a touch sensitive screen, and icons with rounded corners. Litigation arising over design-based patents has increased recently, for example see http://en.wikipedia.org/wiki/Apple_Inc._v._Samsung_Electronics_Co.,_Ltd.

For the research described in this thesis, the key implication of the above changes in patenting patterns was that raw patent data for recent years has shown at best a small and decreasing correlation with innovation levels. This was demonstrated in a recent study by Efrat (2014) that revealed a negative correlation between innovation and individualism based on raw patents (the opposite of most previous study results), but showed a positive correlation between individualism and innovation based on journal publications. A mobile phone-related patent for 'image icon associated with caller' is hardly comparable, in innovation or creativity terms, to a patent for 'a method of characterizing genomic DNA to create a genetic fingerprint'; however, as a 'raw' patent, it is potentially weighted the same.

How culture affects creativity and innovation behaviours

The above two concerns are likely to have contributed to reduced accuracy of results. However, in some cases, the results for apparently similar levels of innovation were the reverse of each other - for example, in the cases of masculinity and uncertainty avoidance. It is difficult to explain such opposing results merely as 'inaccuracies'.

b) Student groups

Research into the performance of student groups has been rightly criticised in the past because neither the students, nor their group environments, were representative of non-student group or team situations. However, such students could be considered to be representative of the sociotechnical system design team members of the future; also, the availability of multiple groups with similar targets in similar settings has provided the equivalent of controlled laboratory experiments. Although many academic publications on student groups were retrieved by the author, relatively few of them had included quantitative analyses of the effects of culture on group performances. In many cases, these studies had examined other variables than performance, e.g. self-efficacy and satisfaction; such variables had been found to be poor predictors of performance, in particular creative performance (Paletz, Peng, Erez, & Maslach, 2003). In other cases, studies had split student groups into two categories – homogenous and culturally-diverse, e.g. Daily et al. (1997), Watson et al. (1993); such a split was too coarse to capture the nuances associated with the varying degrees and different aspects of cultural diversity.

Published studies of culture-moderated performances of student groups are examined in the following paragraphs.

D.C. Thomas (1999) examined the effects of national diversity on the performances of 24 groups of undergraduate student groups; each group was tasked to evaluate five business case studies. Thomas reported that the culturally-homogeneous groups produced better quality solutions for all five case studies than did the culturally-heterogeneous groups; no improvement in the relative performances of the culturally-heterogen-eous groups occurred over the period of the study. Cultural distance was used as a measure of diversity (as was used by the author of this thesis); however, this cultural distance was only measured in terms of collectivism/individualism, based on an eight-item scale developed by Maznevski et al. (1997).

Dahlin et al. (2005) examined the effects of team educational and national diversity on team information use, an important component of potential team performance. Their study results were based on data from 19 MBA student teams that had each been set the task of carrying out four case analyses involving organisational problems. Dahlin et al. reported that national diversity had a 'U' shaped relationship with range of information use, but an inverted 'U' shaped relationship with depth and integration of information use. Range of information has ramifications for the size of the potential solution space, i.e. for the level of creativity of a group; depth and integration probably have greater ramifications for detailed design and implementation. Blau's index (Blau, 1977), which was based on the relative proportions of different nationalities rather than the cultural difference between them[12], was used to calculate both educational and national diversity.

Goncalo & Staw (2006) examined the effects of individualism (vs. collectivism) on the creativity of undergraduate student groups. A total of 68 groups were split into four sets (primed to act 'individualistic' or 'collectivistic' and instructed to act creatively or practically). Individualist (high IDV) groups, when instructed to be creative, were more creative than collectivistic (low-IDV) groups in both the number of ideas generated and the creative quality of the ideas selected.

Wodehouse et al. (2011) examined the effects of average national culture scores on the concept design performance (concept generation and selection) of culturally-diverse student groups. For idea generation, individualism (positive) was the strongest factor, followed by uncertainty avoidance (negative), then power distance (negative). For idea selection (from the previously-generated idea set), individualism (positive) was again the strongest factor, followed by power distance (negative), then uncertainty avoidance (negative). Masculinity appeared to have little effect on the results. Surprisingly, the authors did not take the opportunity to examine the effects of different levels of cultural diversity in the groups.

The above student group results are summarised in Table 3-6; it appeared that the most creative student groups were high in individualism, low in power distance and uncertainty avoidance. Masculinity appeared to have little effect, and the results for cultural diversity were contradictory.

Although the above evaluation of student creativity appeared to confirm the earlier results for creativity in academic and industrial teams, there were grounds for caution. In most or all of the cases, collectivist (low individualist) students were at a disadvantage in that they were typically situated in a foreign environment; this could have had a negative effect on their group performances. It would therefore be informative to be able to compare the above results with those of diverse student groups that were performing in a collectivist environment.

---

[12] As a result, Blau's index is insensitive to *actual* cultural differences within and between teams. A team consisting of three very similar nationalities (e.g. German, Austrian and Swiss-German members) would have the same Blau's index score as a team consisting of three very different nationalities (e.g. Japanese, Serbian and Costa Rican members).

Resear-chers	Group and task types	Optimum cultural dimension scores (low, moderate, high)				
		PDI	IDV	MAS	UAI	Cult. div.
Thomas (1999)	Undergraduate student groups, business case studies.					0
Dahlin et al. (2005)	MBA student groups, business case studies – range of info used.					Low or high** ('U')
	MBA student groups, business case studies – depth & integration of information.					Mod*** ('∩')
Goncalo & Staw (2006)	Undergraduate student groups, creativity of solutions.		High			
Wodehouse et al. (2011) (small sample)	Student groups, design idea generation	Low	High	Little effect	Low	
	Student groups, design idea selection	Low	High	Little effect	Low	
Note: Empty cells = not evaluated. ** U-shaped – low & high diversity teams perform better than moderate diversity teams. *** Inverted U-shaped – moderate diversity teams perform better than low or high diversity teams.						

Table 3-6: Student groups

c) Culture, safety and sociotechnical system accidents

National culture has played a significant role in accident rates (in particular in complex sociotechnical systems such as large transport air-craft, oil refineries and power stations). There were, however, very few quantitative studies of the effects of culture on safety-critical sociotech-nical systems other than aircraft, and some of these had been criticised due to the potential impacts of external factors that were not taken into account, leading to issues with the generalisability of the results (Strauch, 2010). In addition, other studies contained errors that negated their usefulness, for example a paper by H. Park (2011) in which there appeared to be errors associated with uncertainty avoidance.

i) Accident rates in commercial aviation

When carrying out investigations during the 1990s into aircraft accidents, Boeing found a significant relationship between national cultures and accident rates of Western-built commercial passenger jet aircraft, even after taking account of differing fleets, ground facilities and training. In particular, Weener's study of aircraft losses between 1952 and 1992 (E. F. Weener, 1993) linked national scores on several of Hofstede's cultural factors to increases in accidents per million departures.

Also during the 1990s, Merritt & Helmreich conducted a five-year project that surveyed more than 17,000 airline staff, including 8,000 pilots, from 23 countries (A. C. Merritt & Helmreich, 1995); the range of staff included captains, first officers, flight attendants, maintenance staff, managers and trainers. Pilots chose to compete for a high status cross-cultural occupation that required specific combinations of skills, and were therefore not typical members of their ethnic populations. In addition they were subject to regular training and retraining regimes, including simulator-based flying training and crew resource management (CRM). These training facilities were supplied internationally, with minor adaptations. However, despite the large amount of common training across countries, Merritt & Helmreich's surveys of attitudes amongst the 8,000 pilots showed close agreement with three of Hofstede's original national culture results for IBM staff - individualism (vs. collectivism), power distance and uncertainty avoidance. In terms of questions relating to their occupation, pilots across all sampled nations were in closer agreement than would be expected purely from the above cultural survey results[13]. Nevertheless, in specific areas, Merritt & Helmreich reported significant differences between cultural groups; examples of these are listed below:

- Asian pilots preferred order and predictability, whereas most Anglo and North European pilots preferred flexibility and challenging tasks.

- Anglo and North European pilots were the most willing to make their views known in the cockpit, whereas Moroccan, South American and most Asian pilots were the least likely to make their views known; this distinction was associated in part with power distance (low in the case of Anglo and Scandinavian pilots, high in the case of most Asian pilots). The unwillingness of crew members to draw the captain's attention to errors or problems has been a significant factor in many commercial aviation accidents.

- Asian and South American pilots were, in general, neutral or agreed that written procedures should be provided for all in-flight situations and that rules should be obeyed at all times. Anglo pilots strongly disagreed that written procedures should be provided for *all* in-flight situations and also disagreed that rules should be followed when the situation suggested otherwise.

Crew resource management (CRM) training encompasses communication skills, team-working, situational awareness, problem-solving and decision-making in order to ensure the optimum use of all resources, in particular when working under pressure or operating in unusual conditions. Regular CRM training is now mandatory for commercial flying crew covered by most of the World's regulatory bodies, and is also mandatory for an increasing proportion of military crew across the World.

---

[13] This closer agreement reflected their shared professional (or occupational) culture.

However, CRM was pioneered in the USA, and was further developed primarily in the USA and Northern Europe. Because of these origins, CRM was culturally bound (Helmreich, Merritt, & Wilhelm, 1999) as it was based on the assumption of a culture where junior members of the crew were willing to query issues with, or challenge, the captain. As a result, CRM training was most effective when applied to crews of high individualism, low power distance cultures. Flight crews from collectivist, high power distance cultures, e.g. South Korea and China, had considerable barriers to overcome in order to develop the cultural cockpit environment in which subordinates were willing to challenge the captain when they recognized problems or errors. Harris & Li (2008) commented on the much higher commercial aviation accident rates of Asia and Africa compared to the USA and Europe, in particular drawing the reader's attention to the fact that in Asia and Africa, the most frequent circumstantial factor in accidents was a failure in crew resource management. Another paper of theirs (Li, Harris, & Yu, 2008) described an analysis of Taiwanese aircraft accidents that utilised the Human Factors Analysis and Classification System (HFACS); poor CRM was found to result in a 30-to-40-fold increase in decision-making errors, perceptual errors and violations of procedures.

Jing et al. (2000; 2001) examined accident rate information for airlines around the World during the previous twenty years (information is available at http://planecrashinfo.com/rates.htm). They found that the most important cultural variable was *authoritarianism*, which was positively correlated to accident rate and appeared to account for over half the variance (in accident rates) between cultures. From Jing et al.'s descriptions and definitions of authoritarianism, high authoritarianism appeared to be a combination of high power distance and low individualism. Jing et al. stated that authoritarianism was very high in mainland China, Taiwan and Korea; Chinese subordinates in the cockpit would typically agree without query to the captain's demands, even if it meant deviating from the standard procedures. Jing et al. commented that most commercial aircraft and most systems associated with these aircraft were designed by Westerners who had low levels of authoritarianism. Therefore, these Western designers did not understand authoritarianism and were unaware of the degree to which aircraft operations were vulnerable to distortion by authoritarianism.

USA, Anglo and European airlines and their pilots have for many years largely take for granted their incident reporting programmes; the purpose of these programmes has been to improve safety *before* accidents occur. The American Federal Aviation Authority's (FAA's) Aviation Safety Reporting System (ASRS) (Reynard, 1991) was one of the first such programmes; NASA collected data on aviation incidents, analysed them and fed back warnings and recommendations to participating organisations. The FAA also certificated individual airline companies to set up their own Aviation Safety Action Programs (ASAPs) (FAA, 2002), with the agreement of the pilots' unions. Safety reporting programmes have been developed elsewhere with similar success to those of the U.S. ASRS, e.g. the British Confidential Human Factors Incident Reporting Programme (CHIRP) (CHIRP, n.d.) and the British Airways Safety Information System (BASIS) (Holtom, 1998); CHIRP has also been widely used in the international maritime environment, and BASIS has been used by over one hundred airlines. Where these incident reporting and analysis programmes have been effectively implemented, they have made significant contributions to the reduction of serious aircraft accidents (in terms of losses per million flights), and to the improvement of training and standard operational procedures (SOPs).

The assumption behind incident reporting programmes was that all humans made errors, usually unintentionally; therefore aircrews should be encouraged to report errors and incidents within a blame-free environment. Following analysis of these errors and incidents, changes could be put in place to prevent them in the future, or to enable their detection and correction before a safety issue arose. However, unlike the situation in European and USA airline organisations, a significant blame and shame culture existed in many Asian organisations. Therefore Asian pilots were much less willing than their Western counterparts to reveal any errors on their own part if there was a perceived risk of being exposed. Taiwan provided an insight to the effects of culture on the performance of incident reporting programmes: In 1999, the Taiwanese government introduced the TACARE voluntary incident reporting programme in order to improve the country's very poor airline flight safety record. However, the level of incident reporting was low. Therefore Lee & Weitzel (2003) conducted a study of Taiwanese flight crew members' acceptance and usage of TACARE; they found that carriers would attempt to identify and punish flight crews responsible for (reported) incidents, rather than seek to establish and eliminate the root causes of incidents. Lee & Weitzel also commented in their paper on the very high power distance between Taiwanese flight crew captains and first officers, a cultural factor value known to be strongly, positively correlated with flying incidents; this high power distance would also discourage lower ranking officers from reporting incidents associated with their captains' behaviours. A decade-later review of the utilisation of the TACARE system by maintenance personnel (Y.-F. Chen, Metscher, Smith, Ramsay, & Mason, 2014) revealed that fear of punishment and lack of feedback still discouraged personnel from submitting safety reports.

It was clear from the above evidence that Western-designed training, crew resource management and incident reporting systems did not fully meet the needs of non-individualist, high power distance cultures. In addition, aircraft cockpit layouts and standard operating procedures were based on Western individualist cultural assumptions.

49

ii) Accident rates in NATO air forces

Studies of the effects of cultural factors on military aircraft crew performance have revealed very clear links between national cultures and accident rates. Soeters & Boer (2000) conducted a comparative study of fourteen NATO air forces using data based on the years 1988 to 1995. These air forces used similar or identical aircraft and underwent similar training. They used operating procedures and regulations that had been largely harmonized across all NATO countries, and they were also involved in the exchange of personnel between NATO air forces and took part in combined exercises with other NATO countries. The range of NATO aircraft included single-seat tactical fighters and tactical ground attack aircraft (typically operating in pairs or groups of four), two-seat trainers, strategic penetration aircraft and large multiple-crewed aircraft; however, all worked in a larger team environment (i.e. including command & control). Despite the commonality of training, operating procedures and aircraft, strong positive, statistically-validated correlations were found between low individualism, high power distance and high uncertainty avoidance scores and increased accident rates.

As the NATO-wide standardization of training, operating procedures, exchange of personnel, etc., should clearly have produced similar *professional* cultures and (to a lesser extent) similar *organisational* cultures, it is likely that the underlying *national (or ethnic) cultures* exerted a major influence on aircrew behaviour. It is important to note that the NATO standards, regulations, operating procedures, etc., are based on the US/British model; this model has built-in assumptions with regard to aircrew cultures, i.e. that they have an Anglo culture (which scores high in individualism, low in power distance and low in uncertainty avoidance).

iii) Automation of sociotechnical systems

Over recent decades, sociotechnical systems have become increasingly automated, and it is therefore worth examining automation-related issues in a separate subsection; a more detailed examination can be found in Hodgson, Siemieniuch & Hubbard (2013). These issues go beyond the cultures of specific groups or nationalities, although they are affected by certain cultural traits. As sociotechnical systems have become increasingly automated, their very complexity has ensured that not all modes of failure can be predicted. Therefore, given the severe consequences of failure (e.g. for modern passenger transport aircraft or nuclear power stations), it has been necessary to back up these automation systems with humans. However, this automation has brought changes to the activities, workloads, situation awareness and skill levels of human operators or crew. The issues arising from these changes are considered below, with particular reference to the aviation environment.

Automation systems, including flight deck automation, changed the role of the operator from that of active, in-the-loop 'doer' to that of passive, out-of-the-loop monitor. Humans proved to be poor system monitors, in particular if a system was highly reliable (Parasuraman, Molloy, & Singh, 1993), and they reacted more slowly to deviations than when inside the control loop (Kaber & Endsley, 1997). Acting as out-of-the-loop monitors of automation, flight crews typically had reduced situation awareness not only with regard to the current 'flying state' of the aircraft but also, critically, with regard to the detailed mode of the automation system, its constraints and its likely future behaviours (Sarter & Woods, 1995a).

During the 1990s, increasing concerns were expressed about the large number of incidents and accidents arising from pilot confusion with flight automation systems (Kaber & Endsley, 2004), in particular mode confusion (Sarter & Woods, 1995b). In 1996, a U.S. Federal Aviation Administration (FAA) report (Federal Aviation Administration Human Factors Team, 1996) stated that flight crew/automation interface vulnera- bilities adversely affected the crews' situation awareness and manage- ment of automation; the report quoted incidents and crashes due to the automation system changing flight modes without informing the pilots.

The level and complexity of flight automation has increased significantly since 1996, and evidence has emerged that even highly-experienced crews have experienced increasing difficulties with automation (Sarter, Mumaw, & Wickens, 2007). An updated FAA report on flight path management systems (FAA, 2013) found that systemic vulnerabilities remained in the design, user training and operation of modern flight path management systems; the resulting excessive complexity and pilot skill degradation had led to many incidents and accidents. Recent examples of such incidents and accidents have included Hamburg (BFU, 2010), Learmouth (Australian Transport Safety Bureau, 2011) and Schipol (Dutch Safety Board, 2010). Evidence of flight crew loss of skills associated with automation (and automation policy) has been widely reported, for example the UK's Civil Aviation Authority report about flight crew reliance on automation (Wood 2004), the loss of manual flying skills (Ebbatson, 2009; Gillen, 2010), and the relationship between automation experience and manual flying skills (Ebbatson et al., 2010). Following a study of the performance of pilots during refresher training courses, Young et al. (2006) reported that the flight crews who utilized the most flight deck automation also exhibited poorer manual flying skills than others. A recent survey (Zimmermann, Paries, & Amalberti, 2011) revealed that commercial pilots and air traffic controllers believed that flight safety was decreasing. Cases such as the uncontained engine failure on a Qantas Airbus A380 in 2008 (Australian Transport Safety Bureau, 2010) and the successful ditching of an Airbus A300 on the River Hudson after engine failure in 2008 (National Transportation Safety Board, 2010) are indicative of the very high manual skill levels required to survive a major failure – skill levels that few of the latest generation of pilots possess.

Researchers have highlighted the paucity and low quality of interaction between crews and automation systems (Norman, 1990), the need for context-aware systems that emulate CRM principles (Geiselman, Johnson, Buck, & Patrick, 2013) and the need for multisensory feedback to crews (Sarter, 2000). To-date, the automation element of most socio-technical systems has acted as a poorly trained, incommunicative member of the system's crew – thus defeating the purpose of crew resource management (CRM) training. In order for a crew to achieve the level of shared situation awareness required for safe operation, researchers argue that the automated system must become to an adequate degree part of the crew (Christoffersen & Woods, 2002), (G. Klein, Woods, Bradshaw, Hoffman, & Feltovich, 2004).

Sherman et al. (1997) surveyed the attitudes of a sample of 5,879 airline pilots from 12 nations towards flight deck automation. They listed 15 automation-related statements (e.g. *'I am concerned that automation may cause me to lose flying skills'*, *'I look forward to more automation – the more the better'*, *'I prefer flying automated aircraft'*) and, for each country and for each statement, calculated the percentage of pilots who agreed (Sherman et al., 1997, Table 4). Sherman et al. reported that the influence of national culture on the pilots' agreement (or otherwise) was far greater than that of organizational culture or pilot experience[14]. Cultural differences in attitudes to automation are important because they affect crew utilisation of automation and thereby their levels of trust, manual skills and situation awareness.

A summary of sociotechnical system automation safety issues: To-date, increased automation of sociotechnical systems, in particular air-craft automation, has resulted in changes to primary crew functions from 'doing' to 'monitoring', reductions in crew situation awareness and down-grading of crew 'hands-on' skills. As a result of these changes, when failures of automation systems have occurred, manual recoveries have been compromised. Developments in automation, combined with chan-ging airline crew flight training policies, have resulted in an increasing gap between actual and required crew capabilities and situation aware-ness. In terms of Reason's 'Safety Space' model (Reason, 2008), flight automation systems are moving rapidly in the direction of increasing

---

[14] The author of this thesis carried out a further analysis of Sherman's results (see Chapter 5 for more details) in order to gain further insights, for example *'More automation is better'* scores were positively correlated with national power distance (PDI) scores, and *'I prefer automation'* scores were positively correlated with national PDI and uncertainty avoidance (UAI) scores.

vulnerability; similar issues can be found in other complex sociotechnical systems, for example refineries and nuclear power stations.

iv) *Accident rates in industry*

Not all industrial accidents relate to team activities, but many do. Infortunio (2003) carried out a study of the correlations between international industrial fatal accidents and Hofstede's original cultural dimensions, i.e. power distance (PDI), individualism (IDV), masculinity (MAS) and uncertainty avoidance (UAI). Due to the high correlations between PDI and IDV in his initial results, he subsequently utilized the combined factor 'log PDI/IDV'. Chi-squared tests showed no significant correlation between log PDI/IDV and UAI.

Infortunio's results showed that industrial fatal accident rates were correlated with high UAI scores and high PDI/IDV ratios; they were not correlated with MAS scores. Infortunio commented on the particularly high industrial injury rates that were experienced in Guatemala (PDI=95, IDV=6, UAI=101, MAS=37). Note that Infortunio warned that other factors, including country wealth levels, could moderate the results of his study; see Subsection III.B.4 of his thesis for further comments on this.

v) *Road traffic accidents*

Although traffic accidents are not typically the result of team activities, they are worth studying because the cultural factors in road accidents also play a part in other forms of accident and failure. Ozkan & Lajunen (2007) carried out regression analyses on traffic accident data from 46 countries, and identified gross national product (GNP) per capita (negatively related), neuroticism and uncertainty avoidance (both positively related) as being significantly correlated with accident rates. Masculinity (positive) and individualism (negative) were identified as being correlated to a lesser degree.

vi) *Reaction times to anomalies*

G.A. Klein et al. (1999) stated that uncertainty avoidance influenced the threshold for initial reaction to an anomaly, which occurred when an observer mentally 'reframed'; personnel with low uncertainty avoidance scores reframed with less information than did personnel with high uncertainty avoidance scores, i.e. they responded quicker to anomalies. In the context of a complex sociotechnical system, this could provide valuable additional time in which to respond to a deteriorating situation, although it could also lead to false alarms, Vincent and Dubinsky (2004) reported that high-uncertainty-avoidance French students exhibited more maladaptive coping than did low-to-medium-uncertainty-avoidance USA students.

vii) Summary – safety-critical sociotechnical teams

The results of the review of the effects of national culture on the safety of sociotechnical systems are presented in Table 3-7; these include studies of reactions to anomalies. High accident rates appeared to be associated with a particular pattern of cultural dimension scores - low individualism, high uncertainty avoidance and, in most cases, high power distance scores. In the case of uncertainty avoidance, performance in emergency situations was also typically hampered by inadequate practical training and a reluctance to react promptly. A high masculinity score might have been expected to increase the rate of accidents caused by competitiveness and bravado, but little evidence of this was found in the statistics, other than in (non-team) road accidents.

Researchers	Sociotechnical system type or reactions to threats and anomalies	Optimum cultural dimension scores*				
		IDV	PDI	MAS	UAI	Cult div.
Jing et al. (2001)	Commercial transport aircraft	High	Low			
Soeters & Boer 2000)	Military aircraft	High	Low	Little effect	Low	
G. A. Klein et al. (1999)	Thresholds for quick reactions to anomalies				Low	
Vincent & Dubinsky	Maladaptive coping with threats				Low	
* Optimum scores: These refer to *busy or abnormal situations* where the risk to safety is greatest. Note: Empty cells = not evaluated.						

Table 3-7: Safety-critical sociotechnical systems

Finally, a caveat: Wealth (per-capita GDP) is closely correlated with high IDV; therefore it is important to account for wealth before ascribing correlations to cultural traits or scores.

d) Professional sports teams

Professional sports teams might appear at first, in terms of tasks and targets, to be distant from both sociotechnical system design teams and the users of such systems. However, sport provided an opportunity to study the effects of culture and diversity in depth due to the detailed records of multiple projects (i.e. games) for which player details and outcomes were available; indeed Kahn (2000) described professional sport as a 'labour market laboratory' because the life history of every worker (and supervisor) was available (… along with the team performance data). In addition, there were many levels of cultural diversity across teams in most professional leagues.

54

Although many studies have taken place on sports performance and team diversity, very few studies have examined the effects of team member national culture on performance.

i) Football teams

Haas & Nüesch collected data on the performance of the (German) Bundesliga over seven seasons from 1999/00 until 2005/06 (Haas & Nüesch, 2012). They took into account measures of team member skill levels and team national diversity and found that increased national diversity resulted in reduced team performance. Haas & Nüesch utilised the Shannon diversity index as the basis for calculating diversity[15]. On the basis of the researchers' choice of diversity index, the author considers the results to be of limited value. **Note:** The author requested access to the raw data on which the conclusions were based, but this was not forthcoming.

In order to further assess the results obtained by Haas & Nüesch (in the absence of further data from them), the author obtained aggregate Bundesliga player nationality data for the 1999/00 to 2005/06 seasons from a football website (see http://www.transfermarkt.co.uk/en/2-bundesliga/gastarbeiter/wettbewerb_L2_1999.html and the linked web pages). Based on this data, an analysis of the default national cultural dimension scores of Bundesliga players was carried out, which is summarised in Table 3-8.

Season	Proportion of non-German players (%)	Mean weighted cultural dimension scores for non-German nationals			
		PDI	IDV	MAS	UAI
1999/00	39.8	66.6	52.9	43.7	66.6
2000/01	38.1	67.4	49.7	46.5	66.9
2001/02	38.2	67.0	51.3	46.6	66.5
2002/03	36.9	69.3	46.0	44.9	66.2
2003/04	40.9	68.7	47.9	47.3	69.6
2004/05	40.5	64.8	54.8	47.3	65.7
2005/06	41.6	65.0	52.0	44.5	64.0
Average non-German culture scores over 7 years:		**67.0**	**50.7**	**45.8**	**66.5**
German national culture scores:		35	67	66	65
Differences:		**32.0**	**-16.3**	**-20.2**	**1.5**

Table 3-8: Non-German Bundesliga player culture scores

---

[15] As was the case with Blau's index (see earlier footnote), the Shannon diversity index was based in this case on the number or proportion of different nationalities and was, as a result, insensitive to *actual* cultural differences within and between teams.

As can be seen from Table 3-8, over the seven years of Haas & Nüesch's survey the weighted average non-German player individualism (IDV) score was 16 points less than that of the Germans, the average power distance (PDI) score was 32 points greater and the average masculinity (MAS) score was 20 points less; however, the average non-German uncertainty avoidance (UAI) score was only 1.5 points (~1.5%) more than the national German uncertainty avoidance score. It would therefore be reasonable to conclude that, on average, high German team national diversity would result in significant differences in team individualism, power distance and masculinity scores, compared to teams consisting only of German nationals; these differing cultural dimension scores may have influenced match performances as much as the diversity itself. Increased national diversity would have had little effect on German team uncertainty avoidance scores, but the distrust of foreigners (or 'strangers') implied by the higher than average uncertainty avoidance scores of the German players, managers and coaches (G H Hofstede 2001, Ch. 4) would have played a part in reducing the effect-iveness of integrating non-nationals into Bundesliga teams compared to, for example, the case with English Premiership teams.

Brandes et al. (2009) collected and analysed the effects of national diversity on the performance of German Bundesliga teams over the period 2001/02 to 2005/06, as measured by their end-of-season position in the league. They hypothesised that different cultures could bring differing skills to teams. Despite finding skill differences between nation-alities, the results of the analysis indicated that these skill differences (and the associated national diversities) did not appear to have a bearing on team performance over a season. This result is in contrast to that of Haas & Nüesch (see above), who analysed the Bundesliga perfor-mances and national diversity over approximately the same period to find that cultural diversity reduced team performances.

Brandes et al.'s measure of national diversity was similar to that of Haas & Nüesch in that it was based on the number of different nationalities and, therefore, did not reflect the cultural distances between team individuals. Brandes et al. determined players' skillsets from 22 factors (e.g. goals scored, assists, tackle success rate, clearances), and found that there were differences between nationalities. They developed a linear regression model that explained teams' final league position (or rank) in terms of the above 22 factors. One of the problems with these 22 factors was that they were not equally applicable to the various player roles, for example, 'clearances' were more important in the defender role than in the striker role. Therefore, the associations between these factors and team performances were likely to be unclear.

ii) Hockey teams

Phillips & Phillips (2011) tested Blau's paradox of heterogeneity (Blau, 1977) on the USA NHL hockey teams over the ten year period from 1988 to 1998. There was a wide range of heterogeneity across the league, with team heterogeneity from a single nationality to more ten nationalities, representing a total of 28 nationalities. Phillips & Phillips confirmed their hypothesis of a U-shaped relationship between heterogeneity and (winning) performance, i.e. low and high heterogeneity teams were found to win more games than moderate heterogeneity teams, after taking account of control variables.

iii) Summary - sports teams

There were very few quantitative studies on sport, and those that were found had typically concentrated on the effects of diversity, and had utilised measures of diversity that took into account only the number of different nationalities in a team, rather than the actual cultural differences between players (and teams); the results were therefore not very informative. In addition, their results were to some extent contradictory, as can be seen from Table 3-9.

Researchers	Sport and league	Optimum cultural dimension scores (low, high, or [optimum value])				
		IDV	PDI	MAS	UAI	Cult. div.
Haas & Nüesch (2011)	Football (German Bundesliga)					zero
Brandes et al. (2009)	Football (German Bundesliga)					N/E
Phillips & Phillips (2011)	Hockey (United States NFL)					U*
Note: (1) Empty cell = not evaluated. (2) N/E = No effect.						
*U-shaped – low & high diversity teams perform better than moderate diversity teams.						

Table 3-9: Sports teams

e) Further issues of relevance to this review

Culture was only one of several potential reasons for differences in performances between countries. It was therefore important to consider alternative hypotheses in order to avoid misleading results.

i) The effects of per-capita income on outcomes

Per-capita income had a strong negative correlation with accident rates. For example, two research studies demonstrated significant correlations between national power distance scores and aircraft accident rates (Ramsden, 1985; E. F. Weener & Russell, 1994); Hofstede's re-analysis of the data (Hofstede 2001, p.115) found per-capita GNP to be the dominant variable, rather than power distance. Similarly, Helmreich and

Merritt (2001) drew readers' attention to the potential effects on accident rates of factors such as facility quality and government regulation (pp.104-5).

ii) Studies that utilised multiple cultural frameworks

Several published studies on national culture appeared to 'mix-and-match' cultural dimensions from two or more cultural frameworks, for example that of Hasan & Ditsa (1999). Because the introduction of non-orthogonal (i.e. overlapping) dimensions would tend to reduce the strengths of relationships between cultural dimensions and outcomes, or even reverse them, such studies were for the most part discarded.

3.3.2 Effects of culture on intrateam aspects of performance

This section presents an overview from the literature of the intrateam effects of culture on human performance in various team-related situations. The cultural dimensions referred to in this section are primarily the original four of Hofstede's cultural framework.

a) Power distance

In high power distance societies, authority was concentrated in central-ised decision-making structures; there were deep organisational hierar-chies, information flow was constrained by these hierarchies (Hofstede 2001, Ch.3), and there was a lack of informal 'across-the-hierarchy' (horizontal) communications (Khatri, 2009).

Khare (1999) found that that communications between superiors and subordinates in India (a high power distance country) were primarily via formal channels. Kim (1999) found that communications in high power distance South Korea were largely top-down, flowing through the formal chain of command, with little voluntary feedback on the part of subor-dinates; upwards communication tended to occur primarily as responses to superiors in formal settings or to be in the form of indirect, deferential, mitigated speech. Similarly, Offerman & Hellmann (1997) noted that most communication in high power distance settings was in the form of commands, i.e. flowing downwards through the formal hierarchy, and that there was little delegation of authority. Indeed, consultation of subordinates in high power distance organisations was likely to be construed as a sign of incompetence on the part of the superior (Francesco & Chen, 2000). Subordinates in high power distance organi-sations were typically unwilling to participate in decisions; as a result, managers were inundated with routine decisions (Khatri, 2009) and were likely to suffer role overload (M. F. Peterson et al., 1995). The senior person in a team or group was expected to possess all the knowledge relevant to his or her position, even though this was clearly not the case in situations where significant specialisation occurred. As a result, levels of subordinate-initiated communication were low (Khatri, 2009), decisions were made autocratically (Terzi, 2011) and implemented more quickly than in a typical low power distance organisation due to lack of consultation (Graf, Hemmasi, Lust, & Liang, 1990); however, such decisions were likely to be suboptimal (Khatri, 2009), and employees typically dared not point out errors or mistakes.

In low power distance societies, employees expressed a preference for consultation; communication typically flowed freely up and down the formal hierarchy and authority for most decisions was typically delegated to those with the relevant knowledge (Hofstede 2001, Ch.3). Indeed, attempts to implement decisions without consultation in low power distance workplaces could potentially result in employee resistance (Brockner, 2001). Xie et al. (2009) examined the effects of culture on communication effectiveness, finding that low power distance participants were more effective at communication and interaction (as in a work situation) than were high power distance participants. However, there was typically more role ambiguity in low power distance organisations (M. F. Peterson et al., 1995), which could lead to higher job stress.

Helmreich and Merritt's five-year survey of commercial airline staff from 23 countries (Helmreich & Merritt, 2001) revealed that low power distance crew members were willing to make their views known to their captains, whereas high power distance crew members found it much more difficult to raise issues with their captains, even when these were safety-related issues. Asian and South American crews were low in individualism, and this discouraged them further from drawing their captain's attention to errors, as there was also the major issue of loss of face to contend with.

High power distance once offered stability to communities, as every member of society knew his or her position; however, in advanced societies it has discouraged some of the most able people from contributing fully to their organisations, because their potentially useful ideas might never be aired. As a result, decisions have tended to be suboptimal due to the reduced range of options under consideration, and might be seriously flawed due to the unwillingness of subordinates to point out errors. High power distance has also discouraged spontaneous communication between subordinates and leaders; in time-critical situations, for example in the case of sociotechnical system emergencies, this has resulted in reduced shared situation awareness.

To summarise the above: In high power distance societies and organisations, management and decision-making has tended to be strongly centralised with little delegation of authority or discussion with subordinates – this could result in suboptimal decisions, quickly taken. Communication has typically been primarily down the hierarchy, with little cross- or upwards communication (of facts or opinions) by subordinates; shared understandings and shared situation awareness have typically been low because of the resulting lack of interaction. In low power distance societies and organisations, management and decision-making has tended to be much more consensus-based, with delegation of authority to the most capable person, and decisions discussed with subordinates; communication has typically flowed up and down the hierarchy, promoting continuous or frequent interactions and improved shared understandings or shared situation awareness.

b) Individualism

Members of high individualism societies considered 'speaking one's mind' as reflecting honesty, whereas members of low individualism (i.e. collectivist) societies considered that the maintenance of harmony and the avoidance of direct confrontation should always take precedence (Hofstede 2001, Ch.5, p,236). As a result, team members from high individualism societies typically communicated in a direct, low-context manner, where the intended meaning was in the message, whereas team members from low individualism (high collectivism) societies typically communicated in an indirect, high-context manner, where only a small part of the meaning was in the message itself, the remainder was inferred from contextual references and pre-existing knowledge (Ting-Toomey, 1988). Although high-context, indirect communication ensured the maintenance of harmony and reduced the risk of loss of face, it had negative consequences, in particular for urgent safety-critical communications, as it could lead to reduced shared situation awareness at critical times. For example, a low individualism subordinate, on detecting an error on the part of his or her superior, could not typically point this out, but had to attempt to draw the superior's attention to the error in such a way that the superior discovered it for himself or herself. This error discovery process could take a considerable period of time, and could involve the attention of several members of the team (e.g. aircrew, nuclear power station operators) at a critical time; an aircrew might only resort to direct communication with their captain when seconds away from a fatal crash. Evidence for this has been found in flight recorder voice recordings, for example National Transportation Safety Board (2000). One potential explanation for such behaviour has come in the form of theories about chronically-accessible emotion-related schemas based on cultural norms (Weber & Morris, 2010)[16]; frequent activation of

---

[16] The habitual activation of any construct in one's everyday environment leads to chronic accessibility (Bargh, 1984; Higgins, 1996).

such schemas could lead to them taking precedence over important action schemas that had been acquired through training and practice. This was probably the case with face maintenance schemas associated with members of many Far-Eastern societies.

A further effect of the need to maintain harmony in low individualism societies was that a need for consensus discouraged individuals from 'going against the flow', for example to suggest ideas that differed significantly from those that the majority were pursuing. This consensus had an effect on such societies' approaches to innovation, resulting in a focus on market-orientated incremental developments and improvements, rather than on novel ideas and products. In countries such as Japan, Taiwan and South Korea, such a focus was highly successful, and has proved difficult to replicate in the West. Erez & Nouri (2010) identified the differences between the innovation approaches and goals of Eastern (collectivist) societies and Western (individualist) societies in terms of creativity-as-useful/appropriate vs. creativity-as-novel. The low-individualist consensus that led to reduced novelty in ideas proved beneficial when it came to implementing an agreed course of action, as all members typically worked hard to achieve the associated plans.

Many scholars have implied that trust is higher in collectivist countries than in individualist countries because of the greater importance that collectivists place on interpersonal relationships (C. C. Chen, Chen, & Meindl, 1998; Etzioni, 1996). However, this has not appeared to be the case in recent surveys. Realo & Allik (2009) found that trust was higher in individualist societies when measured in terms of social capital. Huff & Kelly (2003) investigated trust of in-groups and out-groups exhibited by American individuals and by individuals of six Asian countries, and found that USA individualists exhibited higher trust of both in-group and out-group individuals and organisations than did Asian collectivists. The results of an earlier cross-national survey of Japanese and American respondents by Yamagashi & Yamagashi (1994) indicated that American respondents were more trusting of people in general than were the Japanese. The relationships between individualism and trust were complicated by the fact that another cultural dimension, uncertainty avoidance, also affected the propensity to trust.

To summarise the above: Low individualism (or high collectivism) reduced the speed and clarity of communications in teams, and also tended to reduce creativity in teams due to the drive for harmony and the need to avoid conflict. However, the harmony and commitment that low individualism engendered enabled teams to perform very effectively at lower creativity tasks. Low individualism also reduced shared situation awareness in organised action teams due to issues of face maintenance. It was not clear as to the role that trust played in team performances, but it appeared that trust in others (not the same as trust in others' abilities) was higher amongst high individualism individuals than amongst low individualism individuals.

c) Masculinity

Hofstede (2001, Ch.6, p.318) described low masculinity employees as 'working in order to live', valuing working conditions and social relationships more than performance, underselling themselves, being unwilling to relocate their families to enhance their careers and preferring the achievement of quality of working life. He described high masculinity employees (in particular, managers) as 'living in order to work', valuing interesting work, performance and pay more than working conditions and social relationships, overselling themselves, being competitive and willing to relocate their families in order to enhance their careers.

Low masculinity (high femininity) appeared to produce some of the behaviours of low individualism, in particular compromise-seeking activities; such behaviours were beneficial to team-working, but suppressed the generation and discussion of contentious issues or novel ideas. Medium-to-high masculinity appeared to encourage the generation and presentation of novel ideas in a team situation. As stated by Hofstede, one of the attributes of a high masculinity society was a high level of competition. It was therefore surprising that little evidence was found that high masculinity contributed to industrial or aircraft accident rates. It was also surprising to find, from a study of medical communication across ten European countries (Meeuwesen, van den Brink-Muinen, & Hofstede, 2009) that general practitioners in high masculinity countries devoted more of their time to psychosocial issues (responding to the emotional issues of patients) and were more satisfied with their work than was the case with practitioners in low masculinity countries. In their three-decade multi-level review of the application of Hofstede's cultural framework, Taras, Kirkman & Steel (2010) examined the relationships between Hofstede's original four dimensions and a wide range of organisationally relevant outcomes. They found that masculinity was strongly correlated with a preference for a compromising approach to conflict management, rather than an avoiding or confrontational approach, or cooperation with opponents.

Helmreich & Merritt's survey of more than 15,000 civil aircraft crew (2001, p.249) found that, although the crew power distance, individualism and (to a slightly lesser extent) uncertainty avoidance scores were reasonably correlated with Hofstede's original IBM country scores, their masculinity scores were not significantly correlated with Hofstede's original scores. Soeters (1997) utilised Hofstede's Value Surveys Module to carry out a survey of student-officers at thirteen European military academies. Surprisingly, the masculinity scores were all lower, in most cases much lower, than the standard scores for the student-officers' civilian compatriots, and were in almost a random ranking compared to the standard Hofstede scores. There may have been certain exceptional issues in play, for example a particularly high level of self-selection for both civil aviation pilots and military officers, but there may be more fundamental issues about the nature of this masculinity dimension.

To summarise the above: Masculinity appeared to play a part in generating (or at least ensuring the presentation of) novel ideas in high creativity teams due to the associated competitiveness and willingness to engage in conflict behaviour (this would also ensure rapid communication), but high masculinity could lead to excessive intra-team conflict. However, there were conflicting results from surveys that utilised default national culture scores, and cultural value surveys of civil aircraft crew and military officers revealed that actual scores for this dimension tended to conform less to default national scores than was the case with other cultural dimensions.

d) Uncertainty avoidance

Compared to members of high uncertainty-avoidance societies, members of low uncertainty-avoidance societies were lower stressed, less anxious, more open to change and innovation, curious about, rather than frightened of, what was different, and were more tolerant of diversity (Hofstede 2001, Ch.4, p.161). High uncertainty avoidance societies coped with the many things beyond human control by reducing *apparent* uncertainties, e.g. by introducing many laws and rules and by adherence to clearly-defined procedures, rituals, etc.

Offerman & Hellman's (1997) survey of the attitudes of mid-level managers of a multinational organisation from 39 countries revealed that high uncertainty avoidance was significantly associated with managers maintaining control, refusing to delegate and lacking approachability.

Joy & Kolb (2009) carried out a research investigation into the effects of cultural dimension scores on preferred learning styles. They reported that students and teachers in high uncertainty avoidance societies preferred abstract conceptualization and reflective observation, whereas those in low uncertainty avoidance societies were comfortable with concrete experience and active experimentation, e.g. training exercises with realistic role play. Effective mental schemas for dealing with situations such as accidents and emergencies could only be developed via realistic role play, so the preferences of high-UAI societies had negative implications for the safety of complex sociotechnical systems. Burke et al. (2008) examined data from 68 organizations from 14 nations in order to assess the effectiveness of training in reducing accidents and injuries; they found that workers from high uncertainty avoiding nations were less well engaged with safety training, that their training was less effective in reducing accidents and injuries and that they responded to critical situations in a rigid manner. Burke et al.'s results supported those of Joy & Kolb.

High uncertainty-avoiding Asian and South-American pilots in Helmreich & Merritt's survey of commercial airline staff (Helmreich & Merritt, 2001, p.84) were either neutral to or agreed with the statement that written procedures should be provided for all in-flight situations and that rules should be obeyed at all times, whereas low uncertainty-avoiding Anglo pilots strongly disagreed with this statement. This tendency of personnel from high uncertainty-avoiding societies to follow standard operating procedures (SOPs) more closely than personnel from low uncertainty-avoiding societies when running complex sociotechnical systems (such as airliners) could reduce the likelihood of errors – a significant benefit in normal operating situations, in maintenance activities and in routine manufacturing situations. However, such personnel would typically persist in following these SOPs (or organisational rules) when they were no longer relevant to the situation (Beckmann, Menkhoff, & Suto, 2008; Helmreich & Merritt, 2001). Vincent and Dubinsky (2004) examined the response-to-threat reactions of students from USA (low-to-medium uncertainty avoidance) and France (high uncertainty avoidance) when faced with threat situations; they reported that the French students exhibited more maladaptive coping than did the USA students.

G. Klein et al. (1999) stated that tolerance for uncertainty (the inverse of uncertainty avoidance) influenced the threshold for initial reaction to an anomaly; this was because problem detection took place when the observer mentally reframed his/her understanding of a situation; see G. A. Klein et al. (2005) for a more detailed discussion of problem detection. Personnel with low uncertainty avoidance scores (high tolerance for uncertainty) changed to a new initial understanding (i.e. reframed) with less information than did personnel with high uncertainty avoidance scores; although this lower information threshold could lead to more false alarms, it alerted an individual to anomalies at an earlier stage.

The effects of differences in capability to deal with uncertainty and unexpected change extended beyond the environment of fast-reaction organised action teams and crews, to academic and industrial teams. Barr & Glynn (2004) administered a survey to 276 participants on graduate or executive management courses (47% U.S. citizens, the remainder from Europe and the Far East). The aim of the survey was to assess the participants' responses to threats and opportunities associated with strategic issues. They were particularly interested in participants' associations between indicators of controllability and threats or opportunities. Their results indicated that participants from high uncertainty avoiding cultures more strongly associated lack of controllability attributes with threats than did those from low uncertainty avoiding cultures. Much weaker associations were found based on the power distance, individualism and masculinity cultural dimensions. These results had implications for the performance of high innovation teams where, due to the presence of 'unknown unknowns', controllability was reduced. Indeed, Cozzi & Giordani's (2011) analysis of the effects of ambiguity aversion on countries' R&D performances (referred to earlier in this thesis) showed that high UAI personnel and organisations were less effective at R&D, with its potential outcome uncertainties and ambiguities.

To summarize the above: High uncertainty avoiding cultures preferred order and routine, in teaching, training, employment and life in general. They were poor at dealing with uncertainty and disliked to 'venture into the unknown', and this had a negative effect on their creativity. Personnel with high uncertainty avoidance scores tended not to delegate and lacked approachability (affecting communications). They followed SOPs more closely than personnel with low scores, which was beneficial to sociotechnical system safety under normal operating conditions. However, high uncertainty avoidance scores tended to hamper decision-making in response to rare emergencies because of reduced situation awareness (due to a lack of realistic training), delayed problem detection and reaction (due to an unwillingness to mentally reframe) and an unwillingness to abandon inappropriate SOPs.

e) Cultural diversity

Researchers have long claimed that the multiple perspectives of cultural diversity provided the potential for higher team creative performance, as suggested by Cox & Blake's 'value-in-diversity' hypothesis, and could also reduce 'groupthink' (Cox & Blake 1991). Nemeth (1986) found that the level of critical analysis relating to decisions amongst alternatives was higher in groups that included minority views than in groups that did not, resulting in improved decision processes. McLeod et al. (1996) found that ethnically diverse groups produced better quality ideas on brainstorming tasks than did ethnically homogeneous groups.

In contrast to the above, Thomas (1999) found that homogenous teams outperformed multicultural teams in a range of tasks, and Wolf (2002) reported on the unexpected problems that managers had faced with multicultural teams. Hambrick (1998) reported that the performance outcomes of multicultural teams had generally been discouraging, particularly in situations that involved coordinative tasks; the promising areas for multicultural teams appeared to be in creative tasks, where heterogeneity in values and cognition could be beneficial. Vodosek (2007) investigated the mediation roles of intra-group relationship, process and task conflict on the relationships between cultural diversity and science research group outcomes; he found that cultural diversity was positively associated with all three forms of conflict, which were in turn associated with unfavourable group outputs.

Niebuhr (2010) carried out a regression analysis of innovation performance in the various German regions; this indicated that diverse cultural backgrounds in the workforce might enhance research & development performance. Kochan et al. (2003) investigated the effects of race and gender diversity on performance, but found few direct positive or negative effects. Earley & Mosakowski (2000) investigated the performance of five teams whose members had a wide diversity in nationalities, but had similar educational and work backgrounds. They found that there were greater communication and conflict problems in moderately heterogeneous teams than in highly heterogeneous teams; they explained their results in terms of Lau & Murnighan's (1998) faultline concept. However, Earley & Mosakowski based their measure of heterogeneity or diversity on the proportions of different nationalities (e.g. as in Shannon's or Blau's index), rather than on the degree of cultural distance between team members. Elron (1997) examined the effects of cultural diversity on the performance of top management teams (TMTs) at 121 subsidiaries of multinational companies. He assigned Hofstede's default country scores to team members, and calculated team cultural diversities based on statistical measures of mean and variance. Elron found a positive relationship between cultural diversity and TMT performance; in particular, he found that only diversities in individualism and masculinity were significant for team *performance*, whereas diversity in uncertainty avoidance was a significant factor for intra-team *disagreements*.

Horwitz & Horwitz (2007) carried out a meta-analysis based on a set of 78 correlations obtained from 35 journal articles on teams; they considered both task-related diversity (functional expertise, education and organisational tenure) and bio-demographic diversity (age, gender and race/ethnicity). They found a positive impact for task-related diversity, but none for bio-demographic diversity (of which race/ethnicity could be associated to culture). Stahl et al. (2007) carried out a meta-analysis of 80 empirical studies of multicultural teams; they concluded that cultural diversity caused process losses due to reduced communication, reduced social interaction and increased conflict, but that these losses could be partially offset by increased creativity. They later carried out a further meta-analysis of 108 empirical studies (Stahl et al. 2010); they concluded that cultural diversity led to process losses through increased task conflict and reduced social integration (in particular, for co-located teams), but led to process gains due to increased creativity and satisfaction. No clear relationship between cultural diversity and overall performance could be demonstrated.

Note that almost all the above-considered teams were 'conventional' teams, e.g. management teams, R&D teams or design teams, where minor delays and temporary misunderstandings due to cultural differences would not (in themselves) have a major effect on team performances. In the case of organised action teams, e.g. aircraft crews, firefighters, military teams, oil platform crews and surgical teams, emergency response time requirements would be much shorter, and communication accuracy and speed would be of paramount importance. The communication delays and losses that are inherent to multicultural teams, e.g. due to native language differences, differing forms of speech (direct, context-independent vs. indirect, context-dependent), differing 'face' issues, etc., could be disastrous in periods of high cognitive load. Orasanu et al. (1997) examined incident reports from the Aviation Safety Reporting System (ASRS) in order to ascertain the relationships between communication and flight safety; they found three main categories that led to error – poor transmission (due to inadequate language skills), ambiguous context, and inadequate understanding (the latter two largely because of cultural differences). Although the misunderstandings that arose from faulty communications could occur between team members of the same culture, Orasanu et al. stated that they were much more likely between team members of differing cultures. In contrast to the above, Merritt & Ratwatte (1997) suggested that multiculturality in crews might result in less complacency, adherence to best crew resource management practices and greater precision in their communications.

Note that the most commonly used measures of cultural diversity appeared to be based on the proportions of different nationalities in the teams (e.g. as in Blau's Index or the Shannon Index) rather than being based on the cultural differences between these nationalities. As a result, studies of multicultural teams (discussed elsewhere in this thesis) could be expected to contribute to widely varying results that would potentially mask any underlying relationships.

To summarise the above: The literature was to some extent contradictory, but the performance results were predominantly negative, compared to homogeneous teams. However, for teams working in non-time-critical situations, a degree of cultural diversity could enable the wider range of experience, knowledge and views that are properties of multicultural teams, to contribute to improved decision options and greater team creativity. For example, in a high technology research environment (e.g. cosmology, particle physics or mathematics), a powerful professional culture, complete with its own symbolism and language, would form the basis of effective communication and common understandings, irrespective of the national cultures of individual team members. For organised action teams, the communication losses associated with multicultural team members would reduce the teams' abilities to handle exceptions and emergencies.

3.3.3 Summarising the effects of culture on team performance

In this subsection, the areas of external team performance and intra-team performance affected by team member cultures are summarised based on Subsections 3.3.1 and 3.3.2. These are grouped under five headings. Note that these are tendencies only - individuals from the same cultural group can display opposite cultural tendencies.

a) Management and decision-making

Culture (as measured via the power distance, individualism and uncertainty avoidance scores) has a major effect on subordinate/superior relationships. Some tasks and missions are best served by high power distance, authoritarian, strongly centralised management, for example highly automated factory systems or missions involving large military manoeuvres; others, for example complex decisions requiring wide or deep knowledge are typically best served by the consensus-based decentralised, delegating management that tends to be a feature of low power distance, low uncertainty-avoiding high individualist cultures. In some environments performance is best served by the rigid adherence to rules or standard operating procedures (SOPs) that tend to be a feature of high uncertainty-avoiding cultures, e.g. in many production and maintenance environments; in other environments, the ability to recognise when to abandon rules or SOPs may 'save the day', for example, when an aircraft is no longer operating within its normal flight envelope. Where it is important to recognise and correct errors (particularly if time is a factor), the improved team communication of low power distance, low uncertainty avoiding cultures, and the context-free communication of high individualism cultures combine to enable prompt accurate responses.

b) Creativity and innovation

Some team goals require an ability to produce (and present) a large number of ideas, go against the consensus and engage in a degree of conflict; others require an ability to take new ideas forward towards usable concepts; yet others require an ability to implement existing technologies into products and processes; in this latter situation, disciplined concentration on the task in hand is better than constantly exploring new ideas. Culture, via pressure to conform, willingness to speak out and attitudes to uncertainty, has a considerable effect on creativeness.

c) Interaction (communication and co-ordination within the team)

Some team situations require rapid, accurate communication and continuous co-ordination, best achieved with low power distance, high individualism and low uncertainty avoidance; other team situations require complex but non-time-critical communication, where cultural factors are less critical, although high power distance will still impede contributions from subordinates. Cultures, due to face issues (in the case of low individualism) and status issues (in the case of high power distance), vary widely in the degree to which rapid, direct, factual communication can occur. Cultural diversity impedes accurate communication due to differences in default assumptions and language.

d) Handling uncertainty and dealing with failures

Some environments and team goals result in highly predictable activities and/or outcomes; other environments result in highly unpredictable activities and/or outcomes that must be accommodated by the team or crew. Cultures (in particular, as measured by their uncertainty avoidance scores) vary greatly in their capabilities to deal with uncertainty.

e) Situation awareness

Some team situations require an ability to reframe and react early based on anomalous cues, others are best served by a preference to stick to standard procedures until there is no alternative but to change. Culture, in particular uncertainty avoidance, heavily influences the communication, training and reframing activities that are required for effective situation awareness. Power distance, individualism, uncertainty avoidance and cultural diversity affect the communications that are vital part of transforming individual situation awareness into joint or shared situation awareness.

Summarising the evidence from subsections 3.3.1(c) and 3.3.2, Figure 3-4 captures the key relationships between culture and sociotechnical system organised action team performance (e.g. aircrews, oil platform operators) when under stress, e.g. due to an emergency or system failure.

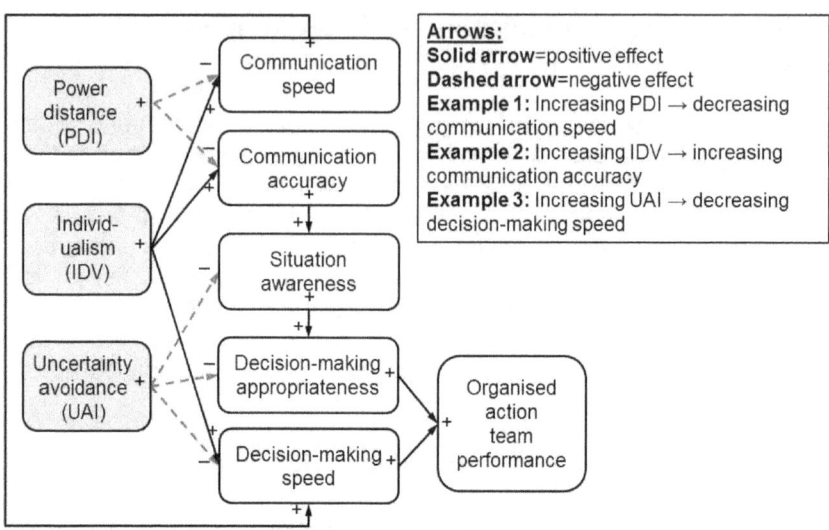

Figure 3-4: Culture's effects on organised action team performance

Despite the large amount of evidence that is available about the effects of culture on team performance, it is worth remembering Hofstede's cautions to his readers. Hofstede (1993), p.89, stated that culture was a construct, i.e. that it was not directly accessible to observation, but could only be inferred from verbal statements and other behaviours; it should only have been used where it proved to be useful, and should have been bypassed where behaviours could have been predicted without it. He went on to remind the reader that his cultural dimensions were also constructs that could be used as tools that might, or might not, clarify a situation.

3.4 Culture-based team performance prediction tools

The original objective of this section of the literature review was to iden-tify and examine existing culture-based performance prediction models and tools, in order to assess their performance capabilities and scope, and to identify any knowledge and performance gaps.

Due to the sparsity of literature on the above models and tools, this section was expanded to include an examination of their potential components, in particular cultural frameworks, measures of cultural diversity and task/mission frameworks.

3.4.1 Tools for the prediction of team performance

The purpose of this subsection was to review methods, models and tools that could predict (or could be adapted in whole or part to predict) team performances at key tasks based primarily on national culture. Such tools would carry out most or all of the functions illustrated in Figure 3-5. Due to the lack of literature on national culture-based models and tools, the review was extended to include organisational culture and safety culture-based models and tools.

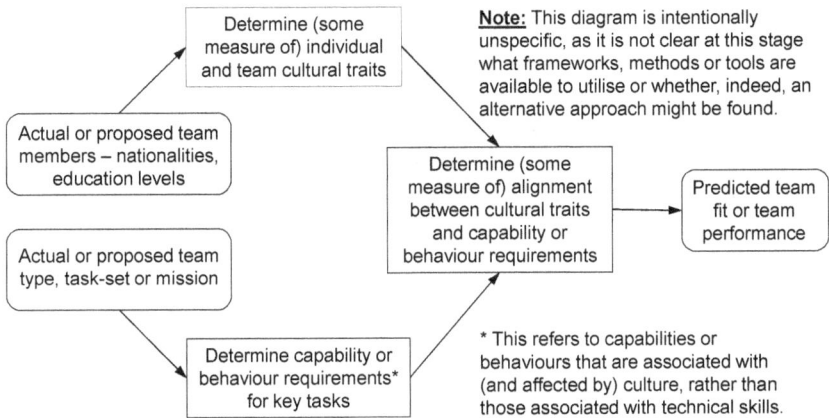

Figure 3-5: A generic flow diagram of a potential method or tool

Note that the flow diagram of Figure 3-5 represented a first attempt to identify, at a generic level, the information and processes that might be required to achieve some measure of culture-based team performance prediction (whether qualitative or quantitative); this was *not* intended to preclude an alternative approach. In the case that the literature review revealed researchers that had devised a significantly different approach to performance prediction from that shown in Figure 3-5, then such an approach would, of course, be examined in detail.

a) National culture models and tools

Only one academic peer-reviewed publication was found on national culture-based methods, models or tools for the prediction of team perfor-mance or the allocation of tasks. This publication, by Sivakumar & Nakata (2003), split the product development process into two stages (initiation and implementation) as recommended by Johne (1984). Using

Hofstede's cultural framework[17], Sivakumar & Nakata found that cultures with scores similar to those of the Nordic countries performed best at the initiation stage, whereas cultures with scores similar to those of the Japan, Taiwan and Mexico performed best at the implementation stage. Sivakumar & Nakata then developed a series of mathematical models that optimised product development success, based on the relative weightings of the initiation and implementation stages of product development; these models assumed that the same team would carry out both stages, leading to significant compromise.

Earley & Gibson (2002) developed a qualitative, two-level model of multi-cultural teams that incorporated six factors at the level of the individual team member (role identity processes, trust and expectations of others, moral character and respect for self and others, interpersonal affect, confidence and efficacy, and social awareness) and five factors at the group level (within-group competition, fractionation, development of a hybrid culture, shared understanding and meaning, and shared goals and priorities). Some very general guidance was provided that particular factors (e.g. high competitiveness) tended to cause certain affects (e.g. fragmentation), but little more.

As a result of the dearth of academic publications of relevance to national culture-based tools, the search was widened to include non-academic sources, and to review organisational culture and safety culture tools. These would not be directly utilisable, but could perhaps offer insights into the measurement of culture, the construction of task typologies and the effects of other factors on team performance.

An examination of non-academic sources of culture tools, in particular, commercial web sites and business management books, revealed three 'national culture' tools. The first, 'The CULTURE Tool' by Catholic Health was a very simple paper-based checklist; it appeared to be targeted primarily at U.S. health workers travelling abroad. This tool was presented as a table which, for three regions and eight countries, listed information under four headings – belief practices, nutritional prefer-ences, communication awareness and patient care. The aim of the tool appeared to be the avoidance of the most obvious cultural blunders and, due to its simplicity and limited coverage, it did not offer a basis for further development.

---

[17] Hofstede's original cultural framework consisted of four cultural dimensions - power distance, individualism, masculinity and uncertainty avoidance; Hofstede provided national (average) numeric scores for these dimensions for many countries, enabling these countries to be compared on a cultural basis. Further details of Hofstede's framework are provided elsewhere in this review (see Table 3-12 and Section 4.2).

The second national culture tool was a software-based tool by Hofstede[18] and the consultancy company *itim international*, and was called 'The Culture Compass Survey' (see http://geert-hofstede.com/cultural-survey.html); due to its commercial nature, only a limited amount of information about its underlying methods could be gleaned. The Culture Compass Survey enabled an individual to state his/her home country, country of interest and to select one of eight roles, then to take a survey (consisting of 42 pairs of statements) that revealed his/her cultural preferences. Scores were then produced internally that indicated cultural differences between the individual and both his/her own country's (default) national culture and that of the country of interest; based on these differences, feedback comments were generated that highlighted potential pitfalls and problems that might occur in both countries. The ranking of these comments appeared to be based on the stated role of the participant. This tool appeared to carry out, to some degree, several of the activities presented in Figure 3-4; it produced a cultural profile (for an individual, not a team), and took limited account of the individual's role (rather than tasks). The tool was aimed at the determination of the degree of fit of an individual 'outsider' to another culture, rather than the degree of fit of a team's culture to a task set. Interestingly, Hofstede has in the past repeatedly warned about the ecological fallacy arising from assigning cultural scores (or cultural preferences) to an individual (Hofstede 2001, p.16). Note that the Culture Compass Survey was released at a very late stage of the work described in this thesis.

The third national culture tool, by *DFA Intercultural Global Solutions*, was an online software-based tool called 'CultureCompass' (see http://dfaculturecompass.com/). As a commercial tool, only a limited amount of information was available about the underlying methods, but it appeared to utilise cultural dimensions from more than one cultural framework. This tool was similar to the Hofstede-based Culture Compass Survey (above); it asked the user to select a role, to take a survey consisting of ten questions (each with a sliding scale between two extremes), and then to enter his/her nationality. The tool then displayed the differences between the user and the national average, and reproduced standard material on the particular dimensions.

b) Organisational culture models and tools

Two published reviews of organisational culture instruments for commerce and industry, public administration (Jung et al., 2009) and health and social care (Scott, Mannion, Davies, & Marshall, 2003) were initially examined. Based on these reviews, several of the more

---

[18] Hofstede's academic contributions are discussed later in this thesis.

interesting instruments were assessed, for example, the Organizational Culture Inventory (Cooke & Szumal, 1993), Competing Values Framework (Cameron & Quinn, 2006). Typically, following the utilisation of checklists, questionnaires, interviews, discussion groups or a combination of these, the culture instrument allocated the organisation's current or proposed culture to one of several types (via a taxonomic or dimensional scheme); these types were clearly related to or affected by national culture, but very little reference was made as to the potential relationships to, and effects of, national culture.

Most of the organisational tools appeared to employ checklists, questionnaires, interviews, discussion groups or a combination of these, in some cases with computer support. There were some overlaps in the above two reviews, but there were differing criteria, e.g. competitive performance improvement in commerce and industry, vs. quality of care in healthcare and intercultural competence in social care. Quantitative organisational culture measurement tool assessments were typically based on typologies (i.e. allocating the culture to one of several predefined types), or on dimensions, where the assessments resulted in scores along each of several dimensions. None of the organisational culture tools contained elements that could be adapted to a national-culture-based tool; in particular, these tools did not enable the consideration of relationships between cultural elements and task performance requirements.

The majority of non-academic sources presented commercial variants on organisational culture tools. Examples included 'lean culture' tools, 'cultural transformation' tools, 'culture alignment' tools and 'customer culture' tools; many of the commercial culture tool web sites offered user training courses.

Only a minority of the publications on organisational culture acknowledged the overriding influence of national culture on organisational culture and most of those that did acknowledge it paid little more than 'lip service'. For example, the book "Diagnosing and Changing Organizational Culture based on the Competing Values Framework", which went into considerable detail on the processes of assessing, diagnosing and changing culture, did not allude to national culture.

Few (if any) of the commercial tools, took account of national cultural differences and, as a result, would have little relevance outside western cultures. In addition, the organisational culture tools appeared not to consider task-related requirements of organisations, rather a target corporate culture that was thought to be conducive from specific viewpoints (e.g. 'the customer').

c) Safety culture models and tools

Several published reviews of safety culture tools were examined. These included a safety culture tool selection guide by the International Association of Oil & Gas Producers (OGP, 2010a), a review of the main safety culture assessment approaches and a selection of tools by the European Agency for Safety and Health at Work (Eeckelaert, Starren, van Scheppingen, Fox, & Bruck, 2011), and a review of patient-related safety culture tools as part of a European Network for Patient Safety project (EUNetPaS, 2010). These tools had many similarities to the organisational culture tools, again employing checklists, questionnaires, interviews, discussion group, etc. However, none of the safety-related dimensions, nor any task-related aspects, appeared to offer any contribution to the culture tool requirements of the author's research. As was the case with organisational culture, none of the safety culture tools could be adapted to a national-culture-based tool, nor did these tools enable the consideration of relationships between cultural elements and the task performance requirements associated with the teams' purposes.

d) Summary on culture tools

No national culture-based models or tools were found that could enable the prediction of the performance of a proposed or current team in a range of team/task situations. No organizational or safety culture tools were found that could be adapted effectively to meet the requirements of the research described in this thesis; indeed, few of the academic or commercial publications on organisational culture appeared to recognise the constraints that national cultures place on organisational and safety cultures. The tool that came nearest to meeting the requirements was that of Hofstede and *itim international*. There appeared to be a signifi-cant gap, in both academia and commerce/industry, in the provision of tools or guidance for culture-based team selection, adaptation and performance prediction for critical tasks.

3.4.2 Cultural frameworks

In the absence of national culture-based models, methods and tools for the estimation or prediction of team performance, the purpose of this section was to ascertain the availability and capabilities of frameworks, models, methods or tools for the capture of national cultural traits of individuals and/or teams. These could form the basis of, or at least provide guidance in the construction of, the 'cultural side' of a perfor-mance prediction model and tool.

Over the last half century, researchers in human culture have developed a variety of quantitative instruments for the measurement of culture.

Typically, these instruments or frameworks encapsulated sets of cultural factors, attributes, orientations or dimensions that were presented as a binary or ternary choice between qualitative alternatives, or in terms of a quantitative scale between two extremes. Although there was no universally-agreed set of cultural dimensions, certain dimensions (and minor variations on them) appeared in several of the cultural frameworks, and were found to be statistically robust.

A review of cultural frameworks was carried out by the author of this thesis, for which the initially-identified authors were Hofstede, House et al., Triandis and Schwartz. Academic books detailing these frameworks represented a useful starting point; these initially-perused books included "Culture's Consequences" (G H Hofstede, 1980), "Cultures and Organizations" (Geert Hofstede, 1991), "Culture, Leadership and Organizations" (House et al., 2004), "Culture and Social Behavior" (Triandis, 1993), "Beyond Individualism/Collectivism" (S H Schwartz, 1994) and "Multinational Work Teams: A New Perspective" (Earley & Gibson, 2002). Academic papers by these authors, and reviews by other authors of their work, were then retrieved and examined before expanding the review via forward- and backward-citations.

There were too many culture-measurement instruments (or frameworks) for all of them to be detailed in this thesis, for example, a recent review paper (Taras, Rowney, & Steel, 2009) identified 121 such instruments. Therefore, this review was limited to the higher impact cultural frameworks, as only these could offer the range of study results that would enable the researcher to extract useful, predictive relationships between culture and performance.

In providing a form of 'cultural location' (see top box of Figure 3-5), the above frameworks could, if combined with task/skill frameworks, provide the basis for a culture-based team performance prediction methodology.

a) National or ethnic culture frameworks

National (or ethnic) culture typically reflects the most profound aspects of culture (compared to occupational, organisational, etc.), as it is inculcated in individuals from a very early age. This section describes the higher impact frameworks.

Kluckhohn & Strodtbeck's value orientations method (VOM) (Hills, 2002; Kluckhohn & Strodtbeck, 1961) was utilised to identify cultural differences between groups; it encapsulated the work of the Harvard Values Project that took place during the 1940s and 1950s (Bahr, 2006). The method was based on five concerns or cultural orientations, each with three descriptive values or responses, see Table 3-10.

Orientations/-preferences	Values - descriptions		
Activity/-behaviour	**Being:** Internal motivation. We need not achieve 'great things'.	**Becoming:** Motivation to improve in ability to our own benefit.	**Doing:** External motivation for activities valued by all.
Basic human nature	**Evil:** Most people are bad, and cannot be trusted.	**Mixed:** There are both good & bad people. One must check people out.	**Good:** Most people are good. "People are born good."
Man-nature relationship	**Subordinate to nature:** We just have to adapt to it.	**Harmony with nature:** We should exercise only partial control.	**Mastery:** We should be dominant over nature.
Social relations	**Hierarchical:** Defer to higher authority.	**Collateral:** Consensus of equals.	**Individual:** Independent decision-making
Time sense	**Past:** Preserving traditional beliefs and ways.	**Present:** Adapting to what is NOW is what matters.	**Future:** Planning ahead, actively seeking new ways.

Table 3-10: Kluckhohn & Strodtbeck's value orientations

Triandis' cultural framework (Triandis 1995; 1996) was composed of five cultural syndromes (or dimensions), each with two descriptive values[19] (the equivalent of low and high) to choose from, i.e. a total of 32 (2^5) cultural categories, see Table 3-11. Whereas many cultural frameworks treated individualism/collectivism as expressing the extremes of a single dimension, Triandis treated *individualism* and *collectivism* as three separate syndromes, including *two* types of collectivism – *horizontal* ('interdependence and oneness') and *vertical* ('serving the group').

Cultural syndrome	Extreme values – descriptions	
Cultural complexity	**Simple:** E.g. hunter-gatherer societies; agricultural societies are slightly more complex.	**Complex:** Industrial societies are complex and information societies even more so.
Cultural tightness	**Loose:** Cultural looseness can arise due to cultural mix; urban populations are often culturally looser than rural ones.	**Tight:** People are required to behave within clear norms, and face sanctions if they deviate. Tight cultures are typically homogeneous.
Individualism	**Low:** Lacking self-reliance and independence.	**High:** Largely treating others as equals, valuing self-reliance and independence.
Horizontal collectivism	**Low:** Lacking a co-operative spirit.	**High:** Placing a high value on interdependence and sharing.
Vertical collectivism	**Low:** Being unwilling to take up one's place within the hierarchy of a group.	**High:** Recognising one's position within the group and being willing to serve the group.

Table 3-11: Triandis' cultural syndromes

---

[19] E.g. cultural tightness has the values 'loose' and 'tight'.

Hofstede's cultural framework (1984) emerged out of a series of research investigations into culture at IBM sites in forty countries, between 1967 and 1973. Based on statistical analyses of responses to a large set of questions, four largely independent cultural dimensions were originally identified and, for these, national scores were derived and normalised to a range between 0 and 100. These four cultural dimensions are listed, with their extreme (descriptive) values, in Table 3-12. More detailed descriptions and explanations of the four dimensions of Table 3-12 can be found in Hofstede (2001), chapters 3 to 6 and Hofstede & Hofstede (2004), chapters 2 to 5. Since Hofstede's original analyses, many further countries have been evaluated and, at the start of this research, scores were available for 76 countries and regions (representing a large proportion of the World's population).

Cultural dimension	Extreme values - descriptions	
Power distance (PDI)	**Low PDI:** Those in authority tend to be consultative, with communications occurring relatively freely up and down the command chain. Decisions are more likely to be made by agents with appropriate knowledge and experience, irrespective of roles.	**High PDI:** Subordinates accept (and even prefer) being ordered with little consultation on the part of leaders. Decisions are made by those in authority, are dispatched downwards through the organization, are rarely questioned and are never overridden.
Individualism (vs. collectivism) (IDV)	**Collectivism (low IDV):** Individuals belong to tightly-knit groups and in return for unquestioning loyalty, gain the protection of their group. Collectivists try to avoid direct, confrontational approaches and speak indirectly (the information is in the context). Hierarchies tend to be rigid, losing face must be avoided at all costs.	**High IDV:** Ties between individuals (other than immediate family members) tend to be loose. Individualists take personal responsibility for their actions, typically speak in a direct manner (the information is in the message), and are willing to argue and to question others' views.
Masculinity (vs. femininity) (MAS)	**Low MAS (high femininity):** There is greater fluidity in roles between the sexes, less differentiation than in high masculinity societies. Quality of life, good relationships and co-operation are important.	**High MAS:** The difference in roles between the genders is high. Competition and recognition are important than quality of life and relationships.
Uncertainty avoidance (UAI)	**Low UAI:** Members have a high tolerance for uncertainty and ambiguity, in many cases preferring situations that offer some uncertainty.	**High UAI:** Members feel discomfort with uncertainty and will seek to reduce it (or at least its apparent manifestation) via laws, rules and other measures.

Table 3-12: Hofstede's original four cultural dimensions

Following work by Chinese researchers, Hofstede (2001, Ch.7) added a further cultural dimension – that of long term orientation; this dimension measured the willingness of a cultural group to persevere over a long time period. Following Minkov's detailed analysis of the World Values

Survey, see Hofstede, Hofstede & Minkov (2010, Ch.8), a sixth cultural dimension, that of indulgence vs. restraint (IVR), was added.

Trompenaars' cultural framework (Trompenaars & Hampden-Turner, 1997) was based on his consultancy experiences. From these, he concluded that cultures are distinguished from each other by the ways that their members solve three fundamental problems - their relationships with other people, with (or to) time, and with nature. Trompenaars developed a questionnaire based on the work of Kluckhohn and Strodtbeck (1961) and Parsons and Shils (1951), and used it to collect data from his international business clients and their employees. In particular, Trompenaars wished to know how these people, from a range of countries, resolved dilemmas. From an analysis of the data, he developed seven cultural dimensions that appeared to explain most of the variations in behaviour that he had observed via his questionnaires (Trompenaars & Hampden-Turner, 1997). These dimensions are listed, with brief extreme value descriptions, in the Table 3-13.

Cultural dimension	Extreme values - descriptions	
Achieved status vs. ascribed status	**Achieved status:** Achieving your status by your continuing accomplishments.	**Ascribed status:** Achieving your status by privilege (e.g. by birth, age or wealth).
Affectivity vs. neutrality	**Affectivity:** People do not hide their feelings, they display their emotions.	**Neutrality:** People are discouraged from displaying feelings and expressing emotions.
Individualism vs. communitarianism	**Individualism:** The individual is placed before the community; self-reliance and initiative are important.	**Communitarianism:** The community is placed before the individual, who must serve the community to satisfy his/her needs.
Inner direction vs. outer direction	**Inner direction:** People can control and change their environment.	**Outer direction:** People should live in harmony with their environment, an organic view.
Sequential time vs. synchronous time	**Sequential time:** Time as an arrow, proceeding irreversibly; do one thing at a time.	**Synchronous time:** Time as circular, with opportunities repeating themselves; do several things at once.
Specificity vs. diffusion	**Specificity:** Plain-speaking, specific, analytic, self-controlled, factual.	**Diffusion:** Mysterious, holistic and passionate. Relationships are key.
Universalism vs. particularism	**Universalism:** Rules - all should be treated equally, the law should not differentiate.	**Particularism:** Relationships - it matters who you are; you might testify falsely for a friend in court.

Table 3-13: Trompenaars' seven cultural dimensions

The GLOBE cultural framework was based on one of the largest recent studies of national culture (House et al., 2004); it examined the attitudes and beliefs of more than 17,000 managers from 950 organisations in 62 countries. The study was primarily focused on cultural influences on organisational leadership. Based on detailed analyses of questionnaire results, the GLOBE researchers classified societies into ten regional clusters - Anglo, Latin Europe, Nordic Europe, Germanic Europe, Eastern Europe, Latin America, Middle East, Sub-Saharan Africa, Southern Asia and Confucian Asia. The GLOBE study identified nine cultural dimensions, which are briefly described in Table 3-14.

Cultural dimension	Extreme values - descriptions	
Assertive-ness	**Low:** Individuals are non-confron-tational and deferential in their social relationships.	**High:** Individuals are assertive and confrontational in their social relationships.
Future orientation	**Low:** Individuals 'live for the day', with relatively little thought for the future.	**High:** Individuals sacrifice some of their current benefits in order to plan and invest for the future,
Gender egalitar-ianism	**Low:** There are significant role differences and inequalities between the genders.	**High:** Society minimises gender role differences and inequality.
Humane orientation	**Low:** Society does not encourage individuals to exhibit altruism, fairness, etc.	**High:** Society rewards individuals well for exhibiting fairness, altruism, generosity and kindness.
Institutional collectivism	**Low:** Institutions do not significan-tly reward collective behaviour.	**High:** Institutions reward collective action and distribution of resources.
In-group collectivism	**Low:** Individuals do not display significant loyalty, pride and cohesiveness in their families and organizations.	**High:** Individuals display significant loyalty, pride and cohesiveness in their families and organizations.
Performance orientation	**Low:** Society does not reward individuals for performance improvement and excellence.	**High:** Society awards individuals for performance improvement and excellence.
Power distance	**Low:** Individuals expect that power will be delegated as appropriate to the situation.	**High:** Individuals expect that power should be concentrated at higher levels,
Uncertainty avoidance	**Low:** Individuals and society tolerate uncertainty.	**High:** Individuals and society strive to avoid uncertainty via social norms, practices and rules.

Table 3-14: The GLOBE Study cultural dimensions

The GLOBE *assertiveness, gender egalitarianism, institutional collec-tivism, in-group collectivism* and *power distance* originated from Hofstede's cultural dimensions (Geert H. Hofstede, 1984). The GLOBE *power distance* and *uncertainty avoidance* cultural dimensions were virtually identical to Hofstede's similarly-named dimensions. A factor analysis of the items intended to measure collectivism (Hofstede's *individualism vs. collectivism*) resulted in two GLOBE dimensions – *institutional collectivism* (a new construct) and *in-group collectivism*. Based on Hofstede's description of his *masculinity vs. femininity* dimension, the GLOBE researchers developed two dimensions – *gender egalitarianism* and *assertiveness*; this enabled them to remove items from the masculinity (gender) dimension that were considered not to be properties of masculinity.

The GLOBE *future orientation* cultural dimension was based on Kluckhohn and Strodtbeck's *time sense* (past, present, future) cultural orientation (Kluckhohn & Strodtbeck, 1961); *future orientation* was also related in concept to Hofstede's *long-term orientation* cultural dimension. The GLOBE humane orientation was based on Kluckhohn and Strodtbeck's *human nature* (evil, mixed, good) cultural orientation, Putnam's civil society work (Putnam, 1993) and McClelland's affiliative motive work (McClelland, 1985).The GLOBE Study was later extended to include in-depth studies of 25 societies (Chhokar, Brodbeck, & House, 2008).

Schwartz's culture-level value scale (or cultural values framework) was based on data collected and analysed data from 49 nations (Shalom H Schwartz, 1999, 2006). He identified seven 'cultural level value types', which could be structured or condensed as 'cultural orientations' along three polar dimensions, see the Table 3-15.

Cultural dimension	Extreme values - descriptions	
Mastery vs. harmony	**Mastery:** self-assertion, seeking to change the world.	**Harmony:** At one with nature and a world at peace.
Embeddedness vs. autonomy	**Embeddedness:** People see themselves in terms of the group, and it is important to maintain the status quo.	**Autonomy:** People see themselves separately from the group, capable of expressing their own opinions and acting independently.
Hierarchy vs. egalitarianism	**Hierarchy:** Roles are ascribed, and rules must be obeyed. Inequality is accepted.	**Egalitarianism:** Members are socialised to co-operate and pursue the wellbeing of all.

Table 3-15: Schwartz' three cultural orientations

A summary of national culture frameworks: The most commonly referenced culture frameworks (described earlier) have been compared to each other in Table 3-16, enabling the reader to observe the differing 'cultural coverage' of the various researchers' offerings. The six vertical columns of the following table represent the cultural dimensions, orientations or syndromes of the six cultural frameworks that are being compared. The table rows associate dimensions that are similar, based on the descriptions of their authors.

Cultural framework dimensions or orientations					
Kluckhohn & Strodtbeck's VOM	Hofstede's original cultural dimensions	Triandis' cultural syndromes	Trompenaars' cultural dimensions	The GLOBE Study cultural dimensions	Schwartz's cultural orientations
Social relations	Individualism vs. collectivism (IDV)	Individualism	Individualism vs. communitarianism	Institutional collectivism	Embeddedness vs. autonomy
		Horizontal collectivism	*Universalism vs. particularism*	In-group collectivism	
		Vertical collectivism			
			Specificity vs. diffusion	*Performance orientation*	
	Power distance (PDI)		*Achieved status vs. ascribed status*	Power distance	Hierarchy vs. egalitarianism
	Masculinity vs. femininity (MAS)			Gender egalitarianism	
				Assertiveness	
	Uncertainty avoidance (UAI)	*Cultural tightness*		Uncertainty avoidance	
Time sense	Long term orientation (LTO)			Future orientation	
Man-nature relationship			Inner direction vs. outer direction		Mastery vs. harmony
			Sequential time vs. synchronous time		
			Affectivity vs. neutrality		
Activity (being or doing)					
Human nature					
		Cultural complexity			
				Humane orientation	

Note that dimensions in *italics* indicate at best an approximate fit.

Table 3-16: A comparison of national cultural frameworks

It can be seen from the table that, for these six widely-publicised cultural frameworks, *individualism vs. collectivism* (or its near equivalent) is the only cultural dimension common to all. Power distance (or its near equivalent) appears in four of the six frameworks. Uncertainty avoidance and man-nature relationships (or their near equivalents), appear in three of the frameworks.

The frameworks of Hofstede and the GLOBE appear to achieve the greatest commonality across all cultural dimensions.

b) Organisational culture frameworks

A brief review was carried out of organisational culture tools (detailed in Section 3.3.1), but this was done with a view to the extraction of useful features for application in the proposed national culture tool. The reason for the review detailed in this subsection was to determine whether it was possible, or reasonable, to adjust default national culture values to take account of organisational differences (where known). Ideally, it should have been possible to allocate certain default organisational culture properties to certain sectors of activity, e.g. to aircraft transport, refining, power generation, medical facilities. These could then have been used to adjust national culture values.

The Competing Values Framework (CVF) emerged out of research work by Cameron and Quinn (Cameron & Quinn, 1999; Quinn & Rohrbaugh, 1981, 1983). The CVF utilised two dimensions - *focused vs. flexible* (differentiating between stability, order and control on the one hand, and flexibility, discretion and dynamism on the other) and *internal vs. external* (differentiating between an internally-orientated focus on unity, integration and collaboration on the one hand, and a focus on competition, rivalry and differentiation on the other). The associated *organization culture assessment instrument* (OCAI) covered six categories of organisation-related statements. By allocating a total of 100 points across the four statements in each category (a total of 600 points), a set of scores emerged that located the organisation within the four CVF quadrants. This allocation exercise was typically carried out for the *'as-is'* organisation, and again for the *'would like to be'* organisation. The two orthogonal dimensions produced four quadrants; companies falling into these four quadrants were identified as hierarchy (focus/internal), market (focus/external), clan (flexible/internal) and adhocracy (flexible/external).

Deal & Kennedy's organisational culture framework (1988) utilised two cultural dimensions - *rapidity of feedback and reward* (the speed with which companies learned whether their actions and strategies have been successful), and *degree of risk or uncertainty* (the amount of risk (or uncertainty) associated with the organisation's key activities). These two dimensions produced four quadrants of culture (as with the earlier-presented CVF); companies falling into these four quadrants were identified as possessing process culture (slow/low-risk), bet-the-company culture (slow/high-risk), work-hard-play-hard culture (rapid/low-risk) and tough-guy-macho culture (rapid/high-risk). Each of these company cultures fitted a particular type of business. For example, the 'tough-guy', macho culture (high risk, rapid feedback) was associated with high-stress organizations that focused primarily on the present, facing constant risk of failing to achieve targets and losing rewards, for example sports and hospital surgery. By way of contrast, the process culture (slow feedback/reward, low risk) was typically a slow plodding bureaucracy intent on maintaining the status quo (past=present=future).

Harrison's organisational culture framework: Harrison (1972) argued that there were six 'interests' associated with organisations, which formed the basis of ideological tension and struggle. He proposed four organisational ideologies that emerged out of these:

- **Power orientation:** Power oriented organisations aspired to dominate their environments and eliminate all opposition. Those who were in positions of power attempted to maintain total control over their subordinates. Although their autocratic structures enabled power-oriented organisations to make quick decisions, the lack of rapid, reliable information flow meant that they were not very flexible or responsive to changes in complex environments.

- **Role orientation:** Role-oriented organisations aspired to rationality and orderliness, and the maintenance of legality, legitimacy and responsibility. Rules and procedures were developed and adhered to. Role oriented organisations were unable to respond quickly to threats and changes in their environments because they were heavily constrained by their rules and standard procedures.

- **Task orientation:** Task-oriented organisations were goal-driven, and all aspects of such organisations were evaluated in terms of their contributions to the goal(s). They typically had a decentralised structure, delegated decisions to those with the appropriate knowledge, and could react quickly to changes in complex environments.

- **Person orientation:** Person-oriented organisations existed to serve their members; only a minimum level of authority was accepted over individual members. Person oriented organisations tended to be slow to respond as they did not have adequate means to organise their members to deal with threats.

Although Harrison did not specify any dimensions associated with the above orientations, there was a degree of exclusivity between two pairs that have some of the qualities of dimensions, i.e.:

- **Role vs. task orientation:** This was very similar to the CVS internal vs. external and Hofstede's process vs. results dimensions (see later).

- **Person vs. power orientation:** This was very similar to Hofstede's organisational culture dimension of employee vs. job-orientation (see later).

Looking to national culture dimensions, Harrison's *power orientation* could (from its description) be associated with high *power distance*, his *role orientation* could be associated with *uncertainty avoidance*.

Hofstede's six dimensional model of organisational culture (Hofstede et al. 1990) was based on studies of organizational cultures in twenty units of ten companies in Denmark and the Netherlands. Following a detailed analysis of the results Hofstede et al. developed a model of organizational cultures consisting of the following dimensions:

- **Process vs. results:** Concern with means (processes, techniques, etc.) vs. concern with the achievement of goals.

- **Employee vs. job-oriented:** Concern about people/employees, delegation of decision-making vs. concern about getting the job done, centralized decision-making, impersonal.

- **Parochial vs. professional:** Employees who derived their identities from the organisation (e.g. 'the company man') vs. employees who derived their identities from their professions (who separate their external lives from the job).

- **Open vs. closed:** Open, welcoming to new employees, easy to gain an insight vs. closed to outsiders; people took a long time to fit in.

- **Loose vs. tight:** Flexible with regard to attitudes, times and budgets vs. highly controlled, serious, adhere to times, budgets.

- **Normative vs. pragmatic:** Implementation of (inviolable) rules vs. maintaining flexibility in order to serve the customer.

Hofstede et al. (2010), p.370, emphasized that, as the research data behind the above six dimensions was based on twenty organisational units in two European countries, it could not be claimed that that the above six dimensions adequately described all types of organisations in all countries. However, they suggested that all organisational cultures could usefully be described by a set of dimensions that would have some resemblance to the above six dimensions.

Schein's organisational culture framework (1996a; 1996b) consisted of the following six dimensions:

- **Relationship to the environment:** The organisation was dominant **vs.** harmonising **vs.** niche-seeking within its business environment.

- **Nature of human activity within the organisation:** The accepted model of behaviour was to control via proactive behaviours **_vs._** to harmonise relationships via passive/fatalistic compromises.

- **Nature of time within the organisation:** Organisation members preferred looking to the past **_vs._** living for the present **_vs._** looking to the future.

- **Reality and truth in the organisation:** Organisation members assessed reality and truth via systematic formulae of motive, means and opportunity **_vs._** experience, wisdom and intuition.

- **The nature of people:** Organisation members assumed that people were good, evil or lazy and perhaps able to change **_vs._** assuming that people were trying to do their best, even when they failed.

- **Distribution of power and affiliation:** Organisation members competed, grabbed resources, worked primarily to further their own goals, and managers were autocratic or paternalistic **_vs._** members cooperated, worked in a team-oriented manner and shared resources.

The reality in most organisations was that they were 'somewhere in the middle' for most of the above dimensions and, also, there would be large differences across different levels and functional areas.

A summary of organisational culture frameworks: The most commonly-referenced organisational culture frameworks (described earlier) are compared to each other via a table, enabling the reader to observe the differing 'organisational cultural coverage' of the various researchers' offerings. The five vertical columns of Table 3-17 represent the cultural dimensions, orientations or syndromes of the five organisational culture frameworks that are being compared. The table rows associate dimensions that are similar, from the five frameworks.

It can be seen from Table 3-17 that, for this sample of organisational culture frameworks, there were two areas of overlap, which could be described as *attitudes to rules* and *power concentration/delegation*[20]. However, even within these groups, there was a wide spread of potential interpretation.

---

[20] The descriptions given here to these common groupings of dimensions are at best approximate.

Organizational cultural framework				
Competing values (organisational culture) framework	Deal and Kennedy's organisational culture framework	Harrison's organisational culture framework	Hofstede's organisational culture framework	Schein's organisational culture framework
Focused vs. flexible			*Loose vs. tight*	*Nature of human activity within the organisation*
		Role vs. task	*Normative vs. pragmatic*	
Internal vs. external			*Process vs. results*	
	Rapidity of feedback			
	Degree of risk or uncertainty			
		Person vs. power	Employee vs. job-oriented	Distribution of power & affiliation
			Parochial vs. professional	
			Open vs. closed	
				4 other dimensions that do not have near equivalents
Note that dimensions in *italics* indicate at best an approximate fit.				

Table 3-17: A comparison of organisational cultural frameworks

c) Occupational culture frameworks

There have been few studies of occupational (or professional) culture, compared to organisational culture. The majority of studies appeared to be comparisons between professions, or comparisons between the culture dimension scores of professionals and the national cultural dimension scores of their compatriots. It was, however, clear that there was a significant degree of self-selection in many professions – different personality types chose to be accountants, teachers, doctors, etc.; this was likely to be reflected to some degree in their quantitative culture scores.

The only study that appeared to offer a replicable, quantitative approach was that by Bosland (G H Hofstede 2001, pp.493-494; Bosland 1985). This adjusted Hofstede's cultural dimension scores based on years in full time education.

A summary of occupational frameworks: Bosland's adjustment of the four dimension scores of Hofstede's original national cultural framework was the only quantitative approach found that was related (via years of full time education) to occupational (or professional) culture.

3.4.3 Measures of team cultural diversity

For the purposes of the work described in this thesis, a measure of cultural diversity of team members was required that provided a quantitative value reflecting the mean cultural differences between team members. It was important that any measure utilised by the researcher would take account, not only of the number of different cultures (e.g. national cultures) in a team, but also the degree of difference between each of those cultures. In addition, it was important that such a measure would enable users of a tool incorporating the measure to identify the diversity associated with each team member.

A review of the literature revealed three main approaches to the determination of cultural diversity, examples of which are briefly discussed below.

a) Diversity based on the number (or proportions) of different nationalities in a team

The **Blau Index** of racial and ethnic diversity (Blau, 1977) , the **Herfindhal-Hirschmann Index** (HHI) (Rhoades, 1993), the **Shannon (or Shannon-Wiener) Diversity Index** (SDI) and **Simpson's Index** (Simpson's D) were based on the number of different types (e.g. plant species, nationalities) and their relative weightings, not the degree of difference (diversity) between types.

Greenberg's Diversity Index (also known as the linguistic diversity index, LDI) was primarily utilised to measure the diversity of a country's languages. In his paper on the measurement of linguistic diversity (Greenberg, 1956), Greenberg described a simple index, GDI(A), based on the probability of two speakers from the selected population, P, speaking the same language, i: $GDI(A) = 1 - \sum (P_i^2)$.

b) Diversity based on a measure of difference between each nationality in a team

Greenberg also described an alternative to his basic diversity index that included a weighting for each language pair based on their linguistic similarities, GDI(B). This **Weighted Monolingual Index** was defined as:

$GDI(B) = 1 - \sum_{i,j} (p_i \, p_j) \, r_{ij}$

Where: p_i, p_j were the proportions of speakers of languages 'i' and 'j' in the population,

and: r_{ij} was a measure of the resemblance between languages 'i' and 'j'.

The GDI(B) took account of quantifiable differences (or distances) between members of a set, so it would be able to distinguish between multicultural teams of similar and dissimilar cultures.

The **Stirling Index** (Stirling, 1999; Stirling, 2007) took account of differences between members of a set by assuming that they were located in Euclidean space, and the distance between any two object types represented their mutual disparity. The Stirling index was defined as:

SI = $\sum_{i,j} d_{ij} p_i p_j$

<u>for</u> i,j = 1 to the number of species (or team member countries),
       d_{ij} = distance (disparity) between species (or country) 'i' and 'j'
<u>and</u> p_i = the proportion of the population belonging to species or country 'i'.

c) Diversity based on standard statistical measures of mean and variance

Statistical measures were utilised by Elron (1997) to derive values for team cultural diversity. Elron calculated the mean and standard deviation of team members based on Hofstede's default national culture scores for team members, the standard deviation providing a measure of team cultural diversity.

d) A summary of measures of cultural diversity

There appeared to be three main approaches to the derivation of diversity within a team or population. The most common approach took account of the number of different members based on some nominal value (e.g. gender, profession or nationality); although this approach was accurate for binary differences such as gender, it was insensitive as a measure of cultural diversity because cultures could be very similar (e.g. Germany, Czech Republic) or very different (e.g. Guatemala, Australia). The second approach utilised a measure of distance or separation in Euclidean space between members (e.g. based on their national culture scores, education and/or ages). However, to combine (in our case) the cultural separation along several axes into a single (Euclidean) distance was to imply that each factor or dimension had a similar effect to each other in every circumstance. The third, statistical approach to the derivation of team or population diversity placed a heavy emphasis on outliers.

3.4.4 Team and task classifications

For the purposes of the work described in this thesis, it was necessary to be able to describe teams and/or their tasks in terms of the behavioural capabilities required for successful performance. Such behavioural capabilities (for want of a better term) could then be associated with team member cultural scores to form the basis of an assessment methodology and tool. The following five culture-modified areas of behaviour/behavioural requirements were identified in Subsection 3.3.3: Management and decision-making, creativity and innovation, interaction (communication and co-ordination), uncertainty handing and achieving shared situation awareness. It was therefore important to examine the literature in order to evaluate team *and* task typologies (taxonomies, classifications) in terms of their abilities to represent the above culture-related requirements.

There have been many detailed reviews of the literature on team theory, in particular on team classifications, for example Guzzo & Dickson (1996), DeMatteo et al. (1998), Wildman et al. (2012) and Hollenbeck et al. (2012). It appeared from an examination of these reviews that team classifications varied greatly depending on the 'central' team type (the classifier's starting point) and on the purpose of the classification. Some of the more interesting approaches to team/task classification (from the point of view of the author's research) are briefly described below.

Cohen and Bailey (1997) carried out a review of research on teams and groups published between January 1990 and April 1996. Their team classification was unsuitable for the approach in this thesis, as they appeared to place some types of organised action team in the same category as routine manufacturing teams. However, they defined team performance along three dimensions – output quantity and quality, member attitudes, and behavioural outcomes. The latter category was of interest, as it could contribute to a link between culture and some aspects of performance. **Marks, Mathieu and Zaccaro** (2001) appeared to concentrate on the classification of industrial and commer-cial work teams but did not provide sufficient details on the task or behavioural aspects of teams to be useful to the work of this thesis; however, their 'team maintenance' processes could perhaps offer a basis for 'layering' the effects of culture onto team performance.

Fernandez et al.'s emergency medicine team taxonomy (2008) utilised the input-process-output (I-P-O) model that is widely used in industry and academia. Inputs represented the team member characteristics (abilities, experience, etc.), processes represented the behaviours and collaborations required to achieve successful outputs in terms of task outcomes and team performances; the various sets of 'task-work' went through the I-P-O cycle, the output of one cycle being an input the next. The emergency medicine process model was proposed as having (in temporal sequence) a planning and preparation phase, action processes and reflection processes. In particular, the taxonomy's 'action process' phase and 'support mechanisms' might have been the locations for culture-affected tasks/behaviours, but insufficient details were available to consider it further. **Steiner** (1972) recognised that the task was one of the key factors in team or group performance. He split unitary (indivisible) tasks into disjunctive, conjunctive, additive and discretionary tasks, and divisible tasks into self-matching, pre-specified and organisationally (externally) allocated tasks; however, the basis of his classification was to enable the optimum allocation of team members on the basis of their technical or experience-based proficiencies, and it would be difficult to associate such tasks with the effects of culture.

McGrath's circumplex (McGrath 1984, Ch. 5) integrated the work of Hackman & Morris (1975), Shaw (1973), Davis and Laughlin, to produce his 'task circumplex' classification framework for group tasks. This circumflex was represented as a circle with eight segments, each segment being one of eight mutually exclusive and collectively exhaustive task categories - planning, creativity, intellective (have 'correct' answers), decision-making (have no 'correct' answers), cognitive conflict, mixed motive, competitive and performance/psycho-motor tasks. McGrath's circumflex listed some of the areas where problems might occur in teams due to the effects of culture, for example in creativity tasks, cognitive conflict tasks, mixed motive tasks and competitive tasks.

Gluesing & Gibson (2003), Chapter 11: Designing and Forming Global Teams, pp. 199-226, claimed that the complexity that global teams, in particular, faced could be described along five dimensions – task, context, people, time and technology. Task complexity appeared to be the most relevant for cultural issues, and could be described in terms of four elements - *workflow interdependence* (based on the degree of interaction required between team members), *task environment (*varying from a static, stable, predictable environment to one that was highly dynamic and unpredictable, causing disruptions and re-evaluations of activities), *external coupling* (which appeared to overlap *task environment), and internal coupling* (which appeared to overlap *workflow interdependence)*. Gluesing & Gibson's approach was extremely complex, but it was perhaps only the communication ramifications of *workflow interdependence* and the uncertainty ramifications of *task environment* that had clear links to culture.

Hollenbeck et al. (2012) reviewed the literature of team taxonomies and classifications, and demonstrated the weaknesses of taxonomies and other categorical systems when attempting to categorise concepts such as team types, which can be placed on a continuum. They proposed three dimensions as forming the basis for a wide range of team types - *skill differentiation* (the degree of knowledge or skill specialisation, which made it difficult to substitute team members), *authority differentiation* (the degree to which decision-making was concentrated, or distributed) and *temporal stability* (the degree to which team members had a shared history and expectations of a shared future). This three-dimensional approach offered a limited degree of flexibility in categorising industrial and commercial work teams, but could not capture the key differences between teams that are related to culture, e.g. creativity or handling uncertainty. Although the dimensions chosen by Hollenbeck et al. were not suitable for a culture-based team performance prediction method-ology, the authors presented a very cogent case for a dimensional, rather than categorical (e.g. taxonomic) approach to team/task classification.

A summary of team and task classifications: Most of the team/task classifications were concentrated on a very small range of teams, and did not include the factors that were mediated by culture. Steiner's approach to task classification was valid for research and production-type teams, but was not very relevant to rapid-reaction (and similar) teams. McGrath's *task circumplex* contained several potentially useful task categories, Gluesing & Gibson's *dimensions of complexity* covered too few of the factors that influence culture-related performance to be usable. The multidimensional approaches of Hollenbeck et al. and Gluesing & Gibson appeared to be the most flexible, but the chosen dimensions excluded most of the key team types of relevance to this author's research, and also did not capture nuances of relevance to culture; however, the workflow interdependence and task environment of Gluesing and Gibson's approach could (in theory) be adapted. None of the team and task typologies identified in the literature covered the range of factors required for this research work. However, the reviews, in particular that of Hollenbeck et al., highlighted the severe limitations of any taxonomic approach – some concepts fit into rigid taxonomic hierarchies (e.g. flora and fauna), others do not (e.g. team and task types, games, word definitions).

3.5 Evidence of the validity of culture-based tools

This section considers the validity and potential applicability of the tools and frameworks presented in Section 3.4. As stated in Section 3.4, due to the sparsity of national culture-based team performance prediction-based tools, the researcher also examined cultural frameworks, measures of diversity and task/mission frameworks.

3.5.1 Validity of tools for the prediction of team performance

As stated in Sub-section 3.4.1, only one academic peer-reviewed publication was found on methods, models or tools for the culture-based prediction of team performance or the allocation of tasks based on national culture – that of Sivakumar & Nakata.

Overall, the Sivakumar & Nakata model was too limited (new product development only), only produced a set of values for an 'optimum culture', and relied on a set of culture 'slope coefficients' that were not clearly justified in the paper. A subsequent examination of all 17 citations of this paper revealed no further culture modelling or culture tool related publications other than one by this author (A. Hodgson, Hubbard, & Siemieniuch, 2013). A precursor paper by the above researchers (Nakata & Sivakumar, 1996) reviewed the area and proposed a general framework for relating national culture values to new product development; an examination of the abstracts of the 470 citations of this paper revealed several studies of the effects of culture on various forms of team performance, but no methodologies or tools related to culture.

The qualitative Earley and Gibson multicultural team model (Earley & Gibson, 2002) provided no more than general guidance to a team's potential internal problems, and was criticised for its excessive complexity and redundancy, for example role processes were modelled at individual and group levels, and as integrative mechanisms (Troyer, 2002). In practical terms, this model was little more than a checklist of factors to consider when evaluating a team of individuals of known personal and cultural traits, and did not offer any capability or basis for developing a predictive cultural tool that took account of team mission and location.

As a very simple paper-based checklist, 'The CULTURE Tool' by Catholic Health was of no significant interest to the research of the author of this thesis. However, it did raise the question as to whether a qualitative culture-based performance prediction tool could be developed. After a brief consideration of requirements, it became clear that such a tool would have to contain a huge amount of text and would not provide any capability for further analysis, unless there was a quantitative basis behind the text.

'The Culture Compass Survey' by Geert Hofstede and the consultancy company *itim international* appeared to carry out, to some degree, several of the activities presented in Figure 3-5; it produced a cultural profile (for an individual, not a team) and took account of the individual's role (rather than tasks). However, the tool was aimed at the determination of the degree of fit of an individual 'outsider' (rather than a team) to another culture (rather than to a task set). In addition, it did not offer role/task choices of key importance to sociotechnical systems (e.g. associated with innovation teams or organised action crews). Nevertheless, the qualitative feedback comments of this tool (clearly based on quantitative differences between national cultural scores and the scores generated from the individual's survey answers) represented a 'user-friendly' way of communicating potential problem areas. Although offering interesting insights about the generation and presentation of cultural information, it did not otherwise represent a means towards the aims of this author's research.

In comparison to The Culture Compass Survey tool, the Culture-Compass tool accepted less information from the user, offered considerably less information in return and was not considered to be of further interest.

With regard to organisational culture 'candidates', few of the models and commercial tools acknowledged the heavy influence of national culture on their likely performances; as a result, they would have had little relevance outside western cultures. In addition, the organisational culture tools appeared not to consider task-related requirements of organisations, instead they compared actual corporate culture with a target culture that was thought to be conducive from specific viewpoints (e.g. 'the customer'). Similar issues arose with safety culture models and tools as with organisational models and tools. As a result, no candidate models, methods or approaches were obtained from these sources.

A summary of the validity of national culture-based tools: As stated in Subsection 3.4.1, (d), no national, organisational or safety culture-based models or tools were found that could be adapted to enable the prediction of the performance of a proposed or current team in a range of team/task situations. It was necessary, therefore, to consider the validities of the potential 'building blocks' of such a tool, instead. These are discussed in the following subsections.

3.5.2 Validity of cultural frameworks

In this section, evidence is presented for the empirical validity and potential applicability (in the researcher's work) of the national cultural frameworks described in Section 3.4.2.

In addition to empirical validity, the author's work placed requirements on a cultural framework to provide default cultural traits (however described or enumerated) for all of the World's major countries or areas, to discriminate adequately between national differences, to enable the linking of a range of team behaviours or task performances to cultural traits[21], to have been validated by researchers and to have been utilised in a large number of studies.

a) Validity of national or ethnic culture frameworks

Kluckhohn & Strodtbeck's five-dimension (or five syndrome) value orientations method (VOM) (Gallagher, 2001a; Hills, 2002; Kluckhohn & Strodtbeck, 1961) was intended primarily as a tool to enable (and train) people to understand their own and other cultures. The VOM had been successfully applied in a range of cross-cultural situations including higher education, healthcare and conflict resolution in public resource management (Gallagher, 2001b), and could be used to train people to be aware of cultural differences. However, its three-value (trinary) syndromes lacked discrimination, did not provide default values for the majority of countries, and would have been difficult to link to behavioural traits that were relevant to task performance assessment. Maznevski et al. (2002) applied the value orientations method (also known as the cultural orientations framework) to 1,600 people in five countries, but this was one of comparatively few studies of reasonable size. Although the VOM served a valid purpose as a thought-provoking introduction to cultural differences, it was not suitable as the basis for a culture-based performance prediction tool.

To summarise – a lack of precision and a paucity of application studies resulted in the VOM being considered as an unsuitable basis for a culture tool.

Triandis' five-dimension (or five syndrome) cultural framework (Triandis 1995; 1996) lacked discrimination due to its two-value (binary) syndromes and, as was the case with the VOM (above), did not provide default values for the majority of countries. In addition, Triandis (1993, p.177) stated that the *tightness* syndrome was related to the *collectivism* syndrome, i.e. that they were not independent of each other; this would lead to increased problems during any statistical analyses.

To summarise – a lack of precision and a paucity of application studies resulted in Triandis' cultural framework being considered as an unsuitable basis for a culture tool.

Hofstede's original cultural framework (1984) consisted of the four dimensions of power distance, individualism-collectivism, masculinity and uncertainty avoidance. Summarised data including default culture

---

[21] This 'enablement' might occur in terms of the extended descriptions and examples provided in relevant texts and/or the applications of the framework to cultural studies as described in publications.

scores for 76 countries and regions (representing a large proportion of the World's population) were available at the start of the author's research, whereas for the later-added 'long-term orientation' dimension, default values were only available for 23 countries; in addition, several criticisms had been made of the dimension (Fang, 2003; Jacob, 2005). A sixth cultural dimension, 'indulgence vs. restraint', was added shortly after the author began his research, but a comprehensive set of default national scores was not available at the time.

Hofstede's original four-dimension framework had been verified many times and in many countries since its original publication for example in Russia (Naumov, 2000), the Gulf States (At-Twaijri & Al-Muhaiza, 1996), New Zealand (Brown, 2003); in addition, individual dimensions had been further evaluated and verified, for example uncertainty avoidance (Merkin, 2006; Minkov & Hofstede, 2014). The framework also had its antagonists based on claims of questionable underlying assumptions (McSweeney, 2002), that Hofstede might not have been actually measuring culture (Baskerville, 2003) and that the framework's dimensions had limited distinctiveness and independence (Blodgett, Bakir, & Rose, 2008). Hofstede answered such antagonists directly (G H Hofstede, 2002, 2003), typically elaborating on the misassumptions that these antagonists had made about his work. Jones (2007) examined publications by scholarly antagonists and protagonists of Hofstede's framework, and also examined published dialogues between Hofstede and his antagonists (see above references); Jones concluded that the weight of evidence supported the majority of Hofstede's work, and that it remained the most valuable contribution on culture to-date for scholars and practitioners. Based on the results of a study of cultural frameworks, Magnusson, Wilson, Zdravkovic, Zhou, & Westjohn (2008) concluded that cultural distance constructs based on Hofstede's and Trompenaar's frameworks[22] had strong convergent validity, whereas those based on the Schwartz and GLOBE frameworks had much weaker validity.

The most important validations of Hofstede's framework were found in meta-studies of the framework's application. Smith & Bond (1998, Ch. 3) examined large scale studies published since Hofstede's original version of 'Culture's Consequences' (1984), and concluded that those studies had supported, rather than contradicted, Hofstede's work. Kirkman et al. (2006) reviewed the use of Hofstede's framework in 180 studies, agreed with Smith & Bond, but drew attention to limitations in the coverage of these studies (in part due to fragmentation and redundancy) and made recommendations for the improvement of researchers' use of Hofstede's framework. In a final example, Taras et al. (2010) utilised data from 598 studies to meta-analyse the relationships between Hofstede's original

---

[22] This is an important consideration for the research described in this thesis.

four dimensions and a range of 'organisationally relevant outcomes'. They found that, at the individual level of analysis, the predictive power of Hofstede's cultural values was lower than those of personality traits and demographics for outcomes such as job performance and absenteeism, but higher for outcomes such as organisational commitment, team-related attitudes and feedback-seeking; the latter were perhaps more strongly related to the team-related aspects of this PhD study than were the former.

To summarise - Hofstede's cultural dimension scores possessed precision (in itself no guarantee of accuracy) and, at the start of this researcher's work, national scores for Hofstede's original four cultural dimensions were available for the majority of the World's population. Also, compared to other cultural frameworks, Hofstede's framework had been subject to much more corroborative research and had been applied in many culture surveys.

Trompenaars' cultural framework did not provide quantitative country scores for each cultural dimension. Multidimensional scaling analysis of Trompenaars' data did not confirm the seven dimensions, and also raised questions about the underlying data sources (G H Hofstede 1996). To summarise – the lack of quantitative country cultural dimension data and a lack of application studies eliminated Trompenaars' framework as a candidate framework for the development of a culture tool.

The GLOBE nine dimension cultural framework appeared to adapt its dimensions from several pre-existing frameworks, including Hofstede's and Kluckhohn & Strodtbeck's. In view of some of the conflicting or indeterminate results in the literature for Hofstede's masculinity dimension, the GLOBE's splitting of Hofstede's masculinity dimension into two – gender egalitarianism and assertiveness – was of particular interest.

As in the case of Hofstede's framework, data from the GLOBE studies were available to the author in summarised form. The primary sources for this data were in the two main books of the project, i.e. House et al. (2004) and Chhokar et al. (2008). Hofstede (2006) statistically analysed this GLOBE data and questioned the basis for deriving the nine GLOBE cultural dimensions, pointing out (amongst other things) that the data suggested the presence of the Hofstede masculinity/femininity dimension. A further issue for this researcher was that, at the start of his PhD research, very few independent researchers had published studies utilising the GLOBE dimensions compared to those utilising Hofstede's framework. Later literature reviews by the author revealed a continuing paucity of studies that utilised the GLOBE cultural scores; the majority of published articles consisted of further papers by the GLOBE's authors, critiques of the GLOBE framework, or comparisons of GLOBE with Hofstede's framework and others, for example Graen (2006) and Peterson & Castro (2006) – a critique that was answered by Hanges & Dickson (2006).

To summarise: The GLOBE's cultural dimensions possessed precision, but the lack of supportive independent verification studies and applications made the GLOBE framework a dubious candidate for the development of a culture tool.

Schwartz's culture-level value scale (or cultural values framework) was condensed from seven 'cultural level value types' into three 'cultural orientations' or dimensions; Schwartz stated that he believed that these types and dimensions were non-independent of each other, which negated the effectiveness of using them as dimensions. As is the case with the GLOBE framework and Trompenaars' framework, there were relatively few published independent research studies that utilised Schwartz's framework, compared to Hofstede's.

To summarise – the interdependency of dimensions and the lack of independent application studies have eliminated Schwartz' framework as a candidate for the development of a culture tool.

A summary of the validity of national culture frameworks: As stated at the beginning of this section, there was a set of minimum requirements for any cultural dimension framework to be viable for the purposes of the research described in this thesis. In particular, a national cultural framework would be required to: (1) provide default cultural traits or scores (however described or enumerated) for all of the World's major countries or areas, (2) be adequately sensitive to national cultural trait differences, (3) enable the linking of a range of team behaviours or task performances to cultural traits[23], (4) be widely validated by researchers and (5) be utilised in a large number of studies. The latter requirement was of particular importance, as these studies would be the sources of qualitative and/or quantitative data for this PhD study.

At the time that this literature review was originally carried out, the national culture framework with the most empirical validation was that of Hofstede's. Hofstede's framework was also the one that was critiqued the most, and the one which appeared to have the most support amongst researchers. There were issues with the framework, but many of these also applied to other frameworks. The potential effects of such

---

[23] This 'enablement' might occur in terms of the extended descriptions and examples provided in relevant texts and/or the applications of the framework to cultural studies as described in publications.

issues needed to be noted, as they could threaten the validity of sub-sequent work.

b) Validity of organisational culture frameworks

An examination of Table 3-17 (in Subsection 3.4.2(b)) revealed that, for the most commonly-cited organisational culture frameworks, there were two areas of overlap, identified as *attitudes to rules* and *power concentration/delegation.* However, as stated in Subsection 3.4.2(b), the dimensions within these groupings were not closely matched (as, for example, they were in the case of national culture dimensions). There was neither sufficient common ground between the various frameworks for any dimensions to emerge as 'clear winners', nor was there common guidance as to the basis for an association between organisational culture traits and industrial or commercial sectors. In addition, other than the competing values framework, they had not been widely applied.

A summary of the validity of organisational culture frameworks: It appeared that existing organisational culture frameworks could not be used as a contributory input to the work of this thesis.

c) Validity of occupational culture frameworks

As stated in Subsection 3.4.2(c), the majority of studies of occupational culture appeared to be comparisons between the cultures or cultural dimension scores of different professions.

The only study that appeared to offer a practicable, replicable, quanti-tative approach was one by Bosland. Bosland's study resulted in a set of adjustments to Hofstede's national cultural dimension scores based on years in full time education. As most professions demanded long periods in education, this provided an indirect means of capturing culture changes associated with professions. However, it did not capture the differences between 'conservative' and 'outgoing' professions that both required (for example) degree-level qualifications. Bosland's tables were validated to some extent when they were used to adjust the culture scores of country elites that were based on a study by Hoppe (1990). Other studies have, in general terms, confirmed Bosland's work. For example, Bosland's tables indicated an increase in individualism score with education; this was supported by Bangwayo-Skeete, Rahim & Zikhali's (2011) analysis of the 2005 World Value Survey data; this analysis found that individuals with higher education attached an increased importance to autonomy vs. conformity to traditional social norms, implying an attitudinal move towards increased individualism.

A summary of the validity of occupational culture frameworks: Bosland's adjustment of the four dimension scores of Hofstede's original national cultural framework was the only quantitative approach found that was related (via years of full time education) to occupational culture. As it adjusted Hofstede's national culture scores, it would be simple to incorporate into a method or tool that utilised Hofstede's national culture framework.

3.5.3 Validity of measures of team cultural diversity

More detailed descriptions of the diversity measures discussed in this section are provided in Subsection 3.4.3. The majority of quantitative publications on multicultural teams appeared to use measures of diversity that were based on the proportions of different nationalities, rather than the degree of difference between those nationalities, for example measures such as the Blau Index, the Herfindhal-Hirschmann Index, the Shannon (or Shannon-Wiener) Diversity Index (SDI) and Simpson's Index. These nominal measures would produce the same diversity score for a four-member team consisting of British, Irish, Australian and New Zealander members as for a team consisting of Chinese, Iraqi, Canadian and Brazilian members. Clearly, such diversity measures were insensitive to the actual cultural differences between team members, and their utilisation had almost certainly contributed to the inconclusive performance results that emerged from meta-studies such those of Stahl et al.

Measures of diversity such as Stirling's index utilised quantitative measures of distance or diversity. However, the assumption implicit in combining several cultural dimension scores into a single Euclidean distance was that all dimensions contributed similarly to each other in every circumstance; this was not a realistic assumption with regard to human culture.

As stated in Subsection 3.4.3(c), Elron (1997) applied the statistics-based measures of mean and variance to Hofstede's cultural scores for team members in order to calculate team cultural diversity; however, although this approach took account of the default national cultural scores of team members, it placed a very high weighting on 'outliers' due to the use of variance; this may have exaggerated the cultural diversity of certain teams. In addition, it was not clear as to how this approach could enable the diversity of each team member to be expressed individually – this would be important if it were required to 'tailor' a team to be more or less diverse.

A summary of the validity of measures of team cultural diversity: The majority of diversity measures (e.g. Blau and Shannon indices) were related to the *number* (or proportion) of different species, ethnic groups, nationalities, etc., not to the amount of *difference* or diversity between them; they were therefore not sufficiently discriminating to be considered valid. Diversity (or heterogeneity) indices such as those of Greenberg and Stirling indices took account of the Euclidean distances between groups or subgroups (e.g. ages, culture scores, years in post), assuming that it did not matter which element of diversity contributed the most; however, this *does* matter. Diversity measures based on statistical measures of variance took into account the *actual* allocated culture scores of individual team or group members, but put excessive weight on outliers, due to the calculation of variance. All of the diversity measures produced an aggregate team diversity value, but none provided any diversity-related information about individual team members – such information would be necessary if a culture tool were required to provide guidance about team composition. None of the currently-utilised measures were considered to be both valid and applicable to the research proposed by this author.

3.5.4 Validity of team and task classifications

As stated in Subsection 3.4.4, to achieve the aims of the research described in this thesis, it was necessary to be able to describe teams and/or their tasks in terms of the behavioural capabilities required for successful performance. Such behavioural capabilities (for want of a better term) could then be associated with team member cultural scores to form the basis of an assessment methodology and tool.

Examination of a range of team and task classifications (see Subsection 3.4.4) revealed no classification that covered an adequate breadth of team types, task types or behaviour requirements that could be moderated by culture. Therefore, it was necessary to develop an alternative team/task typology.

A summary of the validity of task classifications: No task classifi-cations were identified that were both valid and applicable to the research proposed by this author.

3.6　Summary of the literature review and state-of-the-art

This chapter started with an introduction to the literature review method and literature sources that were utilised. Section 3.3 presented evidence of the effects of national culture on team performances. Section 3.4 presented information on culture-related tools and methods. Subsection 3.4.1 highlighted the sparsity of culture-based performance prediction tools, indicating that there was a substantial gap in the literature. In the absence of such tools, Section 3.4.2 presented details of frameworks that allowed us to describe the cultures of teams and individuals, Section 3.4.3 addressed measures of cultural diversity that would be required for a culture-based performance prediction tool and Section 3.4.4 addressed team/task behavioural and performance requirements.

Section 3.5 examined the empirical evidence for the validity of culture-related tools and methodologies, finding that only Hofstede's cultural framework met all the requirements of the researcher's proposed research for discrimination, validity and the availability of published case studies and analyses.

3.6.1 What was not helpful

a) 'Citation disconnect' between disciplines

Researchers have traditionally relied heavily on citation following in order to trace valuable veins of research. However, the research publications of interest to the author were very widely dispersed across disciplines - more than a hundred different journals had been referenced by the completion of the thesis; this count excluded conferences, reports and web-based data sources. Unsurprisingly, there appeared to be little connection in terms of cross-citations between papers published in journals of different disciplines. Also, many related publications tended to have either an extremely high number of citations or a very low number of (or zero) citations, according to World of Science and Scopus; neither of these extremes was helpful.

b) Lack of a creativity/invention/innovation classification

The examination in this review of the effects of culture on innovation-related activities was hampered by the lack of clarity amongst researchers as to the degree of creativity, invention, etc., that their study results were associating particular cultural traits with. There was a need for a common creativity/innovation framework against which such activities could be measured, e.g. one similar to that proposed in Sub-section 3.3.1(a) (ix), Figure 3-3. To add further concerns over the accuracy of recent study results, the use of raw patent numbers as a measure of innovation output must now be called into question due to the increasingly trivial nature of patents that are created as 'foot-soldiers in the commercial litigation wars'. The recent degradation of patents as genuine intellectual property has resulted in the reversal of apparent optimum culture scores − a few years ago, high individualism was associated, via patent output levels, with high innovation; a recently published study demonstrated the opposite result. This reversal was reflected in the recent major increase of Far-Eastern patenting activities. Whereas it was to be expected that other cultures would reduce the longstanding Anglo/European dominance over innovation, there was no evidence other than that of patent numbers that a watershed had been reached.

c) Paucity of material relating safety culture to national culture

A significant part of the research described in this review was concerned with the operational safety of sociotechnical systems, and the effects of national culture on this safety. A large majority of publications relating to safety and culture concerned the topics of safety culture and safety climate; disappointingly, very few of these publications made a connection between safety culture and national culture. Most of those that did mention national culture, failed to identify clear links, for example from national culture, through organisational culture to safety culture/climate.

3.6.2 Gaps identified

a) Culture-based performance prediction tools

No culture-based team performance prediction tools were found in the literature. The most similar method or tool to that proposed by the researcher was a commercial tool offered by Hofstede and the company *itim* that, following completion of a questionnaire, determined an individual's cultural differences from his or her own country and that of a proposed country, and indicated (on the basis of a selection from a small number of general roles) the likely issues that might arise; however, this was neither adaptable to team (rather than individual) level, nor were the general roles adaptable to meaningful team tasks or behaviours.

b) Team/task/mission classifications of relevance to national culture-based tools

No team/task/mission classification was found that could incorporate team member culture as a factor in performance.

c) Creativity/invention/innovation classifications

As stated in Subsection 3.6.1(b) above no satisfactory classification system was found to enable the accurate placement of innovation-related activities to enable the comparison of published culture/-innovation studies.

3.7 Detailed problem statement

The design of complex sociotechnical systems (e.g. oil refineries, power stations, airport systems, large transport aircraft), has been dominated by Western organisations. Even in the case of non-Western-designed systems, the 'blueprint' has typically been based on Western designs, due in part to the constraints imposed by international standards and the associated licencing requirements. As a result, Western cultural assumptions have been built into most complex sociotechnical systems; consequently, they have functioned less effectively when operated by non-Westerners. There are limited quantitative ergonomic tables and tools to assist designers to take account of human physical and mental limitations (if they choose to use them); however, there are no such tables and tools to assist designers to take account of user culture. Whereas we are not yet at a stage where culture-sensitive methodologies could be developed directly to *improve* designs, a 'cultural clash' detection system might *warn* designers where there was a likelihood of mismatch.

Multinational companies increasingly delegate R&D and product improvement projects to foreign subsidiaries, with mixed results to-date. The location, selection or building of teams, as opposed to systems, for various functions (e.g. sociotechnical system design, problem-solving, process improvement, product updating, blue-skies research) could be improved by matching culturally-related strengths to project requirements.

Culture has been shown, in this literature review, to affect behaviour, communication, decision-making, creativity, training and other aspects of team performance, leading in many cases to reduced performance and/or safety. However, current understandings of the effects of various cultural traits are patchy. The effects of power distance and individualism on team performance are better understood and more consistently reported in the literature than are the effects of masculinity and uncertainty avoidance; reports on the performance effects of various levels of cultural diversity in teams are extremely inconsistent and contradictory. There is therefore a need for an improved understanding of the latter three team cultural traits and for the development of methodologies and tools to inform sociotechnical system designers and users about the effects of culture on their teams.

To summarise: The literature review revealed that culture had a significant effect on team efficiency and/or safety; it also revealed that researchers had a patchy understanding of the effects of culture on team performance and that there was a lack of effective quantitative methodologies and tools that took into account culture when designing systems or selecting teams. It was important, therefore, to develop an improved understanding of culture and its effects, and to capture this understanding in models and tools to inform sociotechnical system designers and users about the effects of culture on their teams.

4 Research tools and proposed activities

4.1 Introduction

The key aims of the research described in this thesis were to identify relationships between the observed performances of various team types (based on their tasks/missions) and the cultural backgrounds of their team members, and to develop models, methodologies and tools to aid in the selection of team members and the prediction of team performance-limiting issues.

In order to develop the above aims, it was first necessary to select or define cultural frameworks, methodologies and classifications that would enable the representation (or description) of cultural traits, team and/or task types and to relate them to team performance levels. The primary purposes of activities described in this chapter were therefore:

- to select or define a framework for the representation of team member cultural traits (primarily based on national cultural traits) in quantitative terms,

- to select or define a quantitative measure for team cultural diversity,

- to select or define an initial team/task/behavioural framework that enabled the relationships between team member cultural traits and team performance levels to be explored for various team/task situations,

- to highlight simplifying assumptions related to the choices made in selecting and/or defining elements of proposed tools, and

- to detail the further research activities required to achieve the aims and objectives of the work.

Section 4.2 describes the selection of a cultural framework, and the associated issues, caveats and assumptions. Section 4.3 describes the development of a measure of cultural diversity, and the associated issues, caveats and assumptions. Section 4.4 presents details of a practical team/task/mission framework consisting of five major factors, which is based on the studies of the literature review, in particular Section 3.3. Section 4.5 details additional research activities to be undertaken (based in part on Subsection 3.6.2 of the literature review), and Section 4.6 provides a summary of this chapter.

4.2 Selection of a cultural framework

As was stated in Subsection 3.5.2, Hofstede's original four-dimensional framework (G H Hofstede, 1980) had been shown in the literature to have the widest applicability and replicability of all the cultural frameworks; in addition, there were more studies published that utilised Hofstede's framework than any (or all) other frameworks. Therefore, Hofstede's original four-dimensional framework was chosen to form one of the pillars on which the remaining work of this thesis was based. Note that, for reasons of lack of data and, in the case of long term orientation (LTO), adverse criticism (See Subsection 3.4.2), the two later-added dimensions of Hofstede's framework were not used.

A decision was made that, where appropriate, Bosland's education-related corrections (Bosland, 1985) would be applied as a proxy for the effects of professional or occupational culture.

4.2.1 Hofstede's (original) framework in more detail

Tables 4-1 to 4-4 present descriptions representing the four cultural dimensions utilised in this thesis, i.e. power distance (PDI), individualism (IDV), masculinity (MAS) and uncertainty avoidance (UAI).

Low PDI	High PDI
Families and friends: Parents and children tend to treat each other as equals; children are expected to develop social competence at a relatively early age and to develop a sense of personal and civil morality.	**Families and friends:** Children are expected to be hard-working and obedient, and to respect their elders throughout life; they are not considered to be competent until they are adults.
Education: Teachers and students tend to treat each other as equals, and learning is seen as requiring a two-way process of communication.	**Education:** Teachers are the source of all knowledge and must be treated with respect in all situations; learning depends on the teacher's wisdom, not the student's initiative.
Employment: Managers and workers tend to work in decentralised organisational and decision-making environments. The real decisions are made by those with relevant expertise, rather than those with power in the hierarchy.	**Employment:** Managers and workers tend to work in organisations with centralised organisational structures and decision-making; subordinates expect to be told what to do, and to have little say in decisions, irrespective of their expertise.

Table 4-1: Power distance – expectations and behaviour

See Hofstede (2001), chapters 3 to 6, for his much more detailed descriptions, examples, explanations and statistical studies relating to these cultural dimensions. Note that the descriptions in Tables 4-1 to 4-4 represent extreme locations on the cultural dimension scales, and that most societies are positioned somewhere between these.

Low IDV	High IDV
Families and friends: Extended families live together or in close proximity, strong ties are reinforced by frequent meetings; there is little privacy (but it is not desired); people think primarily in terms of 'we'. Family or clan protection is provided in return for unquestioning loyalty; the world is split into *in-group* and *out-group*; the family choses friendships, marriage partners. It is vital to maintain harmony - direct confrontations must be avoided; the word 'no' is seldom used, and 'yes' does not necessarily mean *yes*. <u>*Being caught*</u> breaking important rules leads to *shame* and loss of *face* for the perpetrator and his/her in-group; morality is primarily a *group* issue.	**Families and friends:** People only live with immediate family members, extended family ties are weak; family members expect to have a degree of privacy; people think primarily in terms of 'I'; children are expected to seek independence; other people are seen as individuals, rather than as in- or out-group members; individuals chose their own friends, marriage partners. Honesty, directness and speaking factually are valued above harmony, ('*yes*' means *yes* and '*no*' means *no*). Breaking important rules leads to *guilt* and loss of *self-respect* for the perpetrator; morality is primarily a *personal* issue.
Education: Students are discouraged from showing individual initiative or speaking up in class (in part due to the risk of being shamed). Students expect to be shown favouritism by in-group teachers. The main purpose of education is to learn how to do.	**Education:** Students are encouraged to show initiative, and are expected to speak up in class. Students expect teachers to treat them impartially. The main purpose of education is to learn how to learn.
Employment: Hiring and promotion of employees is influenced by their in-group associations. Management, discipline and rewards are best directed at the level of the *group*. The need for harmony and consensus leads to 'groupthink', and reduces the generation of novel ideas and the capability for radical innovation.	**Employment:** Hiring and promotion of employees should be based on appropriate skills and talent. Management, discipline and rewards are best directed at the level of the *individual*. A willingness to go against the consensus enables the generation of novel ideas and improves the capability for creativity and radical innovation.

Table 4-2: Individualism - expectations and behaviour

No framework or schema was chosen to reflect organizational culture, as no consensus had been found during the literature review.

Hofstede's cultural framework was originally intended to provide scores in the range 0 to 100 but, following the addition of further countries to the original set, some of these countries were found to have extreme cultural values for their populations; for example, Slovakia scored 104 for power distance and 110 for masculinity, Greece scored 112 for uncertainty avoidance[24]. Nevertheless, treating these scores as representing a

---

[24] Note that in 2013 or 2014 (too late for this author's research), Hofstede made minor adjustments to his cultural dimensions so that, uncorrected for education, they again produced scores between 0 and 100 for all countries; the updated sets of values could be downloaded as an .xls file from Hofstede's website (http://geerthofstede.nl/dimension-data-matrix). Accessibility last checked in July 2014.

percentage (between minimum and maximum), in particular when considering cultural *differences* and cultural diversity, was considered to be a reasonable approximation.

Low MAS	High MAS
Families and friends: Both parents have similar relationships with their children, who are encouraged to be modest, and not to express aggression. **Education:** Socialisation is more important than educational achievement; students are expected to have limited concern for their own performance and to regard the average student as the performance benchmark. **Employment:** Employees *'work in order to live'*, working conditions and social relationships at work are more important than performance. Employees undersell themselves, are unwilling to relocate their families in order to pursue their careers and prefer to achieve quality of working life.	**Families and friends:** Differentiated relationships - fathers deal with the physical world, mothers with the emotional world; girls cry and boys fight back; ambition is encouraged in both sexes. **Education:** Educational performance is very important; students are expected to have significant concern for their own performance and to regard the high-performing student as the benchmark. **Employment:** Employees *'live in order to work'*, working conditions and social relationships at work are less important than interesting work, performance and pay. Employees (in particular managers) are assertive, oversell themselves, are competitive and are willing to relocate their families in order to pursue their careers.

Table 4-3: Masculinity - expectations and behaviour

Low UAI	High UAI
Families: Parents are more relaxed about rules, including those defining what is forbidden or dirty, and there are few 'absolute truths'. Children are encouraged to see the world as a friendly place, and are exposed to situations of uncertainty. **Education:** Teachers are not expected to know everything, and students expect to contribute to discussions in loosely structured learning situations. **Employment:** Employees tend to change jobs frequently, and are happy to work for small organisations. Senior management is primarily focused at the strategic level; a pragmatic approach is taken to running the business and dealing with problems; faith is placed in generalists. Tolerance for uncertainty and ambiguity makes it easier for innovators and inventors to flourish, but a limited faith in technological solutions may be a barrier to adoption.	**Families:** Parents are inflexible about rules, including those that define what is forbidden or dirty; there is a strong belief in 'absolute truths', with little room for alternative views. Children are told that the world is a hostile place, and are sheltered from the unknown. **Education:** Teachers are expected to know everything relating to their subject, and students expect a highly-structured learning situation. **Employment:** Employees seldom change jobs, and prefer to work for large organisations. Senior management is involved at the operational level, and one of its key roles is to limit the level of uncertainty for subordinates; faith is placed in high specialisation. Lack of tolerance for uncertainty and ambiguity makes it difficult for innovators and inventors to flourish, but a greater faith in technological solutions helps widespread adoption, once accepted.

Table 4-4: Uncertainty avoidance - expectations and behaviour

4.2.2 Caveats with regard to Hofstede's cultural framework

Any cultural framework provides, at best, a shorthand representation of cultural traits - a limited set of quantitative cultural dimensions cannot explain every cultural difference between groups or nations. Despite the significant support for Hofstede's framework demonstrated in the literature review, it is no different to other frameworks in this respect. This subsection provides a range of examples to illustrate the limited sensitivities of cultural frameworks.

Firstly, a comparison of British and Americans revealed many significant differences, some of which are listed in Table 4-5.

United Kingdom	United States
General:	**General:**
Limited competitiveness, a dislike of the 'hard sell" approach (e.g. in advertising).	Extreme competitiveness, expectation of the 'hard sell" approach (e.g. in advertising).
A tendency to undersell oneself.	A tendency to self-promotion.
Indirect communication except where direct needed.	Direct communication.
Understatement in speech.	Overstatement in speech.
A liking for satire and irony.	A dislike of satire and irony.
Military:	**Military:**
Minimum force (making do).	Overwhelming force.
Moderately detailed planning that defines commander's intent and the logic behind the plans, leaving considerable flexibility to those carrying out the plans.	Highly detailed planning of what and how, leaving little flexibility to those executing the plans.

Table 4-5: Some differences between UK and USA cultures

See Nevett (1992) for an analysis of American and British television advertising audience preferences; see Fox (2004) for a detailed analysis of the English (rather than British), in particular with regard to irony and understatement; see Rasmussen et al. (2008) for more details about differences between the UK and USA in military planning.

Despite the above (and other) cultural differences between the UK and the USA, the two countries appeared remarkably close across five of six cultural dimensions of the Hofstede framework, with an average of 5 points (effectively 5%) difference across the original four Hofstede dimensions; only in the later version of the long-term orientation dimension (LTO-WVS) was there a significant difference in the countries' scores – the USA and UK scores were, respectively, 25 and 50[25]. Based on anecdotal evidence from the author's experiences and those of colleagues, friends and relatives, the British appeared much closer in cultural terms to other Anglo countries – Australia, New Zealand and, to a lesser extent, Canada, than to the USA.

An inspection and comparison of a range of other country cultural scores revealed further surprising similarities and differences[26] between the default cultural scores of certain countries, based on Hofstede's results. Table 4-6 presents the culture score differences of a selection of countries for each of Hofstede's cultural dimensions, the average differences are based on the four original dimensions (as utilised in this thesis) and also on the full six dimensions (including the two recent additions to the framework).

Countries to be compared		Default culture score differences						Average differences	
Country 1	Country 2	PDI	IDV	MAS	UAI	PRA	IND	4 dims	6 dims
Austria	Japan	43	9	16	22	28	21	23	23
	Portugal	52	28	48	29	32	30	39	37
Germany	Japan	19	21	29	27	5	2	24	17
	Denmark	17	7	50	42	48	30	29	32
France	Thailand	4	51	9	22	31	3	22	20
	United Kingdom	33	18	23	51	12	21	31	26
Brazil	Taiwan	11	21	4	7	49	10	11	17
	Venezuela	12	26	24	0	28	41	16	22

Table 4-6: Culture score differences for selected countries[27]

From Table 4-6, we can observe the following:

- Austria appeared to be culturally far closer to Japan than to Portugal.

- Germany appeared to be culturally far closer to Japan than to its immediate neighbour, Denmark.

- France appeared to be culturally closer to Thailand than to its immediate neighbour, the United Kingdom – despite having

---

[25] Note that Dumitrescu (2012) attributes the differences in rhetoric between the UK and USA, in particular under- vs. overstatement, to their differing LTO-WVS scores.
[26] At the time of writing this thesis, one could visit the website http://geert-hofstede.com/countries.html and select two countries in order to compare their 'Hofstede framework' cultural scores.
[27] To a close approximation, these score differences may be regarded as percentages, i.e. with a maximum potential difference of 100%.

shared a considerable part of its language and history with that neighbour over the last millennium.

- Brazil appeared to be culturally closer to Taiwan than to its immediate neighbour, Venezuela.

We have to bear in mind, with the above results, that some dimensions may play a larger role than others in defining the 'look and feel' of societies; individualism is probably the most important in determining the basic ways that individuals within society interact; however, 'lesser' dimensions such as uncertainty avoidance have critical roles to play in specific situations. Also, the above examples represented unusual cases; by way of contrast, an examination of members of the Germanic cluster (including Germany, Austria, Czech Republic and German-Switzerland) revealed a very close set of scores, as did an examination of members of the Anglo cluster, and of Taiwan and South Korea.

Hofstede and other culture researchers repeatedly warned researchers of the *ecological fallacy*, i.e. the fallacy that inferences could be made about individuals based on aggregate data collected at the group level (Hofstede 2001, p.16), (Brewer & Venaik, 2012); Hofstede emphasised that his cultural framework applied only at the level of *social systems*, not *individuals*. Individuals could vary widely in their cultural dimension scores, for example an individual Indian pilot (high PDI nation) might have a lower PDI score than an individual US pilot (low PDI nation). However, a key aspect of the research described in this thesis related to the prediction of the mismatch between the operators of sociotechnical systems and the requirements of those sociotechnical systems. In many cases, the only knowledge available about operators was their likely nationalities and (perhaps) educational levels. Therefore it was necessary to work with these (default) national-culture-level scores and determine, from the performance of culture tools that were built, whether national culture actually provided a useful basis (in the absence of other measures) for the prediction of performance constraints or benefits. Clearly, if a system were to be designed for users or operators in a particular country, then taking account of those operators' national cultural traits, rather than the cultural traits of the country where the system was designed, would produce a better (if less than perfect) accommodation.

Returning to Hofstede's *ecological fallacy*: Whereas individuals within a culture might vary significantly in terms of their own preferences (as would be reflected in their 'personal' culture dimension scores), the author suggests that these same individuals would vary far less in terms of their *expectations* of the behaviours of others; they would also vary less in their own behaviours when in social situations within their own cultures because cultures impose a behavioural straitjacket, due in part to the strong conformity bias that humans experience with regard to social norms. This straitjacket is particularly strong in low-IDV, high-PDI and high-UAI cultures, where non-conformance is heavily discouraged. In support of the author's view, Gudykunst (1997) stated that, although each member of a culture had a unique view of that culture, the theories that members of that culture shared overlapped sufficiently so that they could co-ordinate their behaviours in everyday life. In addition, researchers have challenged Hofstede's concerns about the ecological fallacy; Fischer & Poortinga (2012) and Huang & Van de Vliert (2003) investigated individual-level and culture-level value structures, and found strong similarities that negated the justification for separate structures. Steel & Ones (2002) attributed stronger predictive powers at the national level to the reduction of measurement error on aggregated data, rather than to the ecological fallacy.

The author of this thesis collected a range of anecdotal information in order to investigate the ecological fallacy and other issues, see Chapter 5 for further details.

4.2.3 Simplifying assumptions

Following on from the caveats presented in Subsection 4.2.2, it is useful at this stage to discuss the assumptions associated with the adoption of Hofstede's dimensional framework and Bosland's educational adjust-ments as key elements of the model and tool. These are presented below:

- **The representational accuracy of a simple four-dimensional cultural framework:** Four integer numbers between 0 and 100 (approximately) clearly cannot capture the nuances of human culture. However, within the constraints of the team environ-ment, the researcher assumed that the scores captured sufficiently the behavioural tendencies of team members that useful general predictions of some aspects of team performance could be made.

- **The ecological fallacy and individual variance within cultures:** Hofstede's cultural scores were determined at the societal level, and Hofstede has repeatedly warned of the fallacy of using them at the level of the individual. However, the researcher assumed that, within the constraints of the team environment, individuals faced strong pressures to conform to the perceived cultural expectations of their colleagues; they would therefore behave in ways that were typical of their cultures.

- **The accuracy of Bosland's educational adjustments:** Educ-ation and occupation have significant effects on culture-based attitudes and, thereby, on potential behaviours. Although only Hofstede and his colleagues directly endorsed Bosland's education-related adjustments, there appeared to be support in the literature for cultural changes in the direction of Bosland's adjustments (increasing education was associated with more individualistic, less uncertainty avoiding attitudes), see Subsection 3.5.2. Although Bosland's educational adjustments failed to capture cultural differences across professions (e.g. accounting vs. acting), they were expected to improve the accuracy of the default Hofstede national culture values.

4.3 Selection or derivation of a measure of cultural diversity

Currently-utilised measures of diversity were examined in Section 3.4.3 of the literature review. None of these measures met the requirements associated with the culture methods and tools proposed in this thesis; therefore an alternative measure has been proposed in Subsection 4.3.2.

4.3.1 Requirements for a measure of cultural diversity

A measure of cultural diversity was required that met the following criteria:

1. It provided a measure of the mean cultural distance of team members from each other and a measure of overall team diversity.

2. It used readily available data, in this case the cultural scores of individuals, (either as default country scores or as manually-entered scores).

3. It enabled the retention and modification of culture scores for each individual team member; this would allow experimentation, and would also allow the entry of both default (country-average) scores and actual individual scores, e.g. those obtained via questionnaire[28].

4. It enabled the identification of individual team members that contributed most to the team's cultural diversity.

---

[28] The author considered, from his past experiences, that there were seldom more twenty members in a meaningfully interacting team. Therefore, it was practicable to consider each team member individually in the calculation without incurring significant overheads.

113

5. It provided diversity values separately for each cultural dimension.

6. It could be implemented on a spread sheet without the use of macros[29].

7. The measure of cultural diversity would be understandable to users as well as to researchers.

4.3.2 Derivation of an expression for cultural diversity

Based on the requirements listed in Section 4.3.1, a measure of cultural diversity was proposed that utilised the separation between team members in cultural space. Figure 4-1 illustrates the location of each member of an imaginary six person team in three-dimensional culture space consisting of power distance, individualism and uncertainty avoidance; in the research described in this thesis, team members will be placed in four-dimensional space (with the addition of the dimension of masculinity).

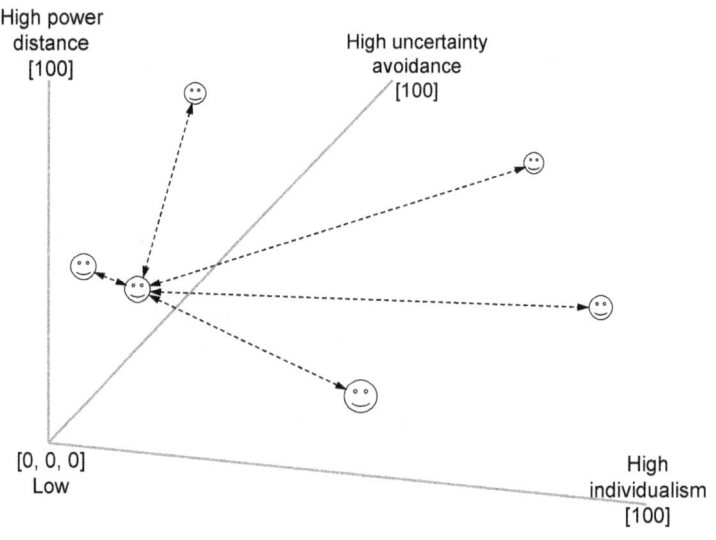

Figure 4-1: Cultural distance or separation

In Figure 4-1, the distances from one of the members of the team to the other five members are represented by arrows; if we calculate the

---

[29] The issue of using spread sheets without macros was important if the tool were to be introduced to industrial companies, as many organisations placed major restrictions on their computer systems' functionalities due to security concerns.

average length for these arrows, we have a measure of the individual's cultural separation from the rest of the team. We can repeat the above calculation for all team members and take an average; we then have a measure of team cultural diversity based on team members' cultural distances from each other.

In practice, in order to maintain cultural diversity values for each of the four cultural dimensions, the cultural separation calculations for each team member and for the team were actually carried out separately for each dimension. The cultural diversity measure derived in this section was utilised in the various studies described later in this thesis.

The expression for cultural diversity was required primarily for the purpose of determining the mean cultural distance between each team member and his or her teammates. For a single cultural dimension, given a set of team member scores along this dimension, the average cultural distance of any team member 'i' (Cd_i) from the other team members could be calculated by summing the absolute values of the score differences between him/her and the other team members, then dividing that sum by the number of *other* team members[30], i.e.:

$$Cd_{ix} = \sum_{j=1}^{N} ABS(Dix - Djx)/(N - 1)$$

Where:

D_{ix}, D_{jx} = Scores for cultural dimension 'x' for team members 'i' and 'j'
N = Total number of team members (including member 'i')

For example, if we had five team members with individualism scores of 30, 40, 50, 60 and 70, then the team members' average cultural distances (in terms of individualism) from their teammates were:

Mbr1: (ABS(30-30)+ABS(30-40)+ABS(30-50)+ABS(30-60)+ABS(30-70))/(5-1) = 100/4 = <u>25</u>
Mbr2: (ABS(40-30)+ABS(40-40)+ABS(40-50)+ABS(40-60)+ABS(40-70))/(5-1) = 70/4 = <u>17.5</u>
Mbr3: (ABS(50-30)+ABS(50-40)+ABS(50-50)+ABS(50-60)+ABS(50-70))/(5-1) = 60/4 = <u>15</u>
Mbr5: (ABS(60-30)+ABS(60-40)+ABS(60-50)+ABS(60-60)+ABS(60-70))/(5-1) = 70/4 = <u>17.5</u>
Mbr5: (ABS(70-30)+ABS(70-40)+ABS(70-50)+ABS(70-60)+ABS(70-70))/(5-1) = 100/4 = <u>25</u>

If we take the average of the team members' average cultural distances (from other team members), we have a useful measure of team cultural diversity (Cd_{team}) in terms of cultural separation for the particular cultural dimension 'x', i.e.:

---

[30] Clearly, one's cultural distance from oneself is zero, hence the term (N-1) in the denominator of the above expression; also, a team of one is not a team.

$$Cd_{teamx} \quad = \quad \sum_{i=1}^{N} \sum_{j=1}^{N} ABS(Dix - Djx)/\big(N \times (N-1)\big)$$

For the earlier five-member team example, the average overall cultural distance for individualism, (or team individualism diversity) was (25+17.5+15+17.5+25)/5 = 100/5 = <u>20</u>.

An overall value for team cultural diversity across all four dimensions (or overall team member average cultural distance) could be obtained by applying the above equation to each cultural dimension and either averaging the values or, if appropriate, weighting the cultural dimensions on some measure of importance, which could vary depending on the type of team.

Table 4-7 illustrates an example (implemented in Microsoft Excel) that applied the proposed diversity expression to an imaginary multicultural team consisting of eight members. For each of the eight team members, the calculation utilised a look-up table to retrieve that team member's four cultural dimension scores (based on nationality), and adjusted these scores based on Bosland's education corrections. Note that, although the team was imaginary, the cultural dimension scores and cultural diversity scores in Table 4-7 were accurate for that mix of nationalities.

Team member number	Team member nationality	Full time education (yrs)	CULTURE SCORES (corr'd for years in full time education)				CULTURAL DIVERSITY (based on proposed diversity expression)				
			PDI	IDV	MAS	UAI	PDI	IDV	MAS	UAI	Mean div.
1	Brazil	16	55	58	37	62	16	33	12	29	22
2	France	16	55	91	31	72	16	30	17	37	25
3	Great Britain	16	25	109	54	21	24	37	10	23	23
4	China	16	65	40	54	16	23	43	10	27	26
5	India	16	63	68	44	26	20	30	10	21	20
6	Australia	15	35	103	56	42	18	34	11	21	21
7	Great Britain	16	25	109	54	21	24	37	10	23	23
8	Pakistan	16	43	34	38	56	16	49	11	25	25
Team scores->			46	77	46	40	20	37	11	26	23

Table 4-7: Example cultural diversity scores

As was the case with all measures of diversity based on separation distances or differences in scores, the theoretical maximum *team* cultural diversity score that the diversity equation could generate depended on the number of team members. For the equation developed in this sub-section, based on the assumption of cultural dimension scores occupying a range of 0 to 100 (as was the case with Hofstede's original set of countries), the theoretical maximum value that overall team diversity could take along any cultural dimension ranged from 100% (of the range of values) for a two-person team to 50% for a very large team, see Table 4-8 for maximum diversity values associated with typical team sizes.

Where individual member scores could take values between 0 and 100, the maximum theoretical diversity (D_{max}) of a team of size 'N' was:

$$D_{max} = (INT\left(\frac{N}{2}\right) * (N - INT\left(\frac{N}{2}\right)) * 2 * 100/N(N-1)$$

Where $INT\left(\frac{N}{2}\right)$ returned the integer part of $\left(\frac{N}{2}\right)$

Number of team members	Maximum team diversity score	Number of team members	Maximum team diversity score
2	100.00	7	57.14
3	66.67	8	57.14
4	66.67	9	55.56
5	60.00	10	55.56
6	60.00	11	54.55

The maximum diversity score approaches 50 for very large teams. For the purposes of the diversity calculations associated with this table, it has been assumed that minimum and maximum cultural scores are 0 and 100 respectively (a small approximation).

Table 4-8: The effect of team size on maximum diversity scores

Maximum team diversity values were not an artefact of the diversity equations, but reflected the fact that, for a team of three or more members, those members could not *all* be separated by maximal cultural distances from each other – all team members were located in the same finite 'cultural space'.

4.3.3 Caveats with regard to cultural diversity

An overall team cultural diversity score represented a simplification of the detailed member diversities and could not capture the detailed pattern of diversity in a typical multicultural team. The very act of calculating a linear average for member diversities and overall team diversity implied an assumption of a linear relationship between the value of any diversity and the effects of that diversity. It was suggested in the literature that innovation could benefit from a moderate amount of team cultural diversity, e.g. a score of 15 (in terms of the cultural diversity scales proposed by this researcher). However, this diversity could arise in (say) a six member team via cultural diversities of 10, 15, 20, 17, 15 & 13, or diversities of 5, 5, 5, 5, 5 & 60; the real contribution of diversity to innovation is likely to be different in each of the two cases. It was likely that 'moderation in cultural diversity' needed to be at *both* the team level and the *individual team member* level, in which case the latter example did not represent 'moderation'.

Problems could arise with particular patterns of team cultural diversity; for example, fragmentation of a team into two or more subgroups could occur if members formed distinct cultural 'blocks' (Cheng, Chua, Morris, & Lee, 2012; Dulaimi & Hariz, 2011), as shown in Figure 4-2. Lau & Murnighan (1998) explored this issue further with their 'fault lines', where several sources of diversity (e.g. national culture, gender and functional background) could combine to cause fragmentation and conflict.

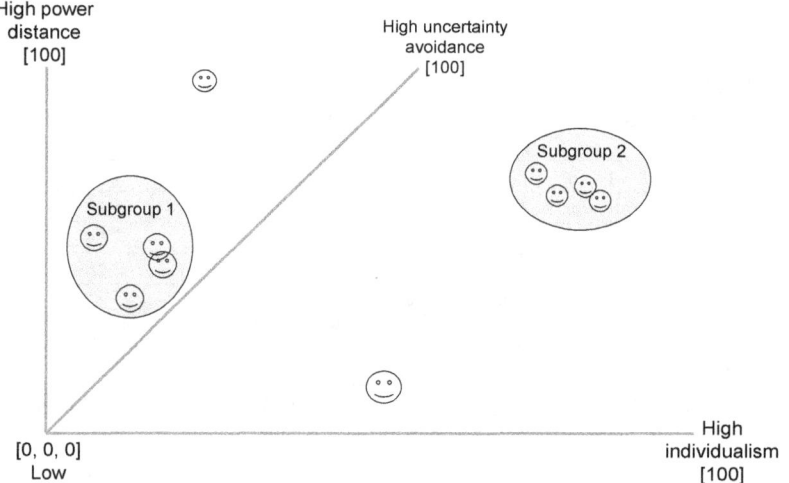

Figure 4-2: Fragmentation into subgroups

The proposed measure of cultural diversity would provide detailed intermediate information about the location of each team member in cultural space. This, in turn, would allow the development of further analyses at a later stage (if required) to determine whether fragmentation into subgroups represented a significant risk for a team.

4.3.4 Simplifying assumptions

Taking into account the comments, descriptions and examples of Subsection 4.3.3, it is useful at this stage to discuss the assumptions associated with the adoption of the proposed measure of cultural diversity as an element of the model and tool:

- **Linearity of diversity effects (see examples in Subsection 4.3.3):** The diversity values for each individual team member, and the mean diversity value for each dimension, were calculated as linear averages. This implied an assumption of the

118

linearity of the effects of cultural distance, i.e. a doubling of cultural distance between two members was assumed to bring twice as much in terms of diversity problems and benefits. In situations where moderate levels of cultural diversity were beneficial, then the diversity expression would be less accurate in terms of its predictions if team member diversities were unevenly distributed, see the example described in Subsection 4.3.3. The author has ignored this potential source of error, other than to incorporate a warning in the tool that was triggered when a single individual's diversity was substantially greater than those of other team members.

- **Limited interactions between culture and diversity:** It was probable that team members from high uncertainty avoiding cultures, with their heightened suspicions of foreigners (Geert H. Hofstede, 2001, p.160, exhibit 4.4), would cope with cultural diversity less effectively than would those from low uncertainty avoiding cultures. This implied that the effects of team diversity were not independent of team average cultural values. The author has ignored this potential source of error, and has assumed, for the purpose of tool-building, that such culture/-diversity interactions had a limited effect compared to those of the average cultural scores and cultural diversity scores.

4.4 Defining teams and tasks from the viewpoint of culture

The team and task classifications identified in the literature review were unsuitable for the purpose of predicting the effects of culture on team task performance. In particular, these team taxonomies were typically applicable to a narrow range of teams, and the task taxonomies did not capture aspects of tasks that were affected by team member cultural traits. Methods of representing team/task combinations had therefore to be developed that were appropriate for the purpose of predicting the effects of culture on performance.

Taxonomic approaches to team classification were very limited in what they could cover (Bacharach, 1989; Hollenbeck et al., 2012); their default assumption (of non-overlapping categories) forced users to assign teams semi-arbitrarily. Even if our teams had five key features that could each take only four values, this would potentially generate more than a thousand slots in the taxonomy if we needed to differentiate between each team type. In reality, team types had overlapping properties, and could often be assigned to several categories. In our case, we needed to distinguish between teams, not only on the basis of their tasks or missions, but also on the basis of the effects of team member cultures on team performance of those tasks or missions.

4.4.1 A practical team/task framework

The five key 'culture-relevant' factors, identified in Section 3.3.3, have been 'fleshed out' into a number of sub-factors (based on the information contained in Sub-sections 3.3.1 to 3.3.3). These factors and their sub-factors are described and summarised below:

a) Management and decision-making

Culture (as measured via the power distance, individualism and uncertainty avoidance scores) had a major effect on subordinate/superior relationships.

Delegation of management authority: High power distance and high uncertainty avoidance cultures both encouraged strong, centralised, directive, non-consultative forms of management and decision-making, whereas low power distance and low uncertainty avoidance cultures encouraged more consensus-based, delegation-based forms of management and decision-making. Some tasks and missions were best served by authoritarian, strongly centralised management, for example highly automated factory systems or missions involving large military man-oeuvres; others, for example complex decisions requiring wide or deep knowledge were typically best served by the consensus-based decentralised, delegating management.

Decision-making under uncertainty: Managers from high uncertainty-avoiding cultures were slow to 'reframe' and tended to have difficulty with decision-making under uncertainty, resulting in delays and non-optimal choices that were made in an attempt to reduce uncertainty. Managers from high power distance cultures typically failed to exploit their subordinates' knowledge, and often made decisions swiftly, based on inadequate information. In some environments performance was best served by the rigid adherence to rules or standard operating procedures (SOPs) that tended to be a feature of high uncertainty-avoiding cultures, e.g. in many production and maintenance environments; in other environments, the ability to recognise when to abandon rules or SOPs could 'save the day', for example, when an aircraft was no longer operating within its normal flight envelope.

Following standard operating instructions (SOPs) (vs. not following them when appropriate): Members of high uncertainty avoidance teams would tend to adhere at all times to SOPs, thus reducing errors under normal conditions; however, they would continue to follow SOPs that were no longer applicable due to their tardiness in 'reframing'.

Members of high power distance teams would not challenge their superiors when they failed to follow SOPs. Members of low individualist teams would not directly challenge their superiors when they failed to follow SOPs, but would attempt, indirectly, to bring their attention to this failure. Members of high individualist teams were willing to challenge their superiors when they deviated from SOPs. Note that cultural dimension scores interact and could produce conflicting constraints on team members.

Recognising and correcting errors: Members of high power distance cultures would typically be unwilling to correct their superiors (e.g. team leaders) when they had made an error. Members of low individualism cultures would not correct others (in particular, leaders) because this would result in a loss of face; instead, they would try, indirectly, to draw the other person's attention to the error so that he/she could discover and correct it. Members of high uncertainty-avoidance teams tended to take more time than others to recognise mistakes or incorrect assumptions; in addition, their leaders or managers tended to discourage feedback from their subordinates. Where it was important to recognise and correct errors (particularly if time was a factor), the improved team communication of low power distance, low uncertainty avoiding cultures, and the context-free communication of high individualism cultures combined to provide prompt, accurate feedback.

Summarising the above sub-factors:

- centralisation of authority and non-consultative decision-making *vs.* delegation of authority and consultative decision-making

- decision-making under uncertainty

- following standard operational procedures (SOPs) at all times *vs.* not following SOPs when circumstances demand

- recognising and correcting errors

b) Creativity and innovation

Culture, via pressure to conform, willingness to speak out and attitudes to uncertainty, had a considerable effect on creativeness. Some team goals required an ability to produce (and present) a large number of ideas, go against the consensus and engage in a degree of conflict; others required an ability to take new ideas forward towards usable concepts; yet others required an ability to implement existing technologies into products and processes; in this latter situation, disciplined concentration on the task in hand was better than constantly exploring new ideas.

Developing new ideas and concepts: High power distance team members would be less likely than low power distance team members to volunteer ideas; high uncertainty avoidance team members would feel uncomfortable with novel ideas ('outside their comfort zone'). Low individualism and low masculinity team members would tend to seek consensus rather than novelty. A degree of cultural diversity offered a wider range of ideas, if they could be 'teased out', e.g. by brain storming.

Developing, improving more conventional ideas, products, processes: In the case of less creative work, well-controlled, ordered organisations and processes appeared to be more effective. In this case, high power distance, low individualist, high uncertainty avoiding and medium-high masculinity cultures appeared to be most effective. Midway between low and high creativity, it appeared that the cultural dimension scores were nearer to the high-creativity scores than the low-creativity scores. In the case of low-creativity teamwork, it was unlikely that the disruption caused by cultural diversity was of any benefit.

Going against the consensus: High power distance team members would normally agree with their leaders, or would say nothing rather than to disagree. High uncertainty-avoiding team members would not generally be encouraged to state differing opinions. Low individualism team members would typically regard consensus as a prior requirement for good performance; low masculinity team members would similarly be driven by a need for consensus. High individualism team members would feel much less constrained to go with the consensus, and high masculinity team members would tend ensure that their views were heard, even if this caused intra-team conflict; however, their scores in other dimensions would affect this willingness to go against the consensus (e.g. low individualist, high masculinity team members in Japan directed their competitiveness externally to the team).

Summarising the above sub-factors:

- developing new ideas and concepts *through to* minor product improvements and following procedures (e.g. in maintenance)

- going against the consensus

c) Interaction (communication and co-ordination within the team)

Cultures, due to face and status issues, varied widely in the degree to which rapid, direct, factual communication could occur. Some team situations required rapid, accurate communication and continuous co-ordination; other team situations required complex but non-time-critical communication. The required speed, complexity and accuracy of communication within a team depended on the tasks that the team had to able to carry out. In a 'blue-skies' research team, occasional interchange of complex information might be required between team members; under emergency conditions in the cockpit of an advanced transport aircraft, or in the control room of a nuclear reactor, rapid, accurate interchange of key information would be required.

Saying what you mean, meaning what you say vs. conveying meaning diplomatically (typically indirectly): In certain circumstances, it was important that team members exchanged information in a prompt, direct, accurate manner, for example in military manoeuvres or rapidly-developing situations, e.g. emergencies, which required immediate responses. High power distance discouraged subordinates from communicating (unless prompted by their superiors); low-individualism demanded high-context communication and, as stated earlier, drawing a superior's attention to a problem or error could only be done indirectly – taking time and attention away from any developing situation. However, when negotiating with low-individualist, high-power-distance or little-understood groups, it was best to proceed with caution and a minimum of commitment to any expression of views. In this case, the low-collectivist, high-power-distance team member might be most effective.

Communicating rapidly and accurately with colleagues, superiors and subordinates when necessary vs. communicating about and discussing in-depth complex concepts in a considered manner: In some forms of teamwork, e.g. in action teams (aircrews, facility operating crews), rapid, accurate communication was required at key times. Conversely, in some other forms of teamwork, for example project planning or research & development, team members came together to discuss problems on an ad-hoc or regular basis; although there might be pressure to achieve specific goals, there was typically time for detailed discussions and deliberations.

Interacting with other team members on a frequent or continuous basis vs. interacting with other team members mainly (or only) at key decision points: When carrying out highly integrated or co-ordinated tasks, continuous interaction might be necessary, for example as part of an assembly or test task, or during a complex manoeuvre such as docking a ship, co-ordinating the landing of aircraft on a carrier or when handling an emergency. Conversely, in some forms of teamwork, team members worked individually for long periods, coming together to discuss progress and key stages, etc., for example in much of research and development work.

Sharing information with other team members whenever possible vs. only sharing information on a need-to-know basis: Keeping others in the team informed of any actions or status changes helped maintain a shared understanding of the situation or stage of development in an ongoing project. Such information sharing was easier in a low power distance, high individualism, low uncertainty-avoiding culture. Conversely, in situations where secrecy (or confidentiality) was important, it might be necessary to limit information-sharing. In such cases, the suspiciousness of high-uncertainty-avoiding team members might be an asset. Also, high-power distance, by discouraging informal information exchange, might be beneficial.

Summarising the above sub-factors:

- saying what you mean and meaning what you say vs. conveying meaning indirectly, diplomatically

- communicating rapidly and accurately with colleagues, superiors and subordinates vs. communicating and discussing in-depth a range of complex topics in a considered manner

- interacting with other team members on a frequent or continuous basis vs. interacting with other team members mainly (or only) at key decision points

- sharing information at all times vs. sharing information only on a need to know basis

d) Handling uncertainty and dealing with failures

Some environments and team goals resulted in highly predictable activities and/or outcomes; other environments resulted in highly unpredictable activities and/or outcomes that had to be accommodated by the team or crew. Cultures (in particular, as measured by their uncertainty avoidance scores) varied greatly in their capabilities to deal with uncertainty.

Highly-predictable activities and outcomes vs. highly unpredictable activities and outcomes: In situations of relatively low uncertainty, for example planned maintenance of sociotechnical systems and the activities of many team games, the inflexibility of high power distance, the commitment to rules and caution of high uncertainty avoidance and the subservience to the group of low individualism might offer benefits. In the opposite case, where both activities and outcomes might be unpredictable, then the flexibility of low power distance, low uncertainty avoidance and high individualism might offer benefits.

Errors and failures must be dealt with quickly vs. errors and failures require careful consideration prior to action: In situations where errors caused rapid deterioration in the situation, they had to be recognised and dealt with promptly. High uncertainty avoidance reduced the speed with which errors were detected, high power distance reduced the willingness of team/crew members to inform their superiors or leaders, and low individualism prevented subordinates from informing their superiors directly due to loss of face issues. Low uncertainty avoidance, low power distance and high individualism contributed to rapid detection of errors and failures (willingness to reframe) and the informing of superiors promptly, in a direct clear manner. In situations where there was time for extended consideration, the effects of culture on performance were less severe than when fast action was required. However, high power distance still tended to reduce the range of solutions under consideration (due in part to lack of consultation), and high uncertainty avoidance tended to limit potential solutions to those that were well-understood.

Summarising the above sub-factors:

- handling highly-predictable activities and outcomes

- handling highly predictable activities and outcomes except under rare circumstances when they become highly dangerous and unpredictable

- handling highly UNpredictable activities and outcomes

- handling errors and failures very quickly

- giving careful consideration to errors and failures prior to action

e) Situation awareness

Individual situation awareness: This applied primarily to organised action teams, e.g. aircrews, power station operators. High uncertainty avoidance tended to reduce individual situation awareness (due to both training issues and reluctance to mentally reframe).

Shared situation awareness: As above, this applied primarily to org-anised action teams. As stated above, high uncertainty avoidance tended to reduce individual situation awareness (due to both training issues and reluctance to mentally reframe) of all operators or crew members. In addition, crew or operator communication difficulties hampered further shared situation awareness – high power distance and high uncertainty avoidance both discouraged unprompted subordinate comm-unication of information. Low individualism caused subordinates to refer indirectly to arising situational issues, rather than directly informing their superiors, often resulting in substantial delays to reactions and reduced shared situation awareness.

Summarising the above sub-factors:

- maintaining individual situation awareness at all times
- maintaining shared situation awareness at all times

4.4.2   An ideal team/task framework

The *cultural* framework described and applied in the work of this thesis utilised four dimensions (PDI, IDV, MAS and UAI) plus cultural diversity, thus enabling us to position team member cultures and team mean culture at locations in continuous culture space. Rather than pursuing a taxonomic or factor approach to team/task classification, it would have greatly simplified matters if a small number of dimensions based on relevant independent factors could have been adopted as the basis for team/task classification, as recommended by Hollenbeck et al. (2012); this would have enabled us to position a team at a location in continuous team/task/mission space, rather than to 'shoehorn' it into an ill-fitting taxonomic slot.

Figure 4-3 illustrates the idealised case, where a task/mission located in task/mission space could be mapped (by a process of transformation) into a 'desirable' location in culture space; for ease of illustration, only three axes are shown in the figure.

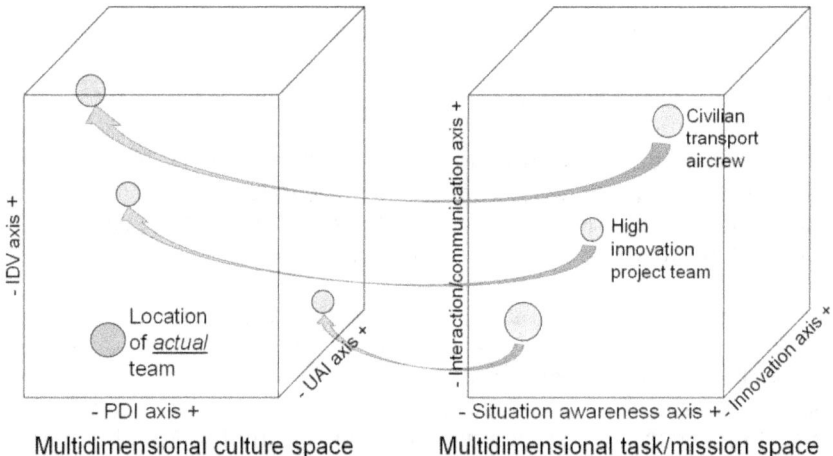

Figure 4-3: Mapping from task/mission space to culture space

Unfortunately, the five earlier-described task/mission factors could not directly be changed into dimensions because each factor was an umbrella for a set of sub-factors whose conglomerate set of weights could not be represented as a single point on a dimension scale.

4.5 Proposed further research activities

As stated in Chapter 2 (Problem statement and research methodology), the proposed research activities included the collection of detailed data from the research literature, the carrying out of a range of pilot studies, the detailed analysis of the resulting data, and the development of performance prediction/culture discrepancy methodologies.

The culmination of the research described in this thesis was to be the development of a culture tool to guide designers and team selectors. However, due to the inconsistent and sometimes contradictory nature of culture study results reported in the literature, see Section 3.7 ('Detailed problem statement'), it was necessary also to consider several specific research questions before constructing the proposed culture models and tools.

4.5.1 Specific research questions

Consistent trends were reported in the literature on the effects of power distance and individualism on human perception, behaviour, decision-making and other aspects of performance; these trends were also reported for some types of team and task. However, the literature on masculinity, uncertainty avoidance and cultural diversity was much less clear. Therefore, the author of this thesis proposed that the following three *research questions* be addressed:

1. **Masculinity (MAS):** There were mixed results in the literature with regard to the effects of MAS on innovation, although low MAS appeared to be associated with compromise and group-think. In areas such as transport and industrial production, there appeared to be remarkably little association between MAS and accident rates; it would be logical to expect that high-MAS, highly-competitive operators and crew would take more risks than low-MAS highly socialising operators and crew. *Could the effects of MAS on team performance in various domains be clarified?*

2. **Uncertainty avoidance (UAI):** High UAI appeared to have a negative effect on most team-related activities, except in the development of low innovation products and services. *Were there other areas where high UAI offered benefits?*

3. **Cultural diversity:** Reports from the literature about the effects of cultural diversity on performance were inconsistent and, in many cases, contradictory. *Were there any cases where clear diversity-linked patterns of effects could be identified?*

4.5.2 Culture models and tools

Based on findings from the literature review and further studies, it was necessary to draw up, at very least, approximate models of the relationships between the four cultural dimensions (plus cultural diversity) and the factors relating to task/mission performance. These, detailed in Chapter 5, would form the information basis of the culture tools.

The first tool (TCT1, Chapter 6) was intended as an initial exploration of approaches to cultural aspects of performance prediction; the later tools were intended to demonstrate increasingly practicable approaches to the assessment of cultural fit and performance prediction.

4.6 Summary of research tools and proposed activities

Hofstede's four-dimension framework was selected as the cultural framework for the proposed research, along with Bosland's educational adjustment factors (Bosland, 1985). A measure of cultural diversity based on team member location in four-dimensional culture space was developed. A team task/mission classification based on five factors and their sub-factors was proposed, based on the literature review.

Knowledge gaps in the cultural landscape were identified, leading to three research questions. These required answers based on the collection and analysis of further data from the literature and from the researcher's proposed qualitative surveys and quantitative pilot studies. In addition to answering the above research questions, this exercise would provide more details of relationships between cultural factors and the above-proposed team/task performance factors.

The above data collection and analysis exercise is presented in detail in Chapter 5.

5 Data collection and analysis

5.1 Introduction

This chapter describes a set of studies, the purpose of which was to identify or clarify culture-performance relationships for various team types. These culture-performance relationships, combined with those found in the earlier literature review, were subsequently utilised in a set of team culture tools described in later chapters.

Section 5.2 describes the collection (via interview and questionnaire) of anecdotal information and its analysis by the author of this thesis. Section 5.3 presents the results of studies carried out by the author, either directly or (in some cases) based on data collected from external sources. Section 5.4 provides partial answers to three research questions posed in Chapter 4. Section 5.5 combines the results of the literature review and the analyses of Sections 5.2, 5.3 and 5.4 in order to derive culture/performance relationships for a set of team culture models and tools described in later chapters. Section 5.6 discusses potential issues that were identified with Hofstede's framework during these studies. Section 5.7 summarises the outcomes of this chapter.

The default assumption behind statistical analyses of data was that relationships between variables were linear. This assumption appeared to be true in some cases, and appeared to be a good approximation over a limited range in other cases; however, it would not be the case where an optimum value (or score) occurred in the middle of a range. As examples of potential non-linear relationships, consider two of the cultural dimensions utilised in this report:

- **Masculinity and innovative or creative team projects:** Very high masculinity could result in excessive competition and reduced co-operation within a research team; low masculinity (high femininity) could result in excessive effort being devoted to the achievement of consensus, at the expense of novelty. As stated in Chapter 3, Halkos & Tzeremes' (2011) results implied an optimum masculinity score of perhaps 70 to 80.

- **Power distance and complex projects requiring high co-ordination:** Very high power distance resulted in much-reduced delegation, potentially resulting in low quality decision-making (based on status rather than knowledge) where subject matter experts were not encouraged to contribute, and also leading to delayed responses to problems (due to lack of feedback from subordinates). However, very low power distance could lead to a loss of leadership and co-ordination.

It was important, therefore, to consider non-linear (or bilinear) relationships where operational logic would indicate the likelihood of such relationships.

Unless otherwise stated, the cultural dimensions referred to in this chapter were those that were identified in Hofstede's original research, i.e. power distance (PDI), individualism (IDV), masculinity (MAS) and uncertainty avoidance (UAI).

In order to determine team member culture scores, to apply Bosland's educational corrections (where appropriate), to calculate cultural diversity scores and to derive average team culture scores, many complex calculations were required. Several tools were developed and incorporated into spread sheets for the purposes of carrying out these calculations.

5.2   Collection of qualitative anecdotal information

The author has worked, and continues to work, in a multicultural university environment. Through contacts via research meetings, research training courses, former colleagues and current friends in other departments and other universities and via sports contacts, the author has been able to gather a range of qualitative anecdotal information. In addition, he has utilised an on-line survey form to collect additional information.

5.2.1 Informal interviews and personal conversations

Note that, as the examples presented in this section were anecdotal, no claim is made to the effect that they were typical or representative. The sources of most of the anecdotes below were the conversations that the author had with other research staff, foreign students, lecturers, fellow footballers and others about their experiences on coming to Britain or travelling elsewhere. In many cases, the anecdotes that the author obtained were potentially traceable to their sources, and in other cases he was asked not to quote them; such anecdotes have not been listed in the selection below. See Appendix 2 for more detailed versions of the conversations.

Examples of culturally-related feedback include the following[31]:

- **Rank and status:** Two high-PDI respondents (from different parts of the World) commented on the lack of respect accorded them by juniors of their own country when in this country.

- **Indirectness:** Despite their high IDV score (which would imply a direct mode of conversation), the British are typically indirect in their commands and feedback. A direct-speaking Scandinavian commented on what he saw as this irritating aspect of dealing with the British; he also commented on the common although declining occurrences of sexist remarks.

- **Face:** Several Chinese respondents commented on guanxi and face-related aspects of their culture (e.g. obtaining jobs, criticism).

- **A British pilot's experiences:** The author carried out an unstructured interview with a pilot who had more than twenty years flying experience on flag carriers, budget airlines and private lease flying services. As a regular pilot trainer, the pilot described one of his key tasks as attempting to minimise the 'power slope' in the cockpit as, for crews of many nationalities, the captain was a considerable distance above the first officer. From the pilot's description, it became clear that 'power slope' was the equivalent of power distance. The pilot also described his concerns about attitudes to standard operational procedures (SOPs), in particular the agitation of some non-UK co-pilots (including experienced ones) when told by him that he would deviate from SOPs in order to maintain a margin of safety, e.g. when landing at difficult airports in bad weather conditions.

The pilot commented on the increasingly multinational nature of the industry, with some airlines employing more than seventy nationalities of flying crews. One such airline used a set of 'watertight' SOPs in order to cope with problems associated with crew national diversity; the pilot expressed concerns about this SOP-fixation and the safety issues that would arise if conditions deviated excessively from the norm, resulting in a loss of safety margin. He commented that the Swissair MD-11 crash of 1998 might have been avoided if the pilots had immediately headed for the nearest airport instead of being preoccupied with following SOPs and going through detailed checklists. The author described the uncertainty avoidance dimension which, the pilot felt, explained some of the above differences he had

---

[31] Note that the cultural values (e.g. high-PDI) referred to the individuals' default national culture scores for the Hofstede cultural framework.

found between various nationalities of pilot, in particular the 'SOP-fixation'.

The pilot went on to describe issues of face that came to the fore when he had to correct pilots of some non-Anglo, non-northern European nationalities, in particular when training or testing pilots. He also commented on the 'gung-ho' attitudes[32] of US pilots, in particular. We discussed this latter point further and it appeared to relate to masculinity; however, this attitude was apparently not common amongst other nationalities. As the USA default masculinity score was lower than that of the UK and many other countries, this supported Merritt's findings that Hofstede's masculinity scores were not closely replicated amongst aircrew (A. C. Merritt, 2000). The pilot also commented on differing preferences for automation, and the issue of loss of flying skills.

To summarise this pilot's experiences, it appeared that national culture played a significant role in civil aviation crewing. The effects of power distance, individualism and uncertainty avoidance appeared to be in line with those reported in the literature; however, the default masculinity scores appeared to be unreliable indicators of attitudes and behaviour.

5.2.2 Questionnaire responses

The author designed a web-based culture questionnaire (taking advice from others as to its format and content) and distributed it via email to a range of students and employees and via Facebook to other contacts. The questionnaire form is shown in Appendix 3. Approximately 75% of answers related to travellers to the UK, and 25% of the answers related to travellers from the UK (to elsewhere). The most common issues and differences commented on in the questionnaire returns included the following:

- **Friendships:** One low-MAS and three low-IDV respondents commented on the disappointing shallowness of English friendships - the apparent initial friendliness did not develop into anything.

- **Formality and power distance (by other names):** Virtually all respondents from countries significantly higher in power distance (compared to the UK) noted this difference; in particular

---

[32] As in over-competitiveness, overenthusiasm, lacking caution and not thinking through potential consequences.

they commented on the reduced formality in meetings and the ease with which they could discuss matters with their team leaders or supervisors.

- **Timing and preparation:** This was remarked on by several respondents. In particular, the high-uncertainty-avoiding German respondents did not like the apparent lack of preparation and the lax time-keeping (including meeting overruns) that were often a feature of meetings in the UK.

5.2.3 Analysis and summary of anecdotal evidence

The comments received from conversations, interviews and question-naire returns appeared to confirm the author's view (based on previous experience) that individuals' culturally-defined *expectations* of behaviour were engrained to such a degree, almost irrespective of their person-alities, that they felt shock and/or disappointment when these expec-tations were not met. Such culturally-defined *expectations* about the behaviours of others (in particular the behaviours of others of the same nationality) almost certainly played a larger role in defining team member interactions than did minor differences in personality and educational background. This represented an *ameliorating factor* with regard to Hofstede's 'ecological fallacy' warning.

5.3 Data from the author's studies

The author carried out a range of pilot studies on commercial and industrial work teams and student groups; in addition, he collected, processed and statistically analysed data from various sources (including websites detailing football fixtures and performances, footballer abilities, aircraft crash data, seafarer fatalities and research performance data). Summary results are presented in the following subsections, and more details can be found in Appendix 4.

As well as contributing to the discovery or confirmation of general rela-tionships, the pilot studies enabled the *relative* contributions of the various cultural dimensions and cultural diversity dimensions to be deter-mined; these contributed to the culture-performance models that formed the basis of the team culture tools described later.

5.3.1 Project and management teams

Many researchers have investigated project and management team success and failure factors, e.g. Pinto & Mantel (1990), Cozijnsen et al. (2000), Belout & Gauvreau (2004) and Iamratanakul et al. (2007). Their results have been extremely variable due in part to the wide disparity in measures of performance effectiveness, the large range of contributing factors (independent variables) taken into account and the wide range of project stages considered. It was therefore with some trepidation that the author gathered data on project team performance via question-naires and (where possible) accompanying interviews. The data was acquired mainly from personnel who were, or had been, involved in technical project and/or management teams. The results, in particular the interview feedback and questionnaire comments sections, revealed some of the issues that plagued researchers in this area; for example, a proven high performance team could find itself with an unattainable target due to external politics. In general, however, it was usually clear from the questionnaire and interview comments as to how well teams performed on a professional and social level, irrespective of the achieve-ment of the externally imposed team goals.

Following further consideration, it was decided to retain the material on project and management teams for the purpose of testing the culture tools rather than for influencing the task-mission/desirable-culture relationships.

5.3.2 Student project groups

The primary data sources for the student group studies were the under-graduate student group projects carried out in Loughborough University's School of Electronic, Electrical & Systems Engineering. These student groups were effectively self-managed project teams.

a) The student group studies

Data was collected on the previous seven years of student group projects; students had been encouraged to comment in these past projects so that additional information on individual views of the groups and their performances were available. The projects had been assessed in part on creativity and innovation.

Table 5-1 presents a summary of the data analysis of student groups, detailed data can be found in Appendix 4A. The results of the statistical analysis indicated that the three main contributors to student group performance (as measured by overall project mark) were student group mean grade point average (GPA)[33], mean uncertainty avoidance (UAI) score and mean UAI diversity score; together, they explained 74.5% of the variance in group performance. Student group project performance

---

[33] Based primarily on the students' individual performances on coursework and examinations.

was positively correlated with average student GPA (as would be expected), negatively correlated with UAI score and positively correlated with UAI diversity score. Other researchers have suggested that *best* student GPA score is more important than *average* student GPA score, e.g. Swigger, Brazile, Harrington, Peng, & Alpaslan (2005); this was tested but not supported by the statistical results.

Prediction factors (of performance) in the student group model	Unstandardised coefficients		Standardised coeff's	t	Sig.	95% confidence limits for B	
	B	Std error	Beta			Lower bound	Upper bound
Constant	42.619	12.045		3.538	.001	18.239	66.909
Average student GPA* (%)	1.136	.101	.845	11.238	.000	.932	1.340
UAI score	-1.711	.414	-.658	-4.131	.000	-2.546	-.876
UAI diversity score	.536	.193	.441	2.778	.008	.147	.925
An adjusted R-squared value of 0.745 was obtained, i.e. the model explained 74.5% of the variance in performance of these student groups. *GPA = grade point average (for the *individual* students).							

Table 5-1: Student group performance – regression model

Based on data from Table 5-1, the relative effects of each cultural/ cultural diversity dimension (in the final model) on student performance are summarised in Table 5-2. Note the use of unstandardised coefficients rather than standardised coefficients as the basis for calculation[34].

Cultural dimension	Unstandardised coefficients	Relative contributions of cultural dimensions
UAI	-1.711	-1.000
UAI diversity	.536	.313

Table 5-2: Culture contributions (student groups)

b) Summary – student groups

The largest contributory factor (for student groups tasked with innovative or creative projects) was average student grade point average; the major

---

[34] *Un*standardised coefficients are used as the basis for calculating relative contributions of cultural dimensions to the dependent variables in all cases. This is because all cultural dimensions have approximately the same *actual* range (of the order of 0 to 100) over the overall global population. A particular sample may have very different ranges for PDI, IDV, MAS and UAI cultural scores (depending on the mix of countries represented); such a situation would result in very different standardised coefficient weightings compared to the unstandardised ones, which would not reflect the real world situation.

cultural factors were UAI, which was negatively correlated with group performance, and UAI diversity, which was positively correlated. Other cultural factors were not statistically significant.

5.3.3 University research groups

Data from the UK's 2008 Research Assessment Exercise (RAE) website was downloaded and analysed by university department for physics & astronomy, and chemical engineering. However, some of the detailed data on the RAE website was removed (or made inaccessible) following initial access, preventing a full analysis. For each department, the author had to assign nationalities to all individuals submitted to the RAE exercise; due to data protection requirements, nationality data were not available from these departments, and the author was obliged to search web sources in order to obtain confirmatory evidence.

a) Physics and astronomy

Details were obtained and processed for a total of twenty-six RAE2008 physics & astronomy submissions. Following processing, they were analysed via the SPSS statistical package.

Table 5-3 presents a summary of the data analysis for physics & astronomy; detailed data can be found in Appendix 4B. Note that, in the statistical model of Table 5-3, an optimum MAS diversity score of '6' had been derived from repeated tests of the model with various proposed optima; the negative sign for MAS diversity indicated that the score of '6' represented a maximum, rather than a minimum, in terms of positive contribution to RAE2008 score in the model.

Prediction factors in final model (Physics & Astronomy)	Unstandardised coefficients		Standardised coeff's	t	Sig.	95% confidence limit for B	
	B	Std error	Beta			Lower bound	Upper bound
(Constant)	10.180	1.088		9.353	.000	7.923	12.437
MAS score	-.142	.020	-1.670	-6.977	.000	-.184	-.100
MAS diversity score*	-.114	.017	-1.632	-6.811	.000	-.149	-.079

* MAS diversity was measured as the absolute distance from an optimum of diversity score of 6.
An adjusted R-squared value of 0.671 was obtained, i.e. the model explained 67.1% of the variance in this sample of the RAE2008 Physics & Astronomy results.

Table 5-3: RAE2008 (physics & astronomy) – regression model

The results of the statistical analysis indicated that the two main contributors to Physics & Astronomy unit performance, as measured by their RAE2008 scores, were the masculinity (MAS) and MAS diversity scores;

together, they explained 67.1% of the variance in research department performance; both were negatively correlated with the RAE2008 score.

Based on data from Table 5-3, the relative effects of each cultural/ cultural diversity dimension (in the final model) on university RAE2008 physics & astronomy performance are summarised in Table 5-4.

Cultural dimension	Unstandardised coefficients	Relative contributions of cultural dimensions
MAS score	-.142	-1.000
MAS diversity score	-.114	-0.803

Table 5-4: Culture contributions to RAE2008 (P&A)

b) Chemical engineering

Details were obtained and processed for all nine RAE2008 chemical engineering submissions; it appeared that many (other) chemical engineering departments had been entered in combination with other engineering departments. Following processing, the data were analysed via the SPSS statistical package.

Given the small number of RAE2008 submissions, the number of predictor variables was limited to one. Table 5-5 presents a summary of the data analysis for chemical engineering; detailed data can be found in Appendix 4C.

Prediction factors in final model (Chemical Engineering)	Unstandardised coefficients		Standardised coeff's	t	Sig.	95% confidence limit for B	
	B	Std error	Beta			Lower bound	Upper bound
(Constant)	3.276	.148		22.186	.000	2.936	3.617
MAS diversity score	-.054	.014	-.810	-3.903	.005	-3.903	.005
An adjusted R-squared value of 0.613 was obtained, i.e. the model explained 61.3% of the variance in this sample of the RAE2008 Chemical Engineering results.							

Table 5-5: RAE2008 (chemical engineering) – regression model

The results of the statistical analysis indicated that the main contributor to chemical engineering facility performance, as measured by their RAE-2008 scores, was the masculinity (MAS) diversity score; it explained 61.3% of the variance in research facility performance, and was negatively correlated with RAE2008 score.

Based on data from Table 5-5, the relative effects of each cultural/cultural diversity dimension (in the final model) on university RAE2008 chemical engineering performance are summarised in Table 5-6. The table is produced for completeness – there is only one cultural dimension.

137

Cultural dimension	Unstandardised coefficients	Relative contributions of cultural dimensions
MAS diversity score	-.054	-1.000

Table 5-6: Culture contributions to RAE2008 (CE)

c) Discussion and summary – RAE2008 results

Only very limited inferences could be drawn, in part due to the nature of the RAE assessment[35] and in part due to the relatively small sample size, as was the case with chemical engineering. The main topic of interest in the RAE2008 results related to cultural diversity. Almost all the measures of cultural diversity that the author of this thesis had previously found in the literature had represented 'total' or 'combined' diversity measures. However, diversity along different cultural dimensions could have produced opposite effects on performance; this may explain why there was little consistency in the academic literature on diversity. However, the above RAE2008 results suggested that MAS diversity was a significant negative contributor to research performance, but that other forms of diversity were not. When a combined measure of diversity was substituted, its contribution was insignificant.

The sizes of the samples limited the number of independent variables that could justifiably be retained in the final model, and therefore limited the inferences that could be drawn from them. MAS, in one model, and MAS diversity in both models appeared to have a significant role (mainly negative) to play in performance as measured by the RAE2008 grade scores. This was perhaps logical if we consider what could happen in discussions and meetings; without formal controls or strong leadership, consensus-seeking low-MAS researchers would be dominated by over-competitive high-MAS researchers.

It is also worth commenting that there appeared to be significant group size effects in both models. Three size-related variables were tested in the early models, but √(group size) was found to contribute the most to the regression model. It was logical that increased group size would tend to broaden experience and enable members to increase their individual knowledge and skills; however, as group sizes increased, groups would tend to become more bureaucratic, thus reducing the positive 'group effect'. The group size variables were removed from both of the final regression models as part of the 'independent variable cull'.

---

[35] Submissions were based on individuals, but the overall academic department or school RAE score was in part an aggregate of these scores, which may have represented several research groups, each potentially with a different cultural profile.

Turning to a different issue, academic research appeared to be 'tagged' onto one end of the' innovation-improvement spectrum' in the literature, yet the author found no evidence in that literature to support such a continuum. As stated in Subsection 3.3.1(a)(ix), three potentially independent activities or processes could be identified – searching for truth (much of academic blue-skies research), creativity/lateral thinking/-invention, and adaptation to needs/markets; these or similar groupings could form the basis of a three (or more) dimension framework, as illustrated in Figure 3-3.

5.3.4 Sports teams

The author carried out a study of the 2010-2011 English Premier Football League season, during which twenty teams played a total of 380 matches. Talent scores were obtained for all Premiership players based on the Castrol EDGE Rankings (Castrol, 2011), and were updated at the halfway stage (beginning of 2011). For each match, team talent scores were calculated based on player talent scores weighted by the proportion of the game that each player spent on the pitch; team mean culture dimension scores were similarly calculated based on weighted player nationality scores. Team cultural diversity and team member average age were also calculated. Talent, cultural and age differences between teams were calculated, and were statistically analysed via the SPSS package, both at the level of the game and at the level of the team over the season.

The measure of performance chosen was *shots-on-goal-difference*; *shots-on-goal-difference* has been shown in the literature to be a more reliable measure of team performance than *goals-scored-difference* or *points* (Miklos-Thal & Ullrich, 2010; Reep & Benjamin, 1968), as *goals scored* and *points* were both significantly affected by inconsistent refereeing decisions. Several models were analysed, initially with a large number of prediction factors; factors with little statistical significance were then eliminated. The final football *match* model contained four prediction factors – team talent difference, home advantage, masculinity difference and uncertainty avoidance difference, see Table 5-7. This model captured 41.3% of the variance in *shots-on-goal-difference* match performance over the season; detailed data can be found in Appendix 4D.

Prediction factors in the final model (Premiership matches)	Unstandar- dised coefficients		Standar- dised coeff's	t	Sig.	95% confidence limit for B	
	B	Std error	Beta			Lower bound	Upper bound
Constant	-1.609	.205		-7.828	.000	-2.012	-1.205
Home advantage	3.217	.291	.308	11.059	.000	2.646	3.788
Team talent difference	.140	.012	.376	11.402	.000	.116	.164
Team MAS difference	.099	.025	.157	3.968	.000	.050	.149
Team UAI difference	.134	.015	.368	8.973	.000	.105	.163

An adjusted R-squared value of 0.413 was obtained, i.e. the model explained 41.3% of the variance in the match-by-match shots-on-target results by Premiership teams during the 380-game season.

Table 5-7: English Football Premiership _match_ performance – regression model

Prior to the final cull of prediction factors, the football match model also contained *MAS diversity difference* and *UAI diversity difference (both positive)*, but their contributions were low compared to the other variables and, therefore, they were eliminated.

Based on data from Table 5-7, the relative effects of each cultural and cultural-diversity dimension (in the final _match_ model) on English Premiership match performance are summarised in Table 5-8.

Cultural dimension	Unstandardised coefficients	Relative contributions of cultural dimensions
Team MAS difference	.099	.739
Team UAI difference	.134	1.000

Table 5-8: Culture contributions to English Premiership _match_ performances

The final football _team_ model contained three prediction factors – team talent difference, home advantage and uncertainty avoidance difference, see Table 5-9; note that UAI diversity and MAS appeared in the football team model (both positive), but their contributions were too low for them to be retained. This football team model captured 82.5% of the variance in *shots-on-goal-difference* performance over the season; detailed data can be found in Appendix 4E.

Prediction factors in the final model (Premiership teams)	Unstandardised coefficients		Standardised coeff's	t	Sig.	95% confidence limit for B	
	B	Std error	Beta			Lower bound	Upper bound
Constant	-1.619	0.271		-5.967	0.000	-2.170	-1.069
Home advantage	3.239	0.385	+0.567	8.414	0.000	.071	.175
Team talent difference	.123	0.026	+0.405	4.772	0.000	2.458	4.020
Team UAI difference	.107	0.025	+0.366	4.329	0.000	.057	.158
An adjusted R-squared value of 0.825 was obtained, i.e. the model explained 82.5% of the variance in the shots-on-target results by Premiership teams *over the season*.							

Table 5-9: English Football Premiership team performance – regression model

From the above models, it was clear that uncertainty avoidance (UAI) was positively associated with a team's performance relative to its rivals. Note that the model of Table 5-9 related to team performance *over the season*, not to individual match performances, where the variance due to random factors was much higher ... a match-by-match prediction ability of 82.5% (even for shots-on-target rather than goals) could earn the wielder of such knowledge a large income!

Regular viewers of English Premiership matches will be aware of the high frequency with which defensive errors occur – slow back passes that are intercepted by opposition players, defenders that are caught with the ball, etc. It is therefore logical to hypothesise that a defensive player would benefit from a high UAI score, as such a player would attempt to reduce or accommodate uncertainty by maintaining greater margins of time and distance. Conversely, an attacking midfielder or striker might benefit from the creativity that comes with low UAI because this could impose increased uncertainty on the opposition defensive players. In order to test the hypothesis 'high UAI benefits defenders rather than attackers', further data processing was carried out to split each of the 380 team/game combinations into a defensive and attacking group of players[36]. Perhaps due to the difficulties of identifying defensive mid-fielders from attacking midfield players, the analysis was inconclusive, and the benefits of high UAI appeared very similar for both defence and attack.

---

[36] Note that this split into defence and attack was to some extent arbitrary as, in a majority of the games, insufficient dedicated defenders were present; in such cases, one or more midfielders played in a defensive role, but it was not clear from the available data as to which midfielders were defending; it was therefore likely that the accuracy of the defence/attack split was limited.

Based on data from Table 5-9, the relative effects of each cultural/ cultural diversity dimension (in the final model) on English Premiership team performance over the season are summarised in Table 5-10.

Cultural dimension	Unstandardised coefficients	Relative contributions of cultural dimensions
Team UAI difference	.107	1.000

Table 5-10: Culture contributions to English Premiership team performances

5.3.5 Organised action teams

Organised action teams were considered to include a range of teams that had to react very quickly to circumstances, in particular 'when things went wrong.' They included high reliability sociotechnical system operators and crews, e.g. airline crews, ship crews, surgical teams, oil rig crews.

a) Aircraft accidents

Data covering the years 1970 to 2009 were collected from the aircraft crash data website Airsafe.com (Airsafe.com, n.d.) and were statistically analysed.

The aircraft accident data were analysed taking into account GDP-per-capita, national corruption via the Corruption Perceptions Index (Transparency International, 2011) and national culture scores. Note that during several trials, the per-capita income was 'topped and tailed' at various levels until optimum results were obtained, by limiting the maximum national GDP-per-capita to £17,000 in the model; this reflected the fact that, above a 'sufficing' level of income, behaviour was not 'proportional' to income. The results of the analysis are shown in Table 5-11 (accidents per million flights) and Table 5-12 (full aircraft loss equivalent, FLE, per million flights); detailed statistical data can be found in Appendices 4F and 4G. Corruption was removed from both analyses, as it was not significant when GDP-per-capita ('topped' at £17,000) was included.

Prediction factors in final model (aircraft accidents per million flights)	Unstandardised coefficients		Standardised coeff's	t	Significance	95.0% confid. limit for B	
	B	Std. error	Beta			Lower bound	Upper bound
(Constant)	6.390	.316		20.241	.000	5.771	7.009
PDI score	.009	.003	.067	2.740	.006	.003	.016
IDV score	-.016	.002	-.215	-7.587	.000	-.021	-.012
MAS score	-.013	.002	-.100	-6.490	.000	-.017	-.009
UAI score	.011	.002	.105	5.168	.000	.007	.015
Per-capita income (£17k max)	.000	.000	-.428	-20.707	.000	.000	.000
An adjusted R-squared value of 0.486 was obtained, i.e. the model explained 48.6% of the variance in aircraft accident rates.							

Table 5-11: Airline accidents per million flights - regression model

The statistical model for accidents per million flights predicted 48.6% of the variance in crash rates, and the statistical model for full (hull) loss equivalent (FLE) per million flights predicted 44.4% of the variance in crash rates.

Prediction factors in final model (full aircraft loss equivalent, FLE, per million flights)	Unstandardised coefficients		Standardised coeff's	t	Significance	95.0% confid. limit for B	
	B	Std. error	Beta			Lower bound	Upper bound
(Constant)	4.128	.234		17.646	.000	3.669	4.587
PDI score	.007	.003	.071	2.801	.005	.002	.012
IDV score	-.010	.002	-.192	-6.509	.000	-.014	-.007
MAS score	-.006	.001	-.069	-4.349	.000	-.009	-.004
UAI score	.009	.002	.115	5.450	.000	.006	.012
Per-capita income (£17k max)	.000	.000	-.416	-19.335	.000	.000	.000
An adjusted R-squared value of 0.444 was obtained, i.e. the model explained 44.4% of the variance in full aircraft loss equivalent rates.							

Table 5-12: Airline full loss equivalent per million flights - regression model

Note that in lower per-capita income countries, inadequate ground facilities, poor quality maintenance, limited skills and commitment of airport staff and other non-flying-related factors all contributed to higher flight accident rates; therefore flight crew culture could only provide a partial explanation.

For both statistical models (accidents per million flights and full loss equivalent per million flights), the most significant factor was per-capita income, and the most significant cultural dimension (even after taking account of its relationship with per-capita income) was IDV. The optimum (low crash rate) cultural configuration appeared to be, from both models, high IDV, low PDI, high MAS and low UAI.

As we would expect, accident rate is greater than FLE rate, as not all accidents cause a full loss of aircraft, passengers and crew; this fact is shown in the above models via the lower value unstandardized coeff-icients for the FLE rate. Based on data from Tables 5-11 and 5-12, the relative effects of each cultural dimension (in the final model) on accident and FLE rates are summarised in the Table 5-13.

Cultural dimension	Accident rate		FLE rate		Relative contributions of cultural dimensions
	Unstand-ardised	Std.	Unstand-ardised	Std.	
PDI	.0095	.576	.0070	.667	.622
IDV	-.0165	-1.000	-.0105	-1.000	-1.000
MAS	-.0130	-.788	-.0065	-.619	-.704
UAI	.0110	.667	.0090	.857	.762

Table 5-13: Culture contributions to aircraft accident/FLE rates

b) Maritime accidents

Data covering the years 1995 to 2004 were extracted from the Inter-national Association of Oil & Gas Producers (OGP) Risk Assessment Data Directory (OGP, 2010b) and were statistically analysed.

The maritime seafarer fatality data were analysed taking into account GDP-per-capita, national corruption via the Corruption Perceptions Index (Transparency International, 2011) and national culture scores. The results of the analysis are shown in Table 5-14; detailed data can be found in Appendix 4H.

Prediction factors in final model (maritime seafarer fatality rates per 100k seafarer-years)	Unstandar-dised coefficients		Standa rdised coeff's	t	Signifi-cance	95.0% confid. limit for B	
	B	Std. error	Beta			Lower bound	Upper bound
(Constant)	96.118	28.959		3.319	0.007	32.379	159.857
IDV score	-1.275	.368	-.677	-3.470	0.005	-2.084	-.466
UAI score	.503	.267	.367	1.880	0.057*	-.086	1.092
An adjusted R-squared value of 0.505 was obtained, i.e. the model explained 50.5% of the variance in maritime seafarer fatality rates. *Slightly above the 5% level.							

Table 5-14: Maritime seafarer fatality rates - regression model

As was the case with the aircraft data, corruption was removed from the analysis as it was not significant when GDP-per-capita was included; however, GDP-per-capita itself was of much lower significance in this (maritime) model than in the earlier aircraft model, and was removed from the final statistical model. This (final) model predicted 50.5% of the variance in fatality rates; the most significant factor was IDV, followed by UAI; the optimum (low fatality rate) cultural configuration appeared, from the model, to be high IDV and low UAI. Note that PDI was positively correlated to fatality rates, whereas MAS was negatively correlated, as in the above analysis of aircraft crash rates. However, both PDI and MAS had a relatively low effect on the model, and were removed from the final statistical model.

Based on data from Table 5-14, the relative effects of each cultural dimension (in the final model) on maritime seafarer rates are summarised in Table 5-15.

Cultural dimension	Unstandardised coefficients	Relative contributions of cultural dimensions
IDV	-1.275	-1.000
UAI	.503	.395

Table 5-15: Culture contributions to maritime seafarer fatality rates

Comparing the results to the aircraft accident results, we can see beyond correlations to probable causations (or lack of them). The less effective maintenance and training associated with lower per-capita GDP countries had a lesser effect on shipping fleets than on aircraft fleets – ships continued to float when engines stopped; high PDI, which reduced inputs from junior members of the crew, was again less problematical in ships than in aircraft due to the lower communication rates required on ships in typical emergencies.

There were issues relating to the accuracy of publically-accessible information on seafarer fatality rates; Nielsen & Roberts (1999) reported that the Institute of London Underwriters (ILU) figures for seafarer casualties due to marine disasters varied from under-reporting by a factor of six (Japan, Chile) to over-reporting by a factor of three (Singapore), compared to those countries' official maritime organisations. This implied that many countries, in particular the 'flag of convenience' countries, did not have a vested interest in maintaining accurate fatality figures.

c) Attitudes to automation

Sherman et al.(1997) surveyed the attitudes toward flight automation of 5879 airline pilots from twelve nations; Sherman et al. produced fifteen automation-related statements and, for each country and for each statement, calculated the percentage of pilots who agreed (Sherman et al. 1997, Table IV). The author of this thesis carried out a further statistical analysis of Sherman et al.'s survey results against pilots' default national cultural scores, which provided additional insights. Table 5-16 presents summary results for the six statements that were statistically significant in the author's analysis; see Appendix 4I for details of the analysis of all fifteen automation-related statements. Note that Sherman et al. had access to the raw data for 5879 pilots, and therefore could produce analyses with much greater statistical confidence than was achieved here by the author.

Model	Pred'n factors in final model	Adj. R Squ.	Unstandardised coeffs B	Std. error	Stdsd coeffs Beta	t	Significance	95.0% conf. limit for B Lower bound	Upper bound
A01: I am concerned that automation may cause me to lose flying skills	(Const.)	.519	86.771	11.964		7.252	.000	59.706	113.836
	PDI		-.279	.130	-.455	-2.153	.060	-.573	.014
	UAI		-.440	.164	-.568	-2.687	.025	-.810	-.069
A02: There are modes and features of the FMC that I do not fully understand	(Const.)	.592	53.199	4.737		11.230	.000	42.644	63.754
	UAI		-.305	.074	-.793	-4.119	.002	-.469	-.140
A03: When workload increases, it's better to avoid reprogramming the FMC	(Const.)	.263	70.961	8.761		8.100	.000	51.441	90.481
	UAI		-.303	.137	-.574	-2.219	.051	-.608	.001
A05: Under abnormal conds, I can rapidly access the info I need in the FMC	(Const.)	.353	58.193	9.668		6.019	.000	36.650	79.735
	UAI		.400	.151	.642	2.647	.024	.063	.736
A10: The effective crew member always uses the automation tools provided	(Const.)	.784	117.941	17.622		6.693	.000	78.077	157.805
	PDI		.392	.101	.565	3.880	.004	.163	.620
	MAS		-1.028	.262	-.572	-3.929	.003	-1.620	-.436
A15: I prefer flying automated aircraft	(Const.)	.389	45.815	13.072		3.505	.006	16.688	74.942
	UAI		.577	.204	.666	2.827	.018	.122	1.032
The adjusted R-squared values indicate the proportion of the variance explained by the cultural dimension scores in each case.									

Table 5-16: Automation preferences – regression model

The strongest correlation appeared to be between national cultural scores and the statement *"The effective crew member always uses the automation tools provided"*; support for this statement was strongly negatively correlated with masculinity (MAS), and was positively correlated with PDI. Of the remaining statements, five were positively or negatively correlated with UAI and nine were not significantly correlated with national cultural scores. From the results shown in Table 5-16, it appears that high-PDI pilots and high-UAI pilots are generally more positive about automation than are their lower-PDI and lower-UAI colleagues. The aforementioned results should be treated with caution as they are based on only twelve countries.

d) Summary – organised action teams

It appeared, from the above results, that fast-reaction-time organised action teams (e.g. flying crews) benefitted from low PDI, high IDV, high MAS and low UAI, whereas relatively low-reaction-time organised action teams (e.g. merchant vessel crews) benefitted primarily from high IDV and low UAI; PDI and MAS appeared to have a much lesser affect when more time was available for decision-making. Similarly, the effects of GDP-per capita on seafarer fatalities were reduced because ship break-downs were much less likely to be fatal mid-voyage than was the case with aircraft piloting errors and breakdowns. With regard to automation – a key factor in the further development of sociotechnical systems – the results indicated that attitudes of high UAI and high PDI crew were strongly positive towards it, and to the maximisation of its application.

5.4 Answers to the earlier research questions

Three research questions relating to masculinity, uncertainty avoidance and cultural diversity were posed in Sub-section 4.5.1; these are considered further in this section.

5.4.1 The effects of masculinity (MAS)

a) Analysis of the literature on MAS

The evidence from the literature review (see Subsection 3.3) about the effects of MAS on team performance was generally inconsistent and, in most cases where found, had a small affect compared to other cultural dimensions.

Creativity and innovation: Low-level innovation projects appeared to benefit from high team MAS scores, whereas medium-level innovation projects appeared to benefit from low/medium team MAS scores; no consensus appeared for high level innovation or academic research and development. In the case of very large projects, in particular those with complex social or political issues, it appeared from qualitative analyses that high team member masculinity scores would tend to contribute to project failure.

b) The author's studies on MAS

Creativity and innovation: High academic research team MAS scores were associated with *reduced* performance (as measured by the UK Research Assessment Exercise). However, as commented in Sub-section 5.3.3, the way that the original RAE data had been collected (at the department or school level) meant that that the effects of culture on individual teams within departments were somewhat masked; also, the sample sizes (in terms of number of schools/departments) were small.

Team sports: MAS was found to have an effect on the performance of professional footballers in the English Premiership. High team MAS scores (compared to the opposing team) were associated with improved shots-on-target-difference performance; note that this MAS effect, though significant, was less pronounced than that of UAI (see Sub-section 5.4.2).

Sociotechnical system operators or crews: High operator or crew MAS scores were associated with reduced sociotechnical accident rates, but MAS was significantly less influential than individualism (an accident-reducing factor) and uncertainty avoidance (an accident-increasing factor). However, in the case of attitudes towards automation, high-MAS aircraft crews were strongly opposed to the use of automation at all times.

c) Summary of findings about MAS

There was general agreement in the literature that a high MAS score was beneficial in project team activities requiring low creativity, e.g. minor product or process improvement, but elsewhere, the evidence was inconsistent. A high team MAS score appeared disadvantageous in some situations where time was not a critical factor, e.g. in multicultural research teams, perhaps because it discouraged some lower-MAS team members from contributing fully; note that *low* MAS scores could have had a similar effect, but for reasons associated with group-think. However, where rapid decisions had to be made, for example in organised action teams, high MAS scores appeared to be associated with benefits – probably in terms of quicker responses to deteriorating situations.

The relationship between MAS and creativity/inventiveness did not appear to be a simple linear one.

5.4.2 The effects of uncertainty avoidance (UAI)

a) Analysis of the literature on UAI

Creativity and innovation: A detailed analysis of reports in the research literature (see Subsection 3.3.1) indicated that a low team UAI score was beneficial to high-level innovation projects, and that a high UAI score was beneficial to low-level innovation projects. Note that UAI did not appear to have a significant effect on academic research, as measured by the UK's RAE2008 scores (see Subsection 5.3.3); this raised a question as to assumptions about the relationships between fundamental research and creativity, inventiveness and innovation.

Sociotechnical system operators or crews: A high crew UAI score was associated with reduced effectiveness of training, and also contributed to increased accident rates in high-reliability sociotechnical systems.

b) The author's studies on UAI

Student project groups: Student group project performances were negatively affected by high student group UAI scores.

Team sports: UAI was found to have a significant effect on the performance of professional footballers in the English Premiership; high team UAI scores were associated with improved shots-on-target-difference performance. Football is a game with simple rules and highly constrained and predictable scenarios; in such an environment, the emphasis (at least for defenders) should be on the avoidance of mistakes. This emphasis on predictability and avoidance of mistakes is paralleled in maintenance organisations, in particular those that are responsible for sociotechnical systems.

Sociotechnical system operators or crews: High crew UAI was found to have a negative effect on sociotechnical system safety; it appeared to have an influence between half and two-thirds that of individualism (IDV). High crew UAI scores were also associated with positive attitudes toward automation, its usage and its capabilities – potentially leading to over-confidence and complacency.

c) Summary of findings about UAI

A high UAI score appeared to be beneficial wherever the emphasis was on following the rules and not taking excessive apparent risks – e.g. in repetitive or low-innovation work, in maintenance and in team games. However, where there was a need to 'reframe', to reassess quickly, a high UAI score appeared to be disadvantageous; high UAI scores also reduced the effectiveness of training. A high UAI score was associated with very positive views of automation and its capabilities.

5.4.3 The effects of cultural diversity

a) Analysis of the literature on cultural diversity

The original literature review (see Section 3.3) revealed a paucity of consistent results in the research literature. This was considered to be due, in part, to the utilisation of inadequate measures of cultural diversity.

Student groups: Studies indicated cultural diversity to be a negative contributor to performance, or to be represented by a 'U-shaped' or 'inverted-U-shaped' distribution, depending on exactly what aspect of performance was measured.

Innovation and creativity: Academic research appeared to benefit from 20-25% non-indigenous researchers or, alternatively, 'low' diversity.

Sports teams: Studies of the German Bundesliga performance indicated that team cultural diversity was either associated with reduced performance, or had no effect on performance; note that the German high UAI nationality score was likely to have a negative effect on the effectiveness of integrating other-culture players within teams[37]. A study of cultural diversity in USA professional hockey teams revealed a 'U-shaped' relationship to team performance; low- and high-diversity teams outperformed medium-diversity teams.

b) The author's studies on cultural diversity

In each of the author's studies, separate statistical analyses were carried out for each of two different representations of cultural diversity:

- Models that initially included the four individual measures of cultural diversities, i.e. PDI, IDV, MAS and UAI.

- Models that initially included only the mean cultural diversity – i.e. the average value of the above four individual diversities.

In no case was the *mean* cultural diversity found to be significant.

---

[37] High uncertainty avoidance is associated with suspiciousness of foreigners (Hofstede et al. 2010, Ch. 6)

Student groups: Diversity in uncertainty avoidance (UAI diversity) appeared to have a significant and positive effect on student group performance.

Innovation and creativity: Diversity in masculinity (MAS diversity) appeared to have a negative effect on academic research team performance (but see earlier-stated caveats). This would be logical in the sense that high-MAS researchers might tend to dominate discussions and meetings, thus discouraging low-MAS researchers from contributing their ideas.

Team sports: MAS diversity and UAI diversity were found to have a small effect on English Premiership team performance over the season, but were removed from the final statistical analysis.

c) Summary of findings about cultural diversity

Mean cultural diversity, taken across all cultural dimensions, appeared to have no net effect on team performance. This result could offer at least a partial explanation for the inconsistent and often contradictory results found in the author's literature survey. However, diversity in individual cultural dimensions was found to play a part in the performance levels of student groups, academic research teams and, to a lesser extent, sports teams (football). This implies that one should consider diversity along each independent cultural dimension.

Note that measures of diversity such as Shannon's index or Blau's index were, as previously stated, fundamentally flawed when applied to multi-cultural teams.

5.5 Establishment of culture-performance relationships

As stated earlier, the literature on culture/performance relationships, including the quantitative studies, was unclear and frequently contradictory; the author's studies supported some studies in the literature, contradicted others and suggested further relationships. Taking all this into consideration, the author, therefore, had to make 'best estimates' of culture-performance relationships in various team situations. These, in turn, formed the basis for the culture/performance associations incorporated in the methodologies and tools described in later chapters.

5.5.1 Optimum 'high' and 'low' culture dimension scores

Neither the studies identified in the literature review, nor the author's own studies, provided *absolute* values in terms of optimum quantitative culture scores for particular missions/tasks; much of the literature, e.g. G. K. Jones & Davis (2000), merely associated general culture dimension scores (e.g. 'high PDI') with particular scenarios (e.g. 'low creativity teamwork'). In other cases (as in the author's studies), a cultural dimension 'slope' was obtained. This would enable the identification of a positive or negative relationship between a cultural dimension and a performance factor (e.g. that uncertainty avoidance (UAI) had a negative relationship with creativity); it would also enable the determination of the relative importance of each cultural dimension to the particular mission (e.g. MAS contributed 23% as much as IDV in the statistical analysis); see Table 5-19 for a summary of the relative effect strengths of the cultural dimensions for each of the author's studies. However, in order for a culture-based performance prediction tool to be effective, it would be necessary to associate specific situations/missions/tasks with specific quantitative optimum culture scores, in order to produce some measure of sub-optimality for any proposed or actual team. For example, what are the optimum PDI, IDV, MAS and UAI scores for a team operating a large ocean-going ship? In order to develop the above culture score/-mission relationships it was necessary to make several assumptions and approximations. These are discussed below and in the following sub-sections.

First of all, a brief examination of the literature: Harzing (1999) stated that, where theory was stated in ordinal terms (e.g. low/high, as above), a simple theoretical approach could be used, e.g. assigning 'low' a zero score, and 'high' a one hundred score; alternatively, empirical 'ideal profiles' could be generated, e.g. by using the mean scores generated from calibration samples, for example the mean scores of high performance organisations, as exemplified by Gresov (1989) and Venkat-raman & Prescott (1990); deviations from such profiles could be calculated to produce 'misfit' scores. In the case of the author's work, there are two complicating factors; these are described further below:

1. **Hofstede's cultural framework:** Hofstede's original cultural scores (based on the data from IBM subsidiaries) were weighted to form a range between zero and one hundred. However, later additions (e.g. Malaysia (PDI), Slovakia (MAS) and Greece (UAI)) extended the range of culture scores beyond one hundred. In addition, the work described in this thesis utilised Bosland's educational corrections, which extended additional scores beyond one hundred (e.g. the Anglo countries' IDV scores) and below zero (e.g. Sweden's MAS score). This complicated the

issue of where to position 'low' scores and 'high' scores for each dimension. See Tables 5-17 and 5-18 for examples of these range changes.

2. **The ramifications of extreme culture scores:** As was the case with all extremes (e.g. in political views or personality), there were potential dangers in the assumption that 'more of a good thing' (or 'less of a bad thing') was better throughout the full range of potential values. For example, extreme masculinity might lead to high intra-team conflict, and extreme uncertainty avoidance might lead to paralysis in decision-making.

The author therefore examined the countries associated with extreme scores in order to evaluate their appropriateness, or otherwise. For example, the countries with the highest uncertainty avoidance scores were Greece (112), Portugal (104), Guatemala (101) and Uruguay (100); these were not countries that were associated with highly effective low-innovation capabilities. Japan (92), South Korea (85) and Taiwan (69) were, however, associated with excellent low-innovation capabilities. They were therefore chosen as the exemplars to represent optimum low-innovation uncertainty avoidance score; their average score, corrected for thirteen years full time education equivalence was selected.

The above-described process was not clear-cut, and the author was obliged to make several subjective best estimates as to which countries to discount and whether to take a maximum (or minimum) or average of a group of countries. Where a particularly high-performing country was at an extreme end, then the author would choose that country's culture score. For example, in the case of low uncertainty avoidance, the high-performing Nordic group was immediately above Jamaica and Singapore (the lowest-scoring countries). A decision was taken to choose the Danish score, as Denmark was the highest performing Nordic country with regard to high originality (e.g. Nobel science awards), and had the lowest Nordic uncertainty avoidance score; the Nordic average uncer-tainty-avoidance score would also have been defensible.

A case of particular difficulty was that of high masculinity; Japan had the highest score (of 95, uncorrected for education), but its aggressive competitiveness appeared to be redirected out from the team or group to focus on competition with other groups and organisations. Note that the individualism score for Japan is significantly higher than those of two West European countries, Portugal and Greece, so an explanation based on collectivism does not appear to be entirely satisfactory. It was decided therefore to base the high masculinity scores on the average of the Germanic group (including Austria), which was the highest mascul-inity scoring *group* of 'high performance' countries.

Tables 5-17 and 5-18 provide information on the countries with the lowest and highest scoring cultural dimension scores; these also include Bosland's corrections for thirteen and sixteen years full time education equivalent, where relevant, representing the most common levels of education amongst sociotechnical operators and system designers. A summary of the reasoning behind the adoption of particular low and high culture scores is also included in these tables.

Cultural dimension	Lowest-scoring countries	Uncorrected range of scores	Corrected scores (13 years FTE)	Corrected scores (16+years FTE)	Comments	Recommended 'low' score(s)
PDI	Austria (11), Israel (13), followed by the Nordics (18-33), Anglos (22-40) and other Germanics (34-35).	11-40	30-57	3-29	The cases for low PDI were primarily associated with high creativity, communication speed, decision-making and situation awareness (mainly FTE16). It was difficult to distinguish amongst this grp, so an average of 16 was proposed.	16
IDV	Guatemala and other Central American countries (6-19), Pakistan (14), Taiwan TW (17), South Korea KR (18), West Africa (20), China (20), Thailand (20), Singapore (20).	6-20 (TW & KR 17-18)	6-20 (TW & KR 17-18)	26-40 (TW & KR 37-38)	The cases for low IDV were primarily associated with low-innovation developments & production (mainly FTE13yrs); also some aspects of diplomatic negotiation (FTE16yrs+). TW & KO were the key producers among these, suggesting a low-IDV of around 17 (FTE13) and 37 (FTE16+).	17 (producers) 37 (negotiation/mgmt)
MAS	Sweden (5), other Nordic countries (8-26), Costa Rica (21), Yugoslavia (21), Chile (28).	5-28 (Nordics 5-26)	12-35	-7to16 (Nordics -7to14)	It was not clear from the data as to where low-MAS was beneficial but, qualitatively, it appeared that complex projects with a social dimension (FTE16yrs) could benefit from low-MAS. Taking the Nordic mean, a value of 4 was proposed.	4
UAI	Singapore (8), Jamaica (13), Denmark (23), Sweden (29), China (30), UK (35), India (40). Other Nordics (29-59) & Anglos (35-51), not included in scores.	8-40	10-42	-6to26 (Denmark 9)	Low UAI appeared to benefit creativity/ high-innovation, communication speed, decision-making and situation awareness (mainly FTE16yrs+). There may be some issues with following SOPs as UAI decreases. It was therefore proposed that the lowest UAI score of the innovative Nordic countries be adopted, i.e. a value of 9, reflecting Denmark FTE16+.	9

Table 5-17: Low scores utilised for cultural dimensions

Based on the information in Table 5-17, the 'low' scores for Hofstede's original four dimensions were proposed as power distance (PDI) = 16, individualism (IDV) = 17 (13yrs FTE) & 37 (16yrs FTE+), masculinity (MAS) = 4, and uncertainty avoidance (UAI) = 9. These recommended optimum scores were best estimates based on limited information, and should not be taken to imply an accuracy to within +/-1 point (or +/-1%).

Cultural dimension	Highest-scoring countries	Uncorrected range of scores	Corrected scores (13 years FTE)	Corrected scores (16+years FTE)	Comments	Recommended 'high' score(s)
PDI	Malaysia (104), Guatemala (95), Panama (95), Philippines (94), Mexico (81), Arab countries (80), ... compared to S.Korea, KR (60), Taiwan TW (58), Japan JP (54)	80-104, JP,KR&TW: 54-60	93-115, 70-75	65-87, 42-47	High PDI appeared to be beneficial for low innovation tasks (mainly FTE13yrs). An examination of high PDI countries revealed that the most productive countries (Japan, Taiwan and South Korea) had FTE13 PDI scores of 70-75. A high-PDI score of 73 was therefore proposed.	73
IDV	Anglos (70, 79-91), Netherlands (80), Italy (76), Belgium (75), France (71), Nordics (63-74), Germanics (55-68)	55-91, Anglos 79-91	55-91, Anglos 79-91	75-111, Anglos 99-111	High IDV appears to be beneficial for creativity/-high innovation, for accurate communication and for rapid decision-making (mainly FTE16+). The highly innovative countries had high IDV scores; a high-IDV score of 105, the average of the Anglos was therefore proposed.	105
MAS	Japan (95), Austria (79), Venezuela (73), Italy (70), Mexico (69), other Germanics (66-70), Anglos (52-68)	52-95	50-102, Germanics 73-77	40-83, Germanics 54-58	High MAS appears to be beneficial for low innovation, routine tasks (mainly FTE13yrs), and for safety in the running of organised action teams (FTE13&16). However, Japan scores much higher than all other countries, and is not a replicable model for MAS; a high-MAS score of 75 (FTE13) and 56 (FTE16) is therefore proposed, based on the Germanics.	75 (producers) (organised action) 56
UAI	Greece (112), Portugal (104), Guatemala (101), Uruguay (100), Belgium (94), Salvador (94), Japan (92), ... South Korea (85), ... Taiwan (69).	69-112	71-114, JP,KW&TW 94,87,71	55-98	High uncertainty avoidance appears to be beneficial in low innovation tasks and routine situations not involving unforeseen events (e.g. following SOPs at all times). A high-UAI score of 84 is proposed based on the average FTE13 scores of JP, KR and TW.	84

Table 5-18: High scores utilised for cultural dimensions

Based on the information in Table 5-18, the 'high' scores for Hofstede's original four dimensions, were proposed as power distance (PDI) = 73 (13yrs FTE), individualism (IDV) = 105 (16yrs+ FTE), masculinity (MAS) = 75 (13yrs FTE) & 56 (16yrs+ FTE), and uncertainty avoidance (UAI) = 84. As is the case with the 'low' scores, these recommended optimum scores were best estimates based on limited information, and should not be taken to imply an accuracy to within +/-1 point (or +/-1%).

The 'low' and 'high' cultural dimension scores listed in Tables 5-17 and 5-18 were used in the models developed in later chapters.

For more extensive details of country cultural dimension scores and distributions, the reader is recommended to examine Hofstede (2001), exhibits 4.2, 5.7, 6.8, 6.17, A5.1 and A5.3. The first four exhibits provide 2-dimensional maps of cultural dimension scores (UAI x PDI, IDV x UAI, IDV x MAS and UAI x MAS) for fifty countries and three regions; the latter two exhibits provide country cultural dimension scores and ranks.

5.5.2 Relative weighting factors for cultural dimensions

The author collected culture dimension predictive powers from his own pilot studies (see Tables 5-2, 5-4, 5-6, 5-8, 5-10, 5-13 and 5-14) and from published studies that were identified in the literature. These are presented in Tables 5-19 and 5-20.

Team type	Cultural dimension	Relative contributions of cultural dimensions	Relative contributions corrected to reflect positive performance
Student groups	UAI	-1.000	-1.000
	UAI diversity	0.313	0.313
RAE2008 (P&A)	MAS	-1.000	-1.000
	MAS diversity	-0.803	-0.803
RAE2008 (CE)	MAS diversity	-1.000	-1.000
English Premiership football (single match)	MAS	0.739	0.739
	UAI	1.000	1.000
English Premiership (team over season)	UAI	1.000	1.000
Aircraft accident/FLE rates	PDI	0.622	-0.622
	IDV	-1.000	1.000
	MAS	-0.704	0.704
	UAI	0.762	-0.762
Maritime accident rates	IDV	-1.000	1.000
	UAI	0.395	-0.395

Table 5-19: Cultural dimension contributions (author's pilot studies)

These culture scores have been normalised in order to provide an option to refine the weightings applied to the cultural dimensions in the models and tools described in the following three chapters.

Researchers/-innovation type	Best estimate of study creativity/-innovation type	Cultural dimension	Predictive powers of cult. dims	Normalised contribution of cultural dimension*
Kaasa & Vadi (2010) – high-tech patents (Eurostat & ESS DB)	Innovation (high end)	PDI	-0.39	-0.736
		IDV	0.22	0.415
		MAS	-0.41	-0.774
		UAI	-0.53	-1.000
Kaasa & Vadi (2010) – all patents (Eurostat & ESS DB)	Innovation	PDI	-0.50	-0.847
		IDV	0.24	0.407
		MAS	-0.43	-0.729
		UAI	-0.59	-1.000
Kaasa & Vadi (2010) – biotech patents (Eurostat & ESS DB	Biotech innovation	PDI	-0.43	0.935
		IDV	-0.1	0.217
		MAS	-0.27	-0.587
		UAI	-0.46	-1.000
Shane (1992) – inventiveness	Inventiveness/-creativity	PDI	-0.38	-0.931
		IDV	0.408	1.000
Rinne & Steel (2012) – GII composite innov'n output	Innovation	PDI	-0.58	-0.879
		IDV	0.66	1.000
		UAI	0.00	0.000
Efrat (2014) – patents/popul'n – no discrimination (SEM)	Innovation DO NOT USE	PDI	-0.07	-0.280
		IDV	-0.14	-0.560
		MAS	0.15	-0.600
		UAI	-0.25	-1.000
Efrat (2014) – scientific & technical journal articles	Searching for knowledge	PDI	-0.61	-1.000
		IDV	0.51	0.8361
		MAS	-0.31	-0.508
		UAI	-0.56	-0.918
Willems (2007) – patents (Euro – EPO, USA – USPTO), 1999-2004	Innovation	PDI	-0.180	-0.571
		IDV	0.315	1.000
		MAS	0.193	0.6127
		UAI	-0.099	-0.314

* The predictive powers of the various cultural dimensions were dependent on the various additional input factors taken into account in the publishing researcher's study (e.g. GDP-per capita or R&D investment intensity); these differed from study to study. Therefore it was necessary to normalise the cultural contributions; this was achieved by dividing the predictive power of each cultural dimension by the absolute value of the predictive power of the biggest cultural contributor.

Table 5-20: Cultural dimension contributions for creativity/-innovation (published studies)

5.6 Potential issues with Hofstede's cultural framework

Following pilot study work and analysis work utilising Hofstede's cultural framework, it would be useful at this stage to consider further some aspects of the framework that could have affected the accuracy of results and could also reduce the effectiveness of the culture tools that are described in the following chapters.

5.6.1 The incremental addition of cultural dimensions

Following work by Michael Bond, a fifth dimension (long-term orientation) was added to Hofstede's framework (Geert H. Hofstede, 2001) and, following Minkov's detailed analysis of the World Values Survey, a sixth dimension (indulgence vs. restraint) was added and the fifth dimension was revised (Geert H. Hofstede et al., 2010). As stated earlier in this thesis, due to the lack of comprehensive country scores when this research began, the latter two dimensions were not used. However, there were issues associated with the addition of extra dimensions – it would have been highly unlikely that the extended framework represented the optimum separation between dimensions. Ideally, the data for all existing dimensions in the framework should have been re-evaluated, and reallocated to a set of new dimensions (with no prior commitment to the number of dimensions); some of these might have been sufficiently similar to the old dimensions to retain their original names and essential characteristics, some might not. Hofstede, in his forward to Minkov's book (Minkov, 2011), commented that, if he were to start again, he would probably begin with the World Values Survey[38]; this is precisely what Minkov did in order to produce his four-dimensional cultural framework. However, Minkov's 2011 publication appeared too late to be utilised in the research described in this thesis. The author of this thesis, if starting two years later, might have chosen Minkov's framework, rather than Hofstede's[39].

5.6.2 The calculation of cultural dimension scores

Hofstede normalised the culture scores he obtained from his original samples so that the countries' scores ranged from zero to one hundred, although this range changed with the addition of new countries to the samples. However, as a consequence of this normalisation, the scores only reflected a country's relative position amongst a group of countries, rather than reflecting (directly) any tendency to think or behave in a certain way. This lack of absolute meaning caused the author of this thesis difficulties in making judgements of optimum 'low' and 'high' scores (see Subsection 5.5.1). This point is discussed further at the end of the next chapter.

---

[38] See Web page http://www.worldvaluessurvey.org/wvs.jsp for information on the World Value Survey (WVS) and for access to WVS data.

[39] But note that the author of this thesis has not yet found any significant studies that have utilised Minkov's framework.

5.7 Summary of data collection and analysis

Relevant studies from the literature were evaluated and, in combination with the author's pilot studies, enabled a number of general relationships between culture dimension scores and team performances in various situations to be identified. In particular, quantitative scores were assigned to the 'low' and 'high' cultural dimension scores identified in the literature review and in the author's studies; these scores formed an essential part of the data basis of the team culture tools that are described in the following chapters.

A contribution was made to current understandings of masculinity, uncertainty avoidance and cultural diversity.

6 A first model and team culture tool

6.1 Introduction

This chapter describes the development of a first model and team culture tool (the TCT1). In this and subsequent chapters, the *terms* 'mission', 'task' and 'task set' are used interchangeably.

The first prototype of the culture tool was intended to produce a direct score of culture-based team effectiveness. The purpose of developing the first prototype was to gain an understanding of the limitations imposed by our current knowledge of the effects of culture, in particular when attempting to quantify these effects directly in terms of team performance. It was therefore expected to represent a step too far, i.e. to be attempting to 'do too much with the limited data available to us'. It also provided a platform to test and assess a vital component of any culture tool – the team cultural profiler.

6.2 Basis of the first model (TCT1)

This section is intended to provide an overview of the model behind the first tool, in particular, the basis on which it generated a measure of team performance, and the assumptions that lay behind the approach.

6.2.1 Overview of the TCT1

The performance prediction model underlying the first team culture tool took the team cultural profile (generated by the team cultural profiler when the user entered the team member details) and applied it to three task/mission factors. The team culture scores reduced the effectiveness of each of the team /mission factors to varying degrees based on how far these scores were away from their optimum scores for each of the factors; the resultant factor effectiveness values were expressed as percentages. The user entered the relative importance of the three task/mission factors as weights (e.g. 50, 100 and 115), and the performance prediction model used those weights to calculate an overall cultural-profile-based efficiency for that team carrying out that task/-mission. Figure 6-1 provides an outline flow diagram of the model.

The three task/mission factors - *creativity and innovation requirements, interaction (communication and co-ordination) requirements* and *requirements for handling uncertainty and dealing with failures and errors*, were considered to cover a sufficiently wide range of team /task/-mission types to enable an initial evaluation of the TCT1 model. The omission of the other two factors - *management & decision-making* and *situation awareness* - from the model would reduce its predictive capability, but it was considered to be important to produce a simple first test-bed for the model and tool.

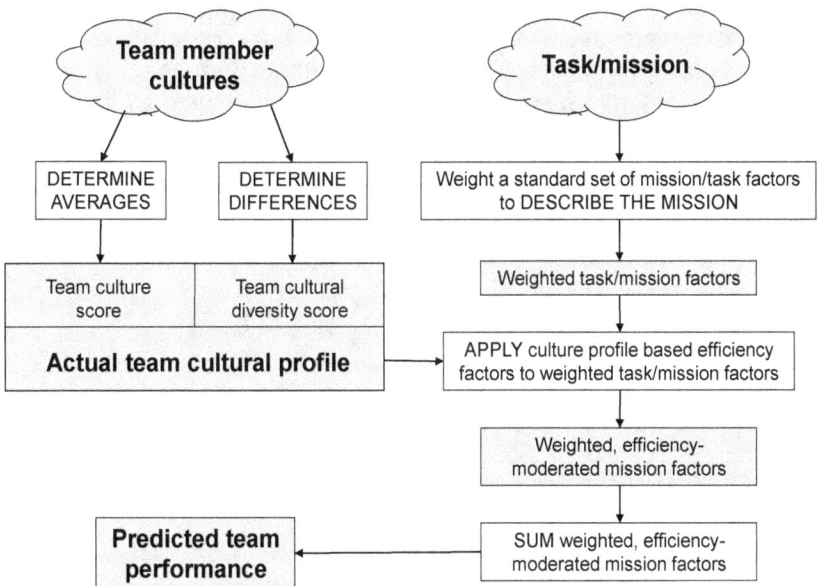

Figure 6-1: Flow diagram of TCT1 culture/mission model

6.2.2 Underpinning assumptions of the TCT1

The three underpinning assumptions of the first performance prediction model are described below.

a) Capturing the cultural traits of an actual or proposed team

It was assumed that the cultural traits of an actual or proposed team could be adequately captured by utilising the default national scores of Hofstede's original four cultural dimensions for each team member (and deriving the team cultural diversity based on these scores).

b) Capturing the actual or proposed team's task/mission

It was assumed that the tasks or mission of the team could be captured sufficiently for the purposes of this 'Aunt Sally'[40] by weighting three 'standard' task/mission factors compared to each other.

c) Calculating the effects of the team's cultural traits on the task/mission factors

For each of the task mission factors, it was assumed that the cultural traits of the team potentially reduced the performance of each task/-mission factor from a theoretical ideal performance (depending how far away the cultural trait was from the ideal trait, as captured by the culture scores), and that a worst-case scenario (in terms of cultural traits) would result in very poor factor performance.

The implications of the above assumptions and the degree to which they were found to be justified are discussed later in this chapter.

6.3   Detailed description of the TCT1

The first model, the TCT1, was based on profiling the team in terms of national culture scores, and profiling the mission in terms of a subset of the factors identified in Subsection 3.3.3 and detailed in Subsection 4.4.1. The task/mission factors chosen were:

- Creativity or innovation requirements
- Communication and co-ordination requirements
- Level of uncertainty/unpredictability

Irrespective of the mission, a particular team cultural profile would affect each of the three task/mission factors the same way, reducing the team's performance (compared to 'ideal') of each of these factors by its own culture-based efficiency factor. It was the relative *weightings* of the mission factors that would determine the overall effects of those culture-based efficiency factors in the final 'performance as a team' value.

Figure 6-2 illustrates the actual TCT1 as implemented in the Microsoft Excel spread sheet program.

---

[40] 'Aunt Sally': A person or thing that is set up as a target for criticism. High accuracy was not a requirement in this model, rather the ability to demonstrate a principle, its weaknesses and limitations.

It can be seen from Figure 6-2, that the team cultural profile (derived from team member nationalities and years in full-time education, see Subsection 6.3.1), was used to derive estimates of internal communication capability and potential innovation capability. These factors were then combined with the task/mission profile weights (manually entered as estimates) and summed to produce an estimate of likely team performance of the given mission profile.

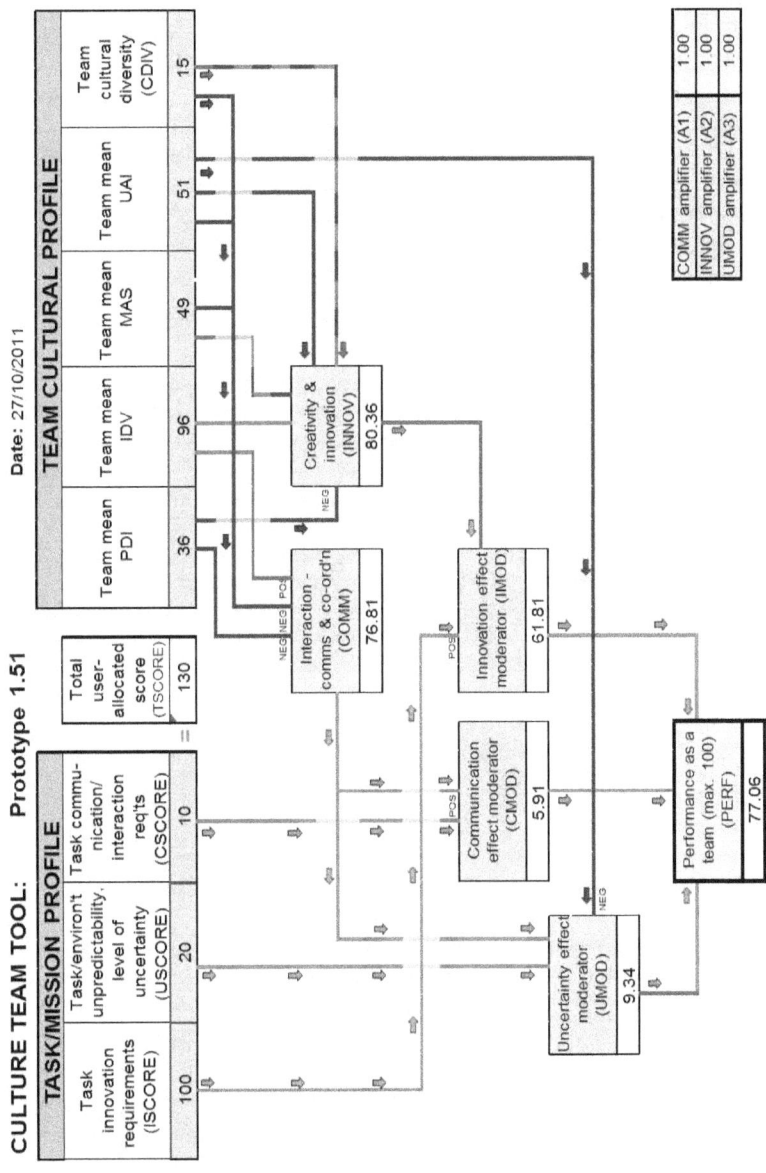

Figure 6-2: Excel implementation of the TCT1

A description of an early version of the TCT1 can be found in Hodgson et al. (2011).

6.3.1 Profiling the team

Because one of the key potential uses of the methodology and tool was to assess the goodness of fit between complex sociotechnical systems and their users, where we might know nothing about potential users other than their likely nationalities and education, the tool's team profiler was designed to operate with default national culture scores.

As stated in Chapter 4, Hofstede's original four-dimensional cultural framework (Geert H. Hofstede, 1984) had been selected as the basis for determining team member culture scores, and a measure of cultural diversity had been developed based on the concept of cultural distance. Table 6-1 illustrates the team cultural profiler.

Team member no.	Nationality	Full time education (years)	CULTURE SCORES (corrected for years in full time education)				CULTURAL DIVERSITY SCORES				
			PDI	IDV	MAS	UAI	PDI	IDV	MAS	UAI	Mean diversity
1	Germany	16	25	87	54	51	12	10	8	17	12
2	France	16	55	91	31	72	22	8	21	24	19
3	Great Britain	16	25	109	54	21	12	15	8	35	17
4	Germany	16	25	87	54	51	12	10	8	17	12
5	Italy	16	38	96	58	61	12	8	10	17	12
6	France	16	55	91	31	72	22	8	21	24	19
7	Great Britain	16	25	109	54	21	12	15	8	35	17
8	Italy	16	38	96	58	61	12	8	10	17	12
...	....	...	...	...	...	...	...	...	...	...	...
14											
15											
	Team scores →		36	96	49	51	15	10	12	23	15

Table 6-1: TCT1 cultural profiler output

In order to profile the team, the user was required to enter, for each team member, nationality and number of years in full time education. The tool then looked up the standard Hofstede culture scores for the relevant country, applied educational corrections, and entered them into the table. The tool then calculated each individual's average cultural distance from other team members, for each of the four dimensions, and also calculated the team's mean culture scores and cultural diversity scores for the four cultural dimensions. Table 6-1 presents an example team; this shows inputs in the form of team member nationalities and years of education (columns 2 and 3), and outputs in terms of culture and diversity scores (columns 4 to 12). The team cultural profile automatically fed into the later calculations of the tool (see upper right-hand side of Figure 6-2), and the performance estimate was calculated based on this.

6.3.2 Profiling the task/mission

To profile the task/mission, the user simply entered estimates of the relative importance of the three mission profile factors. In the spread sheet of Figure 6-2, the factor values have been entered as 100, 20 and 10, as the task is concerned primarily with innovation; note that, as it is the *relative* sizes of the estimates that matter, these could have been entered as 20, 4 and 2.

6.3.3 Interpreting the results

The tool produced a direct estimate of the predicted performance level associated with the team cultural traits. In the example of Figure 6-2, the culture-based performance was estimated to be 77% of the optimum (cultural) performance. A limited amount of other information was available in the other spread-sheet boxes; for example, on the basis of the culture scores, the interaction/communication capability was calculated to be 77% and the innovation/creativity capability was calculated to be 80%.

6.3.4 Basis of the predicted performance equations

The six equations that produced the culture-moderated performance estimate of the TCT1 are explained individually in the following paragraphs. The equations were taken from the Excel implementation of the 1st prototype culture team tool[41], see Figure 6-2. There were no *absolute* measures of performance in the literature, nor could any be gained from the studies, only estimates of *relative* effector strength. Therefore, 'amplifier' variables were placed in the equations that contained culture scores; these enabled the culture effect strengths to be increased or decreased to reflect empirical results. The equations' *optimum* high and low cultural dimension scores (where required) were taken from Tables 5-17 & 5-18.

---

[41] Note that the '10$^{8'}$ and '100' values in the denominators of the following equations corrected the results arising from multiplying percentages together.

a) Team internal communication capability (COMM)

There was little to base this equation on other than the general literature including Hofstede and Helmreich & Merritt (Subsection 3.3 of the literature review). For effective communication, optimum scores for PDI, MAS, UAI and CDIV were low, whereas the optimum value for IDV was high. The literature was in general agreement that the biggest effectors were PDI, IDV and CDIV, with MAS and UAI having a lesser effect. Accordingly, PDI, IDV and CDIV have each been weighted 25%, MAS and UAI have each been weighted 12.5%. These weightings can only be regarded as approximate.

PDI:	Optimum value=16, weighted 25%
IDV:	Optimum value=105, weighted 25%
MAS:	Optimum value=4, weighted 12.5%
UAI:	Optimum value=9, weighted 12.5%
CDIV:	Optimum value=0, weighted 25%

$$COMM = \frac{\begin{array}{c}(100 - A1 * 0.25 * ABS(PDI - 16)) \times \\ (100 - A1 * 0.25 * ABS(105 - IDV)) \times (100 - A1 * 0.125 * ABS(MAS - 4)) \times \\ (100 - A1 * 0.125 * ABS(UAI - 9) \times (100 - A1 * 0.250 * ABS(15 - CDIV))\end{array}}{100000000}$$

Note the amplifier variable, A1, in the above equation; this has been set to '1' (no effect) in the example illustrated in Figure 6-2, but could be used to 'boost' the effects of culture on performance.

b) Team innovation/creativity (INNOV)

The innovation/creativity efficiency equation utilised information from the normalised values that were provided in Table 5-20 of Subsection 5.5.2. Relevant values for the four cultural dimensions were averaged and renormalised, see Table 6-2 for details.

Researchers	Dependent variable	Relative predictive powers			
		PDI	**IDV**	**MAS**	**UAI**
Kaasa & Vadi (2010)	Innovation	-0.847	0.407	-0.729	-1.000
Rinne & Steel (2012)	Innovation	-0.879	1.000	N/E	0
Willems (2007)	Innovation	-0.571	1.000	0.613	-0.314
Average	**(innovation)**	**-0.767**	**0.802**	**-0.058**	**-0.438**
Renormalised (max=1)	**∑ABS=2.574 →**	**-0.956**	**1.000**	**-0.072**	**-0.546**
Renormalised (∑ABS=1)	**∑ABS=1.000 →**	**-0.371**	**0.389**	**-0.028**	**-0.212**

Table 6-2: Cultural dimension predictive powers for innovation

Note: As this subsection was about innovation (not invention or high creativity), only *'innovation'* entries were selected from Table 5-20 (including only one of Kaasa & Vadi's entries, as the datasets overlapped).

PDI: Optimum value=16, weighted 37.1%

IDV: Optimum value=105, weighted 38.9%

MAS: Optimum value=4, weighted 2.8% (but see later comment)

UAI: Optimum value=9, weighted 21.2%

CDIV: Optimum value=15, weighted 25% (the average of the above

$$INNOV = \frac{\begin{pmatrix}(100 - A2 * 0.371 * ABS(PDI - 16)) \times \\ (100 - A2 * 0.389 * ABS(105 - IDV)) \times (100 - A2 * 0.028 * ABS(MAS - 4)) \times \\ (100 - A2 * 0.212 * ABS(UAI - 9)) \times (100 - A2 * 0.250 * ABS(15 - CDIV))\end{pmatrix}}{100000000}$$

Note the amplifier variable, A2, in the above equation; this has been set to '1' (no effect) in the example illustrated in Figure 6-2.

Comment on the weight used for MAS: Although MAS appeared here to have an almost negligible effect, the two scores in Table 6-2 that provided the average were -0.729 and +0.613 (when normalised to a maximum of 1.000), i.e. in each case MAS contributed significantly to the respective predictive model, but in the opposite direction, thus almost cancelling out (the average of the two was -0.072). Further comments on this are included in Subsection 6.5.3(b).

c) Team uncertainty moderator (UMOD)

Handling uncertainty placed a requirement on the team to ensure that members communicated adequately, and was adversely affected by high uncertainty avoidance. The uncertainty moderator (UMOD) took the product of the communication capability (COMM) score and the weighted difference between the actual and optimum UAI score, and factored them by the uncertainty weighting supplied by the user [weighting = score allocated to uncertainty (USCORE) divided by total allocated score (TSCORE)].

$$UMOD = \frac{COMM \times (100 - A3 * 0.500 \times ABS(UAI - 9)) \times USCORE}{TSCORE \times 100}$$

Note the amplifier variable, A3, in the above equation; this has been set to '1' (no effect) in the example illustrated in Figure 6-2.

d) Team communication effect moderator (CMOD)

The team communication effect moderator (CMOD) factored the communication capability (COMM) score by the communication weighting supplied by the user [weighting = score allocated to communication (CSCORE) divided by total allocated score (TSCORE)].

$$CMOD = COMM \times CSCORE/TSCORE$$

e) Team innovation effect moderator (IMOD)

The team innovation effect moderator (IMOD) factored the innovation (INNOV) score by the innovation weighting supplied by the user [weighting = score allocated to innovation (ISCORE) divided by total allocated score (TSCORE)].

$$IMOD = INNOV \times ISCORE/TSCORE$$

f) Performance as a team (PERF)

The *performance as a team* equation simply summed the weighted inputs from the three moderators (unpredictability/uncertainty, communication and innovation).

$$PERF = UMOD + CMOD + IMOD$$

6.4   Evaluation of the TCT1

The TCT1 was tested and analysed on a range of team and mission types (high innovation teams, low innovation teams and aircrew[42]), but was not made available to potential users outside the research team because it was clear that it had several limitations (see Section 6.5).

A paper on the first prototype tool, and the associated culture research was presented at the IEEE System of Systems Conference in Albuquerque (A. Hodgson et al., 2011). The presentation generated considerable interest, and useful discussions with researchers and industrialists took place. Following a demonstration of the tool, several issues about the tool and general approach were raised, and were later taken into account when the second tool was developed.

---

[42] These were specific team *types*, not specific teams, i.e. exemplars that were used to assess whether the tool could produce acceptable results.

6.5 Limitations, and a re-evaluation of the underpinning assumptions

The model performed a useful function in highlighting weaknesses in the general approach to the evaluation of the effects of culture on performance.

6.5.1 Limitations and successes of the tool

It became clear, after testing the tool with a range of mission profiles, that there were several significant problems with the tool, for example:

a) Differentiating between tasks/missions

The tool was unable to differentiate adequately between different tasks/-missions. Low or moderate innovation capability (and a willingness to pursue the mundane) can be more useful than high innovation capability in certain types of team projects, for example when carrying out some forms of process improvement. However, the tool scoring process could not capture this adequately.

b) Relative vs. absolute weighting of cultural dimensions

Subject to the sensitivity limitation stated above, the *relative* weightings of cultural dimensions in the equations could be justified, as they reflected study results from the literature (captured in Tables 5-20 and 6-2). However, the *absolute* weightings[43] (captured in the model and tool by 'tuning' the values of the *amplifier variables* A1, A2 and A3) could only be established by comparisons against the performance of real teams. The author <u>was</u> following the pragmatist principle[44], but in this case, the model was too insensitive for it to be practicable to match its outputs against real-world performances.

c) Providing user guidance

It would be difficult to extend the methodology and tool to provide guidance for team improvement because only limited information was produced. For example, Figure 6-2 indicated a culture-based perfor-

---

[43] In this context, absolute weightings were those weightings applied directly to the task/mission performance measure (e.g. every unit (or 1%) increase in power distance caused a 0.25% reduction in task/mission performance).
[44] See Chapter 2 for a full statement of the pragmatist principle. As Laudan (1978) states, the criteria for assessing the development of a theory should be based on its problem-solving effectiveness, rather than on its falsifiability.

mance rating of 77%. How could we improve this? What were the key problem areas?

d) Increasing sensitivity leads to excessive complexity

To include more task/mission profile factors in the tool, and to split these factors into sub-factors (necessary to capture the nuances of creativity, innovation, etc.), would result in a model of excessive complexity; it would be extremely difficult to maintain the resulting large set of equations, or to modify or to test the model and tool.

e) The cultural profiler

This worked very effectively, and enabled the user to experiment efficiently and effectively with different combinations of team members. However, several researchers (including two researchers at the IEEE System of Systems Conference where the researcher presented a paper on the TCT1) commented on the limitations of being constrained to auto-matically-generated individual cultural profiles based on a single nationality for each team member. Therefore the cultural profiler would be modified in the second culture tool to enable more flexibility.

6.5.2 Re-evaluation of the original assumptions

With regard to the assumptions behind the model, the following conclusions could be drawn:

a) Capturing the cultural traits of an actual or proposed team

It was considered that this was the least problematical part of the model and tool and that, inasmuch as any quantitative modeller of default national culture could capture traits, the cultural profiler performed adequately.

b) Capturing the actual or proposed team's task/mission

This model demonstrated the need for a much more detailed task/-mission profile in order for a realistic, adequately-discriminating tool performance.

c) Calculating the effects of the team's cultural traits on the task/mission factors

Although this assumption (that a worst-case scenario cultural mismatch to mission would likely result in very poor performance) was probably true, the first team culture tool (TCT1) could not reliably demonstrate such an effect because the required data was not available, and the detailed relationships for such a model would be difficult to verify or to incorporate in a tool.

6.5.3 Comments on the application of Hofstede's framework

Some of the problems that arose in the modelling of the TCT1 may have been caused by the nature of the cultural dimensions, others by easily-made assumptions about the nature of the associated statistical distributions. These are discussed below.

a) The 'relative', rather than 'absolute' nature of Hofstede's dimension scores

As discussed in Subsection 5.6.2, Hofstede's cultural scores were normalised based on the range of values obtained in his analysis of the original set of countries in his survey, thus they had no 'absolute' meaning. The lack of meaning associated with these scores made it difficult to develop absolute relationships between cultural values and their effects on communication, conflict, etc.

Instead of the above 'relative' scales, it would have been more informative to have an international set of culture scores that represented the absolute scores (say from zero to one hundred) from answers to cultural dimension-related questions. No individual or group could score less than zero or more than one hundred for a cultural dimension. In such a framework, it would be likely that the distribution of country scores would be much less than the theoretical zero to one hundred range, perhaps thirty to seventy for one dimension, fifteen to sixty for another, but those scores would tell us much more – within the limitations of the original questions – about the cultures of those countries and about human societies in general. We might deduce that (say) human societies are much less variable along certain dimensions than along others.

The difficulties that the author had in assigning maximum and minimum cultural dimension scores (see Subsection 5.5.1) would have been eased if the default culture scores had been absolute rather than relative. A score of one hundred for uncertainty avoidance would have implied a society that was terrified of everything that was less than familiar in its world, a society that rejected all innovations, etc., rather than just 'the most uncertainty-avoiding society'. When building the equations for the TCT1 (Subsection 6.3.4), the author was able to assign relative values to the effects of cultural dimensions on behaviours, but there was no clear basis for the assignment of absolute relationships between cultural dimension scores and behaviours.

Note that the above discussion is not intended to imply that a change to 'absolute' measures would be any form of panacea, merely that a score's meaning would be clear in terms of answering a certain group of questions that were considered to relate to a particular cultural trait.

b) Further issues with the masculinity culture dimension

When developing the innovation equation in Subsection 6.3.4(b), there were large effector scores for masculinity (from the literature), but they were of opposite signs, as was illustrated in Table 3-2 of the literature review and Table 6-2 of this chapter. These scores effectively cancelled each other out, resulting in little input to the innovation equation of the TCT1 on the part of the masculinity cultural dimension. This may have been due to a statistical error in one of the published pilot studies due to the shape of the masculinity/innovation curve[45]; G. Halkos & Tzeremes (2011) suggested that masculinity's beneficial effects on innovation might peak at a score of 70 (that is, 70 uncorrected for FTE, 58 when corrected for 16 years FTE). If this were the case, then samples with low MAS averages would show a positive MAS predictor sign, and samples with high MAS averages would show a negative MAS predictor sign. The authors of one of the studies, Kaasa & Vadi (2010), did not provide a mean value for the MAS samples in their publication, so the above supposition could not be tested. However, there appeared to be extremely variable results in the wider literature with regard to the effects of masculinity, so there were perhaps unrecognised factors associated with this cultural dimension; for example, the masculinity cultural trait might only come into play under certain circumstances or in certain situations.

In the case of a study of airline pilots (A. C. Merritt, 2000) and one of military officers under training (Soeters, 1997), the measured masculinity scores did not correlate with the study samples' default country masculinity scores.

6.5.4 Conclusions

Several conclusions were reached, in particular:

a) The basis of the performance measure was flawed

There were three main problems with the model:

---

[45] E.g. an incorrect assumption that there is a linear relationship between the masculinity score and its effects on innovation performance when the actual shape has a distinct maximum within the range of samples.

i) ***Relative vs. absolute data and relationships:*** At the time of this research, it was not possible to obtain data on absolute relationships between cultural traits (as represented by cultural dimension scores) and aspects of team performance. A methodology based on the relative effects of culture was therefore required for the second model and prototype.

ii) ***Insensitivity and complexity:*** Even if the data had been available, the model was too insensitive to incremental differences between teams. The full range of factors and their sub-factors would have to be utilised to improve the model's sensitivity; however, this would result in excessive model complexity.

iii) ***User information and guidance:*** The tool did not (and could not) provide information to inform the user adequately or to guide him/her in team improvement.

b) The method of obtaining the *team cultural profile* was easy and effective to use

The cultural profiler proved efficient, effective and understandable in use; discussions with other researchers led to proposed improvements in its representational flexibility, to be incorporated in the next tool.

6.6   Summary of the TCT1

Evaluations of the first prototype team culture tool demonstrated the effectiveness of the team cultural profiler, but highlighted issues with the representation of task/mission profiles, raised some issues with regard to the cultural framework, and with the method by which an estimate of potential team performance was obtained. It was therefore decided to carry the cultural profiler (in improved form) across to the second model and prototype team culture tool, but to develop a different assessment methodology, based on transforming the mission/task profile into an ideal or desirable culture profile to form the basis for a comparison with the actual team culture.

7 A second model and team culture tool

7.1 Introduction

This chapter describes the development and evaluation of the second model and team culture tool (TCT2). Unlike the first culture tool (TCT1), this version of the team culture tool was *not* intended to predict the 'absolute' performances of individual teams; instead, it was intended to highlight where culture was *likely* to be a significant factor in under-performance or heightened risk by assessing the goodness of fit between team and mission. This 'fit' was based on the generation of discrepancies between the *desirable* team culture profile (based on the mission) and the *actual* team culture profile.

To use the tool, the user described the team cultural profile, as in the TCT1, and described the team task or mission by weighting a set of factors and their sub-factors; these factors were affected by culture and contributed positively or negatively to the task or mission.

7.2 Basis of the second model (TCT2)

This section is intended to provide an overview of the model behind the second tool, in particular, the basis on which it generated a measure of fit between teams and their task/mission requirements, and the assumptions that lay behind the approach.

7.2.1 Overview of the TCT2

The logic of the second performance prediction model was based on profiling the team via its members' national cultural traits[46] (as was the first model), profiling the task/mission in terms of five task/mission factors and their sub-factors (which were associated with specific cultural traits), and deriving a set of cultural 'discrepancies' that formed the basis for the assessment of team fitness for the task/mission.

---

[46] These 'traits' were captured in shorthand form using Hofstede's cultural framework.

The team cultural profile was created by entering team members' nationalities and their education levels into the model; this then calculated team average cultural scores and diversity scores, based on Hofstede's default national culture scores. The task/mission profile was produced by weighting the set of five task/mission factors identified in Subsection 3.3.3, and their sub-factors (detailed in Subsection 4.4.1). These task/mission factors were:

- Management and decision-making requirements

- Creativity and innovation requirements

- Interaction (communication and co-ordination) requirements

- Requirements for handling uncertainty and dealing with failures and errors

- Situational awareness requirements

The *task/mission profile*, produced by the user by weighting the above factors and their sub-factors, was mapped across to a *desirable cultural profile* based on the 'low' and 'high' scores derived in Subsection 5.5.1 and the effects of national culture described in the literature and captured in Section 3.3. This *desirable cultural profile* was compared to the *actual team cultural profile* generated earlier by entering team member nationalities; discrepancies between the two were then derived. These discrepancies formed the basis for the assessment of mission fit.

Figure 7-1 presents a flow diagram of the above profiling and comparison processes.

A key aspect of this approach was that it allowed the user to define the relative importance of each of the above five team factors *and* their sub-factors to the team task or mission. This approach acknowledged that mission or task requirements could be changed by the utilisation of new processes and/or new technologies. For example, the need for joint (or shared) situation awareness could be met, at least in part, by a future intelligent agent that proactively informed crews of sociotechnical systems (such as aircraft, oil rigs or power stations) of developing hazards.

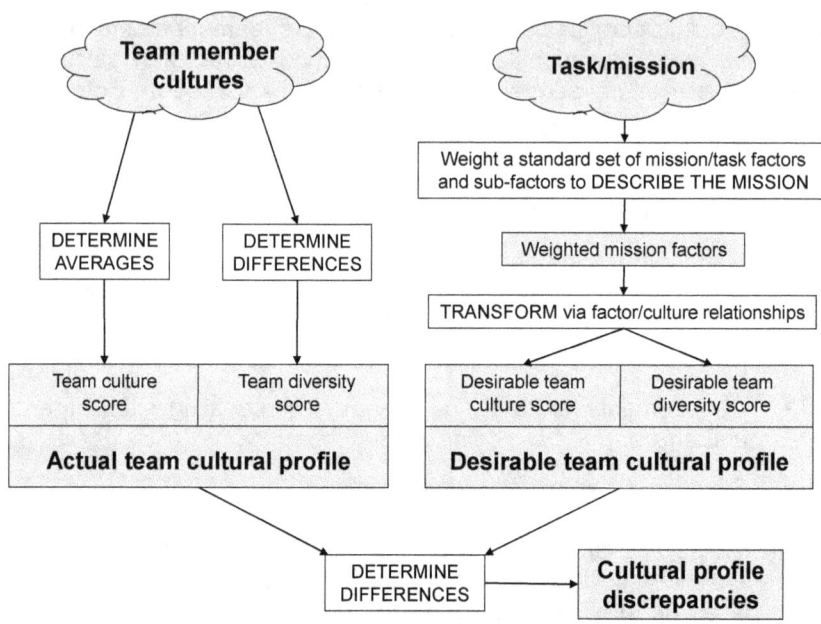

Figure 7-1: Flow diagram of TCT2 culture/mission model

7.2.2 Underpinning assumptions of the TCT2

The underpinning assumptions of the second performance prediction model are described in detail below.

a) Capturing the cultural traits of an actual or proposed team

As with the first model, it was assumed that the cultural traits of an actual or proposed team could be *adequately* captured by utilising the default national scores of Hofstede's original four cultural dimensions for each team member (and deriving the team cultural diversity based on these scores).

b) Capturing the desirable team cultural traits

It was assumed that the tasks or mission of the team could be captured sufficiently by weighting five 'standard' factors and their sub-factors; this required the following:

i) ***Capturing the culture-sensitive elements of team tasks or missions:*** It was assumed that a small number of behavioural factors and their sub-factors could capture the elements of a range of team tasks or missions that were most affected by cultural traits.

ii) Relating culture-sensitive elements of tasks/missions to culture traits: It was assumed that the cultural traits required for optimum performance of the factors/sub-factors of (i) above could be adequately identified and encapsulated in the model.

iii) Describing a particular task or mission in terms of the above factors: It was assumed that users had sufficient knowledge to be able to weight the above five factors and their sub-factors with enough accuracy to define adequately the team's behavioural requirements for the task or mission.

c) Obtaining useful information from the discrepancies

It was assumed that the cultural discrepancies between actual and desirable cultural traits were meaningful, i.e. they informed the user of something useful about potential team performance and/or team problems.

Note: The terms 'adequate' and 'adequately' related to the effects of inaccuracy on the performance of the model and tool. The adequacy issue was complicated by the fact that inaccuracies in various areas would potentially add together to reduce the overall effectiveness of the tool in use. It was therefore difficult to judge the degree of adequacy of individual steps in the process; however, the overall performance could be adjudged from the tool's effectiveness in the hands of users.

The implications of the above assumptions and the degree to which they were found to be justified are discussed later in this chapter.

7.3 Detailed description of the TCT2

The two key elements of the model and tool were the team cultural profiler, and the task/mission profiler. These are further described below.

7.3.1 Team cultural profiler

This was based on the cultural profiler described in Subsection 6.3.1, with the addition of two further options:

- **Hybrid (or dual) cultural nationality:** This facility was provided to enable better alignment for those team members who were bicultural, e.g. because they had emigrated from one cultural area to another. On selecting this option, the user was expected to select not one, but two nationalities when filling in the partic- ular team member's details in the cultural profile table. The relevant culture dimension scores for the two nationalities were then retrieved by the tool (from a table that listed Hofstede's default culture scores by country), corrected for the team member's years in full time education, the four pairs of scores (2 x PDI, 2 x IDV, etc.) were averaged, and these four averaged cultural dimension scores were used in all further calculations for that individual.

- **Manual entry of cultural scores:** This facility was provided for those team members with individually-assessed culture dimension scores, or those with clear deviations from the mean of their culture (e.g. an American pilot with a very high power distance). On selecting this option, the user was expected to enter, manually, the team member's scores for the four Hofstede cultural dimensions. The user's nationality was then ignored by the tool, and the manually-entered cultural dimension scores were used directly in all further calculations for that individual.

7.3.2 Team task/mission profiler

The five-factor team/task profiler framework is described in detail in this subsection. The key aim of this profiler was to enable the user to describe the task/mission profile of the team in terms of factors which were associated with particular cultural dimension scores or ranges. By selecting and weighting the five major factors and their sub-factors (i.e. by indicating how important they were to the team mission), the user enabled the tool to generate an associated set of 'optimum' or 'desirable' cultural dimension scores. Note that, for different aspects of a particular mission (e.g. *communications* and *following standard operational procedures*), contradictory 'desirable' cultural dimension scores could be generated – this reflected the reality of multifaceted tasks and missions.

The five factors were originally described in Subsection 3.3 and expanded in Subsection 4.4.1. The culture dimension scores of Tables 5-17 and 5-18 were used where appropriate to quantify the scores for the sub-factors of the five factors[47].

Figure 7-2 is based on the innovation-related findings of Subsection 3.3 of the literature review, in particular Figure 3.2 and the author's pilot study findings, combined with the 'low' and 'high' cultural dimension scores as derived in Section 5.5.1 This figure was used to obtain quanti-

---

[47] In cases where no evidence was found for the effects of a particular cultural dimension on a sub-factor, no score was allocated to that factor for that cultural dimension.

tative values for 'in-between' sub-factors of the *creativity & innovation* factor.

Two of the relationships in Figure 7-2 were particularly difficult to assess. Firstly, MAS appeared to be strongly positive for low innovation, but not clear for high innovation (but see comment in previous chapter). Secondly, the results for cultural diversity appeared to be inconclusive and frequently contradictory; however, a degree of cultural diversity appeared to be beneficial in the case of high innovation/creativity, but not in the case of low innovation. The value of '15' on the right-hand scale of Figure 7-2 represented the approximate equivalent to 20-25% non-nationals, or equivalent to a Shannon Index score of 0.35, as suggested by Barjak (2006) and Barjak & Robinson (2008).

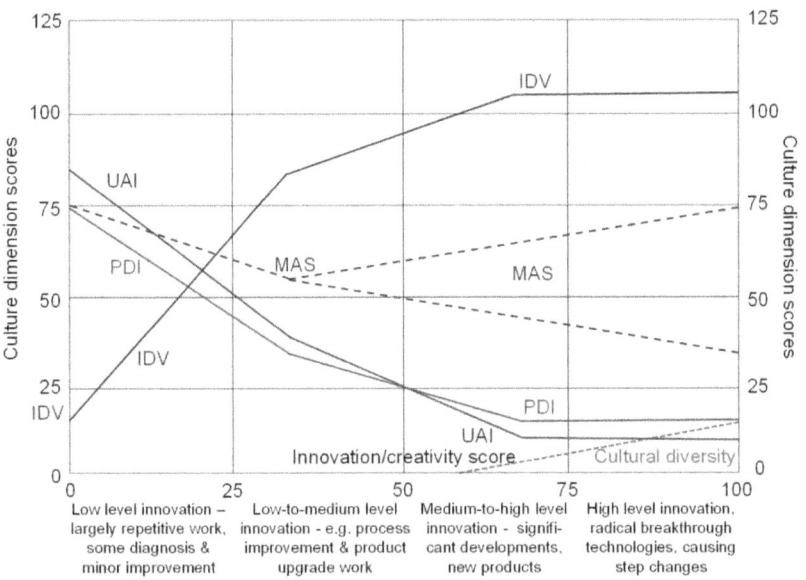

Figure 7-2: Culture/innovation relationships

The detailed scores for the various sub-factors are shown below.

a) Management and decision-making

As stated in Chapter 4, some tasks and missions were best served by authoritarian, strongly centralised management, for example highly auto-mated factory systems or missions involving large military manoeuvres; others, for example complex decisions requiring wide or deep knowledge were typically best served by the consensus-based decentralised, delegating management.

- **Delegation of management and decision-making authority:**

179

- o Centralised, directive, non-consultative management: PDI=high=73; UAI=high=84.

- o Consensus/delegation-based management: PDI=low=16; IDV=high=105; UAI=low=9.

- **Decision-making under uncertainty:** PDI=low=16; UAI=low=9.

- **Following standard operating instructions (SOPs):**

  - o Following SOPs at all times: UAI=high=84.

  - o Abandoning SOPs when appropriate: UAI=low=9.

- **Recognising and correcting mistakes**: PDI=low=16, IDV=high=105, UAI=low=9.

b) Creativity and innovation

Culture, via pressure to conform, willingness to speak out and attitudes to uncertainty, had a considerable effect on creativeness. Some team goals required an ability to produce (and present) a large number of ideas, go against the consensus and engage in a degree of conflict; others required an ability to take new ideas forward towards usable concepts; yet others required an ability to implement existing technologies into products and processes; in this latter situation, disciplined concentration on the task in hand was better than constantly exploring new ideas.

- Developing new ideas and concepts: PDI=low=16; IDV=high=105; MAS=notLow=35to75; UAI=low=9; Cdiv=moderate=15.

- Designing/implementing new products and processes (see Figure 7-2, innovation score=66): PDI=18; IDV=102; MAS=55; UAI=12; Cdiv=3.

- Incorporating ideas developed elsewhere into processes or products (see Figure 7-2, innovation score=33): PDI=35; IDV=80; MAS=55; UAI=38; Cdiv=0.

- Improving, revising designs, processes, process flows, correcting due to failures in the field: PDI=high=75; IDV=low=17; MAS=75; UAI=high=85; Cdiv=0.

- Going against the consensus: PDI=low=16: IDV=high=105: MAS=notLow=35to75.

c) Interaction (communication and co-ordination within the team)

- Say what you mean, mean what you say: PDI=low=16; IDV=high=105; MAS= not applicable (N/A); UAI=low=9.

- Convey meaning diplomatically (typically indirectly): PDI=high=73; IDV=low=17; MAS=N/A; UAI=N/A.

- Communicate rapidly and accurately with colleagues, superiors and subordinates when necessary: PDI=low=16; IDV=high=105; MAS=notLow=35to75; UAI=9; Cdiv=0.

- Communicate about and discuss in-depth complex concepts in a considered manner: PDI=low=16.

- Interact with other team members on a frequent or continuous basis: PDI=low=16; IDV=high=105; Cdiv=0.

- Interact with other team members mainly (or only) at key decision points: *(Any cultural scores.)*

- Share information with other team members whenever possible: PDI=low=16; IDV=high=105; UAI=low=9; Cdiv=0.

- Only share information on a need-to-know basis: *(Any cultural scores)*

d) Handling uncertainty and dealing with failures

Some environments and team goals resulted in highly predictable activities and/or outcomes; other environments resulted in highly unpredictable activities and/or outcomes that had to be accommodated by the team or crew. Cultures (in particular, as measured by their uncertainty avoidance scores) varied greatly in their capabilities to deal with uncertainty.

- Highly-predictable activities and outcomes: PDI=high=73, IDV=low=17, MAS=notLow=35to75, UAI=high=84.

- Highly UNpredictable activities and outcomes: PDI=low=16; IDV=high=105, UAI=low=9.

- Highly predictable activities and outcomes except under rare circumstances when they become highly dangerous and unpredictable: PDI=low=16; IDV=high=105; UAI=low=9; Cdiv=0.

- Must handle errors and failures very quickly: PDI=low=16; IDV=high=105; MAS=notLow=35to75; UAI=low=9; Cdiv=0.

- Should give careful consideration to errors and failures prior to action: PDI=low=16; MAS=notLow=35to75, UAI=low=9.

e) Situation awareness

Operator/crew situation awareness was affected by crew members' willingness to take part in realistic training, their abilities to respond to changing situations (i.e. to reframe) and, in the case of shared situation awareness, their abilities to communicate rapidly and accurately. Situation awareness related primarily to organised action teams, e.g. aircrews, power station operators.

- Must maintain individual situation awareness at all times: UAI=low=9.

- Must maintain shared situation awareness at all times: PDI=low=16; IDV=high=105; MAS=notLow=35to75; UAI=low=9; Cdiv=0.

7.4   Description of the operation of the TCT2

In order to assess the suitability of a team in cultural terms, it was necessary to:

- Profile the team in terms of its cultural traits or characteristics (user input).

- Profile the team mission (including relevant environmental aspects) and thereby generate a desirable cultural profile (user input).

- Compare the two profiles and thus assess the team's suitability or mismatch in terms of discrepancies (tool calculation).

The process of describing the mission was, in reality, a process of weighting the various task-related factors and their sub-factors according to their importance to the performance of the team. The only differences between any two team missions or tasks were the weightings assigned to the factors and sub-factors. The reasons for incorporating weightings of both factors and their sub-factors were:

- The two levels of weighting enabled users to discount, at a high level (i.e. factor level), those items that were not important; for example, for some tasks or missions, *creativity* would not be important, for others, *dealing with uncertainty* or *situation awareness* would not be important.

- Users found it much easier to weight a small number of alternative sub-factors on a comparative basis, rather than the full set of sub-factors.

The following subsections describe the activities and profiles in more detail; as the culture tool represented the implementation of the model, the descriptions are presented in terms of tool usage and processes.

7.4.1 Profiling the team

As stated earlier, the team cultural profiler was based on that used for the first prototype, with the additional options of hybrid nationality and manual entry of cultural dimension scores. The user was first expected to enter team member names or identities, then to select from a dropdown list, for each team member, the choice of input – *single nationality*, *hybrid nationality* or *manual entry*; if 'manual entry' was selected, then the user was expected to manually enter scores for the four Hofstede dimensions. The user was then required to select the number of years in full time education for each team member (from a dropdown list); these factored the scores, based on Bosland's corrections. A field was also provided to record the gender of each team member (M or F), but this was not utilised in the calculations because insufficient data had been found to justify its use.

The team cultural profiler subsequently carried out one of the following courses of action:

- **Single nationality:** Retrieve the four standard culture scores for the relevant country or countries[48], apply educational corrections then enter them into the team culture profile table.

- **Hybrid (dual) nationality:** Retrieve the four standard culture scores for both nationalities, calculate the mean value for each score, apply educational corrections, then enter them into the team culture profile table.

- **Manual entry:** Enter the four user-supplied culture scores into the team culture profile table without further corrections.

Following entry of the above information, the team cultural profiler calculated each individual's average cultural distance from other team members for each of the four dimensions based on the equation described in Subsection 4.3.2, see below:

$$Cd_{ix} \quad = \quad \sum_{j=1}^{N} ABS(Dix - Djx)/(N-1)$$

Where D_{ix}, D_{jx} = scores for cultural dimension 'x' for team members 'i' and 'j', and N = total number of team members

---

[48] Default country scores for the four cultural dimensions were stored in a separate table.

The team cultural profiler also calculated team mean culture scores and mean cultural diversity scores for the four cultural dimensions. See Figure 7-3 for an example team, showing inputs in the form of team member nationalities and education, and outputs in terms of culture and diversity scores.

The example in Figure 7-3 clearly shows the difference between the team cultural profiler of the TCT2 and the earlier version of the team cultural profiler in Table 6-1. Note the facility to enter a single nationality, two nationalities, or to manually enter the individuals' actual culture scores, if known.

7.4.2 Profiling the mission

The task/mission profile in this version of the TCT2 was based on the five major factors and their task-related sub-factors that have been described in detail, along with the associated cultural dimension scores detailed in Subsection 7.3.2.

The team task/mission profiler required the user to:

1. **Select one or more strategic-level descriptions of the team:** This enabled the system to detect large errors in the user's scoring of the factors[49]. If the user's actual or proposed team task/mission was a very close fit to one of the strategic-level descriptions, then the user could just select the strategic level description and ignore the five factors and their sub-factors in order to obtain a default desirable cultural profile.

2. **Weight the five major factors on the basis of their relative importances:** In the 'numeric' version of the TCT2, the user could enter any set of numeric weights, as the tool would recalculate the factor weights to fractional values[50]. A second 'textual' version of the TCT2 utilised dropdown lists in the profiler, enabling users to select a range of options from 'unimportant' to 'extremely important' (or the equivalent); these would be converted to numeric scores.

---

[49] If the user weighted the factors and sub-factors such that the corresponding desirable culture scores were very different from those of the default strategic-level scores, then this was indicative of errors in the user's input; this would result in a warning being shown in the original version of the TCT2.

[50] In the numeric version of the TCT2, the user was recommended to enter '100' or '10' for the most important factor(s), then to enter proportionately lower scores for each of the other factors; following this, the user should do the same for each set of sub-factors. Factors or sub-factors that were of no importance could be ignored by the user, and would be allocated a _zero_ weight by the TCT2.

START HERE >> (INSTRUCTIONS)

(1) Enter team members in table below (top-left table); a minimum of surname, nationality and years full time education are required.

(2) Go to TABLE 2 and follow the instructions at the top of the table >>------>

(3) If the overall discrepancy score is more than 15, then consider changing team membership (see 'TO IMPROVE THE TEAM', below).

Date: 25 March 2012

TEAM CULTURE PROFILE TABLE - enter team member details (in blue areas)

Team ID or description: *Problem solving: Early failure of medium family hatchback brake master cylinder (18 months after release)*

Mbr num	Family name or ID	Fore-name	Choice (of input data)	Nationality 1	Nationality 2 (if applicable)	Gen-der	Full time educ'n (yrs)	CULTURE SCORES (only used with 'Manually enter scores' option) PDI	IDV	MAS	UAI	CULTURE SCORES (corr'd for years in full time education) PDI	IDV	MAS	UAI	CULTURAL DIVERSITY PDI	IDV	MAS	UAI	Mean diversity
1	Appleyard	James	Single nationality	United Kingdom		M	15					34	102	61	26	18	19	4	12	13
2	Chopra	Madhu	Single nationality	India		M	15					72	61	51	31	25	27	7	13	18
3	Field	Susan	Single nationality	United Kingdom		F	15					34	102	61	26	18	19	4	12	13
4	Jarre	David	Hybrid nationality	United Kingdom	France	M	15					49	93	50	52	16	18	9	25	17
5	Jameson	Susan	Single nationality	United Kingdom		F	15					34	102	61	26	18	19	4	12	13
6	Lee	Yan	Hybrid nationality	China *	United Kingdom	F	15					54	68	61	24	17	23	4	14	14
7	McDonald	Anne	Single nationality	United Kingdom		M	15					34	102	61	26	18	19	4	12	13
8	Malik	Adil	Single nationality	India		M	15					72	61	51	31	25	27	7	13	18
9	Posluszny	Borys	Single nationality	Poland *		M	15					64	73	59	84	20	21	4	54	25
10												0	0	0	0	0	0	0	0	0
11												0	0	0	0	0	0	0	0	0
12												0	0	0	0	0	0	0	0	0
13												0	0	0	0	0	0	0	0	0
14												0	0	0	0	0	0	0	0	0
15												0	0	0	0	0	0	0	0	0
	Team scores->											50	85	57	36	19	21	5	19	16
9	*<-No.of mbrs*																			

Figure 7-3: Example TCT2 cultural profiler output

185

3. **Weight the individual sub-factors for each factor:** This was carried out in a similar manner to weighting the major factors; the final weighting of each sub-factor was the product of the factor and sub-factor fractional weightings based on the user-entered numeric weights (or options as selected in the case of the 'textual' version).

TASK/MISSION PROFILE TABLE (general purpose) — describe your team task/mission (in blue areas)		(Relative importance (compared to other subfactors of this factor)	Importance of contextual factor to team (100 max)
Contextual factors	**Contextual subfactors**		
Strategic purpose(s)	Production or service team (e.g. product assembly, maintenance, restaurant)		
	Problem solving team (e.g. following a product failure in the field)	100	
	Product midlife upgrade team (low-medium innovation)		
	New product or service development team (medium-high innovation)		
	Product of the future team (high innovation, medium-high creativity)		25
	Long-term research team (high creativity)		
	Negotiation team (mergers & acquisition, peace treaties, etc.)		
	Organised action team, highly differentiated skills, occasional major risks (e.g. surgery)		
	Organised action team, little differentiated skills, occasional major risks (e.g. aircraft cockpit)		
Management & decision-making	Strong, centralised, directive management/decision-making	100	
	Consensus/delegation-based management/decision-making		
	Decision-making under uncertainty		75
	Following orders and standard operational procedures (SOPs) at all times	60	
	Not following SOPs when circumstances merit		
	Recognising mistakes and correcting them	20	
Creativity & innovation	Develop new ideas, new concepts		
	Design/implement new products or processes		
	Incorporate ideas developed elsewhere into processes or products		100
	Improve or revise designs, processes, process flow, correct failures occurring in the field	100	
	Go against the consensus when necessary		
Interaction (communication & co-ordination) within the team	Say what you mean, mean what you say		
	Convey meaning diplomatically (typically indirectly)		
	Communicate rapidly & accurately with colleagues, superiors & subordinates		
	Communicate about and discuss in-depth complex concepts		100
	Interact with other team members on a frequent or continuous basis		
	Interact with other team members at key decision points	100	
	Share information with other team members whenever possible		
	Only share information on a need-to-know basis		
Handling uncertainty & dealing with failures	Highly predictable activities and outcomes		
	Mostly predictable activities and outcomes	100	
	Highly predictable, except under certain relatively rare conditions		50
	Highly UNpredictable activities and outcomes		
	Errors & failures must be dealt with quickly		
	Errors and failures require careful consideration prior to action	50	
Situational awareness (SA)	Maintain individual situation awareness at all times		
	Maintain shared situation awareness at all times		
	No significant SA requirements (SA applies primarily to organised action teams)		

Figure 7-4: Example user-completed TCT2 task/mission profile

Figure 7-4 illustrates an example task/mission with user-entered numeric weights in the two right-hand columns. The relative weightings of the five factors would be calculated as:

<u>Strategic purpose</u>	= 25/(25+75+100+100+50)	= 7.1%
<u>Mgmt & decision-making</u>	= 75/(25+75+100+100+50)	= 21.4%
<u>Creativity & innovation</u>	= 100/(25+75+100+100+50)	= 28.6%
<u>Interaction (comms, etc.)</u>	= 100/(25+75+100+100+50)	= 28.6%
<u>Handling uncertainty, etc.</u>	= 50/(25+75+100+100+50)	= 14.3%
<u>Situational awareness</u>	= 0/(25+75+100+100+50)	= 0.0%

Within <u>Mgmt & decision-making</u>, the relative weightings of the sub-factors were:

Strong centralised mgmt = 100/(100+60+20) = 55.6% of its parent factor's weighting

Follow SOPs at all times = 60/(100+60+20) = 33.3% of its parent factor's weighting

Listen and analyse ... = 20/(100+60+20) = 11.1% of its parent factor's weighting

The weighting of any sub-factors as a proportion of all five factors (plus strategic purpose) equalled sub-factor (%) weighting multiplied by its factor (%) weighting, for example:

Strong centralised mgmt. = 21.4% x 55.6% = 11.9% of total weighting in the tool.

7.4.3 Deriving cultural discrepancies

Based on the cultural dimension scores listed in Subsection 7.3.2, each of the sub-factors of the 2nd prototype (TCT2) had an associated 'desirable culture score' for each of the four cultural dimensions, four cultural diversity dimensions and one mean diversity dimension[51]; these were stored in a 'desirable culture score' master table. Therefore, for

---

[51] Note that, due to very limited data on the effects of cultural diversity, for most sub-factors, cultural diversity values for these were set to 'NA' (not applicable). Where a reasonable estimate for overall diversity was available from the data, either the same value was also put in each of the individual diversities, or the value was only put into the mean diversity (with the individual diversities set to 'NA'. This was less than satisfactory, but it was intended that, when improved diversity data became available at a later date, they would be entered into the TCT.

each sub-factor, nine discrepancy values (one for each of the above nine culture/cultural-diversity dimensions), were each calculated as the difference between the team's actual culture/cultural-diversity score and the score in the 'desirable culture score' master table. These differences were factored by the sub-factor and factor weights (entered by the user in the task/mission profile table – see Subsection 7.4.2, above), and the results appeared in the team cultural discrepancy table, see Figure 7-5.

Note that a green-amber-red 'traffic light' warning system was implemented in the TCT2; this cannot be seen in Table 7-5, as it is in monochrome, but it was displayed when operating the tool. From this traffic light warning system, it could immediately be seen (in the example relating to Figure 7-5) that the greatest problem areas were *management & decision-making* (red), where the main issue related to the requirement for strong, directive management, and *creativity and innovation* (red), where the main issue related to the requirement to 'improve or revise designs ...'.

7.4.4 Interpreting the results

As stated above, a 'traffic light' system was implemented to highlight discrepant cultural scores:

- **Green:** OK - culture score is within acceptable range.

- **Amber:** Warning - moderate mismatch likely to lead to some reduction in performance; this may be acceptable for non-critical situations.

- **Red:** Danger - high mismatch likely to lead to a significant reduction in performance

The 'traffic light' colours formed the backgrounds of the various discrepancies, enabling users to identify key problem areas at a glance.

TEAM CULTURAL DISCREPANCY TABLE (general purpose) … areas of weakness and strength

| Contextual factor weighting (%) | | 7.14% | 21.43% | 28.57% | 28.57% | 14.29% | 0.00% | 100% |
| Task/mission factor discrepancy scores | | 24.1 | 38.8 | 35.2 | 0.0 | 16.3 | 0.0 | 22.3 |

Cultural diversity score discrepancies

	Overall discrepancy score >
Overall team cultural diversity (IDXdiv)	4.6
Uncertainty avoidance diversity (UAIdiv)	1.0
Masculinity diversity (MASdiv)	0.4
Individualism diversity (IDVdiv)	1.5
Power distance diversity (PDIdiv)	1.4

Cultural dimension score discrepancies

Uncertainty avoidance (UAI)	-22.1
Masculinity (MAS)	-4.6
Individualism (IDV)	23.7
Power distance (PDI)	-9.7

Task/mission factors — Task/mission subfactors

Strategic purpose(s)
- Production or service team (e.g. product assembly, maintenance, restaurant)
- Problem solving team (e.g. follow ing a product failure in the field)
- Product midlife upgrade team (low - medium innovation)
- New product or service development team (medium-high innovation)
- Product of the future team (high innovation, medium-high creativity)
- Long-term research team (high creativity)
- Negotiation team (mergers & acquisition, peace treaties, etc.)
- Organised action team, highly differentiated skills, occasional major risks (e.g. surgery)
- Organised action team, little differentiated skills, occasional major risks (e.g. a/c cockpit)

Management & decision-making
- Strong, centralised, directive management/decision-making
- Consensus/delegation-based management/decision-making
- Decision-making under uncertainty
- Follow ing orders and standard operational procedures (SOPs) at all times
- Not follow ing SOPs w hen circumstances merit
- Recognising mistakes and correcting them

Creativity & Innovation
- Develop new ideas, new concepts
- Design/implement new products or processes
- Incorporate ideas developed elsew here into processes or products
- Improve or revise designs, processes, process flow, correct failures occurring in the field
- Go against the consensus w hen necessary

Interaction (communication & co-ordination) within the team
- Say w hat you mean, mean w hat you say
- Convey meaning diplomatically (typically indirectly)
- Communicate rapidly & accurately w ith colleagues, superiors & subordinates
- Communicate about and discuss in-depth complex concepts
- Interact w ith other team members on a frequent or continuous basis
- Interact w ith other team members at key decision points
- Share information w ith other team members w henever possible
- Only share information on a need-to-know basis

Handling uncertainty & dealing with failures
- Highly predictable activities and outcomes
- Mostly predictable activities and outcomes
- Highly predictable, except under certain relatively rare conditions
- Highly Unpredictable activities and outcomes
- Errors & failures must be dealt w ith quickly
- Errors and failures require careful consideration prior to action

Situational awareness (SA)
- Maintain individual situation aw areness at all times
- Maintain shared situation aw areness at all times
- No significant SA requirements (SA applies primarily to organised action teams)

Figure 7-5: TCT2 team cultural discrepancy table

Figure 7-6 summarises the set of tables and their relationships, and a more detailed process and data flow diagram for the second team culture tool (TCT2) is provided in Figure 7-7.

An understanding of the operation of the TCT2 can be gained by following the sequence of events shown in Figure 7-7, and referring to Figures 7-3 to 7-6 for the individual tables and their contents.

7.5 Validation and evaluation of the TCT2

Initial testing was carried out on the second prototype tool (TCT2) before asking potential users to apply it.

7.5.1 Initial testing and validation

Incident and accident data on commercial aircraft were collected from the website http://aviation-safety.net and input to the TCT2, see Appendix 5 for more details of the data. Table 7-1 presents this aircraft incident data and the discrepancy scores generated by the TCT2, based on crew nationalities.

The results from this limited evaluation of the TCT2 have been plotted in the graph of Figure 7-8. As can be seen, there appears to be a clear relationship between discrepancy score and flying performance. Note that all modern passenger jet incidents (from the first six months of data from the accident site) where the flying crew unambiguously contributed in a significant way to the outcome of the incident (positively or negatively) were selected. Incident reports that provided insufficient details were omitted.

It was not possible to obtain equivalent data to that obtained from aircraft incident reports for other sociotechnical system operations; in particular, it was not possible, in most cases, to ascertain crew or operator nationalities.

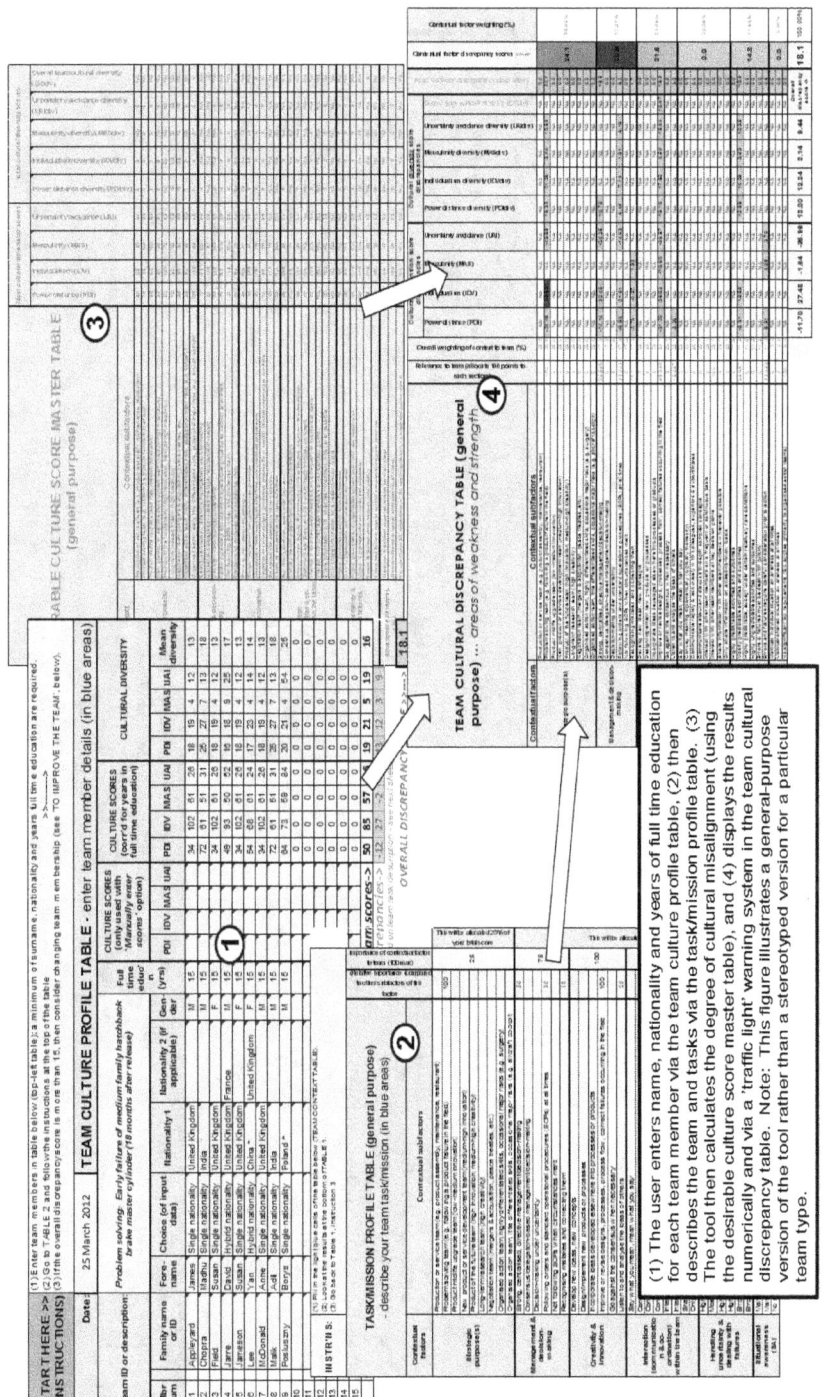

Figure 7-6: The key tables of the TCT2 and their relationships

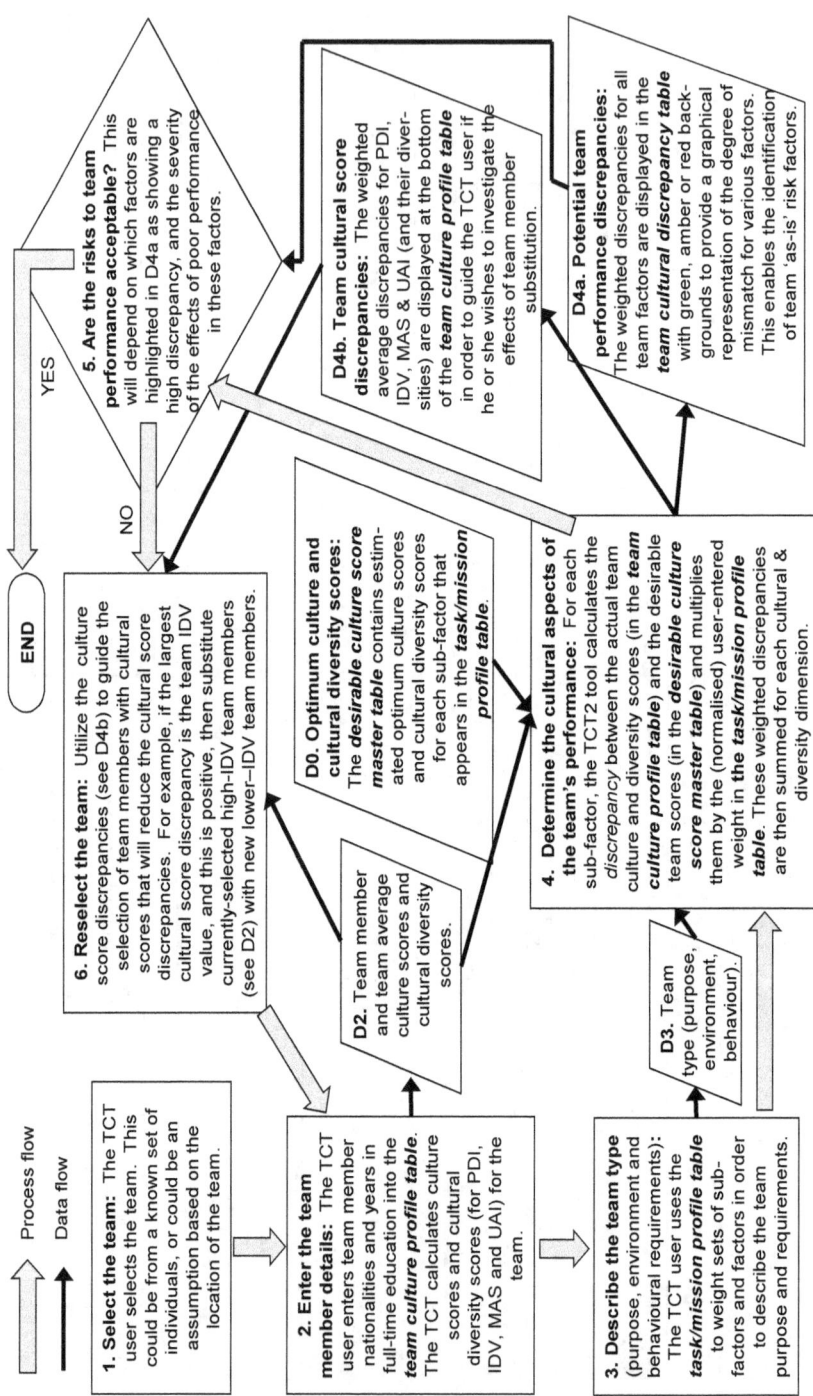

Figure 7-7: Detailed process/data flow diagram for the TCT2

Date & aircraft details	Incident description	Fatalities & damage	Crew performance	Crew nationality	Degree of error/-recovery	Discrepancy scores
Jan 2009, McD-D MD82	Instrument failure, crew became lost	No fatalities, no damage:	Disorientated – loss of situation awareness	Argen-tina	Moderate error	26.0
Jan 2009, Boeing 737	Not warned of landg conditions, river at end of runway	No fatalities, little damage	Quick reaction with max thrust reversers	USA	Good	9.2
Jan 2009, Airbus	Total engine loss over New York, river landing	No fatalities, a/c total loss	Exemplary judgement & flight skills	USA	Exem-plary	9.2
Jan 2009, Boeing 757	FMC misbehaviour, should have aborted	No fatalities, minor damage	Suboptimal decisions, poor communications	Ghana	Moderate error	29.3
Feb 2009, Airbus A321	Poor landing conds, did not abort or use thrust reversers	No fatalities, minor damage	Poor decision making	France	Moderate error	26.2
Feb 2009, Boeing 737	Faulty altimeters, FMC reduced thrust	9 fatalities, a/c total loss	Lack of situation awareness	Turkey	High error	31.0
Mar 2009, Airbus 340	Tail strike during take-off, erroneous calculations	0 fatalities, minor damage	Failure to follow SOPs	Arab world	Moderate + error	29.0
April 2009, BAe-146	Flew into terrain despite repeated instr. warnings	All crew killed, a/c total loss	Lack of SA, cap-tain ignored co-pilot's warnings	Indo-nesia	Extreme error	29.2
April 2009, Boeing 767	Firm landing nose damage	No fatalities, structural damage	Erroneous flight control	Arab world	Moderate error	29.0
Apr 2009, De Hav. DHC-8	Aft fuselage grounded on landing	No fatalities, minor damage	Lack of situation awareness	Canada	Moderate error	11.6
Apr 2009, McD-D MD-81	Left wing tip struck runway on landing	No fatalities, minor damage	Poor flight control	Japan	Moder-ate+ error	31.1
May 2009, Airbus A320	Tail strike after bounced landing	No fatalities, minor damage	Poor flight control	USA	Moderate error	9.2
May 2009, Boeing 747	Flaps retracted without warning on T/O	No fatalities, no damage	Excellent judge-ment & flight skills	UK	Excellent	6.6

Table 7-1: Incident data for commercial passenger aircraft

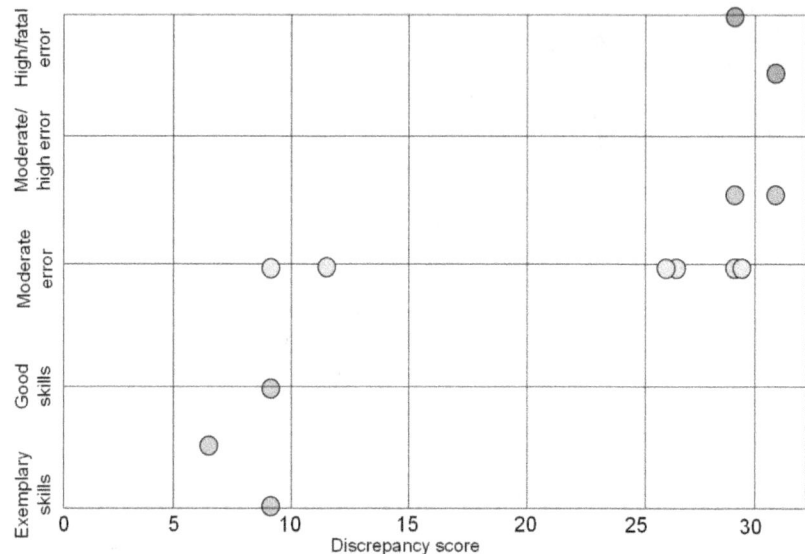

Figure 7-8: Validation of TCT2 via aircraft incident data

7.5.2 User testing and evaluation of the TCT2

After initial testing of the tool on a range of team and task/mission types, the tool was made available to several current and former team leaders, and to others involved with multinational and/or other-national teams. Most, but not all, of these team leaders were British, and their teams had varying proportions of UK and non-UK members.

These users were each asked to fill in a team culture tool questionnaire (see Appendix 6). Information on user and case numbers is summarised in Table 7-2. User feedback on the tool (obtained from their question-naire responses) is summarised in Table 7-3; note that answers based on dropdown lists have been converted into average percentage scores[52].

---

[52] The number of options in each drop-down list was used as the basis for converting answers into percentage scores on the basis of an equi-spaced division of the range of answers. For three options, the answer options (from worst to best) were placed in the centres of 0-33.3%, 33.3-66.7% and 66.7-100%, i.e. at 16.7%, 50.0% and 83.3%. For five options, the answer options were placed at 10, 30, 50, 70 and 90%.

Users	Project management team cases	Organised action team cases
6	8	3

Table 7-2: TCT2 user and case numbers

User	Team cultural profiler			Team task/mission profiler		Discrepancy results		Useful?
	Easy, understandable to use?	Quick/efficient to use?	Meaningful team profile results?	Easy, clear to use?	Quick/efficient to use?	Did the overall results make sense?	Was the standard improvement advice helpful?	Could a TCT2-type tool be useful?
AL	Fairly easy	Fairly fast	Yes	Very difficult	Slow	To some extent	To some extent	To some extent
AMJ	Very easy	Fairly fast	Yes	Somewhat difficult	Slow	Yes	Yes	Yes
JB	Fairly easy	Fairly fast	Yes	Somewhat difficult	Slow	To some extent	Yes	Yes
SN	Fairly easy	Very fast	To some extent	Somewhat difficult	Slow	Yes	To some extent	Yes
PB	Fairly easy	Fairly fast	To some extent	Somewhat difficult	Slow	To some extent	To some extent	To some extent
TW	Fairly easy	Fairly fast	Yes	Very difficult	Very slow	Yes	To some extent	To some extent
No. of answer opt'ns	5	5	3	5	5	3	3	3
Av. score (%)	73	73	72	23	27	67	61	67

Table 7-3: Summary of TCT2 user questionnaire answers

a) Ease of use

For most users, an initial explanation and demonstration of the TCT2 was given, and the users' results were also later discussed with them. Most users considered that it was fairly clear as to what the culture profiling aspect of the tool was doing, that it was easy to use and that it was clear as to where the results (in terms of discrepancies) came from. However, there was less user enthusiasm for the task/mission profiling side, as most users had had difficulty with it (also see later sub-sections for further comments on this). There were clear issues of face validity with the TCT2 task/mission profiler. Several users felt that more case-specific guidance on what to do about the results might have been helpful.

b) Clarity and transparency

One user reported that moderate differences in results occurred when different members of the same team filled in the task/mission profile; this was mainly due to the fact that describing a task/mission profile in terms of management/decision-making, communications, uncertainty, etc., was genuinely difficult. However, following further conversations with the user, it became apparent that the differences in task/mission profile also reflected the differing cultural background of one of the team members who had entered the data into the TCT2.

c) Flexibility and adaptability

One user commented that the task/mission profiling weighting process imposed constraints that prevented him from adequately describing his team.

One user commented positively on the ability to select dual cultural nationality or to enter (directly), as he felt that some team members were 'in-between' or just different to others, e.g. in terms of power distance or uncertainty avoidance[53].

d) Errors and accuracy

There was a spread of opinion from non-committal to enthusiastic, but most felt that the tool would be an adjunct to the team-picking process, rather than the basis of it, and that accuracy was not a particular issue. However one user felt that it was easy to misinterpret the intention or meaning of the task/mission sub-factors and to enter an erroneous task weighting.

There were some issues with regard to the mapping methodology. As the task profile was created by weighting a completely standard profile, the team profile always showed some degree of discrepancy with that standard profile, i.e. there could be no ideal cultural profile for any given task/mission; it was the weighting process that selectively reduced the discrepancies in unimportant areas. However, this also probably reflected the fact that any task-set or mission requires different behaviours at different times, for example closely adhering to standard operational procedures then abandoning them in some types of emergency.

---

[53] He and another user expressed particular interest in the cultural framework, as they felt that it offered an explanation for some of the issues they had previously contended with.

e) Other user-raised points

Political correctness and stereotyping: A user raised the issue of political correctness with regard to the use of nationality-based culture scores.

Clearly, the tool used a process of stereotyping as, in many cases, there would be no other information available. However, it would be unreasonable to use the tool directly as a basis for the inclusion or exclusion of *specific* individuals because such individuals should be personally assessed by their managers as colleagues, rather than being assessed as cultural stereotypes.

Trying to obtain the optimum team values: Several users entered a range of hypothetical teams into the TCT2 in order to gain an under-standing of how it worked. One such user, in particular, complained that it was not possible to get an ideal (zero discrepancy) score, as there was always at least one sub-factor that would be showing discrepancies. Such residual discrepancies occurred because different aspects of tasks or missions were associated with different culture scores.

Using the TCT2 as an adjunct to other tools: Another user suggested that the tool would have to fit in with Belbin-type tools (R Meredith Belbin, 2004, 2010) in order to be accepted.

The tool has already been used at Loughborough University as part of a wider systems engineering toolset.

Variable behaviours by team members: A user commented that he occasionally noticed changes in the behaviours of individual non-UK team members, depending on the composition of the rest of the team. In particular, he noticed that a particular team member would contribute less when one or more other members of his nationality joined the team. He suggested that the TCT2 would not account for this.

This change in behaviour may have been an example of conformity bias (firstly to the wider team culture, then to the team member's own culture), and the TCT2 would not directly account for this.

The task-culture link: Several users commented about cultural aspects, but two users in particular made some particularly interesting comments. The first of these was a pilot, not the same pilot with whom this researcher had an unstructured interview (see Subsection 5.2.1); the pilot's comments have been reproduced below:

> "The culture elements explained a great deal - we're very aware of the problems of culture in the industry but mainly concentrate on

the power gradient. Discussions with crews on the effects of culture (maybe demonstrating with a tool like this) might be valuable - if politically fraught. Some pilots seem to be internationalized so that their own culture is less obvious, but most seem to be at times like the stereotypes in this tool. I may be missing the point in some way but I have noticed that these cultural differences aren't there all the time. Sometimes I suddenly notice the guy is acting differently, he is agitated or not communicating anymore – it's like he's switched some part of his culture on."

There were two parts of this comment that were of particular interest; the first was:

"Some pilots seem to be internationalized so that their own culture is less obvious."

This was perhaps just a reflection of the international jet-setting community (literally), where long, perhaps permanent absence from one's home led to the development of a hybrid culture. The second part was:

"I may be missing the point in some way but I have noticed that these cultural differences aren't obvious all the time. Sometimes I suddenly notice the guy is acting differently, he is agitated or not communicating anymore – it's like he's switched his culture on."

This was of particular interest because it implied the turning on and off of cultural traits. It appeared that, when the situation (or context) changed, a 'dormant' or background cultural trait was 'switched on'.

The second of the two users was a project manager who worked with both academia and industry; his comments have been reproduced below:

"I'm not convinced about the way the task profile works. For instance, I have to deal with industrial engineers and academics of several nationalities. The tasks or missions they carry out may be the same in many ways if they collaborate on a project, but their environments are different and the way they actually respond and carry out the work is different. When one of my experienced academic colleagues works at the industrial partner's premises, his behaviour is different from when at university - and so is mine - I wear my industrial hat!"

This seemed to support the second part of the earlier comment, i.e. that specific (pre-existing) cultural traits were switched on or 'primed' in particular situations or contexts (though they might have been occupational or organisational cultural traits, rather than national cultural traits).

The following paragraph was taken from the anecdotal information referred to in Section 5.2 and detailed in Appendix 2:

"Two high power distance research colleagues have commented to me (and to other British colleagues) that they found it offensive when people junior to themselves from the same region (typically research students who had spent several years in the UK) did not acknowledge their seniority when addressing them."

This was interesting in that these same colleagues did not find it similarly offensive when people junior to themselves of other nationalities did not acknowledge their seniority. It is tempting to conjecture that this is a similar contextual response as the above examples.

Feedback and brief discussions with two of the above people had indicated that they felt that the *actual* behaviours within their teams or crew (in particular, within multicultural teams) could vary significantly and that culture-related behaviours did not always surface. One, in particular, felt that such behaviours were triggered by the context and cues (and perhaps by expectations) within the team and the environment, thus reducing the effectiveness of default culture-based prediction tools such as the TCT2.

f) Comments on user feedback

Evaluations of the second prototype team culture tool (TCT2) demonstrated the flexibility of the task/mission profiler in terms of its ability to represent many team types, but users found the TCT2 quite difficult to apply because, for any particular task, a significant number of sub-factors would have little meaning or relevance, and could be confusing and open to misinterpretation. In addition, because many of the task sub-factors (e.g. management, delegation and decision-making styles) related to team behaviour, these were very likely to be affected by tool user cultural traits. Perhaps more importantly, users raised some critical points about the underlying assumptions (see previous subsection).

The issue of residual discrepancies reported on by one user was worth considering further. 'Tolerance bands' rather than point values for the optimum cultural dimension scores could be utilised; these would much-reduce or eliminate the residual discrepancies reported by users who were experimenting to obtain zero-discrepancy teams (see (e) above). Given the limited accuracy of any culture tool, such tolerances (if not excessive) would be a useful trade-off.

The user comments with regard to contextually-modified behaviours were an important factor to take into consideration. An examination of the literature, for example Oyserman & Lee (2008) suggested that most of the research to-date on cultural priming has concentrated on individualism-collectivism, and there appeared to be little literature associated with priming other cultural dimensions. New research, based on simulating the neural network activities associated with priming automatic social behaviours (Schröder & Thagard, 2013), may improve understandings of the general underlying mechanisms of contextual priming, but there is also a need for direct studies of uncertainty avoidance priming, etc.

7.6 Limitations, and a re-evaluation of the underpinning assumptions

7.6.1 Limitations

It was clear from the feedback from user evaluations that the task/-mission profiler was difficult to use, and that it lacked face validity. Also, issues were raised by users with regard to contextual triggering of cultural traits, which could reduce the predictive accuracy of the tool.

7.6.2 Re-evaluating the assumptions underpinning the TCT2

The underpinning assumptions of the second performance prediction model were originally stated in Subsection 7.2.2. They are reconsidered in this subsection in order to evaluate their validity.

a) Capturing the cultural traits of an actual or proposed team

Within the limits of a simple dimension-based system, the cultural profiler based on Hofstede's framework was effective.

b) Capturing the desirable team cultural traits to achieve a task/mission

It was assumed that the tasks or mission of the team could be captured sufficiently by weighting five 'standard' factors and their sub-factors; this required the following:

i) Capturing the culture-sensitive elements of team tasks or missions: The set of behavioural factors and their sub-factors was not ideal, but the factors captured sufficient key culture-related details to produce results that 'were in the right direction'. However, two users raised issues about the validity about this task-based approach (see following paragraphs).

ii) Relating culture-sensitive elements of tasks/missions to culture traits: The literature review provided enough information, in conjunction with the culture score ranges derived in Subsection 5.5.1, that the author was able to identify and encapsulate in the model the cultural traits required for optimum performance of the sub-factors. There remained question marks over some of the relationships (in particular, those associated with masculinity and cultural diversity), due to lack of data and contradictory published results.

However, as stated in Subsection 7.5.2(e), above, two of the participating managers had questioned the link between culture and *actual* behaviours within their teams or crew (in particular, within multi-cultural teams). Whereas such local-contextual effects would certainly reduce the direct effects of culture (or the reliability with which such effects appeared), cultural traits would still provide a baseline and, given certain mission-related contextual cues, should tend to trigger certain behaviours.

iii) Describing a particular task or in terms of the above factors: Some users found this difficult, as the sub-factors were not necessarily those that they would normally use to describe a team. Although it was very flexible, that very flexibility may have added to confusion (due to lack of focus towards specific tasks/missions) and may have reduced its acceptability.

c) **Obtaining useful information from the discrepancies between desirable and actual cultural traits**

General explanations were provided in the tool and, in addition, context-sensitive (or discrepancy-sensitive) messages were generated to help in the identification of problem areas. The managers who were interested in culture picked up the meanings of the cultural dimensions quickly and appeared to understand the operation of the tool and its outputs (discrepancy figures and comment(s)). However, there was a lack of confidence on the part of the some users in the task/behavioural profile, and therefore in the usefulness of the information.

7.7 Proposed changes to the tool

The proposed changes were based in part on the user comments and on the re-examination of the assumptions. In particular, the comments by two users regarding situations or contexts were of concern. A direct focus on the mission context could, to some extent, sidestep this issue, and also alleviate the practical difficulties that users had with the TCT2.

It was therefore decided that the third prototype would include changes from a task-oriented representation to a dimension-based mission representation that attempted to capture the key context of that mission. This would enable a user to define a mission by locating it in 'mission space', relative to other missions. In addition, the third prototype would incorporate upper and lower bounds to optimum culture dimension scores, rather than single 'optimum' or 'desirable' values.

7.8 Summary of the TCT2

The second model and tool confirmed the effectiveness and face validity of the team cultural profiler. However, it also highlighted issues with the factor/sub-factor representation of task/mission profiles, both in terms of difficulties in use and underlying assumptions. A substantially different approach was therefore needed for the task/mission profiler.

8   A third model and team culture tool

8.1   Introduction

This chapter describes the development of the third and final set of versions of the model and team culture tool (TCT3); these versions utilised a dimension-based approach for both the team cultural profile and mission profile.

The aim of this third exercise was to create a prototype culture tool that did not rely on a task-based approach, and demonstrated the potential for application by *engineers* and *managers*, rather than by researchers who had particular knowledge of culture and its interactions with team performance.

As was the case with the TCT2, this version of the team culture tool was not intended to predict the 'absolute' performances of individual teams, but was intended to highlight where culture was *likely* to be a significant factor in underperformance or heightened risk. Also, as was the case with the TCT2, the goodness of fit (between team and mission) was based on the generation of discrepancies between the *desirable* team culture profile (based on the mission) and the *actual* team profile.

The main difference in the third methodology and tool was that the team mission was selected as *a location in multidimensional mission space*, rather than *described via weighting a set of factors and their sub-factors*.

8.2   Basis of the third model (TCT3)

This section is intended to provide an overview of the model that under-lies the third tool, in particular, the basis on which it generated a measure of fit between teams and their mission requirements, and the assumptions that lay behind the approach.

8.2.1   Overview of the TCT3

The logic of the third performance prediction model was based on profiling the team via its members' national cultural traits (as were the first and second models), profiling the mission by locating it within a set of mission dimensions (rather than via the five *team behavioural* factors of the second model) in order to capture directly the key context of the mission[54], and thereby directly deriving a set of cultural 'discrepancies' that represented the differences between the optimum cultural traits for the mission and the actual cultural traits of the team. These discrepancies formed the basis of team fitness for the mission.

The team cultural profile was created by entering team members' nationalities and their education levels into the model, which then utilised Hofstede's default national culture scores to calculate the team cultural profile; this consisted of the team average cultural scores and team diversity scores. The mission profile was created by selecting the team's location on a two-dimensional (2-D) *team-type* or *mission* grid that was partially populated by exemplar teams; this then generated a *desirable cultural profile*, based on the team's location on the 2-D grid. This desirable cultural profile was compared to the *actual* (or *proposed*) *team cultural profile* and discrepancies between these two profiles were derived. Figure 8-1 illustrates an idealised mapping directly from a selected location in multidimensional mission space to a location in multidimensional cultural space, as proposed in Subsection 4.4.2.

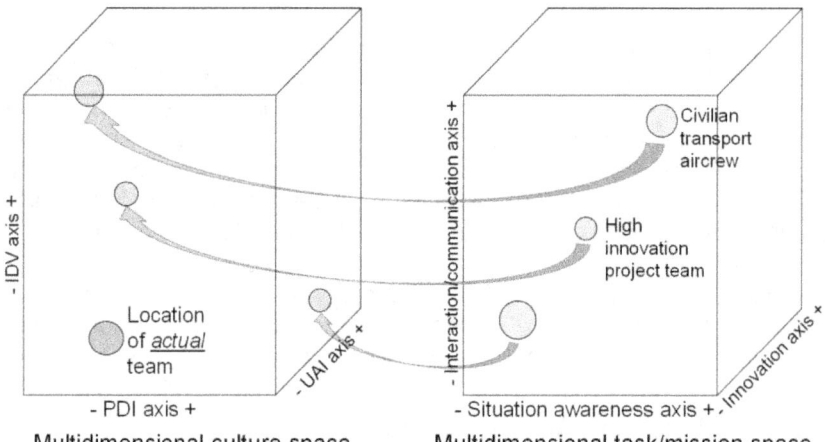

Multidimensional culture space   Multidimensional task/mission space

Figure 8-1: Mapping from task/mission space to culture space

---

[54] The key context was that (or those) which had to be handled appropriately in order to guarantee (or at least promote) the success of the mission. For example, the key context could relate to aspects of creativity or innovation in a scientifically advanced project or to rapid, appropriate responses following a major failure of a sociotechnical system in operation.

The distance in multidimensional culture space, between the location of the actual team and the cultural location resulting from the projection from the mission space, represents the cultural discrepancy.

Figure 8-2 presents an outline flow diagram of the model.

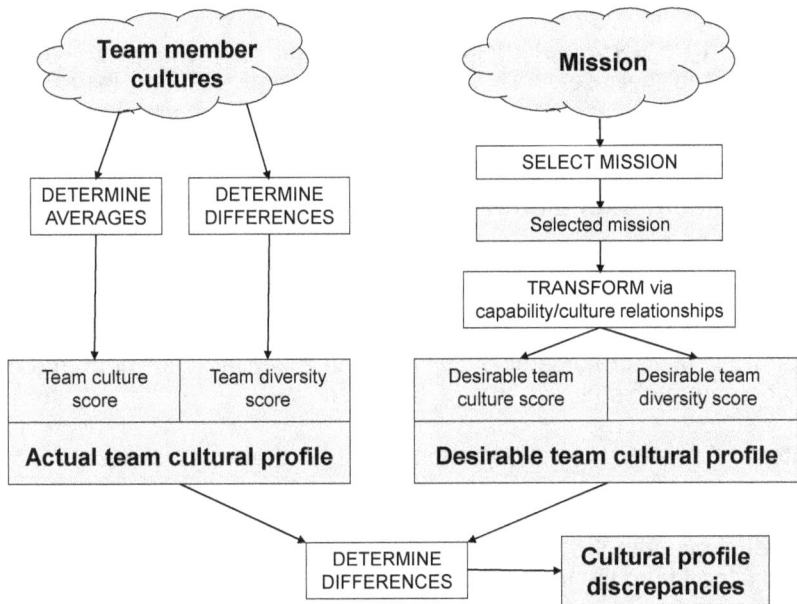

Figure 8-2: Flow diagram of TCT3 culture/mission model

8.2.2 Underpinning assumptions of the TCT3

The *additional* underpinning assumptions of the third performance prediction model (i.e. excluding those that were met in the second model) were as follows:

a) Capturing the desirable team cultural traits

It was assumed that the mission of a team could be captured sufficiently by placing the team or mission on a 'grid' or map containing a range of exemplar teams; this required the following:

i) *Capturing the culture-sensitive elements of team missions:* It was assumed that a small number of mission dimensions could capture the key context (or contexts) of a mission or team with adequate accuracy to enable the cultural traits associated with optimum performance to be identified.

ii) ***Relating culture-sensitive aspects of mission contexts to culture traits:*** It was assumed that the cultural traits required for optimum performance of the teams/missions of (i) above could be adequately identified by the author (based on the literature and his additional studies) and encapsulated in the model; these included the cultural traits of the exemplar teams.

iii) ***Placing a particular team or mission on a grid or map:*** It was assumed that users had sufficient knowledge to locate their teams with adequate accuracy within the grid or map in relation to exemplar teams.

b) Obtaining useful information from the discrepancies

It was assumed that the cultural discrepancies between actual and desirable cultural traits, when combined with the associated comments generated by the model/tool, would be meaningful, i.e. that they would inform the user of something useful about potential team performance and/or team problems.

Note: As stated in Subsection 7.2.2, the terms 'adequate' and 'adequately' related to the effects of inaccuracy on the performance of the model and tool. It was difficult to judge the degree of adequacy of individual steps in the process; however, the overall performance could be adjudged from the tool's effectiveness in the hands of users.

The implications of the above assumptions and the degree to which they were found to be justified are discussed later in this chapter.

8.3   Description of the key elements of the TCT3

The TCT3 team cultural profiler was identical to that used in the TCT2, which was described in Subsection 7.3.1 and illustrated in Figure 7-3. Therefore, no further descriptions of the profiler and the resulting *team cultural profile* have been provided in this section.

The *mission profile*, produced when the user placed the team (in terms of its mission) at an appropriate location in mission space, was mapped across to a *desirable cultural profile*. This *desirable cultural profile* was compared to the *team cultural profile* (generated by entering team member nationalities and educational levels), and discrepancies between the two were derived. These discrepancies, as in the second model, formed the basis for assessing mission fit.

The proposed changes of Subsection 7.6 included the adaptation of the tool to incorporate a valid range of scores, rather than a single point optimum score. This range would reflect the limited accuracy of the optimum culture scores and would provide several benefits:

- It would enable users to find optimum team configurations more easily if that was their intent.

- It would enable the tool to cope with situations where a particular cultural trait was unimportant, simply by expanding the range of 'optimal' scores.

- It would enable the tool to emulate a situation where a cultural trait reduced in importance over a particular range of scenarios (whether or not its optimum score changed); for example, this was the case with the organised action teams – the slower the required response time was, the less important power distance and masculinity were.

On the basis of the limited accuracy of the cultural dimension scores, a decision was made to incorporate a default minimum range of +/-5. That implied, for example, that an optimum cultural dimension score of 25 would become an optimum range of 20-30, and a team score of anywhere between 20 and 30 (for that dimension) would have a discrepancy score of zero.

When this third and final model was initially developed, the aim was to profile all potential tasks/missions by locating them in three or four dimensions. However, this proved extremely difficult for the following reasons:

- It proved impossible to design a simple three/four-dimensional input tool that a user could utilise effectively. It required the user to select a team twice, once on each pair of dimensions, and it proved difficult to place and explain the numerous exemplars required to guide the user in his or her selection.

- Different team/mission types could not effectively be expressed via a common set of dimensions, as at least one dimension would be superfluous and distracting.

As a result, a decision was taken to utilise different underlying dimensions and input forms for the different forms of team mission. The decision to split team types greatly simplified the process of implementation, and produced a mission interface that was extremely simple to use.

The two key team/mission types (and their dimension) selected were the ones of key interest to this research (see Subsection 2.2.2), i.e.:

- **project teams** – typically designing, implementing or improving elements of sociotechnical systems

- **organised action teams** – typically the crew or operators of safety-critical sociotechnical systems

8.3.1 Project teams

These teams were associated primarily with research, development and implementation of complex products and sociotechnical systems.

Section 3.3 of the literature review examined the effects of culture on the performance of teams involved in research, innovation, improvement, etc. The main culturally-moderated issues that appeared to arise with project teams appeared from the literature to be the level of creativity/-innovation, and the additional problems imposed by social complexities on larger projects – i.e. the parties involved, their cultural differences, etc. Whereas the innovation/creativity issues had been quantitatively evaluated by many authors (with varying results and conclusions), the issue of social complexity and its effects on projects had been subject only to limited qualitative analysis. However, the major social problems with complex projects, as identified in Subsection 3.3.1(a) (vii), were failures in communications and understandings across departmental and organisational boundaries. In particular, the very masculine cultures associated with the management of large projects tended to result in impersonal problem-solving, and a failure to form relationships and to adopt a consensus-seeking approach. It appeared that a low-power distance, low-masculinity culture would improve communication and encourage the building of consensual relations between partners, rather than the adversarial relationships that formed the basis of much current project work.

The dimensions for sociotechnical system project teams were therefore defined as:

- creativity/innovation

- social complexity

Note that, in addition to technically-focussed project teams, this configuration of dimensions also enabled the assessment of non-technical management teams. These dimensions are discussed further in the following subsections.

a) Creativity/innovation dimension

The author brought together the findings on innovation from the literature review and from his own studies in order to produce a best estimate of the relationships. The author's pilot study results (subsections 5.3.1 to 5.3.4 & 5.4) broadly supported the innovation results that were obtained from the literature; in particular:

- The student group results demonstrated that uncertainty avoidance was a detractor from innovation performance[55].

- The football results demonstrated that, in an environment of clearly-defined rules and no lethal surprises, high uncertainty avoidance ('sticking to the plans and being cautious') and high masculinity (high competitiveness) were of significant benefit.

The cultural dimension scores of Figure 7-2 were utilised in the second model and tool (TCT2), and that figure has been reproduced here as Figure 8-3, as it is used further in this chapter.

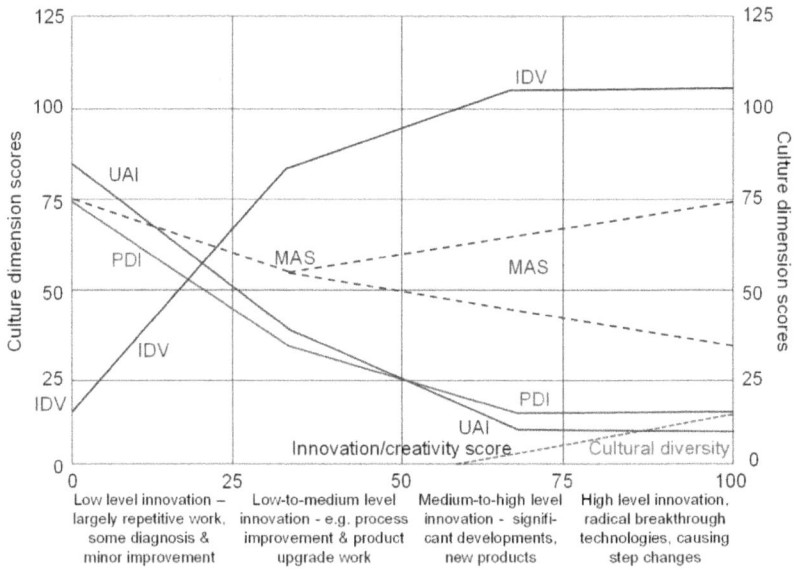

Figure 8-3: Culture/innovation relationships

As stated in Chapter 7, this figure is based on the innovation-related findings of Subsection 3.3 of the literature review, in particular Figure 3.2 and on the author's pilot study findings, combined with the 'low' and

---

[55] Innovation formed a significant part of the student groups' performance assessments.

'high' cultural dimension scores as derived in Section 5.5. Also, as stated in Chapter 7, two of the relationships were particularly difficult to assess. Firstly, the results for masculinity appeared strongly positive for low innovation but unclear for high innovation, with different researchers reporting strong positive and negative effects. Secondly, the results for cultural diversity were highly variable, although there appeared to be some degree of consensus on the positive benefits that multiple points of view brought for high innovation, but not low innovation.

b) Social complexity dimension

As discussed in Subsection 3.3.1(a) (vii), the very masculine cultures associated with the management of large projects tended to result in impersonal problem-solving, and a failure to form relationships and to adopt a consensus-seeking approach. It appeared that a low-power distance, low-masculinity culture could improve communications and could also encourage the building of consensual relations between partners, rather than the adversarial relationships that formed the basis of much current project work. To this end, it was proposed that the 'desirable' MAS score associated with projects should decline to the 'low' value ('4') of Table 5-17 for socially complex projects.

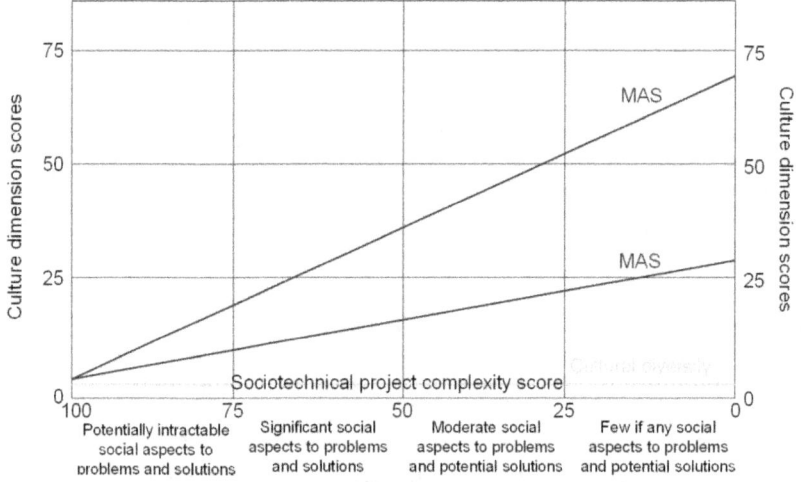

Figure 8-4: Culture/social complexity relationship[56]

Figure 8-4 illustrates this reduction in MAS score; the two values on the right represent the extremes of MAS scores for innovation. In order to produce a 'desirable' overall mission MAS value (one that conformed to

---

[56] The actual value for masculinity (on the right side of the figure) depends on the degree of innovation creativity/required.

Figure 8-4), the culture tool applied the following adjustment to the MAS value associated with innovation[57]:

$$MAS_{COMPLEX} = MAS_{INNOV} - (MAS_{INNOV} - MAS_{LOW}) * complexityScore/100$$

Where:

$\underline{MAS_{COMPLEX}}$ = MAS_{INNOV} adjusted for project social complexity.

MAS_{LOW} = The 'low' value for MAS from Table 5-17 (=4).

$\underline{MAS_{INNOV}}$ = Masculinity score based on level of creativity/innovation required.

$\underline{complexityScore}$ = a measure of social complexity ranging from zero to 100, as shown in Figure 8-4.

8.3.2   Organised action teams

These teams were primarily associated with the crewing (or operating) of sociotechnical systems, for example large transport aircraft, ships, petro-chemical oil refineries or power stations.

Section 3.3.1(c) of the literature review examined the effects of national culture on the performance of crews and operators of sociotechnical systems, in particular, aircraft crews. Although only limited publication data was available in this area, compared to that on innovation, that data was consistent across all researchers: national culture appeared to play a significant role in accident rates. Accident recordings had revealed a range of intra-team issues; low accident rates were associated with low PDI, high IDV, low UAI and high MAS; high accident rates were associated with the opposite set of culture scores. Cultural diversity was not given significant attention in the literature on organised action teams, but it would be reasonable to assume that, because it reduced communication rates and increased misunderstandings, cultural diversity would have added to the risk of accidents.

The author's analysis of aircraft accident data (Subsection 5.3.5(a)) confirmed that high accident rates in fast response time systems were associated with high PDI, low IDV, high UAI and low MAS. In addition, the author's analysis confirmed Hofstede's assertion that per-capita GDP was the most important factor relating to aircraft accident rates (low per-capita GDP is associated with high aircraft accident rates). The author's studies also indicated that, in slower response time systems, e.g. merchant maritime (Subsection 5.3.5(b)), per-capita GDP, MAS and PDI had much-reduced effects compared to IDV and UAI. The author's examination of automation issues (Subsection 3.3.1(c)) and analysis of attitudes to automation (Subsection 5.3.5(c)) provided further insights as

---

[57] But note that the +/-5 range was applied to all culture scores including this MAS score; it was not shown here in order to avoid confusion.

to loss of flying skills, reduced situation awareness and complacency, which are all potential contributors to accident risks.

Although no significant relationships were found in the literature between degree of specialisation within a team and the effects of culture on accident rates, specialisation proved to be a useful way of discriminating teams in order to display them on a two dimensional grid, and to enable users to place their own teams' missions.

To summarise the above, the two dimensions selected were:

- mission response time requirements (rather than *communication and co-ordination* or *situational awareness*, which were team *behavioural* factors)

- mission specialisation amongst team members (a key team-differentiating dimension identified by Hollenbeck et al. (2012))

Figure 8-5 presents a best estimate of the optimum cultural values for sociotechnical system crews based on the accident-related findings of Subsection 3.3 of the literature review and the author's pilot study findings of Subsections 5.3.5(a), (b) & (c), combined with the 'low' and 'high' cultural dimension scores as derived in Section 5.5, (see also Tables 5-11 to 5-18). This forms the basis of the cultural scores in the TCT3 organised action team model.

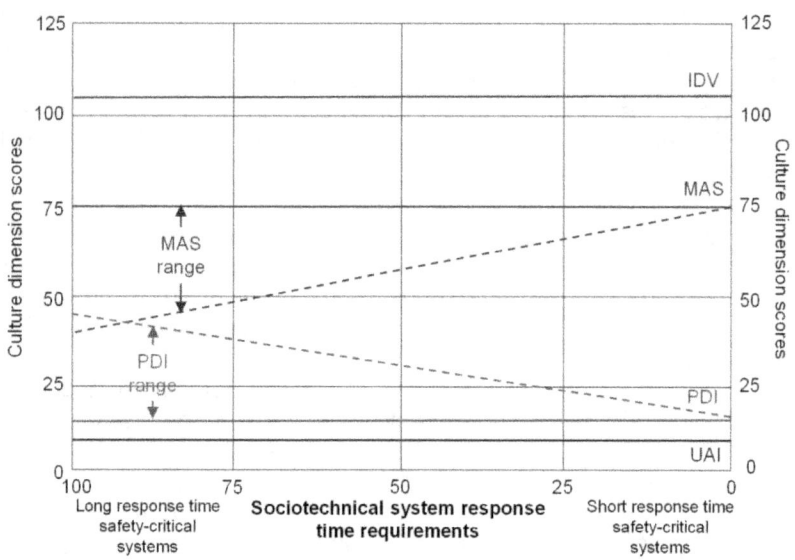

Figure 8-5: Culture/response time relationships

The basis of the culture/response time relationship illustrated in Figure 8-5 is described under the following bullet points:

- **Short response time axis:** This reflected the aircraft accident results:

  PDI=low=16; IDV=high=105; MAS=high=75; UAI=low=9.

- **Long response time axis:** This reflected shipping accident results; here, IDV and UAI remained as key predictors, but PDI and MAS were much reduced as predictors – this reduction was modelled by providing a high and low value for PDI and MAS, rather than a single optimum value for each. In each case, this was calculated as half of the cultural dimension's range between its low and high values[58] (these low and high values were calculated in Subsection 5.5.1):

  PDI_{LOW}=16 & PDI_{HIGH}=16+(73-16)/2=45; IDV=high=105; MAS_{HIGH}=75 & MAS_{LOW}=75-(75-4)/2=40; UAI=low=9.

The issues associated with the operation of high-reliability sociotechnical systems related to relatively rare situations where events combined or failures occurred such that the operators or crew had to 'reframe' and, typically, abandon their normal standard operating procedures (SOPs). However, operators that were willing to abandon their SOPs at an earlier stage might abandon them when such a course was not necessary. Where the balance of risk was weighted towards the consequences of *failure to follow SOPs*, for example when carrying out planned maintenance of an aircraft[59] or of a section of a refinery, then high UAI (following SOPs), high PDI (obeying orders) crews might perform better. Note that *low* IDV (high collectivism) did not guarantee the following of SOPs or orders. Although sport might appear at first consideration to have little to do with sociotechnical systems, the issues associated with a willingness (or otherwise) to take a low uncertainty (high predictability) course of action have been demonstrated in the author's English Premiership pilot study; here, the key contributory cultural dimension to successful performance was found to be high UAI. Due to a lack of publications and data on maintenance operations in sociotechnical systems, this topic has not been included in the TCT3.

---

[58] This was a pragmatic decision because there was insufficient data to estimate an accurate value; note that the +/-5 score range would also be applied (as is the case throughout the model).

[59] For an example of the failure of a UK aircraft maintenance organisation to follow standard operating procedures, see AAIB (2013). The UK score for uncertainty avoidance is low, but is not necessarily a contributing factor to this serious incident.

8.4 Description of the methodology and tool operation

As stated in the previous chapter, in order to assess the suitability of a team in cultural terms, it was necessary to be able to profile the team in terms of its culture, to profile the team mission (including relevant environmental aspects), and to provide a mapping between the team mission and cultural traits that would enable an assessment of team suitability or mismatch to be carried out. The main difference in the third methodology and tool was that the team mission was *selected as a location in multidimensional mission space*, rather than *described via weighting a set of factors and their sub-factors*; Figure 8-1 illustrates an idealised mapping directly from a selected location in multidimensional mission space to a location in cultural dimension space.

Knowing the desirable location in 'culture space' and the actual team's location in the same space, the separation (or discrepancy) along each cultural dimension could be determined.

The following subsections describe the activities and profiles in more detail; as in the last chapter, the descriptions are presented in terms of tool usage and processes.

8.4.1 Profiling the team

The team cultural profiler was identical to that of the TCT2, and was utilised in an identical fashion. See Figure 7-3 for the TCT2 and TCT3 team cultural profiler.

8.4.2 Profiling the mission

In order to utilise the tool, the user was required to place the team mission in the space formed by the two mission dimensions. Note that, in the case of organised action teams, one of the utilised dimensions was there primarily to help the user in his/her selection and produce a more readable spread of exemplars; see Appendix 9 for information on the creation of exemplars. Figure 8-6 illustrates the engineering/-management project team mission profile selector.

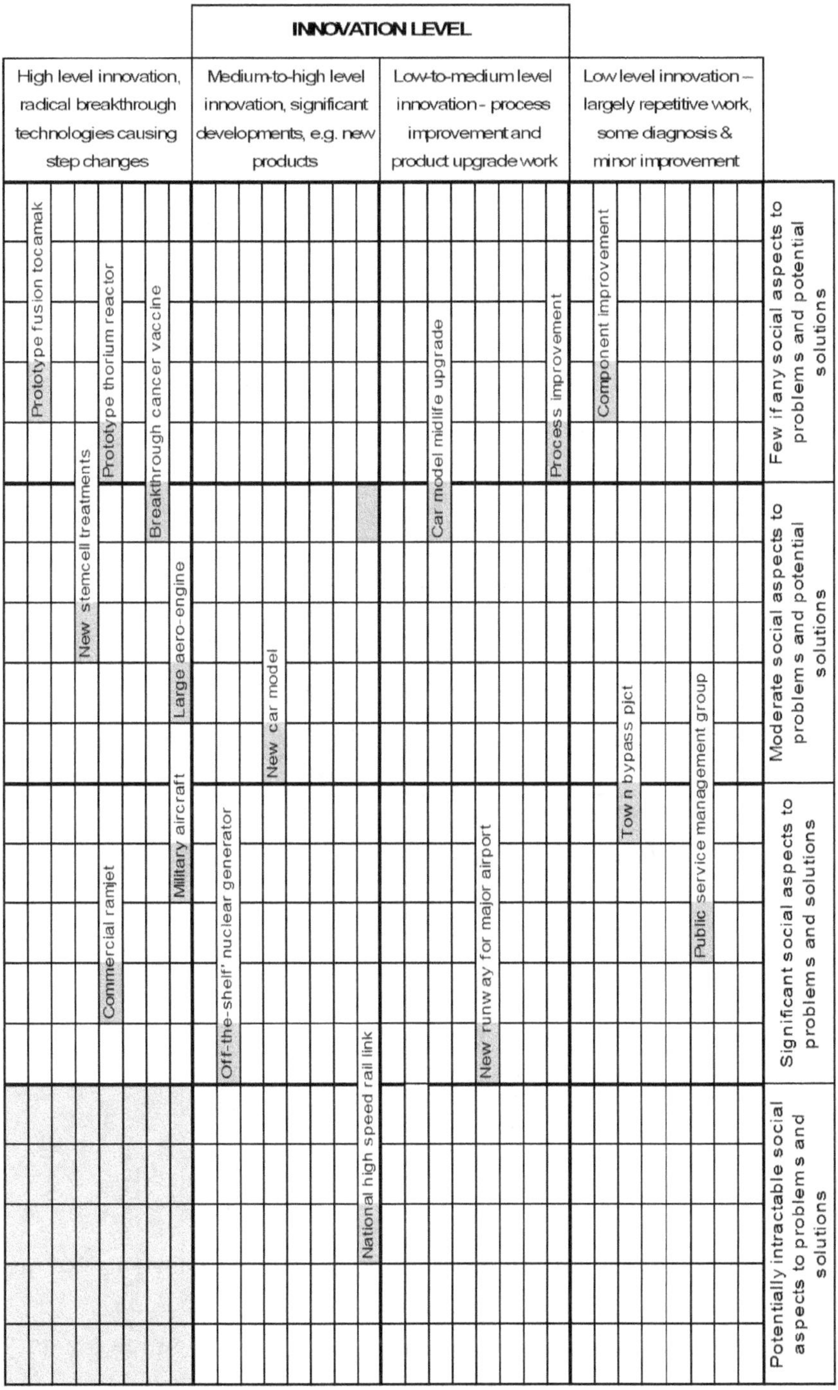

A third model and team culture tool

INNOVATION LEVEL			
High level innovation, radical breakthrough technologies causing step changes	Medium-to-high level innovation, significant developments, e.g. new products	Low-to-medium level innovation - process improvement and product upgrade work	Low level innovation – largely repetitive work, some diagnosis & minor improvement	
Prototype fusion tocamak; Prototype thorium reactor; Breakthrough cancer vaccine		Process improvement; Component improvement		Few if any social aspects to problems and potential solutions
New stem cell treatments; Breakthrough cancer vaccine	Large aero-engine	Car model midlife upgrade		Moderate social aspects to problems and potential solutions
Commercial ramjet; Military aircraft	Off-the-shelf nuclear generator; New car model	New runway for major airport	Town bypass pjct; Public service management group	Significant social aspects to problems and solutions
	National high speed rail link			Potentially intractable social aspects to problems and solutions

Figure 8-6: Profiling the TCT3 mission – project teams

215

Figure 8-7 illustrates the organised action team mission profile selector.

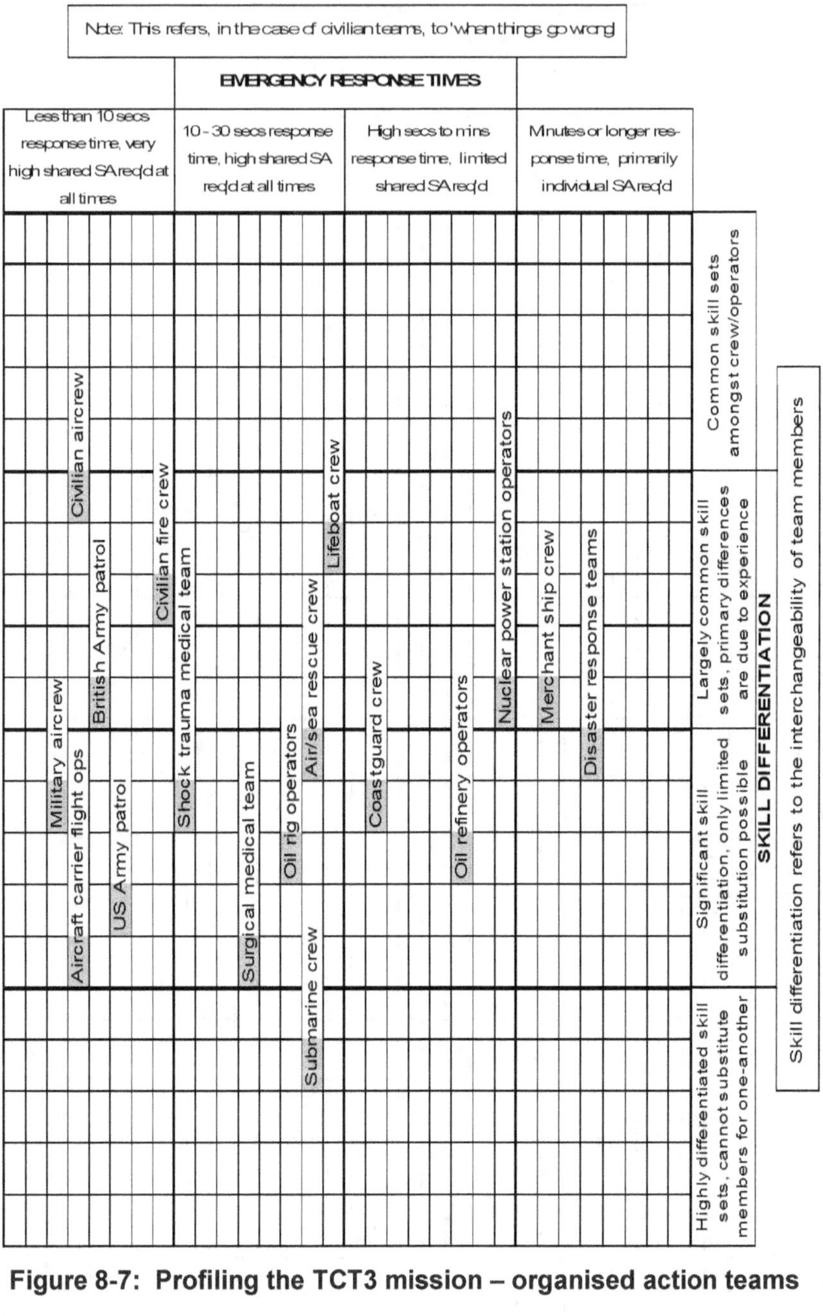

Note: This refers, in the case of civilian teams, to 'when things go wrong'

EMERGENCY RESPONSE TIMES

Less than 10 secs response time, very high shared SA req'd at all times	10 - 30 secs response time, high shared SA req'd at all times	High secs to mins response time, limited shared SA req'd	Minutes or longer response time, primarily individual SA req'd

Military aircrew

Aircraft carrier flight ops

British Army patrol

US Army patrol

Civilian aircrew

Civilian fire crew

Shock trauma medical team

Surgical medical team

Submarine crew

Oil rig operators

Air/sea rescue crew

Lifeboat crew

Coastguard crew

Oil refinery operators

Nuclear power station operators

Merchant ship crew

Disaster response teams

Common skill sets amongst crew/operators

Largely common skill sets, primary differences are due to experience

Significant skill differentiation, only limited substitution possible

Highly differentiated skill sets, cannot substitute members for one-another

SKILL DIFFERENTIATION

Skill differentiation refers to the interchangeability of team members

Figure 8-7: Profiling the TCT3 mission – organised action teams

The locating/profiling process was very quick, and it was easy to place the team amongst the exemplars of different types of action team.

8.4.3 Deriving cultural discrepancies

Each of the active dimensions had an associated set of cultural relation-ships. Following the user's selection of a location in task/mission space, a desirable score (expressed as a range) was generated for each cult-ural dimension and for cultural diversity – resulting in a *desirable cultural profile*. Figure 8-8 illustrates an example desirable cultural profile, based on one of the outputs of a TCT3 spreadsheet.

Cultural dimension ->	PDI		IDV		MAS		UAI		Cdiv	
Desirable profile ->	**24**	**34**	**80**	**90**	**42**	**68**	**21**	**31**	**3**	**6**
	Range (low-hi)		Range (low-hi)		Range (low-hi)		Range (low-hi)		Range (low-hi)	

Figure 8-8: Example desirable culture profile

The elements of the *actual* team cultural profile (i.e. the team's cultural dimension and diversity scores) were then compared to the *desirable cultural profile for the mission* to ascertain whether they lay inside or outside each range; if outside the range, the distance was displayed as a positive or negative discrepancy; if inside the range, the discrepancy was set to zero. See example below, based on Figure 8-8:

If UAI desirable range = 21 to 31, then:

If team UAI = 15, then UAI discrepancy = -6 (6 below bottom of range).

If team UAI = 29, then UAI discrepancy = 0 (within range).

If team UAI = 43, then UAI discrepancy = 12 (12 above top of range).

The overall discrepancy in the standard model underlying the TCT3 was simply the average of the individual discrepancies. However, a modified version of the TCT3 was also developed, which applied relative weights (based on the values presented in Table 5-19) to the individual discrep-ancies. This led to some issues with two users who noticed that the discrepancy values 'didn't add up'. Face validity is important for this tool, therefore the modified version was not used further in the main validation exercise.

8.4.4 Interpreting the results

Following selection of the team mission profile from one of the two TCT3 mission grids, depending on mission type (Figure 8-6 or 8-7), the TCT3 updated a radar diagram in order to present an overview of the degree of fit and to highlight the areas of greatest discrepancy, see Figure 8-9.

The radar diagram example of Figure 8-9 was based on a project team (the culture tool version was displayed in multiple colours); we can see that the actual team PDI and cultural diversity (Cdiv) scores, represented by the lighter line in the diagram, were outside the desirable range. Note that it had not been feasible to generate a radar diagram for the TCT2, as there were no *unique* desirable culture scores to plot.

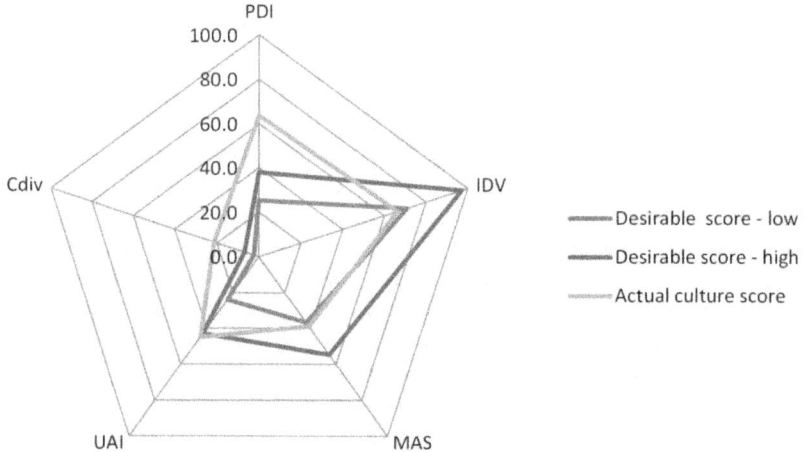

Figure 8-9: Radar diagram showing cultural fit to mission/task

The discrepancies between the desired mission cultural profile and the actual team cultural profile were also shown at the base of the TCT3 Table 1 – team culture profile table, see Figure 8-10. In this particular example, as the team's power distance (PDI) and cultural diversity were significantly higher than was desirable, the team's overall discrepancy was a somewhat high score of 9.4.

In order to improve the situation, we would need to exchange high PDI team members for low PDI members. The three Russian members have the highest PDI and diversity scores, therefore replacing them with (say) Nordic or German members, would cause both PDI and diversity to fall to within the 'desirable' range. However, this may not be feasible due to knowledge/skill/experience constraints or political constraints.

A third model and team culture tool

START HERE >> (INSTRUCTIONS)

(1) Enter team members in table below (top-left table); a minimum of surname, nationality and years full time education are required >>------>
(2) Go to TABLE 2 and follow the instructions at the top of the table
(3) If the overall discrepancy score is more than 15, then consider changing team membership (see 'TO IMPROVE THE TEAM', below).

TEAM CULTURE PROFILE TABLE - enter member details

Mbr num	Family name or ID	Fore-name	Choice (of input data)	Nationality 1	Nationality 2 (if applicable)	Gen-der	Full time educ'n (yrs)	PDI	IDV	MAS	UAI	PDI	IDV	MAS	UAI	PDI	IDV	MAS	UAI	Mean diversity
1	Technology leader		Single nationality	Great Britain		M	16					25	109	54	21	45	49	17	29	35
2	Project mgr		Single nationality	India		M	16					63	68	44	26	12	14	11	26	16
3	Chief scientist		Single nationality	Russia *		M	16					77	59	24	81	15	14	17	41	22
4	Systems engr1		Single nationality	Russia *		M	16					77	59	24	81	15	14	17	41	22
5	Systems engr2		Single nationality	China *		M	16					65	40	54	16	12	14	17	33	23
6	Systems engr3		Single nationality	India		M	16					63	68	44	26	12	14	11	26	16
7	Softw are engr1		Single nationality	India		M	16					63	68	44	26	12	14	11	26	16
8	Softw are engr2		Single nationality	Russia *		M	16					77	59	24	81	15	14	17	41	22
9												0	0	0	0	0	0	0	0	0
10												0	0	0	0	0	0	0	0	0
11												0	0	0	0	0	0	0	0	0
12												0	0	0	0	0	0	0	0	0
13												0	0	0	0	0	0	0	0	0
14												0	0	0	0	0	0	0	0	0
15												0	0	0	0	0	0	0	0	0
8	<-No.of mbrs											64	66	39	45	17	20	15	33	21

Column group headers: CULTURE SCORES (use with 'Manually enter scores' option) [PDI IDV MAS UAI]; CULTURE SCORES (corr'd for years in full time education) [PDI IDV MAS UAI]; CULTURAL DIVERSITY [PDI IDV MAS UAI Mean diversity]

Date: 15 December 2012

Team ID or description: A feasibility study of a military integration platform based on the MODAF standard (industrial R&D)

Team scores-> 64 66 39 45 ... 17 20 15 33 21
Discrepancies-> 26 -5 0 2 ... 15
(based on task/mission)

OVERALL DISCREPANCY SCORE >>---> 9.4

Ignore the discrepancy figures until you have placed your team on the grid (Table 2, to the right >>--->).

WHAT THE SCORES MEAN: In approximate terms, the scores represent deviations from ideal scores, expressed as percentages. An overall discrepancy score of less than 8, is acceptable, a discrepancy score of 8 to 15 is acceptable for non-critical teams (where failures of communication and occasional poor decision-making do not cause physical danger or risk of high financial losses. A discrepancy score above 15 implies that a team that will not function adequately in its role.

TO IMPROVE THE TEAM: Identify the cultural dimension with the greatest discrepancy. If the discrepancy is positive, then the average score of team members is too high; replace high scoring team members with new, lower scoring members (i.e. of different nationality or education) for that cultural dimension. If the discrepancy is negative, then replace low scoring team members with members that score highly for that cultural dimension. Such changes affect the discrepancy scores for other dimensions, so check them afterwards. High (positive) cultural diversity scores are reduced by choosing replacement team members that are more similar to the average in the team, vice versa for low (negative) cultural diversity scores.

Figure 8-10: Applying the tool to a project team (TCT3 Table 1)

219

8.5 Validation and user evaluation of the TCT3

As with the second prototype, initial testing was carried out on the third prototype tool (TCT3) before asking potential users to apply it.

8.5.1 Initial testing and validation

The commercial aircraft incident data that were collected to test the TCT2 were also used to test the TCT3, see Appendix 5 for more details of this data. Table 8-1 presents this aircraft incident data and the TCT3 discrepancy scores based on crew nationalities.

Note that Table 8-1 is similar to Table 7-1, except that the discrepancy scores (in the last column) were generated via the TCT3 methodology rather than via the TCT2 methodology.

The results from this limited evaluation of the TCT3 have been plotted in the graph of Figure 8-11. As was the case with the TCT2, there appeared to be a significant relationship between discrepancy score and flying performance/accident rate, as one would expect. Note that, as stated in the previous chapter, <u>all</u> modern passenger jet incidents (from the first six months of data from the accident website) where the flying crew unambiguously contributed in a significant way to the outcome of the incident (positively or negatively) were selected. Incident reports that provided insufficient details were omitted.

The graph of Figure 8-11 also contains the results for the TCT2 (which utilised the same data). The results are very similar in this case although the TCT3 discrepancies are smaller; this is in part due to the implementation of an optimum culture score (or desirable culture score) *range,* as shown in Figures 8-8 and 8-9, rather than a single point optimum culture score, as was the case with the TCT2.

Date & aircraft details	Incident description	Fatalities & damage	Crew performance	Crew nationality	Degree of error/- recovery	Discrepancy scores
Jan 2009, McDD MD82	Instrument failure, crew became lost	No fatalities, no damage:	Disorientated – loss of situation awareness	Argen-tina	Moder ate error	14.8
Jan 2009, Boeing 737	Not warned of land-ing conditions, river at end of runway	No fatalities, little damage	Quick reaction with max thrust reversers	USA	Good	1.7
Jan 2009, Airbus	Total engine loss over New York, river landing	No fatalities, a/c total loss	Exemplary flight skills	USA	Excel-lent	1.7
Jan 2009, Boeing 757	FMC misbehaviour, should have aborted	No fatalities, minor damage	Suboptimal decisions, poor communications	Ghana	Moder ate error	18.7
Feb 2009, Airbus A321	Poor landing condi-tions, did not abort or use thrust reversers	No fatalities, minor damage	Poor decision making	France	Moder ate error	14.8
Feb 2009, Boeing 737	Faulty altimeters, FMC reduced thrust	9 fatalities, a/c total loss	Lack of situation awareness	Turkey	High error	19.5
March 2009, Airbus 340	Tail strike during dangerous take-off due to erroneous calculations	0 fatalities, minor damage	Failure to follow SOPs	Arab world	Moder ate-to-high	18.4
April 2009, BAe-146	Flew into terrain despite repeated instr. warnings	All crew killed, a/c total loss	Lack of SA, cap-tain ignored co-pilot's warnings	Indo-nesia	High error	18.8
April 2009, Boeing 767	Firm landing, nose damage	No fatalities, structural damage	Erroneous flight control	Arab world	Moder ate error	18.4
Apr 2009, De Hav. DHC-8	Aft fuselage grounded on landing	No fatalities, minor damage	Lack of situation awareness	Cana-da	Moder ate error	1.9
Apr 2009, McDD MD-81	Left wing tip struck runway on landing	No fatalities, minor damage	Poor flight control	Japan	Moder ate+ error	16.9
May 2009, Airbus A320	Tail strike after bounced landing	No fatalities, minor damage	Poor flight control	USA	Moder ate error	1.7
May 2009, Boeing 747	Flaps retracted with-out warning on T/O	No fatalities, no damage	Exemplary flight skills	UK	Excel-lent	0.2

Table 8-1: Data set for evaluation of action team option of TCT3

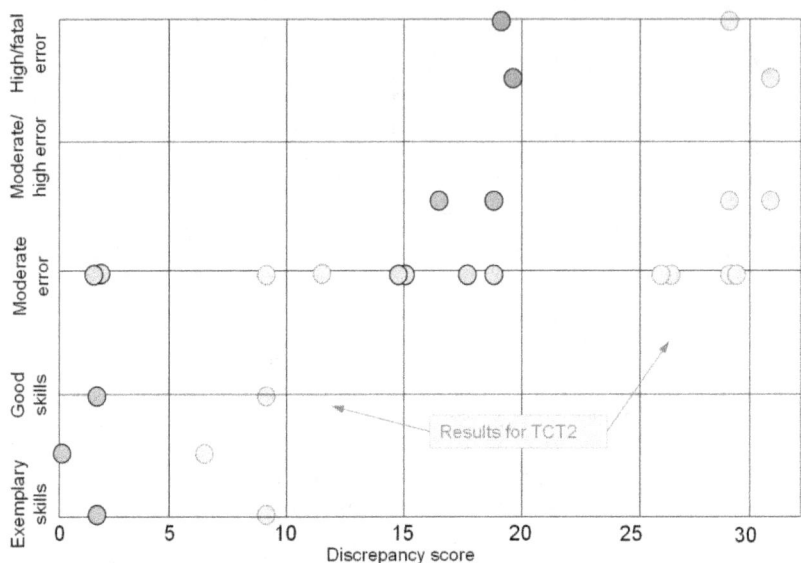

Figure 8-11: Evaluation of TCT3 organised action team option

Several managers who had been involved in various industrial or commercial projects were asked to fill in a team questionnaire (see Appendix 7); in addition, a highly-experienced aircraft pilot was asked to fill in the same questionnaire. The aim of this questionnaire was to collect information on team purpose, activities, team members (including their performances as team members), overall teaming performances, delivery performances and other teaming aspects. The management & engineering design team results and action team (aircraft crew) results from the team questionnaires have been plotted in the graph of Figure 8-12. As can be seen, there appears to be a negative relationship between teaming efficiency and cultural discrepancy score, i.e. the greater the cultural discrepancy (the difference between desirable and actual team culture scores), the less well the team was likely to perform in its key mission areas.

Originally, the author was intending to use external measures of team performance, e.g. output (against requirements) and timeliness, in his evaluation of the TCT3. However, several managers indicated in their questionnaire returns that actual achieved performance was significantly adversely affected by external constraints (e.g. company politics or project partner issues) and, as a result, they did not consider 'performance' always to be a reliable measure of team ability.

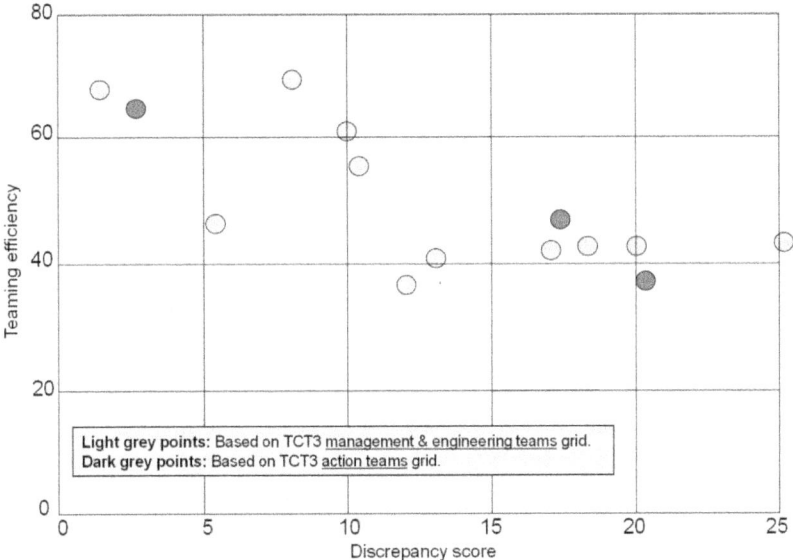

Figure 8-12: Evaluation (primarily) of TCT3 project team option

Therefore, the author used the user-scored measures of teaming ability weighted by the user-perceived importance of each measure to give an overall *teaming efficiency* measure. Teaming efficiency was based on the first six ratings in the 'Team Performance' section of the team questionnaire (Appendix 7) that had been filled in by managers, see Figure 8-13.

TEAM PERFORMANCE		
Rate the team performance as a whole with regard to ...	Rating	Importance
Rapid communication of situational factors needing urgent or prompt attention	Good	Slightly important
Communication between team members of complex factors and concepts	Adequate	Moderately important
Trusting and getting on with each other	Adequate	Moderately important
Creativity/coming up with novel ideas	Adequate	Quite important
Decision-making/selecting courses of action	Poor	Very important
Organising and allocating activities	Poor	Very important
Delivering the right quality and quantity of output (achieving goals or targets)	Adequate	Very important
Delivering in a timely fashion (getting the job done in time)	Good	Very important

Figure 8-13: The basis for calculating teaming ability

Note that the seventh and eighth ratings of Figure 8-13 provided a measure of actual team performance (as would be externally measured). The '*Rating*' and '*Importance*' values were selected from dropdown lists by the user; there were five options in each dropdown list, each assigned a percentage score from 10 to 90[60]. The measure of teaming performance was calculated as:

$$\frac{\sum(Rating \times Importance)}{\sum Importance}$$

The above measure of teaming, when applied to the example of Figure 8-13, produced a teaming ability score of 42%. Note that the same set of ratings (taken from the middle column of Figure 8-13) could produce a wide range of teaming ability scores depending on the relative importance of each factor (right-hand column).

The organised action team and project team results provided positive validation for the discrepancy-based model underlying the TCT3.

Discussions with several of the above managers about their questionnaire responses revealed additional interesting information. One manager brought up the issue of the 'macho' behaviours amongst the predominantly British members of his teams, who defended their 'positions' excessively, delaying progress (they were from a range of departments in a very large company). The introduction of female members to one of the teams produced a much improved level of behaviour in the team, with more consideration being given by the men to all other team members.

8.5.2 User testing and evaluation of the TCT3

Following the initial testing of the TCT3 on a range of team and mission types, the tool was made available to individuals who were or had been involved with British, other-national and/or multinational teams; where feasible, they were given an explanation and demonstration of the TCT3 prior to evaluating it by entering their team and project details. Following their evaluation exercises, users were each asked to fill in a TCT3 questionnaire (see Appendix 8). Information on numbers of users and cases (teams) is summarised in Table 8-2. User feedback on the tool (obtained from their questionnaire responses) is summarised in Table 8-3; note that answers based on dropdown lists have been converted into average percentage scores, as was the case with the earlier-described team questionnaire.

---

[60] As stated in Chapter 7, the number of options in each drop-down list was used as the basis for converting answers into percentage scores on the basis of an equi-spaced division of the range of answers. For three options, the answer options (from worst to best) were placed in the centres of 0-33.3%, 33.3-66.7% and 66.7-100%, i.e. at 16.7%, 50.0% and 83.3%. For five options, the answer options were placed at 10, 30, 50, 70 and 90%.

Users	Qty	Mission cases	Qty
Had used the TCT2	5	Project/design teams	11
Had not used the TCT2	3	Organised action teams	3
Total	8	Total	14

Table 8-2: TCT3 user and case numbers

a) Ease of use

From the TCT3 questionnaire answers, it appeared that all users found the cultural profiling of the team members and team to be straight-forward, as with the previous model.

Users found the mission profiling exercise faster and easier than had been the case with TCT2 as, instead of weighting a significant range of factors and sub-factors in order to produce the profile, it was only necessary to locate the mission context amongst exemplars in a two-dimensional grid. This also had the advantage of avoiding issues relating to the users' cultural backgrounds, which had been a problem with the TCT2. However, several users commented on the need for a wider range of exemplars.

b) Clarity and transparency

From the team culture tool questionnaire returns, it appeared that a majority of users considered that it was fairly clear as to what the TCT3 was doing and where the results (in terms of discrepancies) came from, see Table 8-3 for details of the responses.

c) Flexibility and adaptability

Users did not comment directly on this aspect.

d) Errors and accuracy

Based on the TCT3 questionnaire answers, four of the five users who had used both the TCT2 and TCT3 considered that they were less likely to make errors with the TCT3. As with the second tool, most users considered that the TCT3 would be an adjunct to the team-picking process, rather than the basis of it and that high accuracy was unimportant. The only potential issue associated with accuracy was considered to lie with the locations of the projects/missions on the grids and the resulting desirable cultural profiles.

Users	Team cultural profiler			Team mission profiler		Discrepancy results			Useful?
	Easy, understandable to use?	Quick/efficient to use?	Meaningful team profile results?	Easy, clear to use?	Quick/efficient to use?	Did the overall results make sense?	Was the improvement advice helpful?	Was the radar diagram helpful?	Could a TCT3-type tool be useful?
AL	Fairly easy	Fairly fast	Yes	OK	OK	To some extent	To some extent	Yes	Yes
AMJ	Very easy	Very fast	Yes	Fairly easy	Very fast	Yes	Yes	Yes	Yes
CEJ	Fairly easy	Fairly fast	To some extent	OK	Fairly fast	To some extent	Yes	To some extent	Yes
JB	Fairly easy	Fairly fast	Yes	Fairly easy	OK	Yes	Yes	Yes	Yes
JV	OK	Fairly fast	To some extent	OK	OK	To some extent	To some extent	To some extent	To some extent
MW	Fairly easy	Very fast	Yes	Fairly easy	Very fast	Yes	To some extent	Yes	Yes
SN	Fairly easy	Very fast	Yes	Fairly easy	Fairly fast	Yes	Yes	Yes	Yes
TW	Fairly easy	Fairly fast	Yes	OK	OK	Yes	To some extent	To some extent	To some extent
No. of answer options	5	5	3	5	5	3	3	3	3
Average score (%)	70	78	75	60	65	71	67	71	75

Table 8-3: Summary of TCT3 user questionnaire answers

e) Other user comments

One user commented about the issue of longevity of a team and changing attitudes due to familiarity – something that the culture tools did not adjust for. Another user suggested that additional help in terms drop-down boxes to help chose level of technical complexity or innovation, and more guidance for the social dimension.

Some users again commented about the (political) risks in using a culture tool, particularly one based on stereotypes.

8.6 Limitations, and a re-evaluation of the underpinning assumptions

Limitations were imposed on the scope of the research at an early stage of the study; however, it is worth reiterating these and other limitations that subsequently arose during the study.

8.6.1 Scoping limitations

Team analysis and performance prediction is a very wide area of research, which has been active since the 1950s. In order to complete a meaningful research project on the effects of culture, it had been necessary, from the beginning, to impose severe scoping limitations. As a result, most factors relating to team performance, such as personality (and team member types), leadership, training and stages in team development, were not considered, except where they directly impinged on cultural aspects of team performance. Therefore, the tool had limited applicability in terms of identifying a '*good*' team, but could act as a 'warning light' that might lead to reconsideration in circumstances where culture would be likely to lead to reduced performance.

8.6.2 Data availability

In addition to scoping limitations, the limited availability of detailed data from culture-related studies constrained the degree of progress and tool development that could be achieved, and also the accuracy of the tool.

8.6.3 Re-evaluating the assumptions underpinning the TCT3

A set of underpinning assumptions was listed in Subsection 8.2.2; it is worth reconsidering these at this stage.

(a) Capturing the cultural traits of actual or proposed teams

Feedback and brief discussions with two of the managers had indicated that they felt that the *actual* behaviours within their teams (in particular, within multicultural teams) could vary significantly based on the constraints and cues (and perhaps implied expectations) within the team and the environment, thus reducing the effectiveness of culture-based prediction tools such as the TCT3. This is probably true; however, cultural traits would provide a baseline and, given certain mission-related contextual cues, should trigger certain behaviours.

(b) Capturing the desirable team cultural traits to achieve a mission

It was assumed that the mission of a team could be captured sufficiently by placing the team or mission on a 'grid' or map containing a range of exemplar teams; this required the following:

i) *Capturing the culture-sensitive elements of team missions:* It was assumed that a small number of dimensions could capture the description of a mission or team with adequate accuracy to enable the cultural traits associated with optimum performance to be identified.

   Comments: The two dimensions chosen for each scenario appeared to capture sufficient aspects of missions to enable useful culture-based predictions, if the culture-related data was available (see (ii)).

ii) *Relating culture-sensitive elements of teams/missions to culture traits:* It was assumed that the cultural traits required for optimum performance of the teams/missions of (i) above could be adequately identified by the author; these included the cultural traits associated with the exemplar teams.

   Comments: The data from published studies varied widely, and there were no definitive, high quality studies that could be relied on. As a result, only limited confidence could be placed in the accuracy of the mission → cultural trait score transformation[61]. However, the evaluation results appeared overall to support the relationships between mission context and the cultural traits that were encapsulated in the TCT3.

iii) *Describing a particular team or mission in terms of the above factors:* It was assumed that users had sufficient knowledge to locate their teams with adequate accuracy within the grid or map.

   Comments: In the case of the user evaluation, they appeared to be able to locate their teams, but several expressed the opinion that more exemplars were required. These were, in the main, sophisticated managers with whom I had previously discussed the TCT3 and its purpose; most had also utilised the TCT2. It was therefore clear that more work needed to be done on exemplars (more of them, validation of their placing on the grid, and descriptions of their essential qualities). It was probable that

---

[61] In particular, with regard to masculinity and cultural diversity.

practical versions of a tool such as the TCT3 would need to be specialised for software projects, civil engineering, etc., where the exemplars would be much more meaningful to users.

c) Obtaining useful information from the discrepancies between desirable and actual cultural traits

It was assumed that the cultural discrepancies between actual and desirable cultural traits, when combined with the associated comments generated by the model/tool, would be meaningful, i.e. that they would inform the user of something useful about potential team performance and/or team problems.

Comments: The absolute values of the discrepancies probably meant little to the users at first. However, after experimenting with the TCT3, e.g. entering differing team member nationalities and selecting differing team types, the users appeared to have a feel for the relationships between the discrepancies and the associated messages (which were generated by the tool).

Note: In the above assumptions the words 'adequate' and 'adequately' appeared several times. These should not be confused with accurate/-accuracy. Given the potentially large cultural and personality variations between individuals, any team culture tool can at best only offer generalised information about potential team characteristics, the effects of which can be mollified or encouraged by training, appropriate management and leadership, or by other steps. Many internationally-experienced different-culture or multicultural teams would not be represented accurately (in cultural terms) by any general culture tool.

8.7   Summary of the TCT3

A dimensionally-based approach (as opposed to a factor-weighting or taxonomic approach) to team mission profiling was implemented in the third model and team culture tool (TCT3).

The dimension-based approach to missions had three advantages compared to the TCT2:

- **Ease of use:** The mission profiler was much easier and quicker to use, as it only required the user to select a location in mission space, guided by pre-existing exemplars. However it needed more exemplars, with more associated explanation, to be a practical, effective general user tool.

- **Reduced cultural bias on the part of the user:** Users no longer selected factors that were subject to cultural bias (e.g.

229

management and communication styles); however, the approach may have increased the risks associated with tool designer cultural bias (i.e. the author's western biases).

- **Direct associations between mission context and cultural traits:** This avoided issues associated with tasks and behaviours.

The dimension-based approach to missions had two disadvantages compared to the TCT2:

- **Limited range of teams/missions:** The mission profiler only covered a limited range of teams – if the mission did not lie within one of the two environments (design/project teams or organised action teams) then it could not be culturally assessed.

- **Tool inflexibility in a changing world:** The mission → desirable culture transformation was fixed – i.e. team members of particular cultural backgrounds were and would remain discrepant to a particular degree, depending on the mission. However, in the 'real world', changing systems, in particular the development of intelligent 'automation-as-a-crew-member' systems could obviate, or at least reduce, cultural issues. As long as the tool was only used as a rough guide to potential culturally-related problems, this would not be a major issue.

It proved impracticable to implement a single comprehensive multidimensional system, as the dimensions required by different teams varied to such a degree that a comprehensive system would have been effectively unusable; also additional dimensions were required to assist the user to place the team[62]. It would be worth investigating a 'dimension-hiding' approach using a sophisticated programming environment at a later stage (a topic for future work).

Two dimension-based team types – *design/project teams* and *organised action teams* (or *swift-start action teams*) were successfully validated and user-evaluated. These were the key teams of interest to the stakeholders identified in this thesis.

---

[62] As an example, a dimension relating to team member specialisation was introduced for *action team* mission selection; this spread the team types out and enabled the user to differentiate his/her mission, and place it effectively. In this case, specialisation did not play a significant part in deriving the desirable cultural profile.

The TCT3 could be regarded as an implementation of a theory about the culture-performance relationship, based on the pragmatist principle (Charles Teddlie & Abbas Tashakkori 2009, Table 4.1, p.74), i.e.:

> *"Theories are viewed instrumentally (they are "true" to differing degrees based on how well they currently work; workability is judged especially on the criteria of predictability and applicability)."*

9 Discussion and analysis

9.1 Introduction

The purpose of this chapter is to describe and critically analyse the 'research path' for readers, then to highlight the key achievements, problems and limitations of the research against the objectives and, finally, to detail the contributions to knowledge, limitations, novel outputs and further research opportunities. These are summarised in the conclusions of the following and final chapter.

The use of teams in industry and commerce has increased rapidly over the last several decades. In the case of multinationals, they have increasingly utilised 'other culture' or 'different culture'[63] teams and, in their home countries, multicultural teams. Whereas much research has been carried out on team theory, particularly in the English-speaking world, this has tended to be applied to single culture, typically 'Anglo'[64] teams. The research community's theoretical understanding of the performance of 'other-culture' teams and multicultural teams is much less developed, and many of the earlier-developed team-related assumptions do not apply.

The purposes of the research described in this thesis were to gain an improved knowledge of the relationships between team member cultural traits and team performance for various team/task situations, and to encapsulate this knowledge in models and tools that offered the potential for practicable application by managers and engineers.

---

[63] 'Different culture' as in the majority of subsidiaries of multinational companies being of different national cultures to the head office and to each other, resulting in implications for the effective placement of various forms of research, development and manufacture.

[64] As stated earlier in this thesis, the term 'Anglo' refers to people of British descent, e.g. British, Irish, Canadian, Anglo-American, New Zealander, Australian, Anglo-South African.

9.2 A brief overview of the research activities

Chapter 2 provided a problem statement, identified the key stakeholders and described the research methodology; the need to follow the pragmatist approach was emphasised in order to ensure that a tool of potential practicable use emerged out of the work. The chapter then provided an overview of the solution approach, including the key topic areas for investigation in the literature review. Chapter 3, the literature review, examined the effects of culture on the performance of teams, the availability of culture-based tools to predict the performance of teams, and evidence to support the validity of such tools. Although much evidence of the effects of culture on team performance was found, it was inconsistent, in particular with regard to the cultural traits of masculinity and diversity. Very few national culture based performance prediction tools were found, and those that were identified did not relate to team activities; however, several cultural frameworks were identified that could form the basis of such a tool. No suitable task/mission classification was identified in the literature (an essential part of any performance prediction tool), nor was a suitable diversity measure for the capture of cultural differences between team members. However, the review had earlier identified five culturally-moderated behaviour-related factors that could be used to describe tasks or missions.

Based on the literature review of Chapter 3, Chapter 4 described the researcher's choice of a cultural framework – Hofstede's original four-dimensional framework, chosen due to the large number of validation and application studies associated with the framework – probably more than all other cultural frameworks combined. However, there was also a requirement for an expression for cultural diversity, and for a classifi-cation of teams/tasks/missions that could be utilised for the exploration of cultural aspects of team performance, as nothing suitable had been found in the literature. As a result, the author was required to develop and evaluate an alternative measure of team cultural diversity based on member cultural separations in each of the four dimensions (see Sub-section 4.3.2). The expression produced a <u>separate</u> measure of diversity for <u>each</u> cultural dimension; an average could be taken if an overall diversity figure were required. The expression for cultural diversity along cultural dimension ''x' (CD_{teamx}) was:

$$Cd_{teamx} = \sum_{i=1}^{N}\sum_{j=1}^{N} ABS(Dix - Djx)/(N \times (N-1))$$

Where:

D_{ix}, D_{jx} = Scores for cultural dimension 'x' for team members 'i' and 'j'

N = Total number of team members (including member 'i')

As stated earlier, no team or task/mission classification had been found in the literature that could be utilised for the purpose of distinguishing team performances on the basis of cultural traits. Therefore, the author developed a task/mission classification that was based on the five key culturally-moderated factors that had been identified in the literature review (see subsections 3.3.3 and 4.4.1). As an alternative to the above task/mission factors, an ideal team/task/mission framework was identified to be a continuous multidimensional space (rather than a taxonomy), but it was not clear as to the nature of the minimum set of culture-sensitive dimensions. Three research questions relating to masculinity, uncertainty avoidance and cultural diversity were also posed in Chapter 4; these cultural dimensions and diversity measures were relatively under-researched compared to those of power distance and individualism, and the available evidence of their effects had tended to be contradictory; it was important to include them in the culture models and tools, therefore an improved understanding of their effects on team performance was needed.

Chapter 5 described the data collection and analysis activities. These included the collection of qualitative anecdotal and questionnaire-based data to provide validation (or otherwise) for some of the assumptions behind the proposed models and tools and the completion of a range of pilot studies into the performances of 'other-culture' and multicultural teams. Based on the analysis of all the collected data (both qualitative and quantitative), several novel outputs were produced in answering the three research questions posed in Chapter 4. The analysis also enabled the elaboration of the relationships between cultural dimensions and performance factors, including the identification of optimum 'high' and 'low' culture scores. Further details of these novel outputs are provided in Section 9.6.

Chapters 6, 7 and 8 described the three culture models and team culture tools developed as a key part of the author's research. All models were based on the concept of profiling the team culture to provide estimates of team average culture scores and cultural diversity scores for each cultural dimension (see Table 4-7, and Figure 7-3 for example cultural profiles), but each model utilised a different approach to the generation and application of a team/task/mission profile. The culture model described in Chapter 6 (TCT1) aimed to derive a direct culture-based measure of team efficiency (expressed as a percentage). However, the complex, interrelated calculations were difficult to justify on a theoretical basis; also, the model was not flexible enough to cover an adequate range of teams, nor was it discriminating enough to distinguish between different levels of innovation.

The culture model described in Chapter 7 (TCT2) utilised a more sophisticated version of the team cultural profiler that had been utilised in Chapter 6; this enabled bicultural and culturally-unique team members to be entered into the profile. However, the model adopted a very different approach to the evaluation of the effects of team culture on team performance. A task/mission was profiled by applying weights to the standard set of five task/mission factors and their sub-factors that had been identified in Chapter 3 and elaborated in Chapter 4 (see Section 7.4.2 and Figure 7-4); these user-entered weights indicated which culturally moderated behaviours and capabilities were important and which were not. Each sub-factor in the task/mission profile was associated with a set of desirable culture dimension scores; by determining the differences between actual team dimension scores and desirable scores, and factoring these by both the sub-factor and factor weightings, a set of cultural *discrepancy* scores was obtained. This set of discrepancies formed the basis of the assessment of the team's fit to the task/mission. Whereas the team culture profiler was easy to use, the task profiler was difficult and unclear for those who had not worked on the model and, as a result, had low face validity amongst users. Also several users commented on the efficacy of utilising task or behavioural factors which, some considered, were probably context-dependent anyway (this is discussed later).

Taking into account the difficulties encountered when using the second tool and user concerns about the use of behaviours or behaviourally-related tasks, the culture model described in Chapter 8 (TCT3) utilised a new dimension-based mission context profiler (as suggested in Chapter 4); users merely placed their mission on a two-dimensional grid that included exemplars to aid with the placement process. The TCT3 continued to utilise the same team culture profiler as that of the TCT2. The validations of the TCT3 demonstrated a positive discrepancy/-accident relationship for organised action team accident rates, and negative discrepancy/project performance relationship for project team performances, i.e. both relationships were confirmatory of the tool's prediction capabilities. Users found this tool to be easy to use, and the underlying model to be logical and understandable (see Section 8.5.2 and Table 8-3 for details).

9.3 A critical analysis of the research

Several factors imposed constraints on the research, presented issues, raised requirements for additional work due to the absence of research results, suitable tools or representations, or reduced the effectiveness of the research or accuracy of the tools that were developed during the research. These are discussed further in this section.

9.3.1 The creativity conundrum

The creation and application of new knowledge is a key part of the work of teams associated with the design and development of sociotechnical systems. The lack of a suitable creativity classification methodology in the literature was a major problem – the researchers carrying out culture/creativity studies could not place their studies accurately, and their fellow researchers could not place their results accurately in the context of other work. Basic research, invention, innovation and improvement were significantly different activities that appeared (from the literature) to be performed optimally in different cultures. Therefore, a failure to associate the performance results of a study with an appropriate form of creativity would result in a similar failure to connect particular cultural traits with that form of creativity.

As an indication of the critical nature of this creativity conundrum, there are now problems with the utilisation in many studies of patents (pending or granted) as measures of creative or innovatory output. An increasing proportion of patents have recently been sought (and granted) for designs or functions that, in themselves, were not the products of creativity or innovation but were 'spoilers' designed to prevent rivals from utilising intuitive or simple actions on new technology devices (e.g. smart phones). Such trivial patents have started to distort the conclusions of studies that have used patents as output measures of team or country performance. Evidence has emerged from recent patent-based studies that low individualism appears to be positively associated with creativity rather than improvement – a reversal of the results of earlier studies. Although it is highly likely that Eastern Asian countries have been significantly improving their innovation performances, the recent changes (which are associated with very large increases in the number of Eastern Asian patents) have happened very suddenly.

The author of this thesis has proposed a three dimensional framework, for the placement of creativity/innovation activities (see figure). Such a framework would be designed specifically to enable the placement of creativity-linked activities, for the purpose of being able adjudge the nature of any project[65]. Note that projects would migrate over time in certain directions within this space.

---

[65] Any classification system must have a purpose, which effectively defines it. In this case, the purpose was specifically to place creativity-related activities in relation to each other. If it were a classification intended to assist with the flow of steps through to completion of creativity-related activities, it would be substantially different.

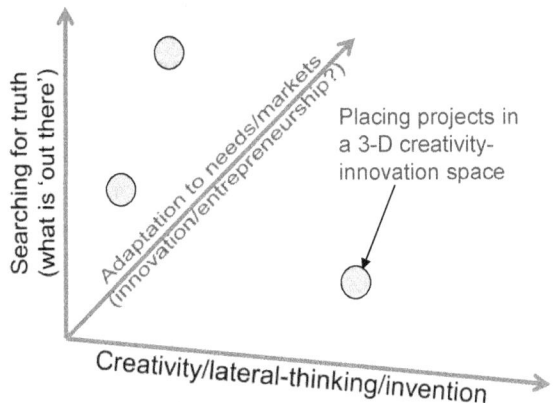

Such a framework would enable more consistent classification of creativity-related activities, leading to a better understanding of the cultural aspects of creativity and, potentially, to an improved allocation of projects around the World. Note that the vertical axis reflects an Eastern view of creativity as the search for, or a revealing of, a truth that is temporarily hidden from view. The successful collaboration of 113 nationalities of scientists and engineers at CERN implies that the search for truth (as in fundamental research) is a task for all nations. Recent history would suggest that the British have been more effective at creativity/lateral-thinking/invention than adaptation-to-markets/innovation, whereas the Japanese have perhaps been the opposite.

To summarise: The lack of an adequate classification that covered the various forms of creativity-related activities has resulted in reduced accuracy of the creativity-linked aspects of this thesis; in particular, the prediction reliability of the sociotechnical project team aspect of the TCT2 and TCT3 team culture tools was reduced.

9.3.2 The representational accuracy of cultural frameworks

Selection of Hofstede's framework: As stated earlier, Hofstede's cultural framework was selected as the basis for culture measurement because of the large number of evaluations of it over the previous two decades, and the large number of studies that had used the framework – more than all other quantitative frameworks combined. When the author's PhD studies began, a wide range of national scores was available for only four of Hofstede's cultural dimensions – power distance, individualism, masculinity and uncertainty avoidance. A fifth dimension, long term orientation was available, but with only twenty-eight or so national scores; in addition, there were criticisms of the validity of this dimension. A revised fifth dimension (LTO-WVS) and a sixth dimension, indulgence vs. restraint (IVR), were identified and published in 2010, eighteen months after the author's PhD research had started. Although many national scores have now been determined for the latter two dimensions, these scores became available too late for incorporation in the work described in this thesis; note also that the author has not been able to locate any quantitative cultural studies that utilised these two additional dimensions[66]. See Appendix 10 for a brief discussion of the fifth and sixth dimensions of Hofstede's framework.

Limitations of any dimensional framework: As elaborated in Section 4.2, a small number of quantitative cultural dimensions cannot explain every cultural difference between groups or nations, and Hofstede's framework is no different to others in this respect; Subsection 4.2.2 provides some surprising examples of cultural bedfellows and strangers.

Extension of the Hofstede framework: There was an obvious issue, commented on in Subsection 5.6.1, about the incremental extension of cultural frameworks – two further dimensions had been added to Hofstede's framework. New dimensions cannot realistically be 'tacked on' to existing frameworks without reducing the independence between dimensions. Ideally, the introduction of the two new dimensions would have resulted in a re-examination of all the original and new factors/-questions, and an optimal reassignment of all of them into potentially new dimensions.

Limited meanings of cultural dimension scores: Hofstede's cultural dimension scores were normalised so that the range between the lowest and highest scoring countries in each dimension was 0 to 100 (this changed with the addition of new countries). How low was low power distance, how high was high? It was difficult to utilise these scores to produce default values for the 'high' and 'low' values claimed in the studies of the literature, as the scores had little intrinsic meaning.

The ecological fallacy: Hofstede repeatedly reminded readers that his cultural framework applied only at the level of *social systems*, and that users of his framework should avoid falling into the *ecological fallacy* trap, i.e. by making inferences about *individuals* based on his data. However, as stated in Section 4.2 of this thesis, a key aspect of the research described in this thesis related to the prediction of the mis-match between the cultures of operators of sociotechnical systems and the cultural requirements of those sociotechnical systems. In many cases, the only knowledge available about operators was their likely

---

[66] In commenting on the lack of studies here, I am referring to the later version of LTO (LTO-WVS) and IVR, not to the earlier version of LTO, for which a limited number of studies were located.

nationalities and (perhaps) their educational levels; it was therefore necessary to work with the default national culture scores. It would only be possible to determine, on the basis of actual culture tool performance, whether these default aggregate national scores provided a useful basis for predicting performance problems. One might reasonably expect that taking account of national culture when designing systems would produce a more culture-friendly product or system than not taking account of national culture.

The author of this thesis suggested, in Section 4.2.2, that whereas individuals within a culture might vary significantly in terms of their own preferences, these individuals would be likely to vary far less in terms of their *expectations* of the behaviour of others, and in their *actual* behaviours in social situations within their own cultures. This lower variance in behaviour was likely because cultures imposed a behavioural straitjacket that was particularly strong in low-individualism, high-power distance or high-uncertainty avoiding cultures, where non-conformance was heavily discouraged. This view appeared to be supported by the anecdotal evidence collected by the author (see Section 5.2 for a summary). No doubt, the use of Hofstede's default country scores for members of small teams (e.g. two or three member crews) could introduce errors, but there was no alternative but to use these default cultural scores.

An alternative to Hofstede's framework: Hofstede's cultural frame-work was probably the only one with a sufficient number of associated studies; therefore it was the only feasible choice to enable the route that was taken in this PhD study. An alternative approach would have been to eschew cultural frameworks. Instead, it may have been feasible, firstly, to access raw (or semi-processed) data on human populations, for example via the World Value Survey, in order to build culture-related constructs. Secondly it would have been feasible to access raw data on innovation, industrial outputs, accident rates and other statistics, for example via The Global Innovation Index, World Intellectual Property Organization, European Patent Office, US Patent & Trademark Office, Airsafe.com and World Health Organization. These would have allowed the building of culture models based on large databases. It would have required considerable statistical analysis, and would probably have been a high risk strategy for a PhD study.

To summarise: It was unlikely that there would have been sufficient research study results available with any other framework but Hofstede's to enable the evidence-based assessment of culture-performance relationships and the consequent building of the culture tools described in this thesis. However, the above points, taken together, imply that the default culture scores, as used in the work of this thesis, were less accurate than would be desirable. An alternative, rather different approach would have been to use large information sets such as that of the World Value Survey (WVS) to build cultural constructs, innovation models, accident models, etc., and to produce predictive tools based on these.

9.3.3 The choice of 'cultural profile discrepancies'

Since the 1950s, a very large body of research has been carried out into team performance, resulting in the identification of many performance-affecting factors and the development of many frameworks, models and theories, for example Tuckman's stages model (Tuckman & Jensen, 1977), Tubbs' systems model (Tubbs, 1995), Belbin's team role theory (R M Belbin, 1993) and the balanced team generating model (van de Water, van de Water, & Bukman, 2007). It was impossible, within the constraints of a PhD, to incorporate, adapt and evaluate these and other team models as part of a larger model and, in any case, such models were not culture-free.

After evaluating the first team culture model and tool, it became clear that a practicable team culture tool should not attempt directly to forecast *overall* team performance because this performance depended on too many non-cultural factors, including those modelled by the above-listed frameworks and models. Instead, following analysis of the first culture tool, the TCT1, it was decided that the team cultural tool should determine the gaps or discrepancies between the actual team cultural profile and an 'ideal' or 'desirable' cultural profile that was generated by the tool; these discrepancies could form the basis for forecasting the likely effects of the team's *cultural* traits on performance.

To summarise: The choice of some of form of discrepancy between actual and desirable team cultural profile appeared to have been the only practicable option, given our current limited understandings of culture.

9.3.4 Task classifications

From an external perspective (e.g. the viewpoint of the customer, the enterprise or the department), the key team performance measures typically related to the effectiveness or safety and/or timeliness with which the team carried out its tasks or missions. It was therefore considered necessary, when defining a team, to consider the key tasks that it had to perform successfully and the behaviours that were required; this appeared to necessitate the adoption of some form of task/behaviour classification scheme. The literature review (Subsection 3.4.4) revealed that there were no team task classification systems that could be adapted to provide a culture-sensitive team task scheme. It also revealed that a taxonomic approach was likely to be ineffective, as it would introduce both complexity and inaccuracy (Hollenbeck et al., 2012). As stated earlier, five task factors were identified and their sub-task/behavioural factors were also identified; each of these behavioural sub-factors had an optimum or ideal set of culture scores associated with it, based on the literature and the author's pilot studies. The first team culture tool (TCT1) task representation was based on three of these factors, the second team culture tool (TCT2) task/mission representation was based on all five of these factors and their sub-tasks/behaviours (see Section 4.4.1 for details).

Evaluations of the five-factor/behavioural sub-factor approach utilised in the TCT2 produced results that were in line with the literature and with the author's expectations. However, two users who evaluated the TCT2 had concerns about the direct associations between sub-factor behavioural requirements and cultural traits, as they felt that these links were conditional on situations. These concerns are discussed further in the next subsection.

9.3.5 Implications for the validity of the initial assumptions

The initial assumptions (stated originally in Chapter 1) are listed below. Some comments are made as to the individual assumptions. However, these assumptions are effectively interlinked, and it is the performance of the overall tool that reveals the validity (or otherwise) of the set of assumptions; therefore, a separate discussion of the overall performance is presented at the end.

The cultural properties (i.e. 'cultural profiles') of teams could be usefully modelled[67] by quantifying team member cultural values along a limited number of 'cultural dimensions':

Based on the analysis of Subsection 9.3.2, the framework was almost certainly less accurate than was originally thought. However, it is probably the way in which the researcher *applies* the framework that is more important than its accuracy, Therefore this assumption largely held true.

The tasks that teams performed (i.e. their task profiles) could be modelled in terms of behavioural factors that were directly affected by team culture:

---

[67] In this context, 'usefully modelled' implied that the cultural profiles captured some significant differences between teams that influenced relative team performance.

As stated earlier, a five-factor/behavioural sub-factor generic represen-tation of mission tasks was produced, the sub-factors of which were clearly identified in the literature as being affected by cultural traits, therefore this assumption largely held true.

Relationships between culture dimension scores and the perfor-mance of task behavioural factors could be established:

Based on the literature and on the results of author's own studies, 'optimum' cultural dimension scores were identified and associated with behavioural factors. This assumption effectively held true.

Models that incorporated team cultural profiles and task/behav-ioural profiles could be used to predict the effect of team culture on team performance:

The second team culture tool incorporated the team cultural profile and task/behavioural profile, and the results of applying these to teams and their tasks appeared encouraging – increasing discrepancies were generally indicative of decreasingly effective performance. However, comments from and discussions with former project team managers who had evaluated the second tool, the TCT, revealed an issue relating to the initiating – or not – of culturally-modified behaviours by contextual cues. Following these discussions, the author looked at the literature in this area. It was realised that the actual triggering of culturally-modified behaviours could not be assumed – it depended on the contextual cues, and degree of prior priming. This implied that the previously assumed culture → behaviour relationships were not as rigid (or reliable) as had been thought. The relationships were still there, but could not be assumed to cause the expected behaviour in all circumstances.

Unfortunately, it was also clear from the literature that researchers' understandings of the effects of contextual cues for culture-related behaviour were concentrated on the collectivism – individualism dimen-sion. A decision was therefore made to replace the task/behavioural factors with direct associations between cultural traits and key mission contexts. Relationships were established for two major team/task/-mission types – organised action teams, and a limited range of project teams. It was not possible to disentangle the many contextual cues that might play a part, as current research-based understandings were not adequate.

Although the second tool, based on these assumptions, demonstrated reasonable predictive power in terms of showing associations between cultural discrepancies and reduced performance or safety, the basic assumption of a direct link between culture and behaviour was not strictly true.

To summarise: The original fourth assumption of a direct link between cultural traits and behaviours was an oversimplification, and could lead to inaccuracies under some circumstances.

9.4 What could have been done differently?

The author underestimated several aspects of the research, and spent too long studying aspects that turned out to be unimportant; with hindsight, more could have been achieved. These aspects are discussed below.

- **Lack of access to published study data:** Although it initially appeared that a significant amount of quantitative data was available in published form, few studies were directly comparable to each other due to the differing combinations of input and output variables, correction factors, etc.; also, in most cases, the datasets used by other authors were not available. The author contacted several researchers with a view to obtaining the raw data that would enable comparative analysis, without success. This is, perhaps, understandable, as the author spent many months collecting, processing and analysing data, and would probably have been less than happy to hand that data over to a stranger unless there was an option of collaborative work.

  With hindsight, the author would have spent more time at an early stage familiarising himself with the key international data sources, e.g. United Nations (UNSD/UNdata), European Union (Eurostat), World Values Survey (WVS) World Intellectual Property Organization (WIPO), United States Patent and Trademark Office (USPTY), and the European Patent Office (EPO). The WVS is the only source (as far as this author was aware) of international comprehensive, timeline data on *attitudes*. A better understanding of the above (and other similar) data sources would have enabled the author to develop a wider range of statistical studies of his own, although this work would have been very time-consuming. The author did access and utilise some international data sources, for example air accident databases.

- **Team/task/mission classifications:** The lack of a suitable classification was a major delaying factor in the research. With hindsight, the author would have spent more time developing and analysing a multidimensional team/task/mission representation. The work on this was started relatively late in the PhD, partially driven by user issues that arose with the classification approach that had been initially adopted.

- **Cognitive neuroscience aspects of culture**: The author has, for many years, been interested in the cognitive neuroscience of affect, the associated behaviour, and (more recently) the culturally-shaped modifications to that behaviour. He spent a significant part of the early phase of the PhD studying this area; in particular, the work of Jaak Panksepp and Peter Richerson appeared to offer a basis for new theories of affect and culture. With hindsight, the author recognises that this, though fascinating, was a step too far. The time should have been devoted to more accessible culture-related work.

9.5   Meeting the research aims and objectives

The original aims of the research were to develop an improved understanding of the factors (in particular cultural factors) that influenced the effectiveness of teams, and to create a methodology and toolset for the evaluation of project teams and sociotechnical system operators and crews. The associated objectives are listed below, with brief descriptions of the associated achievements.

- **To identify the culturally-related factors that contributed most to variances in team attitudes, behaviours and performances:** This was achieved for a limited range of team types, including project teams involved in creative and innovatory work (e.g. sociotechnical system design), sociotechnical system operators and crew. However, due to the extreme variance in the results from published research studies, the effects of the cultural dimension 'masculinity', and the effects of cultural diversity on team performance were less clear than those of the others (power distance, individualism and uncertainty avoidance).

  The author considers that he has only partially met this objective as the high variability of masculinity (in particular) in the published study results has limited the accuracy of the work.

- **To identify a task classification relevant to culturally-moderated team performance:** This proved difficult, as no team/task classification found in the literature was either broad enough or could reasonably be linked to culturally-modified behaviours. The author developed a five-factor team/task/mission classification (based on the literature, see Subsections 3.3.3 and 4.4.1); although there were minor user difficulties and face validity issues, these could have been tackled. Issues associated with the link between culture, contextual cueing and behaviour reduced the potential reliability of the second model; therefore, a dimension-based mission representation was introduced in the third model.

The author considers that he has partially achieved this objective.

- **To build a model that incorporates the above factors for the prediction of the effects of culture on team performance when tackling specified types of task:** Two detailed culture/-mission models and their associated tools were developed based on results from the literature and the author's pilot studies; one of these models covered organised action teams (including socio-technical system operators and crews), the other covered project teams carrying out various levels of innovation (including socio-technical system design & build projects).

The author considers that this objective was achieved, subject to the limitations associated with cultural contexts.

- **To encapsulate the above model(s) in a methodology and tool in order to:**

  o **Facilitate the selection of successful teams in given situations.**

  o **Enable the prediction of the effects of culture on team performance, and likely success or failure, of existing or proposed teams.**

The first team culture tool attempted directly to predict team performance; however, this was not considered to be based on a viable model. The second and third tools encapsulated the above models (in different forms) to enable the selection of team members and the prediction of potential performance reduction, based on cultural discrepancies between actual and desirable team culture. It is considered that, for a restricted set of teams (engineering/management project teams and organised action teams) the tools have successfully encapsulated the models, and have been verified and validated to a limited extent.

9.6 Contributions to knowledge and novel outputs

The contributions to knowledge and novel outputs are listed and described in the following paragraphs.

- **An improved understanding of the relationships between uncertainty avoidance & cultural diversity (as measured by cultural dimension scores) and team performance factors** (see Section 5.4).

  The above results were important, in particular the findings with regard to cultural diversity. The confirmation of the effects of uncertainty avoidance on creative performance and, notably, in situations where 'sticking to the rules' was important, were valuable. In the literature, cultural diversity was typically measured as a single crude value based on the number and proportion of different nationalities. Such a measure was highly insensitive to actual cultural diversity between individuals of different cultures[68], so it is hardly surprising that study results were contradictory. Research by the author indicates that it was specific forms of diversity (e.g. masculinity diversity or uncertainty avoidance diversity) that affected specific task/mission situations; the author's statistical results also showed that overall cultural diversity (taken across the four original Hofstede dimensions) seldom appeared as statistically significant. This result was important and, if other researchers were to adopt similarly sensitive measures, consistent results relating to the effects of cultural diversity might begin to emerge.

- **Significantly greater detail in the relationships between cultural dimension scores and team performance factors**: These were encapsulated in the graphs of Figures 8-3 to 8-5.

- **A theoretically-justifiable model of the effects of team culture on team performance:** The discrepancy-based approach sidestepped the potential issues caused by the many other non-cultural factors associated with team performance. It enabled the prediction of the effects of team culture of the team's potential performance.

- **A practicable user-orientated team culture tool:** The author did not come across any practicable, quantitative culture tools that provided a prediction capability for user-specified teams. The third team culture tool (TCT3) enabled the creation of a

---

[68] A team consisting of one each of British, Irish, Canadian and Australian members would typically be considered maximally diverse, despite the extremely similar cultural dimension scores amongst its members; a team consisting of two Saudi Arabian and two Swedish members would be considered less diverse despite the almost completely opposite cultural dimension scores associated with the two nationalities.

culture profile for any real team (of up to sixteen members), simply by entering team members' nationalities and education levels[69], and enabled the creation of a desirable cultural profile based on the team's task/mission by a single mouse click on a two-dimensional grid that included exemplar teams.

- **A recognition of the limits inherent in simple dimension-based quantitative cultural frameworks**: The issue of contextual cueing (or priming) of culturally-moderated behaviours has yet to be recognised in mainstream research. The author makes no claim to have advanced the understanding of contextual cues on culture-moderated behaviours, but feels that the work described in this thesis has drawn attention to it.

The author claimed, in Chapter 1, that the main contribution to knowledge would be a cultural theory of work team performance and a validated, quantitative methodology and tool that would enable the culturally-based assessment and improvement of teams. It is considered that these contributions have largely been achieved, but see the last point above.

9.7 What questions can we now answer?

The team culture tool enabled engineer and management users to obtain answers to questions such as:

- All other things being equal, would it be better from a cultural point of view to move our early-stage R&D to the subsidiary in the USA, or the subsidiary in Singapore?

- Why?

- Which countries do current flight deck layouts and automation systems pose the biggest cultural threats to?

- Why?

---

[69] The user could instead enter *dual* cultural nationalities (for example to reflect a team member's immigrant background), or could directly enter cultural values based on an individual's answers to a questionnaire or based on knowledge of the person.

9.8 Meeting the requirements of the main stakeholders

The main stakeholders were identified, in Section 1.6, as:

- **Organisations that designed and built complex sociotechnical systems:**

  The third team culture tool could demonstrate the designers/-builders cultural profiles and contrast these with the users' (operators', crews') profiles – enabling designers/builders to recognise the differences between themselves and users - and the potential resulting issues. The tool could also show the discrepancies between the demands of such systems and the culture-moderated abilities of the users.

- **Organisations that used complex sociotechnical systems:**

  The tool could, via the discrepancies, indicate where culture-sensitive crew resource management and other training programmes could potentially reduce cultural mismatches and thereby improve safety.

- **Organisations that assembled and utilised multicultural and other-cultural teams for problem solving and project work:**

  The tool could demonstrate the effects of different team cultural profiles on proposed projects of varying levels of creativity and innovation. This would enable organisations to decide where to place projects and who to select for particular teams.

- **Education and training organisations:**

  The tool could be useful as a general culture teaching aid, and for training students to deal with other cultures.

Note: The team culture tools were prototypes and would need to have improved data collection and storage capabilities to be optimised for regular use.

9.9 Further work

The work described in this thesis produced methodologies and tools that enabled users to explore to a limited degree the effects of team member cultural traits on team performance in certain environments, for certain team/task types. There were several logical avenues for further development, both pragmatic and theoretical.

On a pragmatic basis, extensions of the current work could include the following:

1. **Expansion (or substitution) of the cultural framework**

    During the work described in this thesis, Hofstede's cultural framework was expanded to include a sixth dimension, that of indulgence vs. restraint; culture scores for this and a modified form of the fifth dimension (long term orientation) became available towards the end of the author's research work. Despite the reservations expressed earlier about long term orientation, it would be useful to explore the effects of these two additional dimensions on performance; this could be done initially by statistically reanalysing the existing data used in this thesis with the addition of the two extra cultural dimensions. A search for relevant publications, conducted shortly before the completion of this thesis, revealed no studies utilising either of the two additional Hofstede cultural dimensions that would be relevant to the team types discussed in this thesis. However, this could be considered to indicate a fertile new area of investigation.

    The more recent framework of Minkov (2011) could offer an interesting alternative.

2. **Developing the dimensional representation of tasks/-missions**

    Different sets of task/mission dimensions have been used for the two key team/task/mission types currently available in the third team culture tool. It is desirable to develop a wider-scope set of common dimensions, perhaps incorporating a dimension-hiding technique so that, for a given task/mission type, only dimensions and exemplars of relevance to that type would be displayed.

3. **Incorporating a model of the contextual cueing of culturally-moderated behaviour**

    This is a fascinating area, as there are several directions of development currently taking place. It may be rewarding to explore the cueing (or suppression) of uncertainty-avoiding behaviours, as an understanding of this would be beneficial to safety and safety training.

4. Developing an organisational culture tool

Although there is currently little in the way of effective quantitative organisational culture models or tools, Hofstede discusses the power distance/uncertainty avoidance matrix as a basis for different national and company types. A pragmatic approach based on a power distance/uncertainty avoidance matrix grid could be tested against industrial project data in order to assess the potential of the approach; industrial colleagues have commented several times on the problems caused by projects involving multiple organisations.

On a more theoretical basis, new developments in tools and analytic techniques are offering the scope for the development of completely new understandings of culture, personality, affect and behaviour. These developments provide opportunities to move from statistical correlation-based models to explanatory, causation-based models:

1. Cognitive neuroscience theories of affect, culture and behaviour

Cognitive neuroscience theories and tools have progressed to the stage where we are able to observe in real time, and understand, some of the culture-based emotion moderating pathways and feedback cycles in the brain. The development of causal explanations of culture will help us to understand culture-based limitations, and also help us to develop training techniques to reduce or remove such limitations, or work environments that are more sympathetic to these limitations.

2. Gene/culture interaction and culture-moderating pathways

Clear evidence has already emerged of culture-based selection pressures on human genes, e.g. the S-allele of the serotonin transporter gene SLC6A4; this example hints at relationships with uncertainty avoidance and collectivism, and could lead to a better understanding of the physical and neurochemical pathways through which uncertainty avoidance is played out. It is likely that there are other culture/gene interactions that could reveal further details of the fundamental structures behind cultural and personality traits; in some cases, these interactions could reveal that certain traits are not fundamental, but are statistical ephemera.

3. Epigenetics and the multigenerational expression of early cultural influences

The discovery of epigenetic changes in gene expression that are triggered by environmental conditions has enabled the study of cultural influences on gene expression. The yet-little-understood mechanisms that carry such changes across generations have major ramifications for culture-based changes.

These are exciting times for culture researchers who are willing to look beyond the conventional fields and methods of study.

10 Conclusions and recommendations

10.1 Introduction

This chapter summarises the findings of the previous chapter. The statements below are intentionally brief, more detailed descriptions and supporting material can be found in the previous chapter.

10.2 Meeting the aims and objectives of the research

The original aims of the research were to develop an improved understanding of the cultural factors that influenced the effectiveness of teams, and to create a methodology and toolset for the evaluation of project teams and sociotechnical system operators and crews. The associated objectives are listed below, with brief descriptions of the associated achievements:

- **To identify the culturally-related factors that contributed most to variances in team attitudes, behaviours and performances:**

   This was achieved for a range of team types.

   The author considers that this objective has been partially achieved.

- **To identify a task classification relevant to culturally-moderated team performance:**

   Team/task classifications presented in the literature were neither broad enough, nor could they reasonably be linked to culturally-modified behaviours; therefore, the author developed a five factor team/task/mission classification and later a dimension-based task/mission representation.

   The author considers that this objective has been partially achieved.

- **To build a model that incorporated the above factors for the prediction of the effects of culture on team performance when tackling specified types of task:**

  Two detailed culture/mission models were developed based on results from the literature and the author's pilot studies. These covered organised action teams and innovation-related project teams.

  The author considers that this objective has been largely achieved, subject to the limitations associated with cultural contexts.

- **To encapsulate the above model(s) in a methodology and tool in order to:**

  - o **Facilitate the selection of successful teams in given situations**

  - o **Enable the prediction of the effects of culture on team performance, and likely success or failure, of existing or proposed teams**

  The second and third team culture tools encapsulated the above models (in different forms) to enable the selection of team members and the prediction of potential performance reduction, rather than absolute performance.

  The author considers that this objective has been largely achieved, albeit with limited validation and verification of the tools.

10.3 Summary of the research findings and contributions to knowledge

The author claimed, in Chapter 1, that the main contribution to knowledge would be a cultural theory of work team performance and a validated, quantitative methodology and tool that would enable the culturally-based assessment and improvement of teams. The key research findings are considered to be:

1. **Further relationships between uncertainty avoidance (UAI), MAS-diversity and UAI diversity and various aspects of team performance**

The results associated with cultural diversity were novel and of particular importance. They demonstrated that team performance <u>was</u> affected by cultural diversity constructs that were constrained to (i) single cultural dimensions and (ii) were sensitive to cultural distance.

2. **Detailed relationships between cultural dimension scores and team performance factors were derived for two key types of task/mission**

   The two team/task/mission types - sociotechnical system project teams, and sociotechnical system operators or crew (organised action teams), were the key types of team that were of concern to the research of this thesis.

3. **A theoretically-justifiable model of the effects of team culture on team performance**

   No other equivalent models were found in the literature. In particular, the incorporation of discrepancies (between actual team culture and desirable culture) sidestepped the issues that made team performance prediction extremely difficult.

4. **A practicable user-orientated team culture tool encapsulating the above model and relationships**

   The author did not come across any other practicable, quantitative culture tool that provided a prediction capability for user-specified teams.

The discrepancy-based model of point 3, above, and the team culture tool of point 4, combined to achieve the projected contribution to knowledge stated in Chapter 1.

10.4 Further work

New tools and discoveries are now transforming our understandings of the human mind, and culture is one of the areas that are likely to benefit from these advances. There are several avenues for further development, some pragmatic and related to the models and tools described in this thesis; others are more theoretical and take advantage of new research in the fields of cognitive science, genetics and epigenetics.

On a pragmatic basis, extensions of the current work could include the following:

1. **Expansion of the cultural framework used in the team culture tool to include all six of Hofstede's dimensions**

   This should improve the accuracy of the team culture tool; it would also assist in the re-evaluation of prior statistical results in the light of the new dimensions[70] and in the search for new culture/performance relationships.

2. **Development of the dimensional representation of tasks/- missions to achieve a single set of (say) four or five dimensions that would cover all teams**

   This would enable the tool to tackle almost any task/mission configuration.

3. **Development of an organisational culture tool to enable the examination of issues faced by multiple organisations working together on large projects**

   The development of a practical, empirical, successful tool should encourage the development of a supporting theory in its wake. Also, this what industry wants, now.

On a more theoretical basis, tracking the work and adapting the results of cognitive neuroscientists and others could enable major contributions to the field of human culture:

1. The development of explanations for culture-moderated attitudes and behaviours, based on emerging results from cognitive neuroscience and from simulation tools.

2. The identification of further evidence of culture-based gene selection in order to understand better the physical and neuro-chemical pathways through which cultural and personality traits interact with behaviour.

3. Determination of the effects of epigenetic changes on the reinforcement of cultural traits and the transmission of those traits across generations.

---

[70] In order to process various datasets, including a large football dataset, the author developed a range of spread sheet tools that automatically allocated and processed national cultural dimension scores for the original four Hofstede dimensions. These tools could be extended to process the current six dimensions.

The author considers the above work as providing an alternative causal-based model of culture, rather than the current correlation-based model, which explains little, in itself, about human behaviour.

10.5 Exploitation of the tool

The team culture tool is now part of a package of systems engineering tools that are utilised in soft systems courses at Loughborough University, and has been used by an M.Eng. project student for determining team cultural discrepancies at a major consultancy company.

The author has been in discussion with other researchers with regard to combining 'form' data with culture data in order to improve the prediction of sports results.

The second and third versions of the Team Culture Tool have been made available to the Engineering System of Systems (ESoS) Group's industrial collaborator partners, via the ESoS website.

References

AAIB. (2013). *AAIB Bulletin S3/2013 Special*. Farnborough, UK. Retrieved from http://www.aaib.gov.uk/cms_resources.cfm?file=/AAIB S3-2013 G-EUOE.pdf

Airsafe.com. (n.d.). No Title. *Plane Crashes and Other Significant Airline Safety Events by Airline*. Retrieved February 11, 2013, from http://www.airsafe.com/airline.htm

Ambos, B., & Schlegelmilch, B. B. (2008). Innovation in multinational firms: Does cultural fit enhance performance? *Management International Review, 48*(2), 189–206. doi:10.1007/s11575-008-0011-2

Anderson, C. (2011). Top Ten Causes of Project Management Failures. Retrieved from http://www.bizmanualz.com/blog/top-10-causes-of-project-management-failures.html

At-Twaijri, M. I., & Al-Muhaiza, I. A. (1996). Hofstede's cultural dimensions in the GCC countries: An empirical investigation. *International Journal of Value-Based Management, 9*(2), 121–131. doi:10.1007/BF00440149

Australian Transport Safety Bureau. (2010). *In-flight uncontained engine failure overhead Batam Island, Indonesia 4 November 2010 VH-OQA Airbus A380-842* (No. ATSB Transport Safety Report AO-2010-089). Canberra. Retrieved from http://www.atsb.gov.au/media/2888854/ao-2010-089 preliminary report.pdf

Australian Transport Safety Bureau. (2011). *In-flight upset 154 km West of Learmonth, WA 7 October 2008 VH-QPA Airbus A330-303* (No. ATSB Transport Safety Report AO-2008-070 Final). Canberra.

Bacharach, S. B. (1989). Organizational theories: Some criteria for evaluation. *Academy of Management Review, 14*(4), 496–515.

Bahr, H. M. (2006). Thomas F. O'Dea, the Harvard Values Project, and the mormons: Early lessons on ethnography among the literate. *Human Organization, 65*(4), 343–352.

Balachandra, R., & Friar, J. H. (1997). Factors for success in R&D projects and new product innovation: A contextual framework. *IEEE Transactions on Engineering Management, 44*(3), 276–287. doi:10.1109/17.618169

References

Bangwayo-Skeete, P. F., Rahim, A. H., & Zikhali, P. (2011). Does education engender cultural values that matter for economic growth? *Journal of Socio-Economics, 40*(2), 163–171.

Baregheh, A., Rowley, J., & Sambrook, S. (2009). Towards a multidisciplinary definition of innovation. *Management Decision, 47*(8), 1323–1339.

Bargh, J. A. (1984). Automatic and conscious processing of social information. In R. S. Wyer & T. K. Srull (Eds.), *Handbook of Social Cognition, Vol. 3* (pp. 1–43). New York: Erlbaum.

Barjak, F. (2006). Team diversity and research collaboration in life science teams: Does a combination of research cultures pay off? University of Applied Sciences Northwestern Switzerland. Retrieved from http://www.netreact-eu.org/documents/DPW2006-02_Team Diversity _Barjak_Franz.pdf

Barjak, F., & Robinson, S. (2008). International collaboration, mobility and team diversity in the lifesciences: impact on research performance. *Social Geography, 3*, 23–36. Retrieved from http://www.soc-geogr.net/3/23/2008/sg-3-23-2008.pdf

Barr, P. S., & Glynn, M. A. (2004). Cultural variations in strategic issue interpretation: relating cultural uncertainty avoidance to controllability in discriminating threat and opportunity. *Strategic Management Journal, 25*(1), 59–67. doi:10.1002/smj.361

Baskerville, R. F. (2003). Hofstede never studied culture. *Accounting, Organizations and Society, 28*(1), 1.

Baxter Magolda, M. B. (1992). *Knowing and reasoning in college: Gender-related patterns in students' intellectual development.* (U. Delworth, Ed.)*The JosseyBass higher and adult education series.* Jossey-Bass. Retrieved from http://scholar.google.com/scholar?hl=en&q=Baxter+Magolda,+1992&btnG=&as_sdt=1,9&as_sdtp=#0

Beckmann, D., Menkhoff, L., & Suto, M. (2008). Does culture influence asset managers' views and behavior? *Journal of Economic Behavior and Organization, 67*(3-4), 624–643. Retrieved from http://peer.ccsd.cnrs.fr/docs/00/61/46/85/PDF/PEER_stage2_10.1016%252Fj.jebo.2007.12.001.pdf

Belbin, R. M. (1993). *Team Roles at Work.* Oxford, UK: Butterworth-Heinemann.

References

Belbin, R. M. (2004). *Management Teams: Why They Succeed or Fail. Management Teams Why They Succeed or Fail.* Butterworth Heinemann.

Belbin, R. M. (2010). *Team Roles at Work* (2nd ed.). Oxford: Elsevier Ltd.

Belout, A., & Gauvreau, C. (2004). Factors influencing project success: The impact of human resource management. *International Journal of Project Management, 22*(1), 1–11. doi:10.1016/S0263-7863(03)00003-6

Berthrong, J. H. (1998). *Concerning Creativity: A Comparison of Chu Hsi, Whitehead, and Neville.* Albany, NY: State University of New York Press.

BFU. (2010). *Investigation Report 5X003-0/08.*

Blau, P. M. (1977). *Inequality and Heterogeneity: A Primitive Theory of Social Structure.* New York: The Free Press.

Blodgett, J. G., Bakir, A., & Rose, G. M. (2008). A test of the validity of Hofstede's cultural framework. *The Journal of Consumer Marketing, 25*(6), 339. Retrieved from http://proquest.umi.com/pqdweb?did=1564041431&Fmt=7&clientId=523 8&RQT=309&VName=PQD

Bosland, N. (1985). *An Evaluation of Replication Studies Using the Value Survey Module* (No. 85/2) (Vol. Working Pa). Maastricht, Netherlands: Institute for Intercultural Cooperation, Tilburg.

Bouncken, R. B., & Winkler, V. A. (2008). National and cultural diversity in global innovation teams: Creativity and innovation as a function of cultural team composition. In *PICMET '08 - 2008 Portland International Conference on Management of Engineering & Technology.* doi:10.1109/PICMET.2008.4599795

Brandes, L., Franck, E. P., & Theiler, P. (2009). The effect from national diversity on team production - empirical evidence from the sports industry. *Schmalenbach Business Review, 61,* 225–246. doi:10.2139/ssrn.1406933

Brewer, P., & Venaik, S. (2012). On the misuse of national culture dimensions. *International Marketing Review, 29*(6), 673–683. doi:10.1108/02651331211277991

Brockner, J. (2001). Culture and procedural justice: The influence of power distance on reactions to voice. *Journal of Experimental Social Psychology, 37*(4), 300–315. doi:10.1006/jesp.2000.1451

259

References

Brown, K. (2003). Cultural dimensions of New Zealand entrepreneurial behaviour. In *16th Annual Conference of Small Enterprise Association of Australia and New Zealand* (Vol. University).

Buckle, P., & Thomas, J. (2003). Deconstructing project management: a gender analysis of project management guidelines. *International Journal of Project Management, 21*(6), 433–441. doi:10.1016/S0263-7863(02)00114-X

Budworth, D. (1986). The making (and breaking) of a myth. *New Scientist,* (1503, April 10th), 70. Retrieved from http://books.google.co.uk/books?id=ikRlsIIuZoQC&printsec=frontcover& dq=new+scientist+1986+issue+1503&hl=en&sa=X&ei=Qk8eUZqaGseJ4 ATD6oHADw&redir_esc=y#v=onepage&q=new scientist 1986 issue 1503&f=false

Burke, M., Chan-Serafin, S., Salvador, R., Smith, A., & Sarpy, S. A. (2008). The role of national culture and organizational climate in safety training effectiveness. *European Journal of Work and Organizational Psychology, 17*(1), 133–152. doi:10.1080/13594320701307503

Cameron, K. S., & Quinn, R. E. (1999). Diagnosing and changing organizational culture based on the Competing Values Framework (review). *Response, 59*(3), 1–12. doi:10.1111/j.1744-6570.2006.00052_5.x

Cameron, K. S., & Quinn, R. E. (2006). *Diagnosing and Changing Organizational Culture: Based on the Competing Values Framework.* Jossey-Bass.

Carley, W. M. (1998). Crash of Swissair 111 stirs debate on when to stick to procedure. *Wall Street Journal Europe,* (December 16).

Carter, R. T. (1990). Cultural value differences between African Americans and white Americans. *Journal of College Student Development, 31*(1), 71–79.

Cartwright, S., & Gale, A. (1995). Project management: different gender, different culture? *Leadership & Organizational Development Journal, 16*(4), 12–17.

Castrol. (2011). Castrol EDGE Rankings. Retrieved from http://www.castrolfootball.com/rankings/rankings/

References

Chen, C. C., Chen, X.-P., & Meindl, J. R. (1998). How can cooperation be fostered? The cultural effects of individualism-collectivism. *Academy of Management Review, 23*(2), 285–304. doi:10.5465/AMR.1998.533227

Chen, Y.-F., Metscher, D. S., Smith, M., Ramsay, J., & Mason, R. (2014). The Taiwan Civil Aviation Safety Reporting (TACARE) system in aircraft maintenance: An evaluation of the acceptance of voluntary incident reporting programs. *International Journal of Professional Aviation Training & Testing Research, 6*(1).

Cheng, C., Chua, R. O. Y. Y. J., Morris, M. W., & Lee, L. (2012). Finding the right mix : How the composition of self-managing multicultural teams ' cultural value orientation influences performance over time. *Journal of Organizational Behavior, 411*(January), 389–411. doi:10.1002/job

Chhokar, J. S., Brodbeck, F. C., & House, R. J. (2008). *Culture and Leadership Across the World: The GLOBE Book of In-Depth Studies of 25 Societies. Series in Organization and Management.* New York, NY, USA: Taylor & Francis Group, LLC.

CHIRP. (n.d.). The UK Confidential Reporting Programme for Aviation and Maritime. Retrieved from http://www.chirp.co.uk/information-about.asp

Christoffersen, K., & Woods, D. D. (2002). How to make automated systems team players. *Advances in Human Performance and Cognitive Engineering Research, 2*(2002), 1–12. Retrieved from http://www.emeraldinsight.com/Insight/ViewContentServlet?contentType =Book&Filename=/published/emeraldfulltextarticle/pdf/10_1016_s1 479-3601_02_02003-9.pdf

Cocklin, J. T. (2004). Swissair 111 human factors: Checklist and cockpit communication. *Journal of Air Transportation, 9*(3), 19–42. Retrieved from http://search.ebscohost.com/login.aspx?direct=true&profile=ehost&scope =site&authtype=crawler&jrnl=15446980&AN=14891788&h=79unwMX LU2mry+HMvVWDwMC3c/luQK54zOs6VSpI1raiKGwXOJLKc4owY4 KcEE4lBd662JDZoq571YEdOo0dog==&crl=c

Cohen, S. G., & Bailey, D. E. (1997). What makes teams work: Group effectiveness research from the shop floor to the executive suite. *Journal of Management, 23*(3), 239–290. doi:10.1177/014920639702300303

Cooke, R. A., & Szumal, J. L. (1993). Measuring normative beliefs and shared behavioral expectations in organizations: The reliability and validity of

References

the Organizational Culture Inventory. *Psychological Reports, 72*(3c), 1299–1330. doi:10.2466/pr0.1993.72.3c.1299

Cooper, J. R. (1998). A multidimensional approach to the adoption of innovation. *Management Decision, 36*(8), 493–502.

Cox, T. H., & Blake, S. (1991). Managing cultural diversity: Implications for organizational competitiveness. *Academy of Management Executive, 5*(3), 45–56. doi:10.5465/AME.1991.4274465

Cozijnsen, A. J., Vrakking, W. J., & IJzerloo, M. Van. (2000). Success and failure of 50 innovation projects in Dutch companies. *European Journal of Innovation Management, 3*(3), 150–159. doi:10.1108/14601060010322301

Cozzi, G., & Giordani, P. E. (2011). Ambiguity attitude, R&D investments and economic growth. *Journal of Evolutionary Economics, 21*, 303–319. doi:10.1007/s00191-101-0217-x

d'Iribarne, P., Henry, A., Segal, J.-P., Chevrier, S., & Globokar, T. (1998). *Cultures et Mondialisation: Gérer par-delà les Frontieres.* Paris: Points.

Dahlin, K. B., Weingart, L. R., & Hinds, P. J. (2005). Team diversity and information use. *Academy of Management Journal, 48*, 1107–1123. Retrieved from http://www.stanford.edu/~phinds/PDFs/Dahlin-et-al-AMJ05.pdf

Daily, B. F., Loveland, J., & Stenier, R. (1997). A comparative analysis of reactions from multicultural and culturally homogeneous teams to decision making with and without GDSS technology. *ACM SIGCPR Computer Personnel, 18*(1), 3–14.

Daley, D. M., & Naff, K. C. (1998). Gender differences and managerial competencies. *Review of Public Personnel Administration, 18*(2), 41–56.

Deal, T. E., & Kennedy, A. A. (1988). *Corporate Cultures: The Rites and Rituals of Corporate Life.* Harmondsworth: Penguin.

DeMatteo, J. S., Eby, L. T., & Sundstrom, E. (1998). Team-based rewards: Current empirical evidence and directions for future research. In *Research in Organizational Behavior Vol 20 1998* (Vol. 20, pp. 141–183). JAI PRESS INC.

References

DiStefano, J., & Maznevski, M. L. (2000). Creating value with diverse teams in global management. *Organizational Dynamics*, *29*(1), 45–63. doi:10.1016/S0090-2616(00)00012-7

Dulaimi, M., & Hariz, A. (2011). The impact of cultural diversity on the effectiveness of construction project teams. *Engineering Project Organization Journal*, *1*(4), 213–221. Retrieved from http://www.tandfonline.com/doi/pdf/10.1080/21573727.2011.621419

Dumitrescu, V. M. (2012). The cultural dimension of rhetoric: The use of meiosis and hyperbole in British and American English. *Business and Cultural Studies*, *8*(2), 161–169.

Dutch Safety Board. (2010). *Crashed during approach, Boeing 737-800, near Amsterdam Schiphol Airport 25 February 2009* (No. Project No. M2009LV0225_01, 2010). The Hague. Retrieved from http://www.onderzoeksraad.nl/docs/rapporten/Rapport_TA_ENG_web.pdf

Earley, P. C., & Gibson, C. B. (2002). *Multinational Work Teams: A New Perspective* (Vol. 1). Psychology Press.

Earley, P. C., & Mosakowski, E. (2000). Creating hybrid team cultures: An empirical test of transnational team functioning. *Academy of Management Journal*, *43*(1), 26–49. doi:10.2307/1556384

Eeckelaert, L., Starren, A., van Scheppingen, A., Fox, D., & Bruck, C. (2011). *Occupational Safety and Health Culture Assessment - a Review of Main Approaches and Selected Tools* (No. TE-WE-11-005--EN-N). doi:10.2802/53184

Efrat, K. (2014). The direct and indirect impact of culture on innovation. *Technovation*, *34*(1), 12–20. Retrieved from http://www.sciencedirect.com/science/article/pii/S0166497213001028

Elron, E. (1997). Top management teams within multinational corporations: Effects of cultural heterogeneity. *The Leadership Quarterly*, *8*(4), 393–412. doi:10.1016/S1048-9843(97)90021-7

Erez, M., & Nouri, R. (2010). Creativity: The influence of cultural, social, and work contexts. *Management and Organization Review*, *6*(3), 351–370. doi:10.1111/j.1740-8784.2010.00191.x

Etzioni, A. (1996). *The New Golden Rule: Community and Morality in a Democratic Society*. New York, NY, USA: Basic Books.

References

EUNetPaS. (2010). *Use of Patient Safety Culture Instruments and Recommendations.* Aarhus N, Denmark. Retrieved from http://ns208606.ovh.net/~extranet/images/EUNetPaS_Publications/eunetp as-report-use-of-psci-and-recommandations-april-8-2010.pdf

Everdingen, Y. M. Van, & Waarts, E. (2003). The effect of national culture on the adoption of innovations. *Marketing Letters, 14*(3), 217–232. doi:10.3727/109830403108750786

FAA. (2002). *Aviation Safety Action Program (ASAP)* (No. 120-66B). Retrieved from http://www.faa.gov/documentLibrary/media/Advisory_Circular/AC120-66B.pdf

FAA. (2013). *Operational Use of Flight Path Management Systems.* Washington, DC, USA. Retrieved from http://www.faa.gov/about/office_org/headquarters_offices/avs/offices/afs/afs400/parc/parc_reco/media/2013/130908_PARC_FltDAWG_Final_Rep ort_Recommendations.pdf

Falagas, M. E., Pitsouni, E. I., Malietzis, G. A., & Pappas, G. (2008). Comparison of PubMed, Scopus, Web of Science, and Google Scholar: strengths and weaknesses. *The FASEB Journal : Official Publication of the Federation of American Societies for Experimental Biology, 22*(2), 338–342. doi:10.1096/fj.07-9492LSF

Fang, T. (2003). A critique of Hofstede's fifth national culture dimension. *International Journal of Cross Cultural Management, 3*(3), 347–368. doi:10.1177/1470595803003003006

Federal Aviation Administration Human Factors Team. (1996). *The Interfaces between Flightcrews and Modern Flight Deck Systems.* Retrieved from http://ocw.mit.edu/courses/aeronautics-and-astronautics/16-422-human-supervisory-control-of-automated-systems-spring-2004/readings/interfac.pdf

Fellows, R. (2011). Culture in construction. *ARCOM Newsletter, 28*(2), 2–3. Retrieved from http://www.arcom.ac.uk/-docs/newsletter/2011_28-2.pdf

Fernandez, R., Kozlowski, S. W. J., Shapiro, M. J., & Salas, E. (2008). Toward a definition of teamwork in emergency medicine. *Academic Emergency Medicine, 15*(11), 1104–1112. Retrieved from http://www.ncbi.nlm.nih.gov/pubmed/18828831

References

Fisch, C. O., Block, J. H., & Sandner, P. G. (2013). *Chinese university patents: Quantity, quality, and the role of subsidy programs.* Trier, Germany. Retrieved from http://papers.ssrn.com/sol3/papers.cfm?abstract_id=2304224

Fischer, R., & Poortinga, Y. H. (2012). Are cultural values the same as the values of individuals? An examination of similarities in personal, social and cultural value structures. *International Journal of Cross Cultural Management, 12*(2), 157–170. doi:10.1177/1470595812439867

Fox, K. (2004). *Watching the English: The Hidden Rules of English Behaviour* (1st ed.). London, UK: Hodder & Stoughton.

Francesco, A. M., & Chen, Z.-X. (2000). Cross-cultural differences within a single culture: Power distance as a moderator of the participation-outcome relationship in the People's Republic of China. In *BRC Papers on Cross-Cultural Management.* Hong Kong, PRC: Hong Kong Baptist University. Retrieved from http://ied.hkbu.edu.hk/publications/ccmp/CCMP200007.pdf

Gallagher, T. (2001a). The value orientations method: A tool to help understand cultural differences. *Journal of Extension, 39*(6). Retrieved from http://www.joe.org/joe/2001december/tt1.php

Gallagher, T. (2001b). Understanding other cultures: The Value Orientations Method. In *Association of Leadership Educators Conference* (Vol. Minneapoli). Minneapolis, MN, USA. Retrieved from http://www.leadershipeducators.org/Resources/Documents/Conferences/Minneapolis/Gallagher.pdf

Geiselman, E. E., Johnson, C. M., Buck, D. R., & Patrick, T. (2013). Flight deck automation: A call for context-aware logic to improve safety. *Ergonomics in Design: The Quarterly of Human Factors Applications, 21*(4), 13–18. doi:10.1177/1064804613489126

Giustini, D., & Boulos, M. N. K. (2013). Google Scholar is not enough to be used alone for systematic reviews. *Online Journal of Public Health Informatics, 5*(2), 214. doi:10.5210/ojphi.v5i2.4623

Gluesing, J. C., & Gibson, C. B. (2003). Designing and forming global teams. In *Handbook of Cross-Cultural Management.* Retrieved from http://ceo.usc.edu/pdf/G035433.pdf

References

Goncalo, J. A., & Staw, B. M. (2006). Individualism–collectivism and group creativity. *Organizational Behavior and Human Decision Processes*, *100*(1), 96–109. doi:10.1016/j.obhdp.2005.11.003

Graen, G. B. (2006). In the eye of the beholder: cross-cultural lesson in leadership from project GLOBE: A response viewed from the third culture bonding (TCB) model of cross-cultural leadership. *Academy of Management Perspectives*, *20*(4), 95–101. doi:10.5465/AMP.2006.23270309

Graf, L. A., Hemmasi, M., Lust, J. A., & Liang, Y. (1990). Perceptions of desirable organizational reforms in Chinese state enterprises. *International Studies of Management & Organization*, *20*(1/2), 47–56. Retrieved from http://search.ebscohost.com/login.aspx?direct=true&db=buh&AN=58136 17&site=ehost-live

Greenberg, J. H. (1956). The measurement of linguistic diversity. *Language*, *32*(9), 109–115.

Gresov, C. (1989). Exploring fit and misfit with multiple contingencies. *Administrative Science Quarterly*, *34*, 431–453. doi:10.5465/AMBPP.1987.17534088

Gudykunst, W. B. (1997). Cultural variability in communication: An introduction. *Communication Research*, *24*(4), 327–348. doi:10.1177/009365097024004001

Guzzo, R. A., & Dickson, M. W. (1996). Teams in organizations: recent research on performance and effectiveness. *Annual Review of Psychology*, *47*(1), 307–338. Retrieved from http://www.ncbi.nlm.nih.gov/pubmed/15012484

Haas, H., & Nüesch, S. (2012). Are multinational teams more successful? *International Journal of Human Resource Management*, *23*(15), 3105–3113.

Hackman, J. R., & Morris, C. G. (1975). Group tasks, group interaction process, and group performance effectiveness: A review and proposed integration. *Advances in Experimental Social Psychology*, *8*, 45–99. doi:10.1016/S0065-2601(08)60248-8

Halkos, G. E., & Tzeremes, N. G. (2013). Modelling the effect of national culture on countries' innovation performances: A conditional full frontier approach. *International Review of Applied Economics*, *27*(5), 656–678. doi:10.1080/02692171.2013.778819

References

Halkos, G., & Tzeremes, N. (2011). *The effect of national culture on countries' innovation efficiency (MPRA Paper 30100)*. Munich. Retrieved from http://mpra.ub.uni-muenchen.de/30100/1/MPRA_paper_30100.pdf

Hambrick, D. C., Davison, S. C., Snell, S. A., & Snow, C. C. (1998). When groups consist of multiple nationalities: Towards a new understanding of the implications. *Organizational Studies, 19*(2), 181–206.

Hanges, P. J., & Dickson, M. W. (2006). Agitation over aggregation: Clarifying the development of and the nature of the GLOBE scales. *Leadership Quarterly, 17*(5), 522–536.

Harris, D., & Li, W.-C. (2008). Cockpit design and cross-cultural issues underlying failures in crew resource management. *Aviation, Space, and Environmental Medicine, 79*(5), 537–538. doi:10.3357/ASEM.2271.2008

Harrison, R. (1972). Understanding your organization's character. *Harvard Business Review, 50*(3), 119–128. Retrieved from http://search.ebscohost.com/login.aspx?direct=true&db=buh&AN=3866987&site=ehost-live

Harzing, A.-W. (1999). *Managing the Multinationals: An International Study of Control Mechanisms*. Cheltenham, UK: Edward Elgar.

Hasan, H. M., & Ditsa, G. (1999). The impact of culture on the adoption of IT: An interpretative study. *Journal of Global Information Management, 7*(1), 5–15.

Helmreich, R. L., & Merritt, A. C. (2001). *Culture at Work in Aviation and Medicine: National, Organizational and Professional Influences* (Vol. 2nd). UK: Ashgate Publishing Limited.

Helmreich, R. L., Merritt, A. C., & Wilhelm, J. A. (1999). The evolution of crew resource management training in commercial aviation. *The International Journal of Aviation Psychology, 9*(1), 19–32. Retrieved from http://www.ncbi.nlm.nih.gov/pubmed/11541445

Herbig, P. A., & Miller, J. C. (1992). Culture and technology: Does the traffic move in both directions. *Journal of Global Marketing, 6*(3), 75. Retrieved from http://search.ebscohost.com/login.aspx?direct=true&db=buh&AN=5353375&site=ehost-live

Herbig, P., & Dunphy, S. (1998). Culture and innovation. *Cross Cultural Management: An International Journal, 5*(4), 13–21.

267

References

Herbig, P., & Jacobs, L. (1998). Culture as an explanatory variable for the Japanese innovative processes. *Cross Cultural Management An International Journal, 5*(3), 5–30. doi:10.1108/13527609810796808

Higgins, E. T. (1996). Knowledge activation: Accessibility, application and salience. In E. T. Higgins & A. W. Kruglanski (Eds.), *Social Psychology: Handbook of Basic Principles* (pp. 133–168). Ney York: Guilford Press.

Hills, M. D. (2002). Kluckhohn and Strodtbeck's Values Orientation Theory. *Online Readings in Psychology and Culture, Unit 4*. Retrieved from http://scholarworks.gvsu.edu/orpc/vol4/iss4/3

Hodgson, A., Hubbard, E.-M., & Siemieniuch, C. E. (2011). Culture and the performance of teams in complex systems. In *2011 6th International Conference on System of Systems Engineering* (pp. 95–100). IEEE. doi:10.1109/SYSOSE.2011.5966580

Hodgson, A., Hubbard, E.-M., & Siemieniuch, C. E. (2013). Toward an understanding of culture and the performance of teams in complex systems. *IEEE Systems Journal, 7*(4), 606–615.

Hodgson, A., Siemieniuch, C. E., & Hubbard, E.-M. (2013). Culture and the safety of complex automated sociotechnical systems. *IEEE Transactions on Human-Machine Systems, 43*(6), 608–619.

Hodgson, D., & Cicmil, S. (2008). The other side of projects: The case for critical project studies. *International Journal of Managing Projects in Business, 1*(1), 142–152. Retrieved from http://eprints.uwe.ac.uk/16734/

Hofstede, G. (1986). Cultural differences in teaching and learning. *International Journal of Intercultural Relations, 10*(3), 301–320. doi:10.1016/0147-1767(86)90015-5

Hofstede, G. (1991). *Cultures and Organizations: Software of the Mind. Development*. McGraw-Hill Publishing Co.

Hofstede, G. (1993). Cultural constraints in management theories. *Academy of Management Perspectives, 7*(1), 81–94. doi:10.5465/AME.1993.9409142061

Hofstede, G. (2006). What did GLOBE really measure? Researchers' minds versus respondents' minds. *Journal of International Business Studies, 37*(6), 882–896. doi:10.1057/palgrave.jibs.8400233

References

Hofstede, G. H. (1980). *Culture's Consequences: International Differences in Work-Related Values*. Beverly Hills: Sage.

Hofstede, G. H. (1984). *Culture's Consequences: International Differences in Work-Related Values*. Beverly Hills: Sage Publications Inc.

Hofstede, G. H. (2001). *Culture's Consequences: Comparing Values, Behaviors, Institutions, and Organizations across Nations. Cultures Consequences Comparing Values Behaviors Institutions and Organizations across Nations* (2nd ed., Vol. 2nd ed.). Thousand Oaks, CA: Sage Publications. Retrieved from http://books.google.com/books?id=w6z18LJ_1VsC

Hofstede, G. H. (2002). Dimensions do not exist: A reply to Brendan McSweeney. *Human Relations, 55*(11). Retrieved from http://www.geert-hofstede.com/dimBSGH.pdf

Hofstede, G. H. (2003). What is culture? A reply to Baskerville. *Accounting, Organizations and Society., 28*(7), 811.

Hofstede, G. H., Hofstede, G. J., & Minkov, M. (2010). *Cultures and Organizations: Software of the Mind: Intercultural Cooperation and its Importance for Survival. Publish* (3rd ed.). McGraw-Hill. Retrieved from http://books.google.com/books?id=o4OqTgV3V00C

Hofstede, G., & Hofstede, G. J. (2004). *Cultures and Organizations: Software of the Mind* (Vol. 2). McGraw-Hill Professional.

Hofstede, G., Hofstede, G. J., Minkov, M., & Vinken, H. (2008a). VSM 08. Retrieved from http://www.geerthofstede.nl/vsm-08

Hofstede, G., Hofstede, G. J., Minkov, M., & Vinken, H. (2008b). VSM08. Retrieved December 8, 2010, from http://www.geerthofstede.nl/vsm-08

Hofstede, G., Neuijen, B., Ohayv, D. D., & Sanders, G. (1990). Measuring organizational cultures: A qualitative and quantitative study across twenty cases. *Administrative Science Quarterly, 35*(2), 286–316. doi:10.2307/2393392

Hollenbeck, J. R., Beersma, B., & Schouten, M. E. (2012). Beyond team types and taxonomies: A dimensional scaling conceptualization for team description. *Academy of Management Review, 37*(1), 82–106. Retrieved from http://search.ebscohost.com/login.aspx?direct=true&db=bah&AN=69705782&site=ehost-live

References

Holtom, M. (1998). BASIS - British Airways Safety Information System. In *Proceedings of the ISASI 29th Seminar* (pp. 51–53). ISASI.

Hoppe, M. H. (1990). *A Comparative Study of Country Elites: International Differences in Work-related Values and Learning and their Implications for Management Training and Development*. University of North Carolina at Chapel Hill.

Horwitz, S. K., & Horwitz, I. B. (2007). The effects of team diversity on team outcomes: A meta-analytic review of team demography. *Journal of Management, 33*(6), 987–1015. doi:10.1177/0149206307308587

House, R. J., Hanges, P. J., Javidan, M., Dorfman, P. W., & Gupta, V. (2004). *Culture, Leadership, and Organizations: The GLOBE Study of 62 Societies. GLOBE study of 62 societies*. Sage Publications, Thousand Oaks, CA, USA: Sage Publications.

Huang, X., & Van de Vliert, E. (2003). Comparing work behaviors across cultures: A cross-level approach using multilevel modeling. *International Journal of Cross Cultural Management, 3*(2), 167–182. doi:10.1177/14705958030032002

Huff, L., & Kelley, L. (2003). Levels of trust in individualist versus collectivist societies: A seven-nation study. *Organization Science, 14*(1), 81–90.

Iamratanakul, S., Hernandez, I. P., Castilla, C., & Milozevic, D. Z. (2007). Innovation and factors affecting the success of NPD projects: Literature explorations and descriptions. *IEEE International Conference on Industrial Engineering and Engineering Management*. doi:10.1109/IEEM.2007.4419353

Infortunio, F. A. (2003). *An Exploration of the Correlations Between Fatal Accident Rates Across Nations and the Cultural Dimensions of Power Distance, Uncertainty Avoidance, Individuality and Masculinity*. Argosy University, Sarasota.

INSEAD. (2009). Global Innovation Index 2008-2009. Retrieved June 5, 2011, from http://elab.insead.edu

Jacob, N. (2005). Cross-cultural investigations: Emerging concepts. *Journal of Organizational Change Management, 18*(5), 514–528.

Jacso, P. (2005). As we may search – Comparison of major features of the Web of Science, Scopus, and Google Scholar. *Current Science*.

References

Jing, H.-S., Lu, C. J., & Peng, S.-J. (2001). Culture, authoritarianism and commercial aircraft accidents. *Human Factors and Aerospace Safety, 1*(4), 341–359.

Jing, H.-S., Peng, S.-J., & Lu, C. J. (2000). On the correlation between cultural background and the commercial aircraft accidents. In *ICAS 2000 Congress.* Retrieved from http://www.icas-proceedings.net/ICAS2000/PAPERS/ICA0674.PDF

Johne, F. A. (1984). How experienced product innovators organize. *Journal of Product Innovation Management, 1*(4), 210–223. doi:10.1111/1540-5885.140210

Jones, G. K., & Davis, H. J. (2000). National culture and innovation: Implications for locating global R&D operations. *Management International Review, 40*(1), 11–39. doi:10.2307/40835865

Jones, M. L. (2007). Hofstede - culturally questionable? In *Oxford Business & Economics Conference* (pp. 24–26). Oxford, UK.

Joy, S., & Kolb, D. A. (2009). Are there cultural differences in learning style? *International Journal of Intercultural Relations, 33*(1), 69–85. doi:10.1016/j.ijintrel.2008.11.002

Jung, T., Scott, T., Davies, H. T. O., Bower, P., Whalley, D., McNally, R., & Mannion, R. (2009). Instruments for exploring organizational culture: A review of the literature. *Public Administration Review, 69*(6), 1087–1096. doi:10.1111/j.1540-6210.2009.02066.x

Kaasa, A., & Vadi, M. (2010). How does culture contribute to innovation? Evidence from European countries. *Economics of Innovation and New Technology, 19*(7), 583–604. doi:10.1080/10438590902987222

Kaber, D. B., & Endsley, M. R. (1997). Out-of-the-loop performance problems and the use of intermediate levels of automation for improved control system functioning and safety. *Process Safety Progress, 16*(3), 126–131. doi:10.1002/prs.680160304

Kaber, D. B., & Endsley, M. R. (2004). The effects of level of automation and adaptive automation on human performance, situation awareness and workload in a dynamic control task. *Theoretical Issues in Ergonomics Science, 5*(2), 113–153. doi:10.1080/1463922021000054335

Kahn, L. M. (2000). The sports business as a labor market laboratory. *Journal of Economic Perspectives, 14*(3), 75–94. doi:10.1257/jep.14.3.75

References

Kedia, B. L., Keller, R. T., & Julian, S. D. (1992). Dimensions of national culture and the productivity of R&D units. *The Journal of High Technology Management Research, 3*(1), 1–18. doi:10.1016/1047-8310(92)90002-J

Khare, A. (1999). Japanese and Indian work patterns: A study of contrasts. In H. S. R. Kao, D. Sinha, & B. Wilpert (Eds.), *3rd Symposium on Indigenous Behaviors in Effective Management and Organizations* (pp. 121–136). Guangzhou, Peoples Republic of China: Sage Publications, Thousand Oaks, CA, USA.

Khatri, N. (2009). Consequences of power distance orientation in organisations. *Vision - The Journal of Business Perspective, 13*(1), 1–9.

Kim, S. U. (1999). Determinants and characteristics of the corporate culture of Korean enterprises. In H. S. R. Kao, D. Sinha, & B. Wilpert (Eds.), *Management and Cultural Values - the Indigenisation of Organisations in Asia* (pp. 86–101). New Delhi, India: Sage Publications.

Kirkman, B. L., Lowe, K. B., & Gibson, C. B. (2006). A quarter century of Culture's Consequences: A review of empirical research incorporating Hofstede's cultural values framework. *Journal of International Business Studies, 37*(3), 285–320. doi:10.1057/palgrave.jibs.8400202

Kirton, M. J. (1976). Adaptors and innovators: A description and measure. *Journal of Applied Psychology, 61*, 759–762.

Klein, G. A., Pliske, R. M., Crandall, B. W., & Woods, D. D. (2005). Problem detection. *Methods, 7*(1), 14–28. doi:10.1007/s10111-004-0166-y

Klein, G. A., Pliske, R. M., Crandall, B., & Woods, D. (1999). Features of problem detection. In *Proc. Human Factors and Ergonomics Society 43rd Annual Meeting, Vol. 1* (pp. 133–137). Sage.

Klein, G., Woods, D. D., Bradshaw, J. M., Hoffman, R. R., & Feltovich, P. J. (2004). Ten challenges for making automation a "team player" in joint human-agent activity. *IEEE Intelligent Systems, 19*(6), 91–95.

Kluckhohn, F. R., & Strodtbeck, F. L. (1961). *Variations in Value Orientations*. Evanston, IL, USA: Row, Peterson.

Kochan, T., Bezrukova, K., Ely, R., Jackson, S., Joshi, A., Jehn, K., … Thomas, D. (2003). The effects of diversity on business performance: Report of the diversity research network. *Human Resource Management, 42*(1), 3–21. doi:10.1002/hrm.10061

272

References

Lau, D. C., & Murnighan, J. K. (1998). Demographic diversity and faultlines: The compositional dynamics of organizational groups. *Academy of Management Review*, *23*(2), 325–340. doi:10.5465/AMR.1998.533229

Laudan, L. (1978). *Progress and its Problems: Toward a Theory of Scientific Growth*. New Delhi: Ambika Publications.

Lee, P. I., & Weitzel, T. R. (2003). Air carrier safety and culture: An investigation of Taiwan's adaptation to Western incident reporting programs. *Journal of Air Transportation*, *10*(1), 20–37. Retrieved from http://swissair.wikispaces.com/file/view/17265480.pdf

Lee, S., & Saw, S. H. (2011). Nuclear fusion energy - mankind's giant step forward. *Journal of Fusion Energy*, *30*(5), 398–403.

Levy, Y., & Ellis, T. J. (2006). A systems approach to conduct an effective literature review in support of information systems research. *Science Journal*, *9*(1), 181–212. doi:10.1049/cp.2009.0961

Li, W.-C., Harris, D., & Yu, C.-S. (2008). Routes to failure: analysis of 41 civil aviation accidents from the Republic of China using the human factors analysis and classification system. *Accident; Analysis and Prevention*, *40*(2), 426–434.

Lichtenberg, S. (1983). Alternatives to conventional project management. *International Journal of Project Management*, *1*(2), 101–102. Retrieved from http://www.sciencedirect.com/science/article/pii/0263786383900078

Lin, L.-H. (2009). Effects of national culture on process management and technological innovation. *Total Quality Management Business Excellence*, *20*(12), 1287–1301. doi:10.1080/14783360903250621

Lubart, T. I. (1999). Creativity across cultures in R.J. Sternberg . In R. J. Sternberg (Ed.), *Handbook of Creativity* (pp. 339–350). Cambridge, UK: Cambridge University Press.

Magnusson, P., Wilson, R. T., Zdravkovic, S., Zhou, J. X., & Westjohn, S. A. (2008). Breaking through the cultural clutter: A comparative assessment of multiple cultural and institutional frameworks. *International Marketing Review*. doi:10.1108/02651330810866272

Marks, M. A., Mathieu, J. E., & Zaccaro, S. J. (2001). A temporally based framework and taxonomy of team processes. *Academy of Management Review*, *26*(3), 356–376. doi:10.2307/259182

References

Maslow, A. H. (1943). A theory of human motivation. *Psychological Review*, *50*(4), 370–396. doi:10.1037/h0054346

Maslow, A. H. (1997). *Motivation and Personality* (3rd ed.). Pearson.

Maznevski, M. L., DiStefano, J. J., Gomez, C. B., Nooderhaven, N. G., & Wu, P. (1997). Variations in cultural orientations within and among five countries. In *Academy of International Business Annual Meeting*. Monterrey, Mexico.

Maznevski, M. L., Gomez, C. B., DiStefano, J. J., Noorderhaven, N. G., & Wu, P.-C. (2002). Cultural dimensions at the individual level of analysis: The cultural orientations framework. *International Journal of Cross Cultural Management*, *2*(3), 275–295. doi:10.1177/147059580223001

McClelland, D. C. (1985). How motives, skills, and values determine what people do. Vol 40(7), Jul 1985, 812-825. . *American Psychologist*, *40*(7), 812–825.

McGrath, J. E. (1984). *Groups: Interaction and Performance. Groups: Interaction and Performance*. Englewood Cliffs, NJ: Prentice Hall.

McLeod, P. L., Lobel, S. A., & Cox, T. H. (1996). Ethnic diversity and creativity in small groups. *Small Group Research*, *27*(2), 248–264. doi:10.1177/1046496496272003

McSweeney, B. (2002). Hofstede's model of national cultural differences and their consequences: A triumph of faith – a failure of analysis. *Human Relations*, *55*(1), 89–118. Retrieved from http://www.uk.sagepub.com/managingandorganizations/downloads/Onlin e articles/ch05/4 - McSweeney.pdf

Meeuwesen, L., van den Brink-Muinen, A., & Hofstede, G. (2009). Can dimensions of national culture predict cross-national differences in medical communication? *Patient Education and Counseling*, *75*(1), 58–66.

Meho, L. I., & Yang, K. (2007). Impact of data sources on citation counts and rankings of LIS faculty: Web of Science versus Scopus and Google Scholar. *Journal of the American Society for Information Science and Technology*, *58*(13), 2105–2125. doi:10.1002/asi.20677

Menzel, H. C., Krauss, R., Ulijn, J. M., & Weggeman, M. (2006). *Developing Characteristics of an Intrapreneurship-Supportive Culture* (No. Working

References

Paper 06.10). Eindhoven. Retrieved from
www.uquebec.ca/observgo/fichiers/17943_gdo-2.pdf?

Merkin, R. S. (2006). Uncertainty avoidance and facework: A test of the
Hofstede model. *International Journal of Intercultural Relations*, *30*(2),
213–228. doi:10.1016/j.ijintrel.2005.08.001

Merritt, A. C. (2000). Culture in the cockpit: Do Hofstede's dimensions
replicate? *Journal of Cross-Cultural Psychology*, *31*(3), 283–301.
doi:10.1177/0022022100031003001

Merritt, A. C., & Helmreich, R. (1995). Culture in the cockpit: A multi-airline
study of pilot attitudes and values. In *Proceedings of the Eighth
International Symposium on Aviation Psychology* (Vol. 8, pp. 676–681).
Columbus, Ohio, USA.

Merritt, A., & Ratwatte, S. (1997). Who are you calling a safety threat?! A
debate on safety in mono- versus multicultural cockpits. In *9th
International Symposium on Aviation Psychology*. Columbus, Ohio, USA.

Mihaela, H., Ogrean, C., & Belascu, L. (2011). Culture and national
competitiveness. *African Journal of Business Management*, *5*(8), 3056–
3062.

Miklos-Thal, J., & Ullrich, H. (2010). *Effort incentives in nomination contests:
Evidence from professional soccer (unpublished discussion paper)* (No.
MPRA Paper 24340). Munich, Germany.

Minkov, M. (2011). *Cultural Differences in a Globalizing World* (First., Vol.
840). Bingley, UK: Emerald Group Publishing Limited.
doi:10.1097/PSY.0b013e31815b002c

Minkov, M., & Hofstede, G. (2014). A replication of Hofstede's uncertainty
avoidance dimension across nationally representative samples from
Europe. *International Journal of Cross Cultural Management*, *14*(1).
doi:10.1177/1470595814521600

Morris, M. W., & Leung, K. (2010). Creativity East and West: Perspectives and
parallels. *Management and Organization Review*, *6*(3), 313–327.
doi:10.1111/j.1740-8784.2010.00193.x

Nakata, C., & Sivakumar, K. (1996). National culture and new product
development: An integrative review. *Journal of Marketing*, *60*(1), 61–72.
doi:10.2307/1251888

References

National Transportation Safety Board. (2000). *Controlled Flight into Terrain, Korean Air Flight 801, Boeing 747-300, HL7468, Nimitz Hill, Guam, August 6, 1997*. Washington, D.C., USA. Retrieved from http://www.ntsb.gov/doclib/reports/2000/AAR0001.pdf

National Transportation Safety Board. (2010). *Loss of thrust in both engines after encountering a flock of birds and subsequent ditching on the Hudson River US Airways Flight 1549 Airbus A320-214, N106US Weehawken, New Jersey January 15, 2009* (No. Accident Report NTSB/AAR-10/03). Washington.

Naumov, A. I. (2000). Measuring Russian culture using Hofstede's dimensions. *Applied Psychology: An International Review*, *49*(4), 709–718.

Nemeth, C. J. (1986). Differential contributions of majority and minority influence. *Psychological Review*, *93*(1), 23–32. doi:10.1037/0033-295X.93.1.23

Nevett, T. (1992). Differences between American and British television advertising: Explanations and implications. *Journal of Advertising*, *21*(4), 61. Retrieved from http://proquest.umi.com/pqdweb?did=585386&Fmt=7&clientId=57458&RQT=309&VName=PQD

Niebuhr, A. (2010). Migration and innovation: Does cultural diversity matter for regional R&D activity? *Papers in Regional Science*, *89*(3), 563–585. doi:10.1111/j.1435-5957.2009.00271.x

Nielsen, D., & Roberts, S. (1999). Fatalities among the world's merchant seafarers (1990 - 1994). *Marine Policy*, *23*(1), 71–80. Retrieved from http://www.sciencedirect.com/science/article/B6VCD-3W0GB9Y-C/2/3cbf8901c65c88b9b18ac0cbe6725c23

Niu, W., & Sternberg, R. (2002). Contemporary studies on the concept of creativity: The East and the West. *The Journal of Creative Behavior*, *36*(4), 269–288. Retrieved from http://creativeeducation.metapress.com/index/A351L756HX7R2831.pdf

Norman, D. A. (1990). The "problem" with automation: inappropriate feedback and interaction, not "over-automation". *Philosophical Transactions of the Royal Society of London - Series B: Biological Sciences*, *327*(1241), 585–93. doi:10.1098/rstb.1990.0101

References

Offermann, L. R., & Hellmann, P. S. (1997). Culture's consequences for leadership behavior: National values in action. *Journal of Cross-Cultural Psychology*, *28*(3), 342–351. doi:10.1177/0022022197283008

Office of Government Commerce. (2005). *Common Causes of Project Failure* (No. CP0015/01/05). London. Retrieved from http://www.swan.ac.uk/media/cp0015.pdf

OGP. (2010a). *A guide to selecting appropriate tools to improve HSE culture.* London & Brussels. Retrieved from http://www.ogp.org.uk/pubs/435.pdf

OGP. (2010b). *Risk Assessment Data Directory* (No. 434 – 10). London: International Association of Oil and Gas Producers. Retrieved from http://www.ogp.org.uk/pubs/434-10.pdf

Orasanu, J., Fischer, U., & Davison, J. (1997). Cross-cultural barriers to effective communication in aviation. In C. S. Granrose & S. Oskamp (Eds.), *Cross-Cultual Work Groups* (pp. 134–160). Thousand Oaks, CA, USA: Sage Publications Inc.

Oyserman, D., & Lee, S. W. S. (2008). Does culture influence what and how we think? Effects of priming individualism and collectivism. *Psychological Bulletin*, *134*(2), 311–342. Retrieved from http://www.sciencedirect.com/science/article/B6WY5-4S3FH73-7/2/4a7df5360117c055f8b814e1c1dc9931

Ozkan, T., & Lajunen, T. (2007). The role of personality, culture, and economy in unintentional fatalities: An aggregated level analysis. *Personality and Individual Differences*, *43*(3), 519–530.

Paletz, S. B. F., Peng, K., Erez, M., & Maslach, C. (2003). Ethnic composition and its differential impact on group processes in diverse teams. *Small Group Research*, *20*(10), 1–31. Retrieved from http://iew3.technion.ac.il/~merez/papers/paletz_2004.pdf

Parasuraman, R., Molloy, R., & Singh, I. (1993). Performance consequences of automation-induced "complacency." *The International Journal of Aviation Psychology*, *3*(1), 1–23. doi:10.1207/s15327108ijap0301_1

Park, H. (2011). Man-made disasters: A cross-national analysis. *International Business Review*, *20*, 466–476. doi:10.1016/j.ibusrev.2010.08.004

Parsons, T., & Shils, E. (1951). *Toward a General Theory of Action.* Cambridge, USA: Harvard University.

References

Pearce, R. D. (1990). *The Internationalization of Research and Development by Multinational Enterprises*. New York: Palgrave Macmillan.

Peterson, M. F., & Castro, S. L. (2006). Measurement metrics at aggregate levels of analysis: Implications for organization culture research and the GLOBE project. *Leadership Quarterly, 17*(5), 506–521.

Peterson, M. F., Smith, P. B., Akande, A., Ayestaran, S., Bochner, S., Callan, V., ... Setiadi, B. (1995). Role conflict, ambiguity, and overload: A 21-nation study. *Academy of Management Journal, 38*(2), 429–452. doi:10.2307/256687

Phillips, K. W., & Phillips, D. J. (2011). *National Heterogeneity, Status, and Blau's Paradox: The Case of NHL Hockey Team Performance 1988-1998*. Evanston, IL. Retrieved from web.mit.edu/sloan/.../KWP and DJP Hockey.doc

Pinto, J. K., & Mantel, S. J. J. The causes of project failure. , 37 IEEE Transactions on Engineering Management 269–276 (1990). IEEE. doi:10.1109/17.62322

PMI. (2000). *A Guide to the Project Management Body of Knowledge 2000*. Newtown Square, Pennsylvania, USA: Project Management Institute, Inc.

Putnam, R. D. (1993). *Making Democracy Work*. Princetown, NJ, USA: Princetown University Press.

Quinn, R. E., & Rohrbaugh, J. (1981). A competing values approach to organizational effectiveness. *Public Productivity Review, 5*(2), 122–140. Retrieved from http://www.jstor.org/stable/3380029

Quinn, R. E., & Rohrbaugh, J. (1983). A spatial model of effectiveness criteria: Towards a competing values approach to organizational analysis. *Management Science, 29*(3), 363–377. doi:10.1287/mnsc.29.3.363

Ramsden, J. R. (1985). World airline safety audit. *Flight International*, 29–34.

Rasmussen, L. J., Sieck, W. R., & Smart, P. R. (2008). US/UK mental models of planning: The relationship between plan detail and plan quality. *Framework*, 1–12. Retrieved from http://eprints.ecs.soton.ac.uk/14911/

Realo, A., & Allik, J. (2009). On the relationship between social capital and individualism–collectivism. *Social and Personality Psychology Compass, 3*(6), 871–886. doi:10.1111/j.1751-9004.2009.00226.x

References

Reason, J. T. (2008). *The Human Contribution: Unsafe Acts, Accidents and Heroic Recoveries*. Farnham, Surrey: Ashgate Publishing Limited.

Reep, C., & Benjamin, B. (1968). Skill and chance in association football. *Journal of the Royal Statistical Society, 131*(4), 581–585.

Repiso-Caballero, R., & Delgado-López-Cózar, E. (2013). The impact of scientific journals of communication: Comparing Google Scholar metrics, Web of Science and Scopus. *Comunicar, 21*, 45–52. doi:10.3916/C41-2013-04

Reynard, W. (1991). *The acquisition and use of incident data: Investigating accidents before they happen* (No. 51). Washington DC, USA. Retrieved from http://asrs.arc.nasa.gov/docs/rs/51_Acquisition_and_Use_of_Incident_Data.pdf

Rhoades, S. A. (1993). The Herfindahl-Hirschman index. *Federal Reserve Bulletin, 79*(3), 188. Retrieved from http://www.justice.gov/atr/public/testimony/hhi.htm

Rinne, T., Steel, D., & Fairweather, J. (2013). The role of Hofstede's individualism in national-level creativity. *Creativity Research Journal, 25*(1), 129–136. doi:10.1080/10400419.2013.752293

Rinne, T., Steel, G. D., & Fairweather, J. (2012). Hofstede and Shane revisited: The role of power distance and individualism in national-level innovation success. *Cross-Cultural Research, 46*(2), 91–108. doi:10.1177/1069397111423898

Rothwell, R., & Wissema, H. (1986). Technology, culture and public policy. *Technovation, 4*(2), 91–115. doi:10.1016/0166-4972(86)90002-7

Russo, K. W. (2000). A sharing of subjectivities: the values project Northwest. In K. W. Russo (Ed.), *Finding the Middle Ground: Insight and Applications of the Value Orientations Method* (pp. 165–177). Yarmouth, ME, USA: Intercultural Press.

Sarter, N. B. (2000). The need for multisensory interfaces in support of effective attention allocation in highly dynamic event-driven domains: The case of cockpit automation. *International Journal of Aviation Psychology, 10*(3), 231–245. doi:10.1207/S15327108IJAP1003_02

Sarter, N. B., Mumaw, R. J., & Wickens, C. D. (2007). Pilots' monitoring strategies and performance on automated flight decks: an empirical study combining behavioral and eye-tracking data. *Human Factors*, *49*(3), 347–357. Retrieved from http://hfs.sagepub.com/cgi/doi/10.1518/001872007X196685

Sarter, N. B., & Woods, D. D. (1995a). *'Strong, Silent, and Out-of-the-Loop: Properties of Advanced (Cockpit) Automation and Their Impact on Human-Automation Interactions* (No. CSEL 95-TR-01). Columbus, OH.

Sarter, N. B., & Woods, D. D. (1995b). How in the world did we ever get into that mode? Mode error and awareness in supervisory control. *Human Factors*, *37*(1), 5–19. doi:10.1518/001872095779049516

Schein, E. H. (1996a). Culture: The missing concept in organization studies. *Administrative Science Quarterly*, *41*, 229–240.

Schein, E. H. (1996b). Three cultures of management: The key to organizational learning. *Sloan Management Review*, *38*(1), 9–20.

Schröder, T., & Thagard, P. (2013). The affective meanings of automatic social behaviors: Three mechanisms that explain priming. *Psychological Review*, *120*(1), 255–80. doi:10.1037/a0030972

Schwartz, S. H. (1994). Beyond individualism/collectivism: New cultural dimensions of values. In U. Kim, H. C. Triandis, C. Kagitcibasi, S. C. Choi, & G. Yoon (Eds.), *Individualism and Collectivism Theory Method and Applications* (Vol. 18, pp. 85–119). Sage.

Schwartz, S. H. (1999). A theory of cultural values and some implications for work. *Applied Psychology*, *48*(1), 23–47. doi:10.1111/j.1464-0597.1999.tb00047.x

Schwartz, S. H. (2006). A theory of cultural value orientations: Explication and applications. *Comparative Sociology*, *5*(2), 137–182. doi:10.1163/156913306778667357

Scott, T., Mannion, R., Davies, H., & Marshall, M. (2003). The quantitative measurement of organizational culture in health care: a review of the available instruments. *Health Services Research*, *38*(3), 923–945. Retrieved from http://dx.doi.org/10.1111/1475-6773.00154

Shane, S. (1993). Cultural influences on national rates of innovation. *Journal of Business Venturing*, *8*(1), 59–73. doi:10.1016/0883-9026(93)90011-S

References

Shane, S. (1995). Uncertainty avoidance and the preference for innovation championing roles. *Journal of International Business Studies, 26*(1), 47–68. Retrieved from http://www.jstor.org/stable/155477

Shane, S. A. (1992). Why do some societies invent more than others? *Journal of Business Venturing, 7*(1), 29–46. doi:10.1016/0883-9026(92)90033-N

Shaw, M. E. (1973). Scaling group tasks: A method for dimensional analysis. *JSAS Catalog of Selected Documents in Psychology, 3*(8).

Sherman, P. J., Helmreich, R. L., & Merritt, A. C. (1997). National culture and flight deck automation: Results of a multination survey. *The International Journal of Aviation Psychology, 7*(4), 311–329. Retrieved from http://dx.doi.org/10.1207/s15327108ijap0704_4

Simonton, D. K., & Ting, S.-S. (2010). Creativity in eastern and western civilizations: The lessons of historiometry. *Management and Organization Review, 6*(3), 329–350.

Sivakumar, K., & Nakata, C. (2003). Designing global new product teams: Optimizing the effects of national culture on new product development. *International Marketing Review, 20*(4), 397–445. doi:10.1108/02651330310485162

Smith, P. B., & Bond, M. H. (1998). *Social Psychology Across Cultures* (2nd ed.). Harlow, UK: Pearson Education Limited.

Snow, C. C., Snell, S. A., Davison, S. C., & Hambrick, D. C. (1996). Use transnational teams to globalize your company. *Organizational Dynamics, 24*(4), 50.

Soeters, J. L. (1997). Value orientations in military academies: A thirteen country study. *Armed Forces Society, 24*(1), 7–32. doi:10.1177/0095327x9702400101

Soeters, J. L., & Boer, P. C. (2000). Culture and flight safety in military aviation. *International Journal of Aviation Psychology, 10*(2), 111–133. doi:10.1207/S15327108IJAP1002_1

Spikes Cavell Research Company. (1998). *The Bull Survey*. London.

Stahl, G. K., Mäkelä, K., Zander, L., & Maznevski, M. L. (2010). A look at the bright side of multicultural team diversity. *Scandinavian Journal of Management, 26*(4), 439–447. doi:10.1016/j.scaman.2010.09.009

References

Stahl, G. K., Maznevski, M. L., Voigt, A., & Jonsen, K. (2007). Unraveling the diversity-performance link in multicultural teams: Meta-analysis of studies on the impact of cultural diversity in teams. *Journal of International Business Studies, 36*, 1–49. Retrieved from http://scholar.google.com/scholar?hl=en&btnG=Search&q=intitle:Unraveling+the+diversity-performance+link+in+multicultural+teams:+Meta-analysis+of+studies+on+the+impact+of+cultural+diversity+in+teams#0

Steel, P., & Ones, D. S. (2002). Personality and happiness: A national-level analysis. *Journal of Personality and Social Psychology, 83*, 767–781.

Steiner, I. D. (1972). *Group Process and Productivity*. Academic Press, Inc.

Stirling, A. (1999). On the economics and analysis of diversity. Brighton: Science Policy Research Unit, University of Sussex.

Stirling, A. (2007). A general framework for analysing diversity in science, technology and society. *Journal of the Royal Society Interface the Royal Society, 4*(15), 707–719. Retrieved from http://rsif.royalsocietypublishing.org/content/4/15/707.full

Strauch, B. (2010). Can cultural differences lead to accidents? Team cultural differences and sociotechnical system operations. *Human Factors, 52*(2), 246–263. doi:10.1177/0018720810362238

Swigger, K., Brazile, R., Harrington, B., Peng, S., & Alpaslan, F. (2005). A case study of student software teams using computer-supported software. In *Proceedings of the 2005 International Symposium on Collaborative Technologies and Systems 2005*. doi:10.1109/ISCST.2005.1553309

Taras, V., Kirkman, B. L., & Steel, P. (2010). "Examining the impact of Culture's Consequences: A three-decade, multilevel, meta-analytic review of Hofstede's cultural value dimensions": Correction to Taras, Kirkman, and Steel (2010). *The Journal of Applied Psychology, 95*(5), 888. doi:10.1037/a0020939

Taras, V., Rowney, J., & Steel, P. (2009). Half a century of measuring culture: Review of approaches, challenges, and limitations based on the analysis of 121 instruments for quantifying culture. *Journal of International Management, 15*(4), 357–373. doi:10.1016/j.intman.2008.08.005

Teddlie, C., & Tashakkori, A. (2009). *Foundations of Mixed Methods Research: Integrating Quantitative and Qualitative Approaches in the Social and Behavioral Sciences. Book* (Vol. 1). Sage Publications. Retrieved from http://www.amazon.com/dp/0761930124

References

Terzi, A. R. (2011). Relationship between power distance and autocratic-democratic tendencies. *Educational Research and Reviews*, *6*(7), 528–535. Retrieved from http://www.academicjournals.org/err/PDF/Pdf 2011/July/Terzi.pdf

Thomas, D. C. (1999). Cultural diversity and work group effectiveness: An experimental study. *Journal of Cross-Cultural Psychology*, *30*(2), 242–263. Retrieved from http://jcc.sagepub.com/cgi/reprint/30/2/242

Ting-Toomey, S. (1988). Intercultural conflict styles: A face negotiation theory. In Y. Kim & W. Gudykunst (Eds.), *Theories in Intercultural Communication* (pp. 213–235). Newbury Park, CA: Sage.

Tokimatsu, K., Fujino, J., Konishi, S., Ogawa, Y., & Yamaji, K. (2003). Role of nuclear fusion in future energy systems and the environment under future uncertainties. *Energy Policy*, *31*(8), 775–797.

Transparency International. (2011). Corruption Perceptions Index. *Criticism*. Transparency International. Retrieved from http://www.transparency.org/policy_research/surveys_indices/cpi

Triandis, H. C. (1993). *Culture and Social Behavior*. McGraw-Hill Inc.

Triandis, H. C. (1995). *Individualism and Collectivism*. HarperCollins.

Triandis, H. C. (1996). The psychological measurement of cultural syndromes. *American Psychologist*, *51*(4), 407–415. doi:10.1037//0003-066X.51.4.407

Trompenaars, F., & Hampden-Turner, C. (1997). *Riding the Waves of Culture: Understanding Cultural Diversity in Business* (2nd ed.). Nicholas Brealey Publishing.

Troyer, L. (2002). Review: Multinational work teams: A new perspective. *American Journal of Sociology*, *108*(3), 704–706.

Tubbs, S. L. (1995). *A Systems Approach to Small Group Interaction* (Vol. 5th). McGraw-Hill.

Tuckman, B., & Jensen, M. (1977). Stages of small group development. *Group and Organizational Studies*, *2*, 419–427.

Van de Water, T., van de Water, H., & Bukman, C. (2007). A balanced team generating model. *European Journal of Operational Research*, *180*, 885–906.

283

References

Vecchi, A., & Brennan, L. (2009). A cultural perspective on innovation in international manufacturing. *Research in International Business and Finance, 23*(2), 181–192. doi:10.1016/j.ribaf.2008.03.008

Venkatraman, N., & Prescott, J. E. (1990). Environment-strategy coalignment: An empirical test of its performance implications. *Strategic Management Journal, 11*(1), 1–23. doi:10.1002/smj.4250110102

Vincent, A.-M., & Dubinsky, A. J. (2004). Impact of fear appeals in a cross-cultural context. *Journal of Euromarketing, 15*(1), 17 – 32. Retrieved from http://search.ebscohost.com/login.aspx?direct=true&db=aph&AN=16881 035&site=ehost-live

Vodosek, M. (2007). Intragroup conflict as a mediator between cultural diversity and work group outcome. *International Journal of Conflict Management, 18*(4), 345–375.

Watson, W. E., Kumar, K., & Michaelsen, L. K. (1993). Cultural diversity's impact on interaction process and performance: Comparing homogeneous and diverse task groups. *Academy of Management Journal, 36*(3), 590–602. doi:10.2307/256593

Weber, E. U., & Morris, M. W. (2010). Culture and judgment and decision making: The constructivist turn. *Perspectives on Psychological Science, 5*(4), 410–419. doi:10.1177/1745691610375556

Weener, E. F. (1993). Crew factor accidents: Regional perspective. In *Proceedings of the IATA 22nd Technical Conference on Human Factors in Aviation* (Vol. Montreal, pp. 45–61). International Air Transport Association.

Weener, E. F. (Boeing C. A. G., & Russell, P. D. (1994). Aviation safety review: Regional perspectives. In *22nd International Air Transport Association Technical Conference*. Seattle, WA: IATA.

Wildman, J. L., Thayer, A. L., Rosen, M. A., Salas, E., Mathieu, J. E., & Rayne, S. R. (2012). Task types and team-level attributes: Synthesis of team classification literature. *Human Resource Development Review, 11*(1), 97–129.

Willems, M. J. T. (2007). *The Influence of Social Capital and Cultural Dimensions on Innovation*. Universiteit Maastricht.

References

WIPO. (2013). *WIPO IP Facts and Figures (WIPO Publication No. 943E/13)*. Geneva, Switzerland: World Intellectual Property Organization. Retrieved from http://www.wipo.int/export/sites/www/freepublications/en/statistics/943/w ipo_pub_943_2013.pdf

Wodehouse, A., Maclachlan, R., Grierson, H., & Strong, D. (2011). Culture and concept design: A study of international teams. In *International Conference on Engineering Design*. Kabenhavn, Denmark. Retrieved from https://pure.strath.ac.uk/portal/files/10203357/Culture_and_concept_desig n_conference_resubmission_v2.pdf

Wolf, J. (2002). Multicultural workgroups (editorial). *Management International Review, 42*, 3–5.

Wood, S. J. (2004). *Flight Crew Reliance on Automation: CAA Paper 2004/10* (No. 2004/10). London, UK. Retrieved from http://www.caa.co.uk/docs/33/2004_10.PDF

Xie, A., Rau, P. L. P., Tseng, Y., Su, H., & Zhao, C. (2009). Cross-cultural influence on communication effectiveness and user interface design. *International Journal of Intercultural Relations, 33*(1), 11–20.

Yamagishi, T., & Yamagishi, M. (1994). Trust and commitment in the United States and Japan. *Motivation and Emotion, 18*(2), 129–166. doi:10.1007/BF02249397

Young, J. P., Fanjoy, R. O., & Suckow, M. W. (2006). Impact of glass cockpit experience on manual flying skills. *Journal of Aviation/Aerospace Education and Research, 15*(2), 27–32.

Zimmermann, K., Paries, J., & Amalberti, R. (2011). Distress call from the flight deck: Cross-cultural survey of aviation professionals reveals perception that flight safety is decreasing. *Safety Science Monitor, 15*(2).

Appendices

Appendix 1: Keywords and review sources

This appendix provides additional information associated with some aspects of the literature review and the literature review methodology; it also provides a more detailed view of the data collected from the review, and its analysis.

Appendix 1A: Keywords and their synonyms

There were significant overlaps of keywords between the three literature review areas; however, the keyword/key phrase combinations tended to differ between the review areas.

Although they were not strictly synonyms, it was important to interchange a range of similar terms and phrases when carrying out keyword searches; examples of these are provided below (inverted commas signify phrases):

- "national culture"/"ethnic culture"/"regional culture"

- tools/methodologies/instruments

- "action teams"/"organized action teams"/crews/operators

- multicultural/multinational

Note that in the following list of keywords, inverted commas signify phrases, and forward slashes ('/') signify alternative phrases, e.g. "culture/cultural frameworks/tools" implies a total of four phrases – "culture frameworks", "culture tools", "cultural frameworks" and "cultural tools", Example keywords and phrases are listed below:

Culture, cultural, "cultural traits", "cultural diversity", "culture tool(s)", "culture/cultural frameworks/methodologies/methods/-tools", "cultural dimensions/factors/attributes", "national culture", multicultural, tool(s), team, crew(s), operator(s), "team culture", "team type(s)", teamwork, task(s), "task type(s)", performance, "team/operator/crew performance", effects, effectiveness, "team/operator/crew effectiveness", "organized action teams", "research teams", aviation, aerospace, marine, shipping, refineries, power generators, creativity, invention, innovation, "product development", "product improvement", "process improve-ment".

Keywords and key phrases were assembled to direct the search, depending on whether the author was 'painting a broad brush' as in the early stages, or focusing on a limited area, as in the late stages of the literature review. Examples, expressed in Boolean logic are presented below, but the actual form of a submitted search query would vary depending on the targeted database, as each database (or search engine) had its own representation of logic.

Literature review area 1 – Example query when searching for publications on the effects of culture on team performance:

- "national culture" AND "team performance" AND prediction

- "national culture" AND "team performance" AND tool

- culture AND (framework OR tool OR methodology) AND team AND performance NOT ("safety culture" OR "organizational culture")

Note the requirement (specified in the above search phrase) to exclude safety culture and organisational culture, for which there are many checklists and tools – these had been retrieved and examined in earlier searches.

Literature review area 2 – Example query when searching for publications on frameworks, methodologies and tools for the (culture-based) prediction of team performance:

- "national culture" AND tool AND performance

- culture AND (framework OR tool OR methodology) AND team AND (performance OR assessment OR prediction) NOT ("safety culture" OR "organizational culture")

Queries such as the first example typically returned hundreds or thousands of unhelpful citations. Unfortunately, none of the traditional literature resource search engines appeared to be able to handle complex queries such as the second example above, and it was necessary to break it down into smaller, simpler queries.

Literature review area 3 – Having identified specific frameworks methodologies and tools, their descriptions and/or authors were entered into search engines with additional terms such as validity:

- Hofstede AND (validation OR evaluation OR criticism)

- culture AND dimension AND (validation OR evaluation OR criticism)

Appendix 1B: Thesauri and search engines

The following literature thesauri and search engines were accessed and evaluated, in part by targeting previously-identified research papers in relevant areas:

- CiteSeer^X: This was a free-to-use search engine that accessed publically available websites, not publisher websites; although this reduced the number of articles accessed, it was claimed that it provided a higher proportion of open-access than other search engines. However, when tested by the author, *CiteSeer*^{X} was found to be exceedingly poor at retrieving previously-identified papers, and was therefore not frequently utilised.

- **EBSCO:** Initial test searches on the *EBSCO* database confirmed that it would only retrieve literature from a limited range of subject areas; highly relevant papers on culture were not retrieved if published in non-social science/anthropology journals. *EBSCO* was therefore not frequently utilised.

- **ERIC (Education Resources Information Center):** Following detailed examination of the thesaurus of *ERIC* descriptors, several search tests were carried out on the *ERIC* database using various descriptors and non-descriptor search terms. Although many descriptors within the *ERIC* thesaurus were related to culture, only two potentially-relevant papers (both on creativity) were returned by the *ERIC* database, due probably to its extreme focus on education-related research. *ERIC* was therefore not frequently utilised.

- **Google/Google Scholar:** The *Google/Google Scholar* free-to-use search engine suffered from the opposite problem to EBSCO and ERIC, in that it retrieved information from all sources and in all forms (e.g. blogs, wikis, bulletin boards, discussion forums, newsletters, in addition to the standard academic sources). As a result, searches required careful 'tuning' in order to limit the number of search results to a manageable level. However, the ability to express the search logic more precisely in Google searches than was the case with the other sources, combined with the extreme breadth of disciplines within which culture-related articles appeared, resulted in *Google/Google Scholar* being the most useful search engine, overall.

The citation tracking feature of Google Scholar proved to be very fast and efficient for retrieving abstracts of citing articles for publications, although these were not always accurate. In addition, Google Scholar's 'live' author citation-tracking facility allowed the selection of key authors, following which, regular updates were sent via email as new citations of those authors' works were discovered by Google Scholar. In the case of Hofstede, this was somewhat overwhelming (new citations added daily to the 100,000-plus existing citations list) but, for other authors – e.g. Salas, Helmreich, Hollenbeck, this was found to be a useful facility.

- **Mendeley:** *Mendeley* was a reference manager system with access to a large database of publication details. The author used this system to maintain his collection of references and to organise the references in this thesis because the university-recommended reference manager proved unreliable. *Mendeley*'s publication database was found to be incomplete - the author had to enter approximately 25% of references manually, rather than just to select them from the *Mendeley* database. In addition, a higher proportion of publications retrieved by *Mendeley*'s search engine were irrelevant than was the case with most alternative sources. However, it was convenient to conduct searches within Mendeley because relevant search results could be entered into the author's list of references at the touch of a button; in addition, *Mendeley* offered good (full) document retrieval facilities via its links to Google Scholar and other sources.

- **PubMed:** *PubMed* was a free-to-use search engine that accessed the *MEDLINE* references and abstracts database. When evaluated against a range of articles of relevance to author's work, *PubMed* produced a surprisingly high return rate considering the apparent limited range of sources, and was therefore frequently utilised by the author.

- **PsycINFO:** The *PsycINFO* bibliographic database provided abstracts and citations covering scholarly literature in the fields of psychology, social sciences, behavioural sciences and health sciences. The student was only able to access a limited subset of the *PsycINFO* database, as the university did not have a full subscription to the database.

- **ResearchGate:** ResearchGate was a networking site for scientists and academics. It enabled members to enter details of their publications on the site, to upload copies of them and any associated statistical or other datasets, and to make them available to other ResearchGate members. The site's growing membership resulted in it becoming an increasingly useful source of publications during the period of this PhD research. Even in the case where a publication had not been uploaded to the site due to copyright restrictions, it could be requested via the website and would usually be made available to the requestor by the author within a few days. The author of this thesis found an increasing number of papers (rather than just citation details) on ResearchGate, usually via Google searches. A further benefit of visiting ResearchGate to download a paper was the opportunity to rifle through the particular ResearchGate author's other papers

- **Scopus:** The *Scopus* bibliographic database was claimed have access to 20,000 journals and 5.5 million conference proceedings. It provided abstracts and citations of peer-reviewed literature in the fields of science, technology, arts, humanities, social sciences and medicine. However, it appeared to have less coverage of earlier articles than *Web of Science*.

- **SSCI** (Social Science Citation Index): This was accessed only as part of the *Web of Science.*

- **Web of Science:** The *Web of Science* was claimed to have access to 12,000 journals and 150,000 conference proceedings. It provided advanced search facilities for its 'core' collection, but only basic search facilities for the full collection. It also provided (via the *Web of Knowledge* citation mapping tool) a capability to produce one- or two-level forward and backward citation trees, presented in graphical form; these could be inspected in order to follow up promising authors and titles. This graphical citation tree tool proved to be very effective and fast for discovering further research via citations. In addition, the search facility was efficient.

- **Individual journal searches:** In the late stages of the literature review, the author of this thesis wished to ascertain the thoroughness of his literature search process. He located two journals with relevant coverage, for which all issues (or all modern issues) were available on-line. These journals were then subjected to a 100% article-by-article examination of abstracts (when in doubt, the whole paper was perused); the results were as follows:

  - **International Journal of Cross Cultural Management (all issues, i.e. 2001 to 2013):** 31 papers of potential interest were identified, of which 26 had previously been located and selected via forward or backward citations or keyword searches. One of the 'new' five papers offered a sufficient contribution to be cited in the final literature review.

○ **Journal of Cross-Cultural Psychology (all issues, i.e. 1970 to 2013):** 77 papers of potential interest were identified, of which 72 had previously been located via citations or keyword searches. None of the 'new' five papers offered a sufficient contribution to be cited in the final literature review.

Whereas it is impossible to guarantee complete coverage in a literature review, the above 100% check of journals in the field of national culture provided a degree of confidence that the key-word and citation based searches had been reasonably thorough. Clearly, such an article-by-article search was not dependent on citation chasing 'starting points', nor was it dependent on the choice of appropriate search key words.

Further comments on Google

Over the period of this author's PhD research, Google Scholar (GS) started to change the landscape of literature reviewing and citation following. Earlier publications on the relative performance of citation sources tended to identify GS as less reliable and accurate than other sources, e.g. Jacso (2005) and Falagas et al. (2008), although others identified Google's greater coverage of non-English language journals and conference proceedings in certain disciplines, e.g. Meho & Yang (2007).

Following the launch of Google Scholar Metrics in 2012, Repiso-Caballero & Delgado-López-Cózar (2013) carried out a comparative survey of GS Metrics, Web of Science (WoS) and Scopus in the field of communication studies. They concluded that GS Metrics had twice the coverage of WoS and Scopus, less bias towards English language publi-cations, and that its results were as reliable and valid as those of WoS and Scopus. However, Giustini & Boulos' review of retrieval perfor-mance in the field of social media in health led them to the conclusion that GS was less effective than the traditional citation databases in the case where the titles and authors of articles were already known (Giustini & Boulos, 2013),

Google/GS' comprehensive indexing of 'everything' on the Web has brought further benefits to researchers because it has enabled them to gain free access to authors' personal copies[71] and to research institutions' pre-published copies of academic publications. This free access has been directly beneficial to researchers, but it has also been the catalyst for a rapid increase in open access publications.

---

[71] For example, via the author's ResearchGate account.

Appendix 1C: Main literature sources cited in this thesis

A very wide range of literature sources was accessed. Due to the nature of the work, it was necessary to extend the range of sources beyond academic journals and conferences to include accident reports, government statistical websites, blogs, etc.

The following tables contain an incomplete list of the peer-reviewed journals, learned society publications, professional journals and (occasional) magazines, totalling 109 different publications. They do not include refereed conferences, formal accident reports, government papers, academic reports, national and international data sources or private communications.

Publication title	No. of papers
Academy of Management Executive	1
Academy of Management Journal	4
Academy of Management Perspectives	2
Academy of Management Review	5
Accounting, Organizations and Society	2
Administrative Science Quarterly	3
Advances in Experimental Social Psychology	1
Advances in Human Performance and Cognitive Engineering Research	1
Aerosafety World	1
African Journal of Business Management	1
American Journal of Sociology	1
American Psychologist	3
American Sociological Review	1
Annual Review of Psychology	1
Applied Psychology: An International Review	2
Armed Forces Society	1
Aviation, Space, and Environmental Medicine	1
(BMC) Health Services Research	1
Communication Research	1
Comparative Sociology	1
Creativity Research Journal	1
Criticism	1
Cross Cultural Management	2
Cross-Cultural Research: The Journal of Comparative Social	1

Appendix 1: Keywords and review sources

Publication title	No. of papers
Sci.	
Current Science	1
Economics of Innovation and New Technology	1
Educational Research and Reviews	1
Engineering Project Organization Journal	1
European Journal of Innovation Management	1
European Journal of Operational Research	1
European Journal of Work and Organizational Psychology	1
Flight International	1
Group and Organizational Studies	1
Harvard Business Review	1
Human Factors	4
Human Factors and Aerospace Safety	1
Human Organization	1
Human Relations	2
Human Resource Development Review	1
IEEE Transactions on Engineering Management	2
IEEE Transactions in Human Machine Systems	1
International Business Review	1
International Journal of Aviation Psychology	5
International Journal of Conflict Management	1
International Journal of Cross Cultural Management	5
International Journal of Human Resource Management	1
International Journal of Intercultural Relations	4
International Journal of Managing Projects in Business	1
International Journal of Project Management	3
International Journal of Value-Based Management	1
International Marketing Review	3
Journal of Air Transportation	2
Journal of Aviation/Aerospace Education and Research	1
Journal of Applied Psychology	2
Journal of Business Venturing	2
Journal of College Student Development	1
Journal of Consumer Marketing	1
Journal of Creative Behavior	1
Journal of Cross-Cultural Psychology	3
Journal of Economic Perspectives	1
Journal of Euromarketing	1
Journal of Evolutionary Ergonomics	1
Journal of Experimental Social Psychology	1

Appendix 1: Keywords and review sources

Publication title	No. of papers
Journal of Global Information Management	1
Journal of Global Marketing	1
Journal of High Technology Management Research	1
Journal of International Business Studies	4
Journal of International Management	1
Journal of Management	2
Journal of Marketing	1
Journal of Organizational Behavior	1
Journal of Organizational Change Management	1
Journal of Personality and Social Psychology	1
Journal of Product Innovation Management	1
Journal of the Royal Society – Interface	1
Journal of the Royal Statistical Society	1
JSAS Catalog of Selected Documents in Psychology	1
Leadership and Organizational Development Journal	1
Language	1
Management and Organization Review	3
Management International Review	3
Management Science	1
Marine Policy	1
Marketing Letters	1
Methods	1
Organizational Behavior and Human Decision Processes	1
Organizational Dynamics	2
Organization Science	1
Organization Studies	1
Papers in Regional Science	1
Patient Education and Counseling	1
Personality and Individual Differences	1
Perspectives on Psychological Science	1
Philosophical Transactions of the Royal Society of London – Series B: Biological Sciences	1
Philosophical Transactions of the Royal Society B: Biological Sciences	1
Psychological Review	2
Public Administration Review	1
Public Productivity Review	1
Research in Organizational Behavior	1
Response	1
Review of Public Personnel Administration	1
Scandinavian Journal of Management	1
Science Journal	1

Appendix 1: Keywords and review sources

Publication title	No. of papers
Small Group Research	2
Social Geography	1
Technovation	2
Theoretical Issues in Ergonomics Science	1
Total Quality Management Business Excellence	1
Vision – the Journal of Business Perspective	1

Appendix 2: Interviews and conversations

Note that, as the examples in this section are anecdotal, no claim is made to the effect that they are typical or representative. The sources of most of the anecdotes below are the conversations that the author has had with other research staff, foreign students, lecturers, fellow footballers and others about their experiences on coming to Britain or travelling elsewhere. In many cases, the anecdotes that the author obtained were potentially traceable to their sources, and in other cases the author was asked not to quote them; such anecdotes have not been listed in the selection below.

English indirectness: A Swedish PhD student who had spent some time in the USA recounted his initial difficulties on coming to the UK. He commented to me that his British supervisors or managers would never tell him to do anything, but would use phrases such as "It would be useful if a summary of the data was available by ...", "It would be helpful ...". Just _tell_ me what you want me to do!

English yob culture: A Palestinian student commented on his shock at both the number of young men and women behaving in a drunken manner most evenings near his UK Midlands accommodation, and at the number of single young women with children. Middle-Eastern, Indian and Chinese students have all asked me "Why do you allow this?"

Expectations violated: Two high power distance research colleagues have commented to me (and to other British colleagues) that they found it offensive when people junior to themselves from the same region (typically research students who had spent several years in the UK) did not acknowledge their seniority when addressing them.

Face and politeness (China): A Chinese fellow student/footballer remarked to me that I would have difficulty obtaining useful answers from his countrymen because they would not be willing to make critical comments about China, as that was an issue of losing face, nor would they make critical comments about the UK as that would be considered to be rude to their British hosts.

Face and politeness (Singapore): The author of this thesis lectured for many years on the topic of manufacturing management; the second year course had a large intake of Singaporean students. Most UK students would regularly ask questions, and would answer my questions; however, the Singaporeans avoided such interaction in front of the class, even when encouraged by me. However, during the break in the middle of a two hour lecture presentation, they would quickly confer and send a delegate to me with a list of questions to be answered. I never had time to grab that desperately needed cup of coffee! The issue was apparently about face – no Singaporean student would risk asking a question for which, in retrospect, the answer appeared obvious.

Face, meetings (China): When arranging academic and administrative meetings at a Chinese mainland university, the Chinese secretary of an English professor that I worked for had to plan the seating arrangements very carefully in order to avoid offence, which would hinder the purpose of the meeting. Face issues were associated with where a person sat in relation to the head of the table, whom he or she sat next to, and whether another person of perceived lower status sat further up the table.

Jobs (China): A Chinese PhD student, who was completing his write-up, told me that he hoped to obtain a lectureship at a university near his home. However, it all depended on guanxi - the influence that his relatives would be able to bring to bear on the university decision-makers.

Meetings (UK): I was the only British member of a multinational research group at a UK university. It was difficult to persuade some Middle-Eastern student-members to contribute to meetings, so we instigated a policy that every attendee at the meeting was required, in turn, to state his or her views on each significant item discussed at the meeting. This had the additional benefit that most of us made more effort to prepare for the meeting.

Meetings (UK and Eastern Europe): An Eastern European commented to me that when he first came to this country, he was very surprised to find that things were achieved at meetings in Britain; this had not been the case in his country, where meetings were somewhat of a charade, and the real decisions were made elsewhere. He was also surprised, when he first joined a university department, by the high level of concern that members of staff at meetings showed for individual (usually struggling) students.

Rote education (Egypt): An Egyptian commented to me on the tradition of rote education in Egypt – the need to score in the mid-90's or better in order to gain a place at a prestigious university resulted in parents and students concentrating on the ability to regurgitate the material they had learned verbatim.

Trust (Egypt): An Egyptian former construction engineer commented to me that one of the first things Egyptian workers would do when operating on a new construction site was to hide vital construction-related items in order to ensure that they (the workers) could not be dismissed without inflicting pain on the management.

Trust (UK): An East European colleague remarked that the British were too trusting, and the opportunities for cheating were quite obvious; the British needed to adjust their tax and welfare systems to accommodate immigrants, many of whom would have no compunction about cheating the system.

Uncertainty avoidance - rules and regulations (Germany-1): A German former co-researcher commented to me that the British seemed to consider any action legal unless a rule forbad it, whereas the Germans considered any action illegal unless a rule allowed it. He also commented that both the Germans and British made plans, but the British seemed to abandon them almost as soon as work started. Note that the British and Germans have very similar culture dimension scores except for uncertainty avoidance (UAI), where the Germans score is much higher.

Uncertainty avoidance - rules and regulations (Germany-2): We had been 'bumped off' our regular slot on the University football pitches without warning. As we were all kitted up, eight of us decided to play on a spare grass pitch; however, our German footballing colleague was very nervous about this and insisted that we play on the grass next to the pitch, as we did not have permission to play on the pitch.

Uncertainty avoidance? At a research establishment where I had previously worked, we researchers were asked to attend a meeting to plan new research activities. Several research areas were considered, and researchers were asked to come up with general topics and, within them, specific examples of potential research projects. Following presentations, formation into groups and further discussions, the various topics were put to the vote. I was disappointed to see that not a single radical proposal survived; all the successful proposals seemed to contain nothing more mysterious than 'known unknowns', usually continuations of current research activities. Perhaps I am reading too much into the low individualism, high uncertainty avoidance cultures of the majority of our researchers at that time.

Unfriendly British (1): A female Thai PhD student told me that Italian men seemed much friendlier and open than British men. I made no comment.

Unfriendly British (2): A Scandinavian PhD student remarked that initial friendliness on the part of the British never 'carried through' – they never invited one over to their house, and seldom arranged out-of-work activities.

Unfriendly British (3): An East European PhD student commented similarly to the above, in that raised expectations on the basis of initial friendliness never came to anything.

Unfriendly British (4): A Middle-Eastern colleague also commented on the fact that he was never invited over to British colleagues' homes whereas, when he had lived and worked in the USA, he had frequently been invited to colleagues' homes.

Internationally-shared stereotypes - the Euro (or EuroSwiss) joke – Heaven vs. Hell: National differences and stereotypes, widely recognised across Europe, are captured in various versions of this joke; to avoid potential copyright issues, it will not be quoted here. Please visit one of the following URLs:

http://ploum.net/post/the-european-joke

http://fistfulofeuros.net/afoe/european-stereotypes-and-jokes/

In the case of the latter URL, scroll down the page to "In Heaven, the police are British ..."

The World's most important inventions – the myth: A widely-quoted survey by MITI (Japan's DTI) concluded that, of the world's most important inventions, 54% were British, 25% were American and 5% were Japanese.

The World's most important inventions – a little closer to reality: The author carried out a Web search to locate the original MITI survey, but was unsuccessful; the author did, however, find an article in the New Scientist (Budworth, 1986) that traced the myth back to an original 1976 article by the US National Science Foundation (NSF). The NSF article presented innovation-related estimates for the period 1953 to 1973, split into "radical breakthrough,", "major technical shift", "improvement" and "unclassified". The UK's percentage split between these categories was 55/40/5/0, respectively, the USA 25/28/38/7, West Germany 13/47/34/4, France 23/64/11/0 and Japan 7/51/37/3. Note that in actual *numbers* of radical breakthrough innovations (the UK's best performing category), the USA produced almost six times as many innovations as the UK. However, the NSF based the above figures on *new introductions to the market* – a stage in the invention/innovation chain at which the UK appears to be particularly poor.

The interesting aspect of the invention myth is just how many UK publications and other articles assumed the myth's validity without checking the origin of the claims. I discovered over fifty "... according to MITI ... " articles in a few minutes of 'googling'.

301

A British pilot's experiences – an unstructured interview

The author carried out an interview with a pilot with more than twenty years flying experience on flag carriers, budget airlines and private flying services. As a regular trainer, the pilot described one of his key tasks as attempting to minimise the 'power slope' in the cockpit as, for crews of many nationalities, the captain was a considerable distance above the first officer. Following further discussions it became clear that 'power slope' was the equivalent of power distance.

The pilot also described the issues he had come across with regard to issues related to following standard operational procedures (SOPs) yet retaining flexibility of action when needed. He described the preparations to land at difficult airports in bad weather conditions, and how some co-pilots would become agitated when he explained that he was going to deviate from SOPs in order to maintain a safe margin of control. He went on to comment on the Swissair MD-11 crash of 1998, which he considered likely to be due in part to the pilots' decisions to follow SOPs and to go through detailed checklists, rather than to turn immediately and head for the nearest airport; interestingly Carley (1998) expressed the same view, which appeared to be supported by Cocklin (2004). The pilot mentioned that the members of the civil aircrew community frequently discussed accidents and read and commented on them on a range of on-line blogs; in some cases, he and others had been at a loss to understand the behaviours of pilots in the stages leading up to accidents. Following this part of the discussion, I introduced and described the uncertainty avoidance dimension which, he suggested, explained some of the above differences he had found between various nationalities of pilot.

The pilot commented on the increasing levels multinational employment in the aviation industry, as a result of which some airlines employed more than seventy nationalities of flying crews. In at least one such case, the company had implemented, very rigidly, a comprehensive set of watertight SOPs in order to cope with crew national diversity. The pilot expressed concerns about this SOP-fixation (as he saw it) and the safety issues that would arise when internal or external conditions deviated excessively from the norm, resulting in a loss of margins.

The pilot went on to describe issues of face that came to the fore when he had to correct pilots of some nationalities, in particular when training or testing pilots. He also commented on the 'gungho' attitudes of US pilots, in particular. We discussed this latter point further and it appeared to relate to masculinity; this 'gungho' attitude was not common amongst other nationalities. As the USA default masculinity score was lower than that of the UK and many other countries, this supported Merritt's findings that Hofstede's masculinity scores were not closely replicated amongst aircrew (A. C. Merritt, 2000).

I asked the pilot about automation preferences amongst his colleagues, and he said that he had noticed that, whereas most British (plus other Anglos and North Europeans) preferred a more hands-on approach, pilots of other nationalities were keen to utilise the FMC as much as possible. He also commented, unprompted, about the loss of flying skills associated with increasing automation use, particularly as the generation of pilots with pre- or low-automation experience was retiring. Unlike the older generation of pilots, new recruits typically had no other significant flying experience to fall back on.

To summarise the above, it appeared that national culture played a significant role in civil aviation crewing, although the default masculinity scores appeared to be an unreliable indicator of attitudes and behaviour.

Appendix 3: On-line culture survey form
Culture Survey

This survey is part of a PhD project, and will help me to understand the effects of cultural differences.
The survey aims to collect information about what people find most different when they travel to another culture e.g. as a student or worker.

1. What is your nationality?

2. What country did you travel to?

3. What differences did you notice (compared to home) about your boss' or teacher's behaviour to you?

4. What differences did you notice about other workers' or students' behaviour to you (compared to home)?

5. In what way were meetings different from meetings in your home country (e.g. more casual, more formal)?

6. Did you work in a team? If so, was that different from teams at home?

7. What differences (compared to home) surprised you the most?

8. What were the biggest differences compared to home?

9. What did you like about the country or the people that you met there?
What did you DISLIKE?

10. Please add any other comments about your experiences

Done

Appendix 4: Detailed statistical results

Appendix 4A: Loughborough 2nd year student group data

Model Summary[b]

Model	R	R Square	Adjusted R Square	Std. Error of the Estimate	Change statistics	
					R Square Change	F Change
1	.873[a]	.762	.745	4.43596	.762	45.786

a. Predictors: (Constant), UAIdiversity, Individual_marks, UAI
b. Dependent Variable: GroupPerformance

ANOVA[a]

Model		Sum of Squares	df	Mean Square	F	Sig.
1	Regression	2702.882	3	900.961	45.786	.000[b]
	Residual	846.144	43	19.678		
	Total	3549.026	46			

a. Dependent Variable: GroupPerformance
b. Predictors: (Constant), UAIdiversity, Individual_marks, UAI

Coefficients[a]

Model		Unstandardized Coefficients		Stndrdzd Coeffs	t	Sig.	95.0% Conf. Interval for B	
		B	Std. Error	Beta			Lower Bound	Upper Bound
1	(Constant)	42.619	12.045		3.538	.001	18.329	66.909
	Individual_marks	1.136	.101	.845	11.238	.000	.932	1.340
	UAI	-1.711	.414	-.658	-4.131	.000	-2.546	-.876
	UAIdiversity	.536	.193	.441	2.778	.008	.147	.925

a. Dependent Variable: GroupPerformance

Coefficient Correlations[a]

Model		UAIdiversity	Individual_marks	UAI
1	Correlations			
	UAIdiversity	1.000	.016	-.582
	Individual_marks	.016	1.000	-.078
	UAI	-.582	-.078	1.000
	Covariances			
	UAIdiversity	.037	.000	-.070
	Individual_marks	.000	.010	-.003
	UAI	-.070	-.003	.172

a. Dependent Variable: GroupPerformance

Appendix 4B: UK physics & astronomy RAE2008 data

Model Summary[b]

Model	R	R Square	Adjusted R Square	Std. Error of the Estimate	Change statistics R Square Change	F Change
1	.836[a]	.698	.671	.16473	.698	25.438

a. Predictors: (Constant), MASdiversityOpt, MAS
b. Dependent Variable: RAE2008

ANOVA[a]

Model		Sum of Squares	df	Mean Square	F	Sig.
1	Regression	1.381	2	.690	25.438	.000[b]
	Residual	.597	22	.027		
	Total	1.978	24			

a. Dependent Variable: RAE2008
b. Predictors: (Constant), MASdiversityOpt, MAS

Coefficients[a]

Model		Unstandardized Coefficients B	Std. Error	Standardized Coefficients Beta	t	Sig.	95.0% Confidence Interval for B Lower Bound	Upper Bound
1	(Constant)	10.180	1.088		9.353	.000	7.923	12.437
	MAS	-.142	.020	-1.670	-6.997	.000	-.184	-.100
	MASdiversityOpt	-.114	.017	-1.631	6.811	.000	-.149	-.079

a. Dependent Variable: RAE2008

Coefficient Correlations[a]

Model		MASdiversityOpt	MAS
1	Correlations MASdiversityOpt	1.000	.572
	MAS	.572	1.000
	Covariances MASdiversityOpt	.000	.000
	MAS	.000	.000

a. Dependent Variable: RAE2008

Appendix 4C: UK chemical engineering RAE2008 data

Model Summary[b]

Model	R	R Square	Adjusted R Square	Std. Error of the Estimate	Change statistics	
					R Square Change	F Change
1	.810[a]	.656	.613	.19922	.656	15.237

a. Predictors: (Constant), MASdiversity
b. Dependent Variable: RAE2008

ANOVA[a]

Model		Sum of Squares	df	Mean Square	F	Sig.
1	Regression	.605	1	.605	15.237	.005[b]
	Residual	.318	8	.040		
	Total	.922	9			

a. Dependent Variable: RAE2008
b. Predictors: (Constant), MASdiversity

Coefficients[a]

Model		Unstandardized Coefficients		Standardized Coefficients	t	Sig.	95.0% Confidence Interval for B	
		B	Std. Error	Beta			Lower Bound	Upper Bound
1	(Constant)	3.276	.148		22.186	.000	2.936	3.617
	MASdiversity	-.054	.014	-.810	-3.903	.005	-.086	-.022

a. Dependent Variable: RAE2008

Coefficient Correlations[a]

Model			MASdiversity
1	Correlations	MASdiversity	1.000
	Covariances	MASdiversity	0.000

a. Dependent Variable: RAE2008

Appendix 4D: English Premiership match performance data

Model Summary[b]

Model	R	R Square	Adjusted R Square	Std. Error of the Estimate	Change statistics	
					R Square Change	F Change
1	.645[a]	.416	.413	4.001	.416	134.606

a. Predictors: (Constant), HomeAdv, MASdiff, TalentDiff, UAIdiff
b. Dependent Variable: ShotsOnTargetDiff

ANOVA[a]

Model		Sum of Squares	df	Mean Square	F	Sig.
1	Regression	8617.78	4	2154.445	134.606	.000[b]
	Residual	12084.222	755	16.006		
	Total	20702.000	759			

a. Dependent Variable: ShotsOnTargetDiff
b. Predictors: (Constant), HomeAdv, MASdiff, TalentDiff, UAIdiff

Coefficients[a]

Model		Unstandardized Coefficients		Standardized Coefficients	t	Sig.	95.0% Confidence Interval for B	
		B	Std. Error	Beta			Lower Bound	Upper Bound
1	(Constant)	-1.609	.205		-7.828	.000	-2.012	-1.205
	TalentDiff	.140	.012	.3776	11.402	.000	.116	.164
	MASdiff	.099	.025	.157	3.968	.000	.050	.149
	UAIdiff	.134	.015	.368	8.973	.000	.105	.163
	HomeAdv	3.217	.291	.308	11.059	.000	2.646	3.788

a. Dependent Variable: ShotsOnTargetDiff

Coefficient Correlations[a]

Model			HomeAdv	MASdiff	TalentDiff	UAIdiff
1	Correlations	HomeAdv	1.000	-.005	-.068	.027
		MASdiff	-.005	1.000	.159	.609
		TalentDiff	-.068	.159	1.000	-.308
		UAIdiff	.027	.609	-.308	1.000
	Covariances	HomeAdv	.085	-3.95E-005	.000	.000
		MASdiff	-3.95E-005	.001	4.89E-005	.000
		TalentDiff	.000	4.89E-005	.000	-5.630E-005
		UAIdiff	.000	.000	-5.630E-005	.000

a. Dependent Variable: ShotsOnTargetDiff

Appendix 4E: English Premiership team performance data

Model Summary[b]

Model	R	R Square	Adjusted R Square	Std. Error of the Estimate	Change statistics	
					R Square Change	F Change
1	.916[a]	.838	.825	1.20986	.084	18.742

a. Predictors: (Constant), UAIdiff, HomeAdv, TalentDiff
b. Dependent Variable: ShotsOnTargetDiff

ANOVA[a]

Model		Sum of Squares	df	Mean Square	F	Sig.
1	Regression	273.439	3	91.146	62.268	.000[b]
	Residual	52.696	36	1.464		
	Total	326.135	39			

a. Dependent Variable: ShotsOnTargetDiff
b. Predictors: (Constant), UAIdiff, HomeAdv, TalentDiff

Coefficients[a]

Model		Unstandardized Coefficients		Standardized Coefficients	t	Sig.	95.0% Confidence Interval for B	
		B	Std. Error	Beta			Lower Bound	Upper Bound
1	(Constant)	-1.619	.271		-5.697	.000	-2.170	-1.069
	TalentDiff	.123	.026	.405	4.772	.000	.071	.175
	HomeAdv	3.239	.385	.567	8.414	.000	2.458	4.020
	UAIdiff	.107	.025	.366	4.329	.000	.057	.158

a. Dependent Variable: ShotsOnTargetDiff

Coefficient Correlations[a]

Model			UAIdiff	HomeAdv	TalentDiff
1	Correlations	UAIdiff	1.000	.071	-.611
		HomeAdv	.071	1.000	-.110
		TalentDiff	-.611	-.110	1.000
	Covariances	UAIdiff	.001	.001	.000
		HomeAdv	.001	.148	-.001
		TalentDiff	.000	-.001	.001

a. Dependent Variable: ShotsOnTargetDiff

Appendix 4F: Aircraft accident data (per million flights)

Model Summary[b]

Model	R	R Square	Adjusted R Square	Std. Error of the Estimate	Change statistics R Square Change	F Change
1	.698[a]	.487	.486	1.30776	.487	472.771

a. Dependent Variable: AccPerMillflights
b. Predictors: (Constant), PerCapGDP, UAI, MAS, PDI, IDV

ANOVA[a]

Model		Sum of Squares	df	Mean Square	F	Sig.
1	Regression	4042.736	5	808.547	472.771	.000[b]
	Residual	4254.367	2488	1.710		
	Total	8297.103	2493			

a. Dependent Variable: AccPerMillflights
b. Predictors: (Constant), PerCapGDP, UAI, MAS, PDI, IDV

Coefficients[a]

Model		Unstandardized Coefficients B	Std. Error	Standardized Coefficients Beta	t	Sig.	95.0% Confidence Interval for B Lower Bound	Upper Bound
1	(Constant)	6.390	.316		20.241	.000	5.771	7.009
	PDI	.009	.003	.067	2.740	.006	.003	.016
	IDV	-.016	.002	-.215	-7.587	.000	-.021	-.012
	MAS	-.013	.002	-.100	-6.490	.000	-.017	-.009
	UAI	.011	.002	.105	5.168	.000	.007	.015
	PerCapGDP	.000	.000	-.428	-20.707	.000	.000	.000

a. Dependent Variable: AccPerMillflights

Coefficient Correlations[a]

Model			PerCapGDP	UAI	MAS	PDI	IDV
1	Correlations	PerCapGDP	1.000	-.419	.063	.338	-.400
		UAI	-.419	1.000	-.241	-.170	.526
		MAS	.063	-.241	1.000	-.095	-.316
		PDI	.338	-.170	-.095	1.000	.457
		IDV	-.400	.526	-.316	.457	1.000
	Covariances	PerCapGDP	1.450E-010	-1.086E-008	1.504E-009	1.361E-008	-1.037E-008
		UAI	-1.086E-008	4.639E-006	-1.036E-006	-1.223E-006	2.440E-006
		MAS	1.504E-009	-1.036E-006	3.995E-006	-6.377E-007	-1.359E-006
		PDI	1.361E-008	-1.223E-006	-6.377E-007	1.120E-005	3.292E-006
		IDV	-1.037E-008	2.440E-006	-1.359E-006	3.292E-006	4.636E-006

a. Dependent Variable: AccPerMillflights

Appendix 4G: Aircraft accident data (FLE per million flights)

Model Summary[b]

Model	R	R Square	Adjusted R Square	Std. Error of the Estimate	Change statistics	
					R Square Change	F Change
1	.667[a]	.445	.444	.96910	.445	398.460

a. Dependent Variable: AccPerMillflights
b. Predictors: (Constant), PerCapGDP, UAI, MAS, PDI, IDV

ANOVA[a]

Model		Sum of Squares	df	Mean Square	F	Sig.
1	Regression	1871.088	5	374.218	398.460	.000[b]
	Residual	2336.254	2488	.939		
	Total	4207.342	2493			

a. Dependent Variable: AccPerMillflights
b. Predictors: (Constant), PerCapGDP, UAI, MAS, PDI, IDV

Coefficients[a]

Model		Unstandardized Coefficients		Standardized Coeff's	t	Sig.	95.0% Confidence Interval for B	
		B	Std. Error	Beta			Lower Bound	Upper Bound
1	(Constant)	4.128	.234		17.646	.000	3.669	4.587
	PDI	.007	.002	.071	2.801	.005	.002	.012
	IDV	-.010	.002	-.192	-6.509	.000	-.014	-.007
	MAS	-.006	.001	-.069	-4.349	.000	-.009	-.004
	UAI	.009	.002	.115	5.450	.000	.006	.012
	PerCapGDP	.000	.000	-.416	-19.335	.000	.000	.000

a. Dependent Variable: AccPerMillflights

Coefficient Correlations[a]

Model			PerCapGDP	UAI	MAS	PDI	IDV
1	Correlations	PerCapGDP	1.000	-.419	.063	.338	-.400
		UAI	-.419	1.000	-.241	-.170	.526
		MAS	.063	-.241	1.000	-.095	-.316
		PDI	.338	-.170	-.095	1.000	.457
		IDV	-.400	.526	-.316	.457	1.000
	Covar-iances	PerCapGDP	1.450E-010	-1.086E-008	1.504E-009	1.361E-008	-1.037E-008
		UAI	-1.086E-008	4.639E-006	-1.036E-006	-1.223E-006	2.440E-006
		MAS	1.504E-009	-1.036E-006	3.995E-006	-6.377E-007	-1.359E-006
		PDI	1.361E-008	-1.223E-006	-6.377E-007	1.120E-005	3.292E-006
		IDV	-1.037E-008	2.440E-006	-1.359E-006	3.292E-006	4.636E-006

a. Dependent Variable: AccPerMillflights

Appendix 4H: Maritime fatality rate data

(per 100k seafarer years)

Model Summary[b]

Model	R	R Square	Adjusted R Square	Std. Error of the Estimate	Change statistics	
					R Square Change	F Change
1	.762[a]	.581	.505	30.1993	.581	7.624

a. Dependent Variable: FatalAccidentRate
b. Predictors: (Constant), UAI, IDV

ANOVA[a]

Model		Sum of Squares	df	Mean Square	F	Sig.
1	Regression	13905.441	2	6952.720	7.624	.008[b]
	Residual	10031.988	11	911.999		
	Total	23937.429	13			

a. Dependent Variable: FatalAccidentRate
b. Predictors: (Constant), UAI, IDV

Coefficients[a]

Model		Unstandardized Coefficients		Standardized Coefficients	t	Sig.	95.0% Confidence Interval for B	
		B	Std. Error	Beta			Lower Bound	Upper Bound
1	(Constant)	92.118	28.959		3.319	.007	32.379	159.857
	IDV	-1.275	.368	-.677	-3.470	.005	-2.084	-.466
	UAI	.503	.267	.367	1.880	.057	-.086	1.092

a. Dependent Variable: FatalAccidentRate

Coefficient Correlations[a]

Model			UAI	IDV
1	Correlations	UAI	1.000	-.026
		IDV	-.026	1.000
	Covariances	UAI	.072	-.003
		IDV	-.003	.135

a. Dependent Variable: FatalAccidentRate

Appendix 4I: Aircraft automation preferences

Preference A01: "I am concerned that automation will cause me to lose flying skills"

Model Summary[b]

Model	R	R Square	Adjusted R Square	Std. Error of the Estimate	Change statistics	
					R Square Change	F Change
1	.779[a]	.606	.519	11.232	.606	6.931

ANOVA[a]

	Model	Sum of Squares	df	Mean Square	F	Sig.
1	Regression	1748.680	2	874.340	6.931	.015[b]
	Residual	1135.320	9	126.147		
	Total	2884.000	11			

Coefficients[a]

	Model	Unstandardized Coefficients		Standardized Coefficients	t	Sig.	95.0% Confidence Interval for B	
		B	Std. Error	Beta			Lower Bound	Upper Bound
1	(Constant)	86.771	11.964		7.252	.000	59.706	113.836
	PDI	-.279	.130	-.455	-2.153	.060	-.573	.014
	UAI	-.440	.164	-.568	-2.687	.025	-.810	-.069

Note: a. Dependent Variable: A01; b. Predictors: (Constant), PDI, UAI

Preference A02: "There are modes and features of the FMC that I do not fully understand"

Model Summary[b]

Model	R	R Square	Adjusted R Square	Std. Error of the Estimate	Change statistics	
					R Square Change	F Change
1	.793[a]	.629	.592	5.134	.629	16.965

ANOVA[a]

	Model	Sum of Squares	df	Mean Square	F	Sig.
1	Regression	447.114	1	447.114	16.965	.002[b]
	Residual	263.553	10	26.355		
	Total	710.667	11			

Coefficients[a]

	Model	Unstandardized Coefficients		Standardized Coefficients	t	Sig.	95.0% Confidence Interval for B	
		B	Std. Error	Beta			Lower Bound	Upper Bound
1	(Constant)	53.199	4.737		11.230	.000	42.644	63.754
	UAI	-.305	.074	-.793	-4.119	.002	-.469	-.140

Note: a. Dependent Variable: A02; b. Predictors: (Constant), UAI

Preference A03: "When workload increases, it is better to avoid reprogramming the FMC"

Model Summary[b]

Model	R	R Square	Adjusted R Square	Std. Error of the Estimate	Change statistics	
					R Square Change	F Change
1	.574[a]	.330	.263	9.494	.330	4.922

ANOVA[a]

Model		Sum of Squares	df	Mean Square	F	Sig.
1	Regression	443.668	1	443.668	4.922	.051[b]
	Residual	901.332	10	90.133		
	Total	1345.000	11			

Coefficients[a]

Model		Unstandardized Coefficients		Standardized Coefficients	t	Sig.	95.0% Confidence Interval for B	
		B	Std. Error	Beta			Lower Bound	Upper Bound
1	(Constant)	70.961	8.761		8.100	.000	51.441	90.481
	UAI	-.303	.137	-.574	-2.219	.051	-.608	.001

Note: a. Dependent Variable: A03; b. Predictors: (Constant), UAI

Preference A04: "It's easy to forget how to do FMC operations that are not performed often" *(no correlations)*

Model Summary[b]

Model	R	R Square	Adjusted R Square	Std. Error of the Estimate	Change statistics	
					R Square Change	F Change
1	.533[a]	.284	.213	11.811	.284	3.970

ANOVA[a]

Model		Sum of Squares	df	Mean Square	F	Sig.
1	Regression	553.809	1	553.809	3.970	.074[b]
	Residual	1395.108	10	139.511		
	Total	1948.917	11			

Coefficients[a]

Model		Unstandardized Coefficients		Standardized Coefficients	t	Sig.	95.0% Confidence Interval for B	
		B	Std. Error	Beta			Lower Bound	Upper Bound
1	(Constant)	72.348	8.462		8.549	.000	53.493	91.204
	PDI	-.269	-1.992	-.533	-1.992	.074	-.569	.032

Note: a. Dependent Variable: A04; b. Predictors: (Constant), PDI

315

Preference A05: "Under abnormal conditions, I can rapidly access the information I need in the FMC"

Model Summary[b]

Model	R	R Square	Adjusted R Square	Std. Error of the Estimate	Change statistics	
					R Square Change	F Change
1	.642[a]	.412	.353	10.478	.412	7.006

ANOVA[a]

Model		Sum of Squares	df	Mean Square	F	Sig.
1	Regression	769.174	1	769.174	7.006	.024[b]
	Residual	1097.826	10	109.783		
	Total	1867.000	11			

Coefficients[a]

Model		Unstandardized Coefficients		Standardized Coefficients	t	Sig.	95.0% Confidence Interval for B	
		B	Std. Error	Beta			Lower Bound	Upper Bound
1	(Constant)	58.193	9.668		6.019	.000	36.650	79.735
	UAI	.400	.151	.642	2.647	.024	.063	.736

Note: a. Dependent Variable: A05; b. Predictors: (Constant), UAI

Preference A06: "In order to maintain safety, pilots should avoid disengaging automated systems" *(no correlations)*

Model Summary[b]

Model	R	R Square	Adjusted R Square	Std. Error of the Estimate	Change statistics	
					R Square Change	F Change
1	.593[a]	.351	.286	16.468	.351	5.416

ANOVA[a]

Model		Sum of Squares	df	Mean Square	F	Sig.
1	Regression	1468.862	1	1468.862	5.416	.042[b]
	Residual	2712.055	10	271.205		
	Total	4180.917	11			

Coefficients[a]

Model		Unstandardized Coefficients		Standardized Coefficients	t	Sig.	95.0% Confidence Interval for B	
		B	Std. Error	Beta			Lower Bound	Upper Bound
1	(Constant)	5.493	15.196		.361	.725	-28.366	39.352
	UAI	.552	.237	.593	2.327	.042	.024	1.081

Note: a. Dependent Variable: A06; b. Predictors: (Constant), UAI

Preference A07: "I regularly maintain flying proficiency by disengaging automation" *(no correlations)*

Model Summary[b]

Model	R	R Square	Adjusted R Square	Std. Error of the Estimate	Change statistics	
					R Square Change	F Change
1	.373[a]	.139	.053	17.337	.139	1.614

ANOVA[a]

Model		Sum of Squares	df	Mean Square	F	Sig.
1	Regression	485.044	1	485.044	1.614	.233[b]
	Residual	3005.873	10	300.587		
	Total	3490.917	11			

Coefficients[a]

Model		Unstandardized Coefficients		Standardized Coefficients	t	Sig.	95.0% Confidence Interval for B	
		B	Std. Error	Beta			Lower Bound	Upper Bound
1	(Constant)	76.525	12.422		6.161	.000	48.848	104.202
	UAI	-.252	.198	-.373	-1.270	.233	-.693	.190

Note: a. Dependent Variable: A07; b. Predictors: (Constant), UAI

Preference A08: "I feel free to select the level of automation at any given time" *(no correlations)*

Model Summary[b]

Model	R	R Square	Adjusted R Square	Std. Error of the Estimate	Change statistics	
					R Square Change	F Change
1	.441[a]	.194	.114	10.951	.194	2.414

ANOVA[a]

Model		Sum of Squares	df	Mean Square	F	Sig.
1	Regression	289.526	1	289.526	2.414	.151[b]
	Residual	1199.141	10	119.914		
	Total	1488.667	11			

Coefficients[a]

Model		Unstandardized Coefficients		Standardized Coefficients	t	Sig.	95.0% Confidence Interval for B	
		B	Std. Error	Beta			Lower Bound	Upper Bound
1	(Constant)	67.234	6.655		10.103	.000	52.406	82.062
	IDV	.184	.118	.441	1.554	.151	-.080	.447

Note: a. Dependent Variable: A08; b. Predictors: (Constant), IDV

Preference A09: "My company expects me to always use automation" *(no correlations)*

Model Summary[b]

Model	R	R Square	Adjusted R Square	Std. Error of the Estimate	Change statistics	
					R Square Change	F Change
1	.326[a]	.106	.017	19.875	.106	1.188

ANOVA[a]

Model		Sum of Squares	df	Mean Square	F	Sig.
1	Regression	469.317	1	485.044	1.614	.233[b]
	Residual	3950.350	10	300.587		
	Total	4419.667	11			

Coefficients[a]

Model		Unstandardized Coefficients		Standardized Coefficients	t	Sig.	95.0% Confidence Interval for B	
		B	Std. Error	Beta			Lower Bound	Upper Bound
1	(Constant)	42.846	18.340		2.336	.042	1.982	83.711
	UAI	.312	.286	.326	1.090	.301	-.326	.950

Note: a. Dependent Variable: A09; b. Predictors: (Constant), UAI

Preference A10: "The effective crew member always uses the automation tools provided"

Model Summary[b]

Model	R	R Square	Adjusted R Square	Std. Error of the Estimate	Change statistics	
					R Square Change	F Change
1	.907[a]	.823	.784	8.511	.823	20.922

ANOVA[a]

Model		Sum of Squares	df	Mean Square	F	Sig.
1	Regression	3030.803	2	1515.401	20.922	.000[b]
	Residual	651.864	9	72.429		
	Total	3682.667	11			

Coefficients[a]

Model		Unstandardized Coefficients		Standardized Coefficients	t	Sig.	95.0% Confidence Interval for B	
		B	Std. Error	Beta			Lower Bound	Upper Bound
1	(Constant)	117.941	17.622		6.693	.000	78.077	157.805
	PDI	.392	.101	.565	3.880	.004	.163	.620
	MAS	-1.028	.262	-.572	-3.929	.003	-1.620	-.436

Note: a. Dependent Variable: A10; b. Predictors: (Constant), PDI, MAS

Preference A11: "I make sure the other pilot acknowledges programming changes I make in the FMC" *(no correlations)*

Model Summary[b]

Model	R	R Square	Adjusted R Square	Std. Error of the Estimate	Change statistics	
					R Square Change	F Change
1	.416[a]	.173	.091	5.135	.173	2.095

ANOVA[a]

Model		Sum of Squares	df	Mean Square	F	Sig.
	Regression	55.233	1	55.233	2.095	.178[b]
1	Residual	263.683	10	26.368		
	Total	318.917	11			

Coefficients[a]

Model		Unstandardized Coefficients		Standardized Coefficients	t	Sig.	95.0% Confidence Interval for B	
		B	Std. Error	Beta			Lower Bound	Upper Bound
1	(Constant)	94.558	3.121		30.301	.000	87.605	101.511
	IDV	-.080	.055	-.416	-1.447	.178	-.204	.043

Note: a. Dependent Variable: A11; b. Predictors: (Constant), IDV

Preference A12: "Automated cockpits require more verbal communication between crew members" *(no correlations)*

Model Summary[b]

Model	R	R Square	Adjusted R Square	Std. Error of the Estimate	Change statistics	
					R Square Change	F Change
1	.447[a]	.200	.120	15.476	.200	2.500

ANOVA[a]

Model		Sum of Squares	df	Mean Square	F	Sig.
	Regression	598.861	1	598.861	2.500	.145[b]
1	Residual	2395.139	10	239.514		
	Total	2944.000	11			

Coefficients[a]

Model		Unstandardized Coefficients		Standardized Coefficients	t	Sig.	95.0% Confidence Interval for B	
		B	Std. Error	Beta			Lower Bound	Upper Bound
1	(Constant)	68.087	9.405		7.239	.000	47.131	89.042
	IDV	-.264	.167	-.447	-1.581	.145	-.636	.108

Note: a. Dependent Variable: A12; b. Predictors: (Constant), IDV

Preference A13: "Automated cockpits require more cross-checking of crew member actions" *(no correlations)*

Model Summary[b]

Model	R	R Square	Adjusted R Square	Std. Error of the Estimate	Change statistics	
					R Square Change	F Change
1	.258[a]	.067	-.027	12.450	.067	.715

ANOVA[a]

Model		Sum of Squares	df	Mean Square	F	Sig.
1	Regression	110.823	1	110.823	.715	.418[b]
	Residual	1550.093	10	155.009		
	Total	1660.917	11			

Coefficients[a]

Model		Unstandardized Coefficients		Standardized Coefficients	t	Sig.	95.0% Confidence Interval for B	
		B	Std. Error	Beta			Lower Bound	Upper Bound
1	(Constant)	76.213	7.566		10.073	.000	59.355	93.071
	IDV	-.114	.134	-.258	-.846	.418	-.413	.186

Note: a. Dependent Variable: A13; b. Predictors: (Constant), IDV

Preference A14: "I look forward to more automation-the more the better" *(no correlations)*

Model Summary[b]

Model	R	R Square	Adjusted R Square	Std. Error of the Estimate	Change statistics	
					R Square Change	F Change
1	.778[a]	.605	.565	16.193	.605	15.306

ANOVA[a]

Model		Sum of Squares	df	Mean Square	F	Sig.
1	Regression	4013.485	1	4013.485	15.306	.003[b]
	Residual	2622.181	10	262.218		
	Total	6635.667	11			

Coefficients[a]

Model		Unstandardized Coefficients		Standardized Coefficients	t	Sig.	95.0% Confidence Interval for B	
		B	Std. Error	Beta			Lower Bound	Upper Bound
1	(Constant)	-.375	11.602		-.032	.975	-26.226	25.475
	PDI	.724	.185	.778	3.912	.003	.311	1.136

Note: a. Dependent Variable: A14; b. Predictors: (Constant), PDI

Preference A15: "I prefer flying automated aircraft"

Model Summary[b]

Model	R	R Square	Adjusted R Square	Std. Error of the Estimate	Change statistics R Square Change	Change statistics F Change
1	.666[a]	.444	.389	14.167	.444	7.992

ANOVA[a]

Model		Sum of Squares	df	Mean Square	F	Sig.
1	Regression	1603.987	1	1603.987	7.992	.018[b]
	Residual	2006.930	10	200.693		
	Total	3610.917	11			

Coefficients[a]

Model		Unstandardized Coefficients B	Unstandardized Coefficients Std. Error	Standardized Coefficients Beta	t	Sig.	95.0% Confidence Interval for B Lower Bound	95.0% Confidence Interval for B Upper Bound
1	(Constant)	45.815	13.072		3.505	.006	16.688	74.942
	UAI	.577	.204	.666	2.827	.018	.122	1.032

Note: a. Dependent Variable: A15; b. Predictors: (Constant), UAI

Appendix 5: Test data - aircraft incidents

This dataset formed part of a suite of test data based on information from the website http://aviation-safety.net that was obtained for the purpose of evaluating the performance of the team culture tool (TCT), versions 2 and 3.

The records in this dataset relate to aircraft incidents during the first six months of 2009, and were selected on the following basis:

- They represented incidents that occurred (or were exacerbated) due to crew behaviour, or

- They represented incidents that were mitigated due to crew behaviours and/or abilities.

Jan 2009, Andes Lineas Aereas McDonnell Douglas MD-82 (LV-BHF)

No fatalities. Had to be guided to safety after loss of instruments and became seriously disorientated: Loss of situation awareness (Argentinian crew).

13 Jan 2009, Alaska Airlines Boeing 737-400 ()

No fatalities. Runway more slippery than crew were told by airport; applied maximum reverse thrust for much longer to avoid ending up in Buskin River: Excellent quick reaction to safety problem (United States crew).

15 Jan 2009, US Airways Airbus A320-214

No fatalities. Lost both engines at 3,200ft over New York and had to make an emergency landing in the River Hudson: Exemplary practice by all crew (United States crew).

28 Jan 2009, Ghana International Airlines Boeing 757-258 (G-STRZ)

No fatalities. Problems with a blocked pitot led to FMC misbehaviour and problems of shared situation awareness; A rejection of take-off would have been more appropriate: Suboptimal decision-making and inadequate communication between crew (Ghanaian crew).

09 Feb 2009, Air Mediterranee Airbus A321-211 (F-GYAJ)

No fatalities. The aircraft overran the runway in light snowfall. The accident was due to the continuation of the landing on discovery of the conditions, exacerbated by non-use of thrust reversers: Poor decision-making (French crew).

25 Feb 2009, THY Turkish Airlines Boeing 737-8F2 (TC-JGE)

9 fatalities. Faulty altimeters led to the aircraft's autopilot throttling back AND raising the nose to maintain lift; the crew realised too late what was happening: Autopilot error and lack of situation awareness (Turkish crew).

20 Mar 2009, Emirates Airlines Airbus A340-541 (A6-ERG)

No fatalities. Tail strike – due to incorrect take-off weight calculations which were not checked; the crew failed to carry out all pre-departure SOPs: Failure to follow SOPs (Arabian crew).

09 Apr 2009, Aviastar Mandiri British Aerospace BAe-146-300 (PK-BRD)

All crew killed. Crew did not respond to repeated 'terrain terrain', 'pull up', 'sink rate' and 'too low terrain' aural alerts, and the aircraft flew into the ground: Captain lacked situational awareness, and was unwilling to react to co-pilots warnings (Indonesian crew).

20 April 2009, Royal Air Maroc – RAM Boeing 767-36NER (CN-RNT)

No fatalities. During a firm landing, the first officer's input of full nose down elevator caused substantial structural damage to the aircraft: Erroneous flight control (Moroccan crew).

21 Apr 2009, Porter Airlines de Havilland Canada DHC-8-402 q400 (C-GLQD)

No fatalities. Aft fuselage touched the runway on landing (minor damage); power settings were not checked leading to an excessive descent rate: Lack of situation awareness (Canadian crew).

22 Apr 2009, Japan Airlines (JAL Express) McDonnell Douglass MD-81 (JA8260)

No fatalities. The aircraft struck its left wing tip on the runway during a landing in steady winds of 10kts (minor damage): Poor flight control (Japanese crew).

Appendix 5: Test data - aircraft incidents

04 May 2009, Northwest Airlines Airbus A320-211 (N311US)

No fatalities. There was an 11 knot tailwind which necessitated a higher approach speed, and the aircraft suffered a tail strike after a bounced landing: Poor flight control by first officer (USA crew).

11 May 2009, British Airways Boeing 747-436 (G-BYGA)

No fatalities. Spurious thrust reverser lock signals caused the flaps to retract without warning or (significant) signal during the take-off run (faults in the flight control logic); the crew were commended for their flight skills: Exemplary practice by crew (UK crew).

10 August 2009, Air Nippon Boeing 737-881 (JA56AN)

No fatalities. Multiple tail strikes caused damage to lower tailpiece, three major scratch marks on runway. Poor flight control (Japanese crew).

22 August 2009, Aeroflot-Don Boeing 737-400 (VQ-BAN)

No fatalities. Very heavy landing and tail strike causing substantial damage to the aircraft. Poor flight control (Russian crew).

29 August 2009, Air Algerie Boeing 737-8D6 (7T-VJK)

No fatalities. The aircraft left the runway, continued on the grass for 250 meters, rejoined the runway and took off; minor damage occurred to right engine, airframe and nose gear: Inadequate control and failure to follow SOPs (Algerian crew).

04 September 2009, Air India Boeing 747-437 (VT-ESM)

No fatalities, 21 passenger injuries, aircraft damaged by fire. Fuel leak from no. 1 engine, crew had turned off company channel (against SOPs) and also switched from ground frequency to tower frequency; engineer signalled CCIC, who ignored him; by the time the flight crew reacted, engine 1 was on fire and the passengers panicked; the cabin crew evacuated the passengers successfully, but both pilots evacuated the upper deck (did not come down to the lower deck) and left the aircraft before the evacuation of passengers was complete: Failure to follow SOPs, poor CRM (Indian crew).

Appendix 6: TCT2 questionnaire form

The questionnaire form below was used to obtain feedback on the experiences of users of the second team culture tool (TCT2).

Team Culture Tool (TCT2) User Questionnaire

Purpose of this questionnaire: To find out the views of users of the culture tools, in order to enable changes and improvements.

Please fill in pale blue boxes - most of the small boxes have dropdown lists to select from.

TEAM DESCRIPTION	Information provider:	PB	Date:	23/04/2012	No. in team:	7
Team type:	Academic/industrial collaboration project (communication)					
Team description - purpose, longevity, etc.:	3 years + 3 years (poss)					

USING THE TEAM CULTURE TOOL (TCT2)

Team cultural profiler

How easy and understandable was it to use the team culture profiler (to input the team member details)?	Fairly easy
How quick and efficient did you find the team culture profiler to use?	Fairly fast
Did you find the team cultural scores meaningful (shown at the bottom of Table 1 in yellow highlight)?	To some extent

Team task/mission profiler

How difficult was it to use the task/mission profile table?	Somewhat difficult
How quick and efficient did you find the task/mission profile table to use?	Slow

The discrepancy results

Did the discrepancy results (shown at the bottom of the team culture profile table) make sense?	To some extent
Did the grey boxes ('what the score means' & 'to improve the team') help in explaining what to do?	To some extent

General questions

Have you come across any culture-related problems with any form of team?	To some extent
Could a tool like the team culture tool (TCT2) be useful in reducing or anticipating problems?	To some extent

Any further comments on using the tool?

It was easy to put the team in, and it was interesting running through some other teams that I had been involved in. It was very difficult to use the task-mission profile table, and it would be easy to misinterpret what the subfactors meant and end up with a wrong task-mission. I think that training would be required to do this part reliably.

Any further comments on the results from the tool?

I'm not convinced about the way the task/mission profile works. For instance, I have to deal with industrial engineers and academics. The tasks they carry out may be the same in many ways if they collaborate on a project, but their environments are different and the way they actually respond and carry out the work is different. When one of my experienced academic colleagues works at the industrial partner's premises, his behaviour is different from when at university - and so is mine - I wear my industrial hat!

Any other comments, e.g. on improving the tool, issues with using it, or other factors?

Anything that distinguishes between employees on the basis of nationality is likely to be a hot potato. Irrespective of the tool's benefits, we might be seen as discriminatory - someone is guaranteed to pick up on it and embarrass us (or worse). This may be the biggest limitation of the culture tool. It may be safer to do a tool based on company culture and professional culture.

© Allan Hodgson

Appendix 7: Team questionnaire form

This questionnaire was used to obtain team-related information.

Team Questionnaire

Purpose of this survey: To collect anonymous data on many different types of teams in order to find out what factors affect the performance of multicultural teams (we also need to collect data on single-culture teams for comparison).

Background to our research: Teams containing people from many cultural backgrounds are used widely in service and manufacturing industries. These multicultural teams typically perform less effectively than single-culture teams; however, sometimes multicultural teams perform extremely well due to the wide range of points of view and experience of team members. If we can better understand the effects of culture on single-culture and multicultural team performance, we can build better teams.

TEAM DESCRIPTION	Information provider:	JT-SI	Date:	08/11/2011	No. in team:	
Team type:	A major integration project to bring disparate services under integrated control					
Team description - purpose, longevity, etc.:	A five year project that involved a range of organisations and authorities. Although significant software development was required, it was essential to bring all key parties on board, in part by ensuring that their core requirements were met. Note - team roles and nationalities are those of group leaders (over 100 people involved).					
What can/could/did go wrong:	Project failure. Too many egos, not enough serious negotiating. No-one with enough authority to ensure that negotiations and project activities stayed on track. Team leaders lacked the qualities required for the complex balance required between stakeholders.					

On average, how long have team members known each other?		3 years
EXTERNALLY IMPOSED CONSTRAINTS & PROBLEMS	How realistic were the team objectives?	Utterly unrealistic
Was the team given adequate authority?	Insufficient	Were adequate **personnel & resources** provided?	Plenty enough
How often did external interference occur?	Frequently	Was the team given adequate time?	Plenty enough

TEAM MEMBER DESCRIPTIONS (maximum 16 team members)

I/D	Team role	Experience	Gender	Nationality	2nd nationality	Occupational background	Age or qual's when left FT education	Ability to do team tasks
1	Project manager	5 years+	M	English			BSc. or BA degree	Adequate
2	Liaison (technical)	5 years+	M	English			BSc. or BA degree	Excellent
3	Liaison (stakeholder)	5 years+	M	English			18	Poor
4	Stakeholder (service providers)	5 years+	M	English			BSc. or BA degree	Adequate
5	Stakeholder (customers)		F	English			BSc. or BA degree	Poor
6	Business analysis		F	English			BSc. or BA degree	Good
7	S/w analysis		M	English			BSc. or BA degree	Excellent
8	Subcontractor (s/w)		M	Poland			UNKNOWN	Good
9	Subcontractor (n/w)		M	English			UNKNOWN	Good
10	Financial planning & control	5 years+	F	English			BSc. or BA degree	Poor
11								
12								
13								
14								
15								
16								

TEAM PERFORMANCE

Rate the team performance as a whole with regard to ...	Rating	Importance
Rapid communication of situational factors needing urgent or prompt attention	Adequate	Not important
Communication between team members of complex factors and concepts	Poor	Very important
Trusting and getting on with each other	Poor	Very important
Creativity/coming up with novel ideas	Adequate	Moderately important
Decision-making/selecting courses of action	Poor	Quite important
Organising and allocating activities	Adequate	Quite important
Delivering the right quality and quantity of output (achieving goals or targets)	Poor	Very important
Delivering in a timely fashion (getting the job done in time)	Very poor	Very important

Looking in detail at conflict within the team ...	Rating
Relationship conflict (not getting on with others in the group)	Occasionally
Task conflict (disagreements about the team goals and WHAT the team should do)	Occasionally
Process conflict (disagreements about HOW the team should do the work)	Occasionally
Rate the team with regard to fragmentation (where the team breaks up into disagreeing subgroups or factions)	A minority of members split into subgroups

FURTHER COMMENTS THAT YOU THINK ARE RELEVANT

Although there were some technical issues, these were relatively small - the organisational/people issues were much more important. A failure of organisation and trust due in part to the personalities of the key people involved

© Allan Hodgson

Appendix 8: TCT3 questionnaire form

The questionnaire form below was used to obtain feedback on the experiences of users of the third team culture tool (TCT3).

Team Culture Tool (TCT3) User Questionnaire

Purpose of this questionnaire: To find out the views of users of the culture tools, in order to enable changes and improvements.

Please fill in pale blue boxes - most of the small boxes have dropdown lists to select from.

TEAM DESCRIPTION	Information provider:	AMJ	Date:	05/02/2013	No. in team: 7,10
Team type:	1. Sales/mktg team 2. Softw are/w eb project team				
Team description - purpose, longevity, etc.:	Mktg teams - w eb sales partnerships Integr w eb bkg system specification				

USING THE TEAM CULTURE TOOL (TCT3)

Team cultural profiler

How difficult w as it to use the team culture profiler (to input the team member details)?	Very easy
How quick did you find the team culture profiler to use?	Very fast
Did you find the team cultural scores meaningful (show n at the bottom of Table 1 in yellow highlight)?	Yes

Team task/mission profiler

How difficult w as it to use the team task/mission profiler?	Fairly easy
How quick and efficient did you find the task/mission profiler to use?	Very fast
Did you use the engineering management project team or action team option?	Project team

The discrepancy results

Did the discrepancy results (show n at the bottom of the team culture profile table) make sense?	Yes
Did the grey boxes ('w hat the score means' & 'to improve the team') help in explaining w hat to do?	Yes
Did the radar diagram (spider's w eb below grey boxes) provide useful information about the team?	Yes

General questions

Have you come across any culture-related problems w ith any form of team?	Yes
Could a tool like the team culture tool (TCT3) could be useful in reducing or anticipating problems?	To some extent

Any further comments on using the tool?

As before, the team cultural profile was easy to use. The task profiler was easier than the previous version but the teams were a bit difficult to place. It needs more examples in software and web areas.

Any further comments on the results from the tool?

The results were again reasonably in line with my experience, reflecting the issues caused by certain members. Having said that, I have worked in multinational teams that caused none of the problems that we had with these two teams-not everyone feels a need to behave in line with their nationality. It seems to me that if the team leader is fair and considerate the rest of the team will follow his lead and junior members will behave themselves anyway. In one case, the guy with the power had a high power distance according to your program and he was obnoxious to everyone most of the time! Maybe it was just his personality.

Any other comments, e.g. on improving the tool, issues with using it, or other factors?

The new task mission matrix seems to get round the problem of who fills in the tool. The scores should be more consistent.

Have you used the previous culture tool (TCT2)? If so, please comment on the different 'user experience', including ease of use, likelihood of errors and accuracy.

Yes. Much easier to use (task profiler), but see comments about examples.

Appendix 9: Generating exemplars for the TCT3

The exemplars were an essential part of the TCT3 tool because they allowed users to place their teams or missions in an appropriate context based on relative rather than absolute assessments of that context – a much easier process that also reduced the likelihood of gross errors of assignment.

In order to derive a set of exemplars and to locate them in each of the two mission areas (project and operation), the researcher initially collected a set of mission exemplars for each of the scenarios from the literature and from news articles and blogs. It was important that these exemplars were as unambiguous as possible to the majority of users, so the researcher discussed this set of exemplars with a colleague and, having made minor changes, created two 'grids', similar in appearance to Figures 8-6 (projects) and 8-7 (crews/operators). Each of these grids was populated with just four 'extreme' exemplars; a set of explanations of the placement of each exemplar was written, and a list was provided of exemplars that might be placed on each grid.

The researcher then organised meetings with former industrial acquaintances or emailed the project grids to them (as Excel files), and these acquaintances were persuaded (a) to revise or add to the list of exemplars, (b) to place the set of revised exemplars on the grid, and (c) to move or remove the originally-placed exemplars as seemed appropriate. The researcher then produced a composite version of the project grid based on the returned, populated 'mission grids'. Following comments from one of the exemplar providers about the paucity of software projects, that provider was persuaded to produce a computer systems/software/webware grid; this was not used in this thesis, but was incorporated in an alternative version of the TCT3 and sent back to him.

In the case of the organised action team grid, there was less access to useful sources of information and advice. The researcher utilised the earlier-interviewed pilot, who commented on his views with regard to various crews, but the main sources were from the general and academic literature, including comparative accident analyses.

From the comments of the above provider of software-related exemplars, it would appear fruitful to produce more industry-focused mission grids, which would provide an enhanced user experience.

Appendix 10: Hofstede's 5th and 6th dimensions

As stated elsewhere in this thesis, when the research began, sets of national cultural scores covering the majority of nations were only available for four dimensions of Hofstede's framework – power distance (PDI), individualism (IDV), masculinity (MAS) and uncertainty avoidance (UAI). For the fifth dimension, long vs. short term orientation (LTO), culture scores were available for only twenty-three nations (primarily Asian), and attempts to extend the scores to other countries had produced disappointing results. For the sixth dimension, indulgence vs. restraint (IVS), a full set of national scores was not presented in any of Hofstede's publications until the release of the third edition of Cultures and Organizations (Geert H. Hofstede et al., 2010) approximately eighteen months after the start of this PhD. However this dimension was included in the 2008 Values Survey Module (Geert Hofstede, Hofstede, Minkov, & Vinken, 2008b), along with a seventh dimension, monumentalism vs. flexhumility (MVF). This latter dimension was found to be inversely correlated with long term orientation, see Chapter 4 of Minkov (Minkov, 2011). Therefore, rather than adding MVF to the previous six dimensions, Hofstede introduced, in his 2010 book, a modified form of long term orientation, LTO- WVS[72], which took account of the MVF findings - see also Minkov's analyses (Geert Hofstede, Hofstede, Minkov, & Vinken, 2008a) .

Due to time pressure, the author was not able retrospectively to include the fifth (revised) dimension and sixth dimension of Hofstede's framework into his statistical work; in addition, there was very little published material on these dimensions that was of relevance to the author's studies. A further literature review at the time of thesis completion, revealed no publications on LTO-WVS/pragmatism or IVS that were of relevance to the research work described in this thesis.

---

[72] This was later renamed 'pragmatism'.

www.ingramcontent.com/pod-product-compliance
Lightning Source LLC
Chambersburg PA
CBHW060447290526
45791CB00001B/12